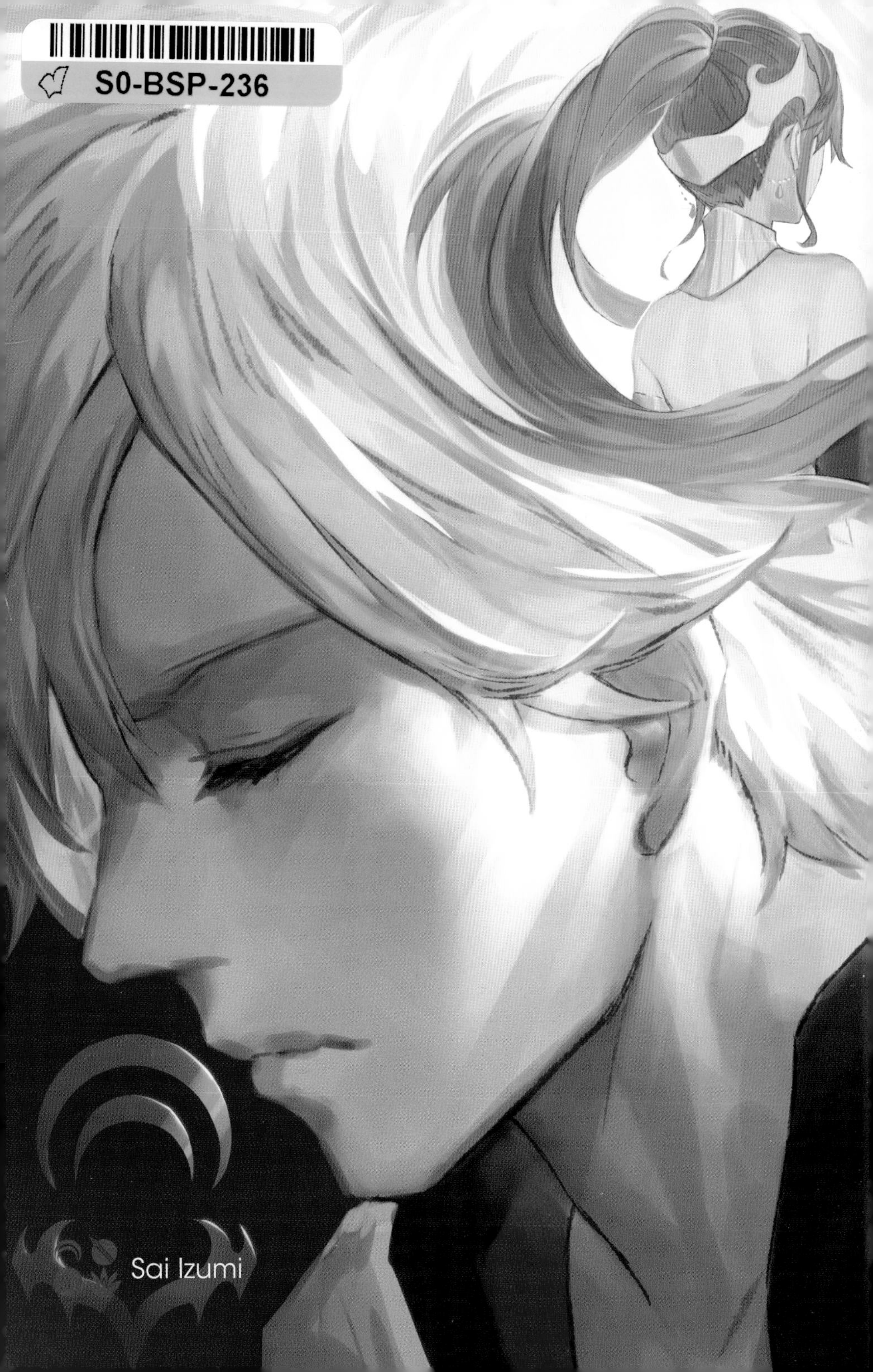
Sai Izumi

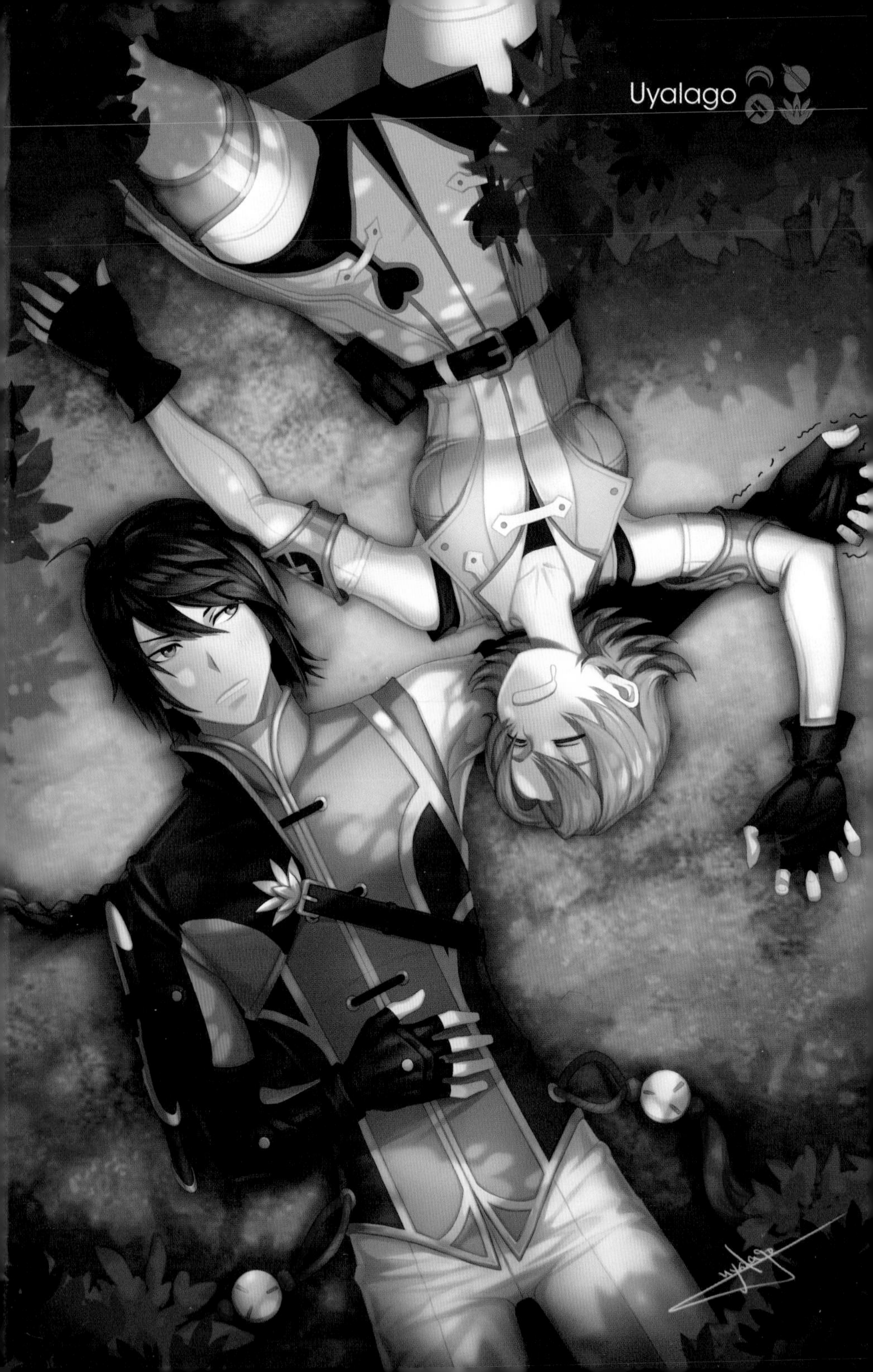
Uyalago

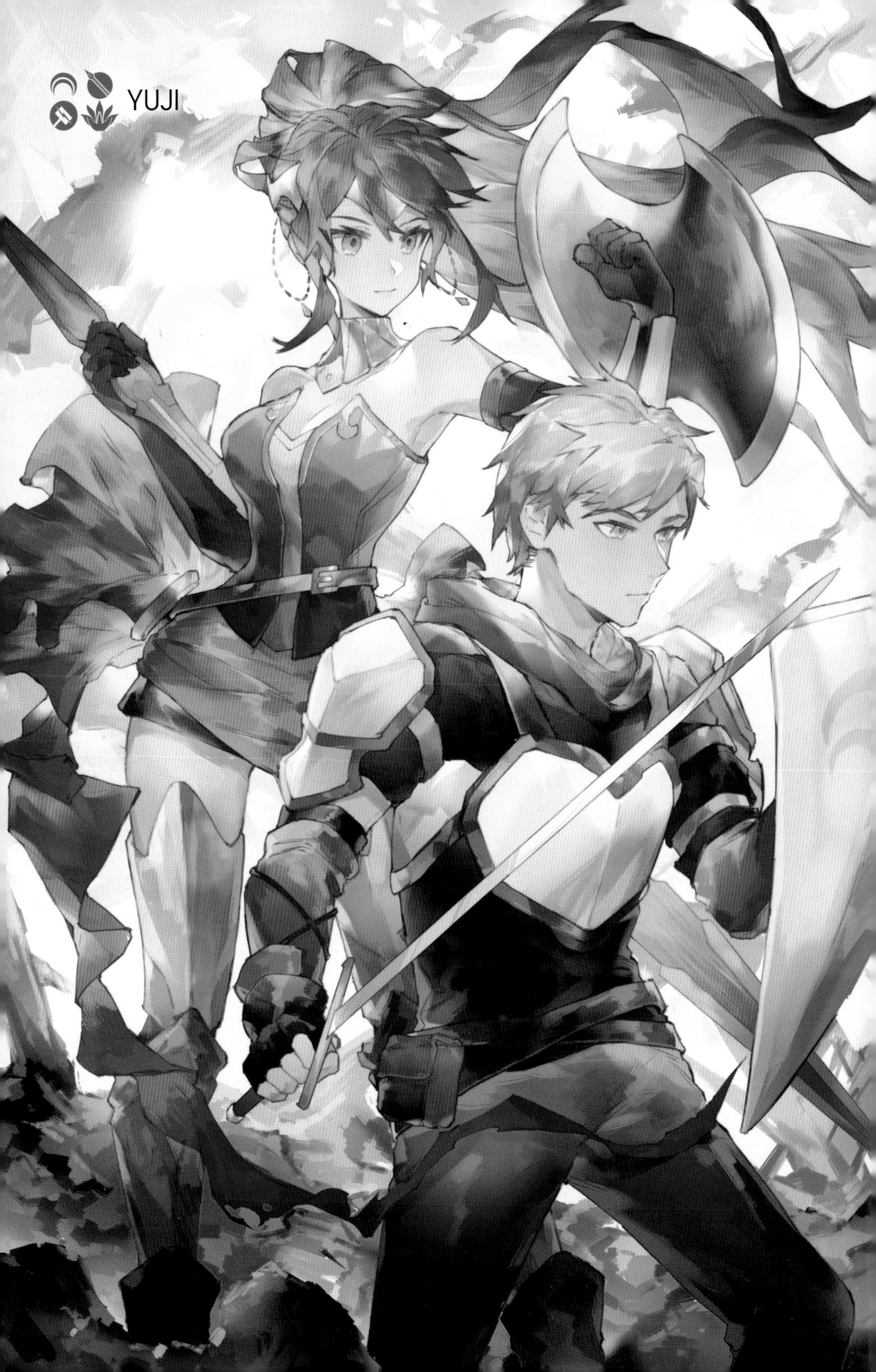
YUJI

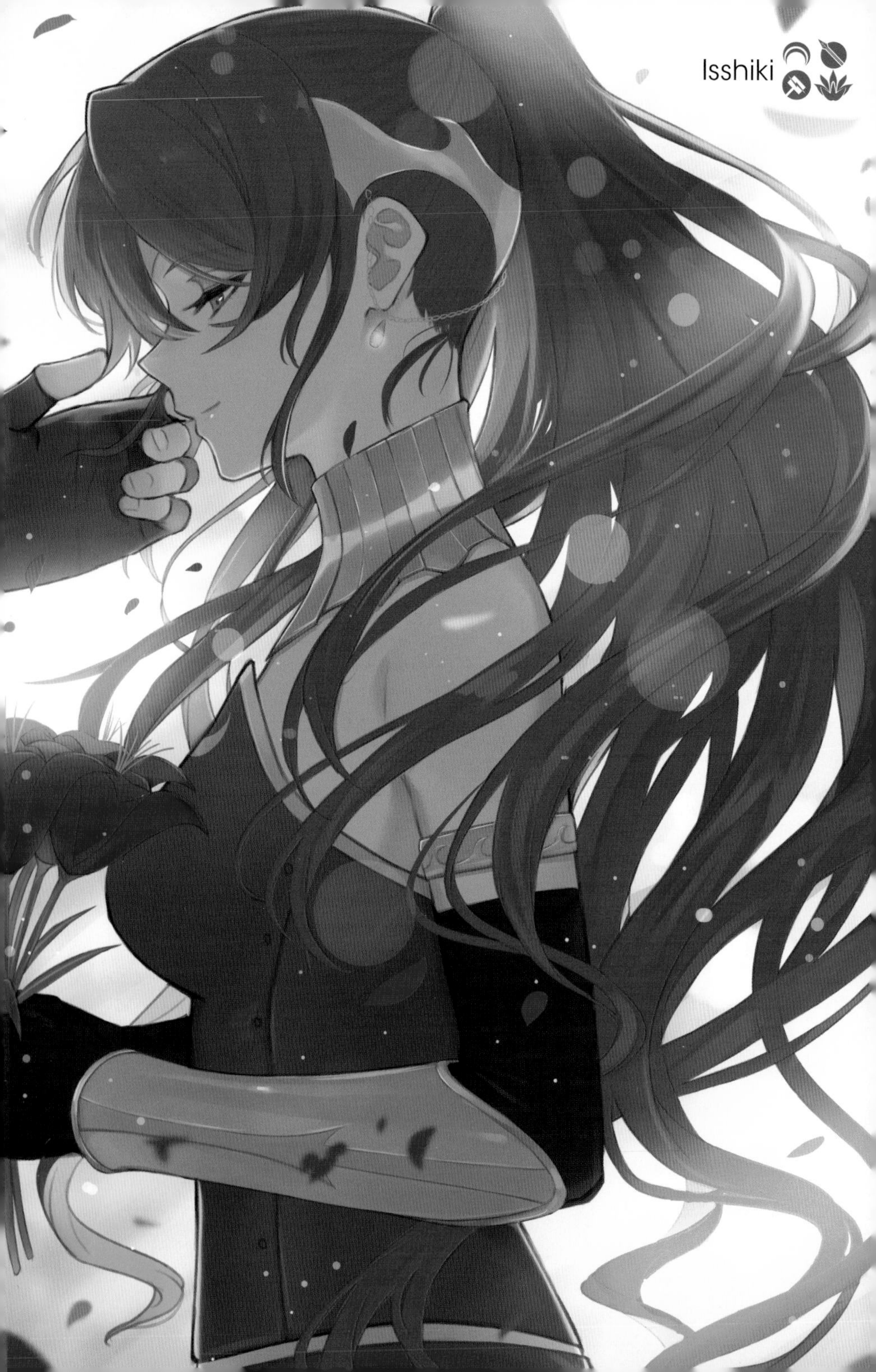
Isshiki

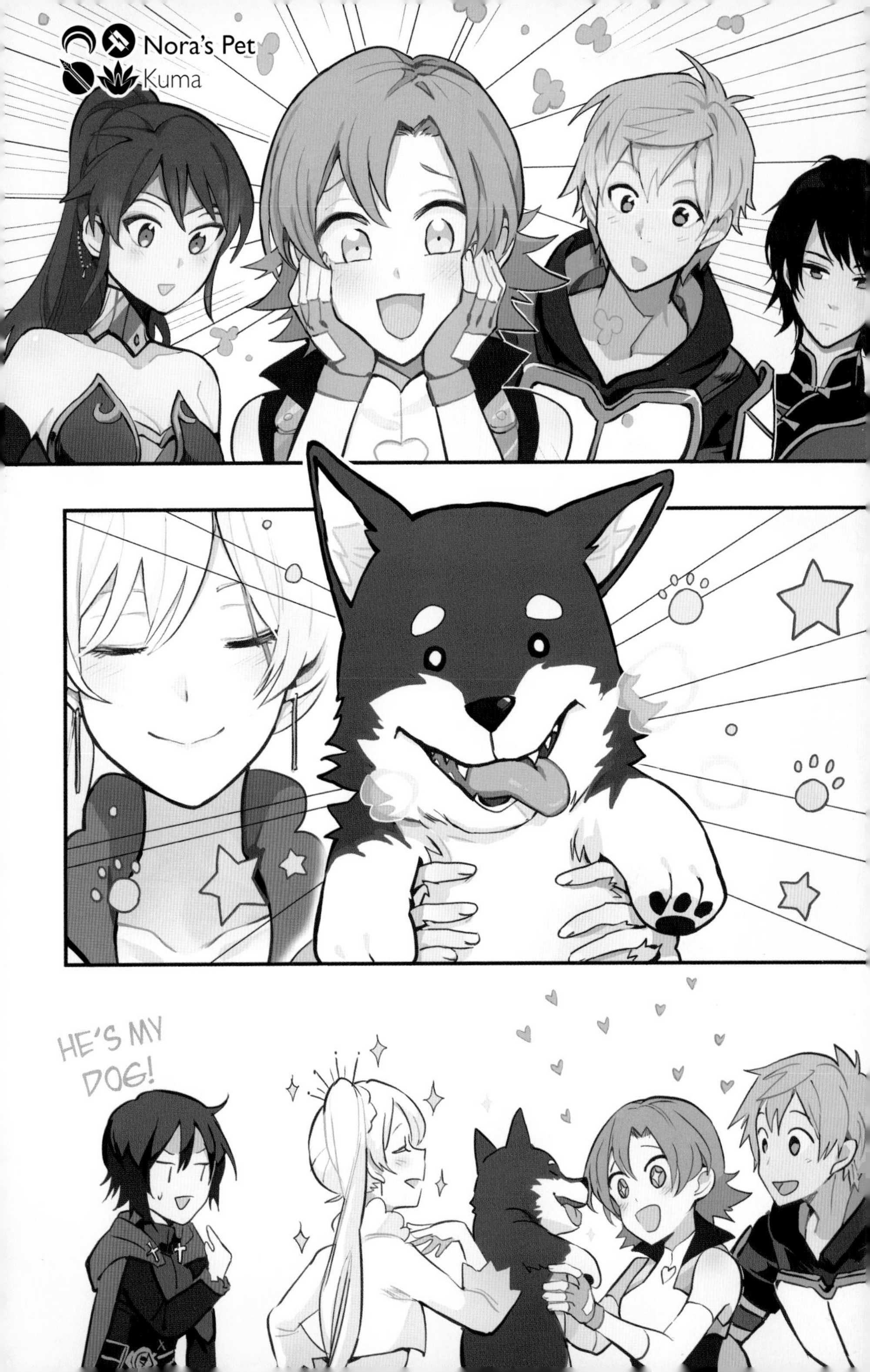
Nora's Pet
Kuma
HE'S MY DOG!

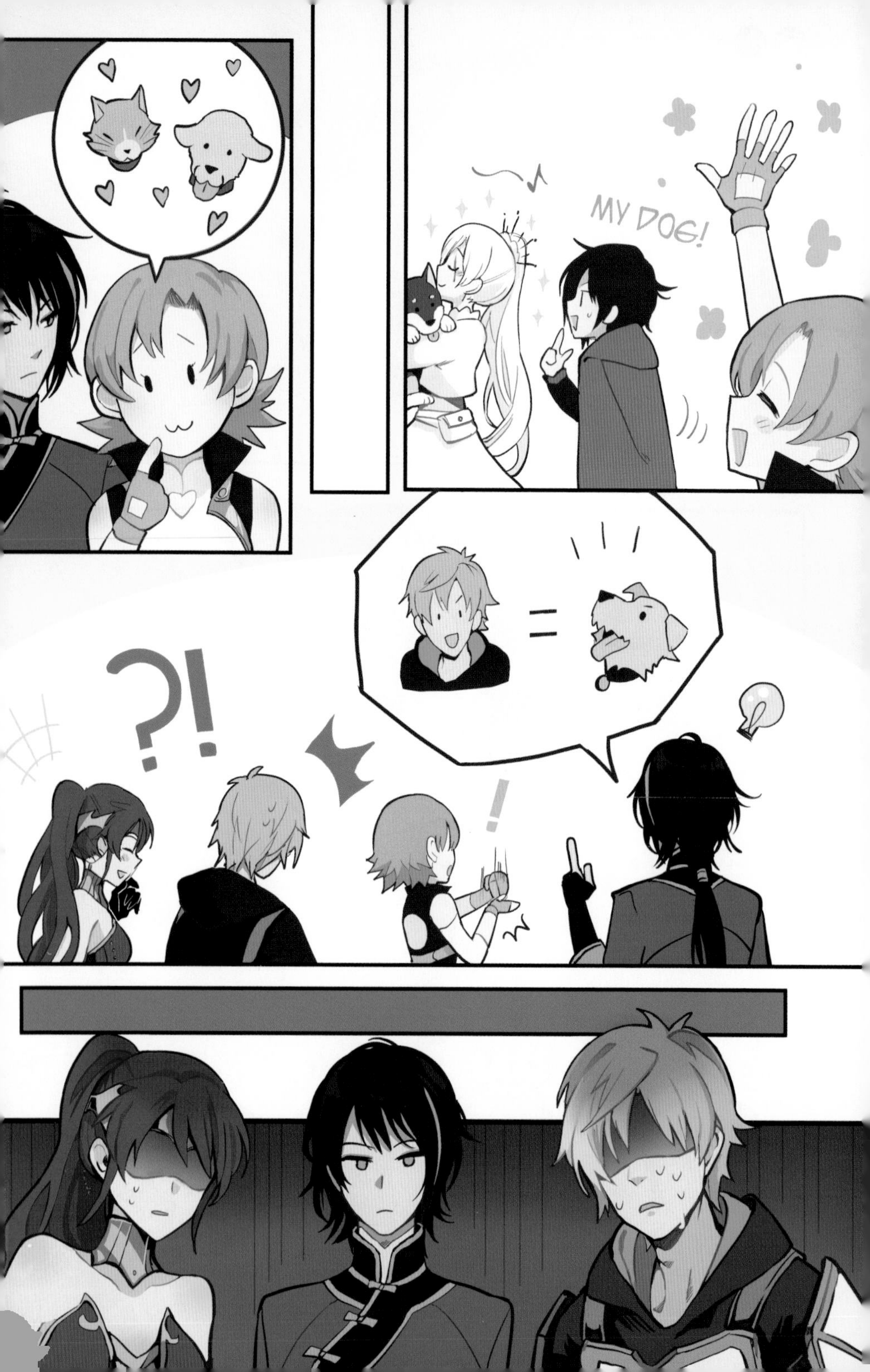
MY DOG!
?!
!

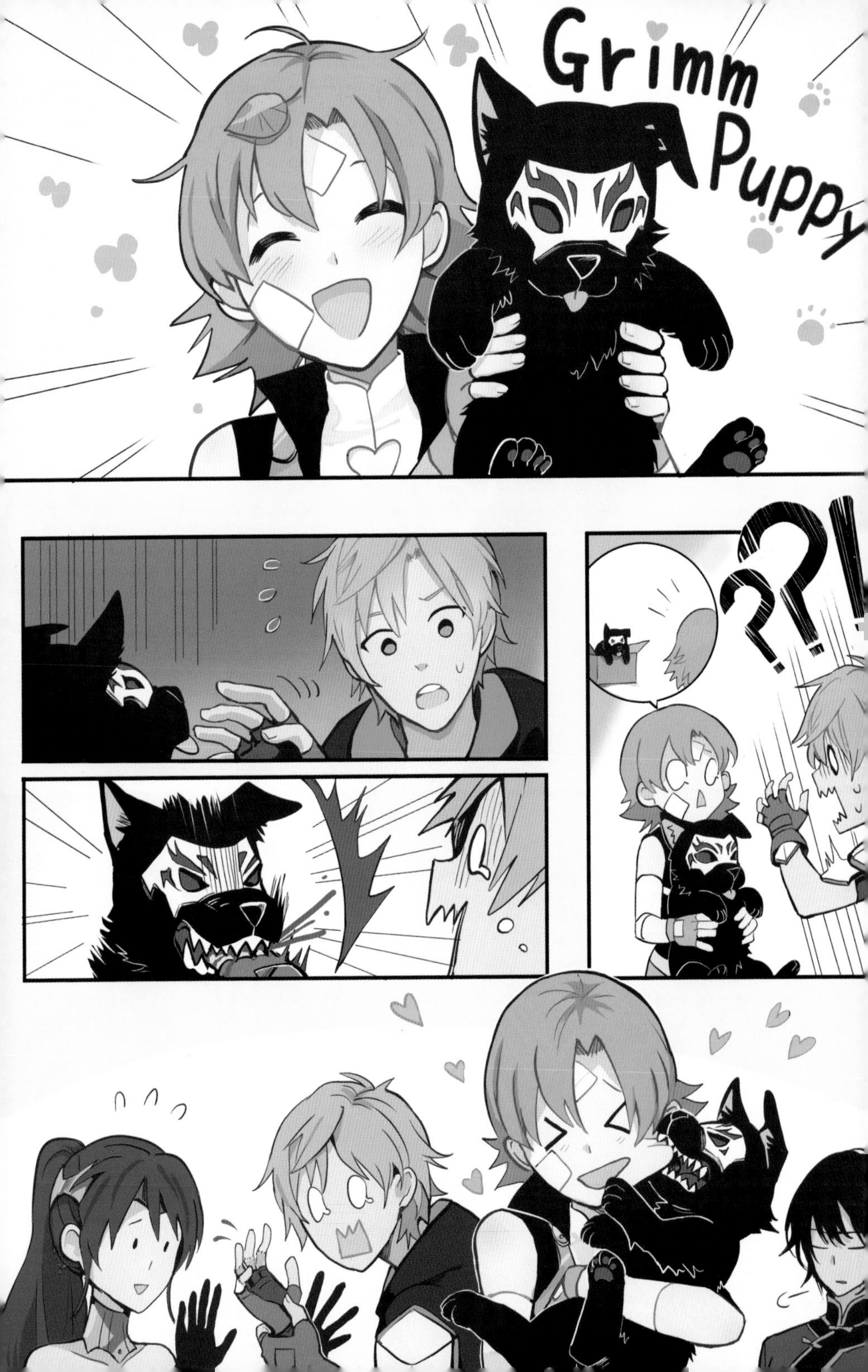
Grimm Puppy
??!

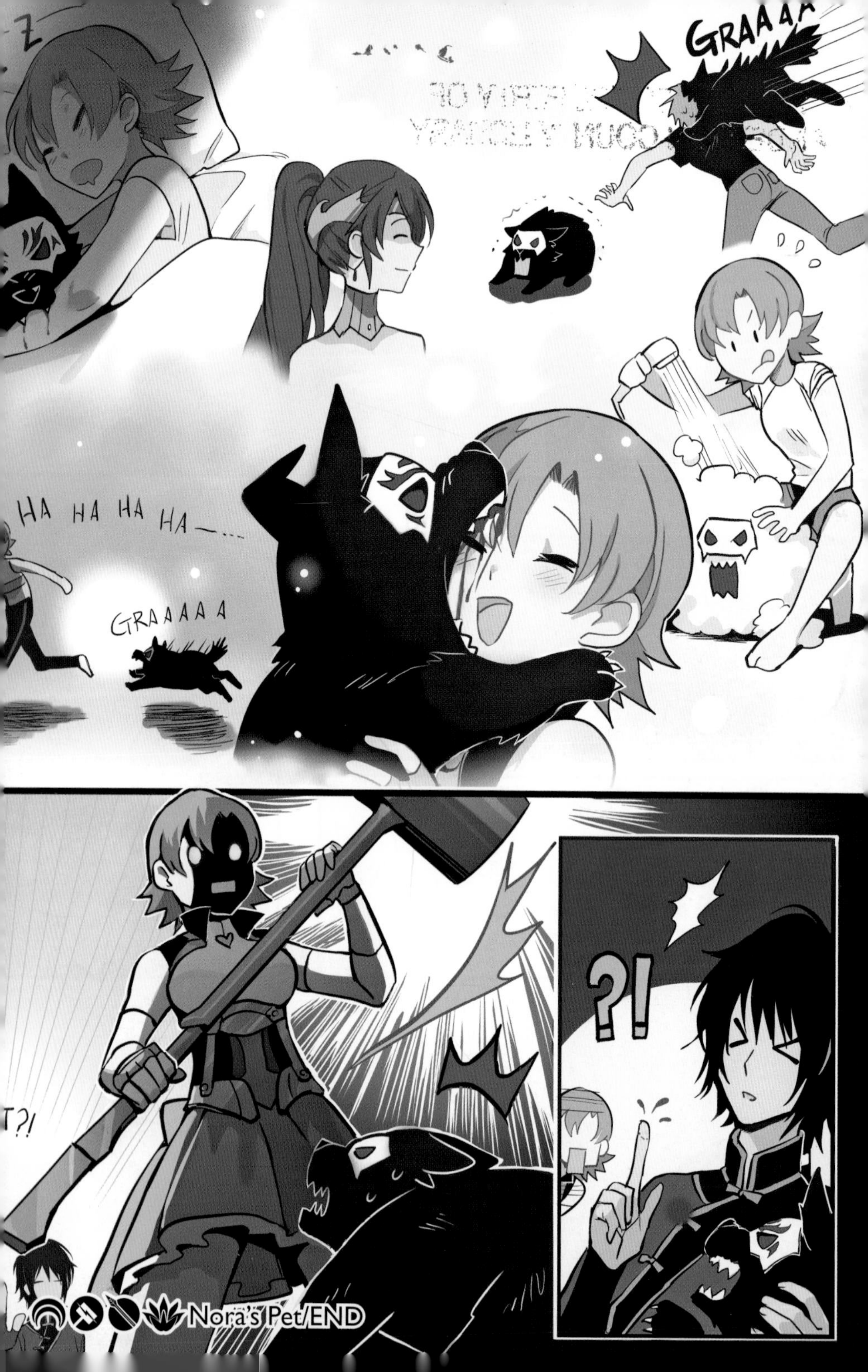
GRAAAA
HA HA HA HA—...
GRAAAAA
?!
T?!
Nora's Pet/END

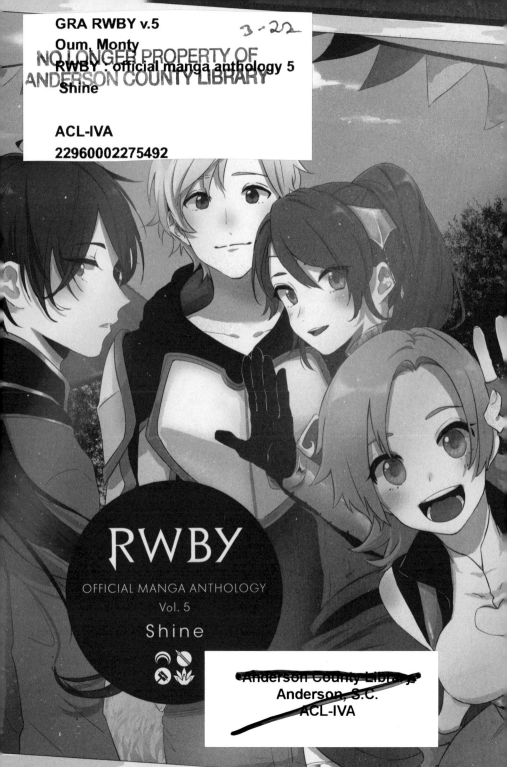

RWBY

OFFICIAL MANGA ANTHOLOGY

Vol. 5

Shine

RWBY
OFFICIAL MANGA ANTHOLOGY 5

Shine
CONTENTS

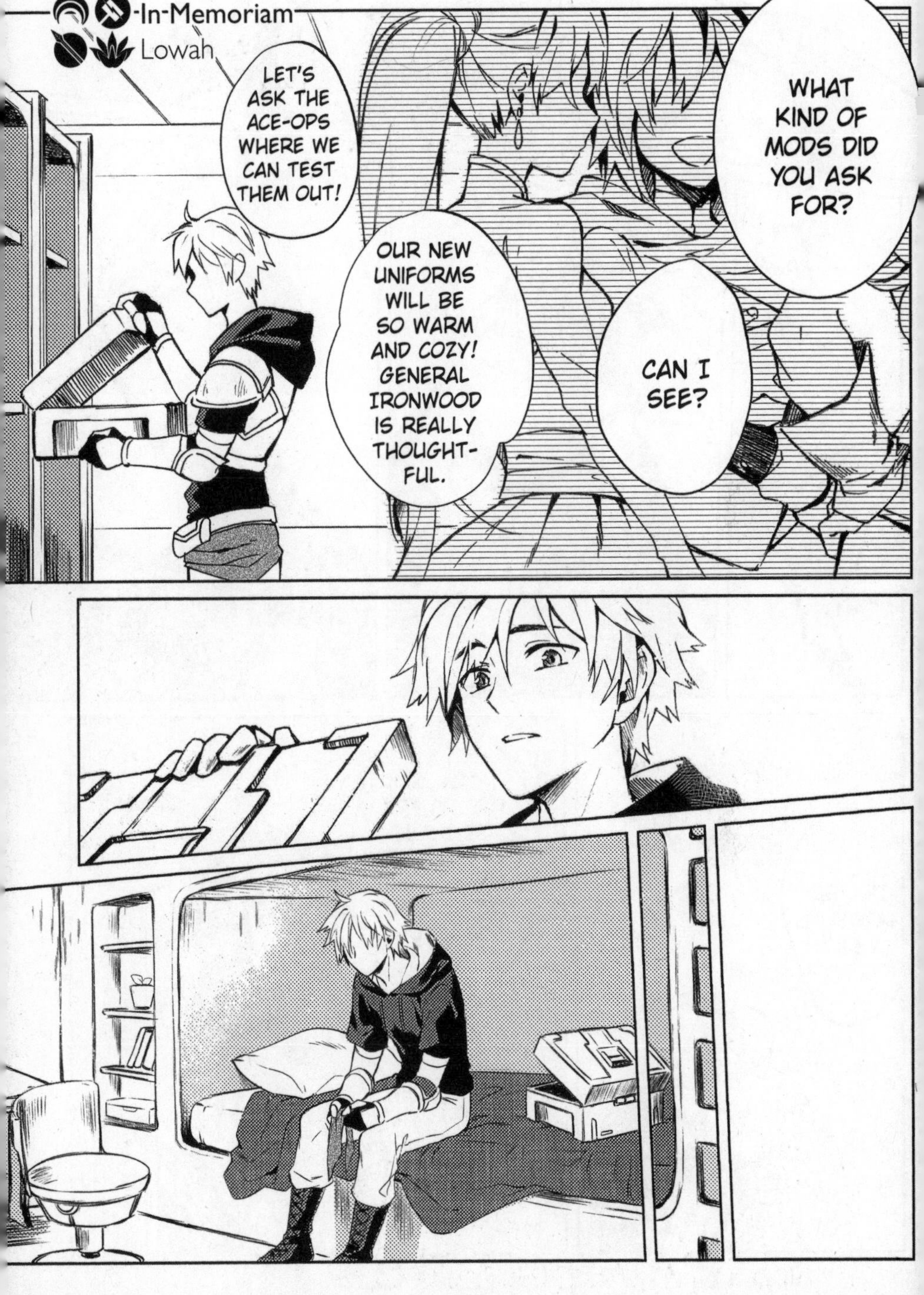
WHAT KIND OF MODS DID YOU ASK FOR?
CAN I SEE?
OUR NEW UNIFORMS WILL BE SO WARM AND COZY! GENERAL IRONWOOD IS REALLY THOUGHT-FUL.
LET'S ASK THE ACE-OPS WHERE WE CAN TEST THEM OUT!

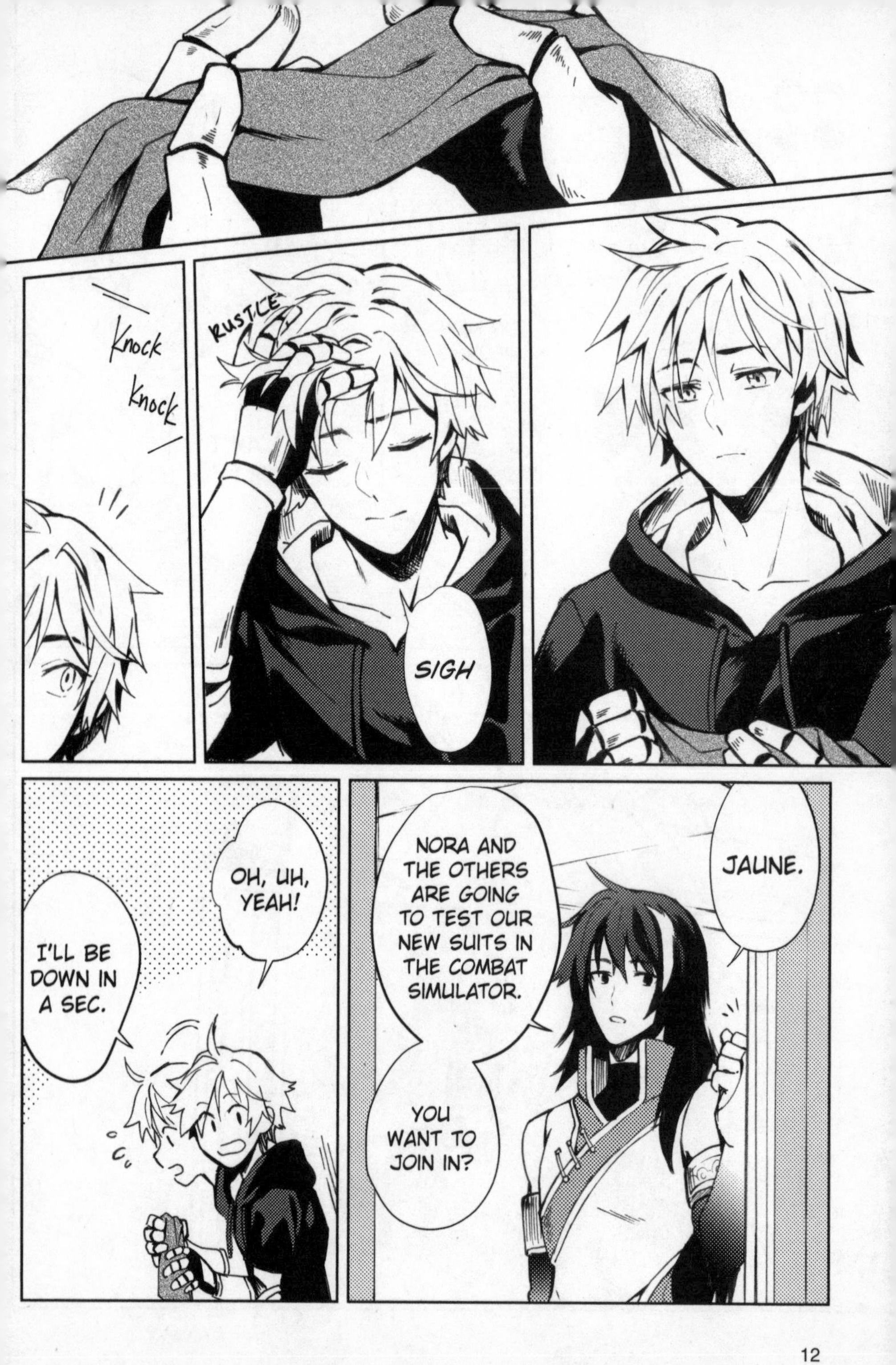
RUSTLE
SIGH
Knock
Knock
JAUNE.
NORA AND THE OTHERS ARE GOING TO TEST OUR NEW SUITS IN THE COMBAT SIMULATOR.
YOU WANT TO JOIN IN?
OH, UH, YEAH!
I'LL BE DOWN IN A SEC.

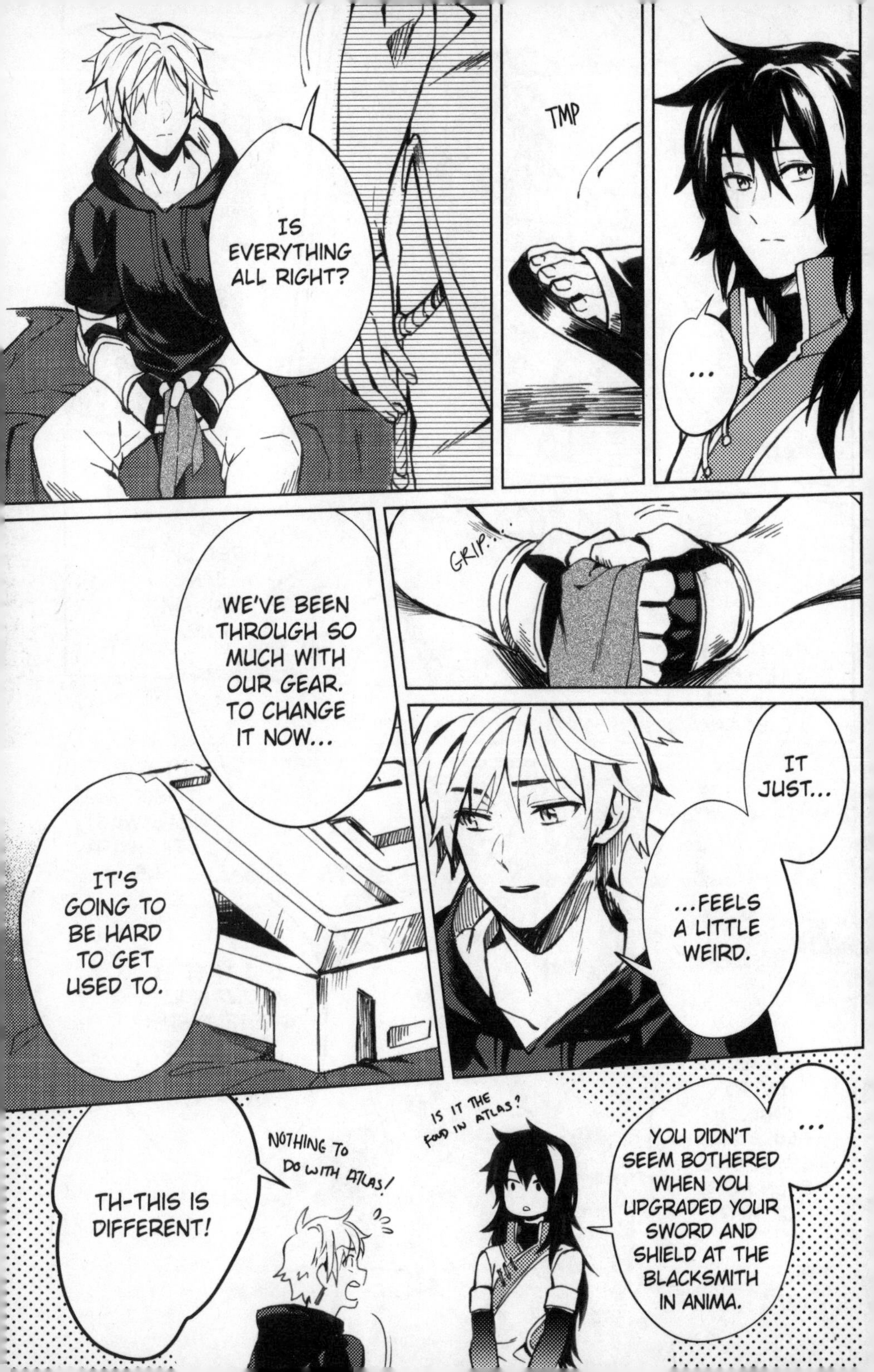
...
TMP
IS EVERYTHING ALL RIGHT?
GRIP...
IT JUST...
...FEELS A LITTLE WEIRD.
WE'VE BEEN THROUGH SO MUCH WITH OUR GEAR. TO CHANGE IT NOW...
IT'S GOING TO BE HARD TO GET USED TO.
...
YOU DIDN'T SEEM BOTHERED WHEN YOU UPGRADED YOUR SWORD AND SHIELD AT THE BLACKSMITH IN ANIMA.
IS IT THE FOOD IN ATLAS?
TH-THIS IS DIFFERENT!
NOTHING TO DO WITH ATLAS!

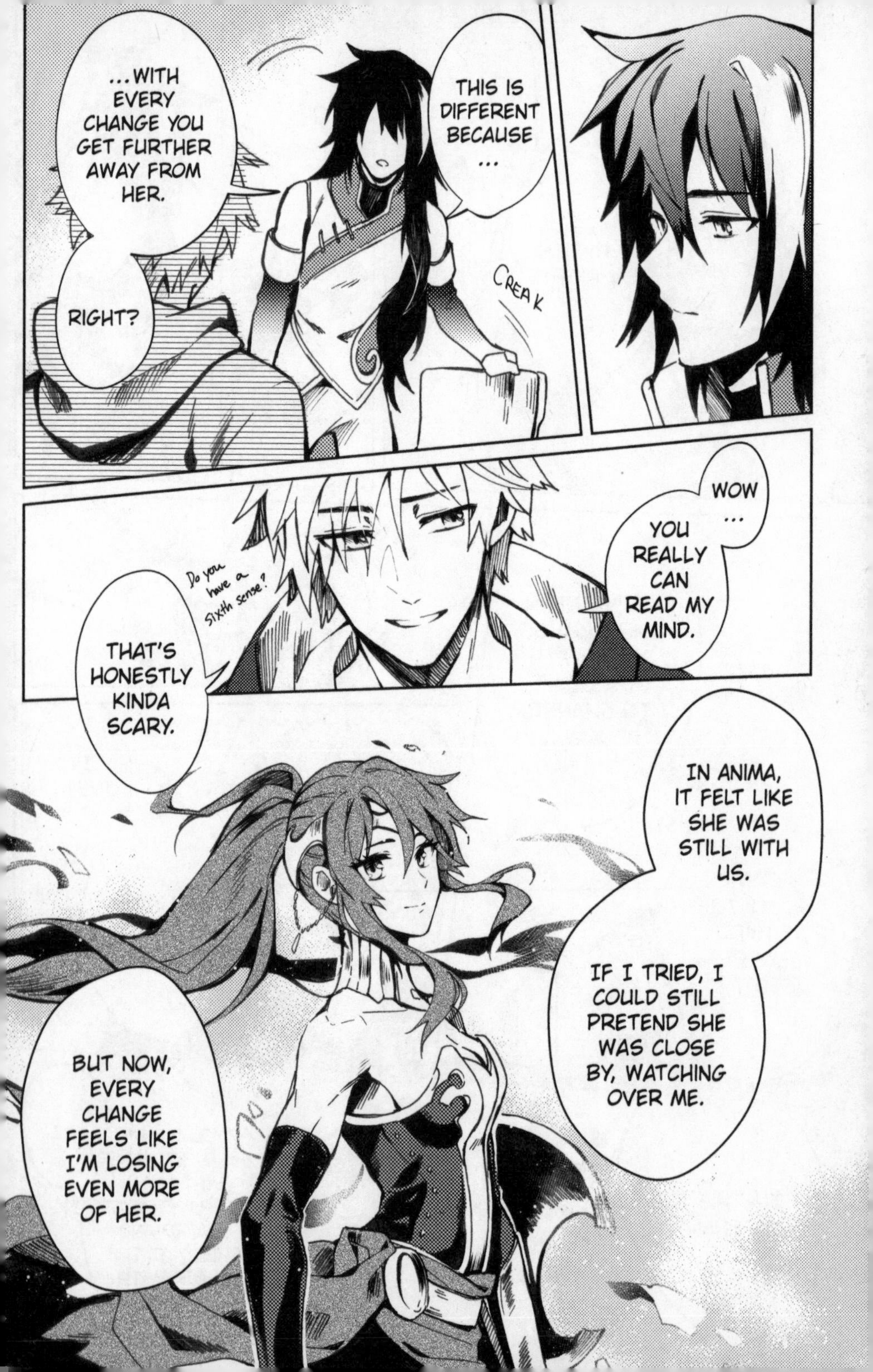
THIS IS DIFFERENT BECAUSE ...
...WITH EVERY CHANGE YOU GET FURTHER AWAY FROM HER.
CREAK
RIGHT?
WOW ...
YOU REALLY CAN READ MY MIND.
Do you have a sixth sense?
THAT'S HONESTLY KINDA SCARY.
IN ANIMA, IT FELT LIKE SHE WAS STILL WITH US.
IF I TRIED, I COULD STILL PRETEND SHE WAS CLOSE BY, WATCHING OVER ME.
BUT NOW, EVERY CHANGE FEELS LIKE I'M LOSING EVEN MORE OF HER.

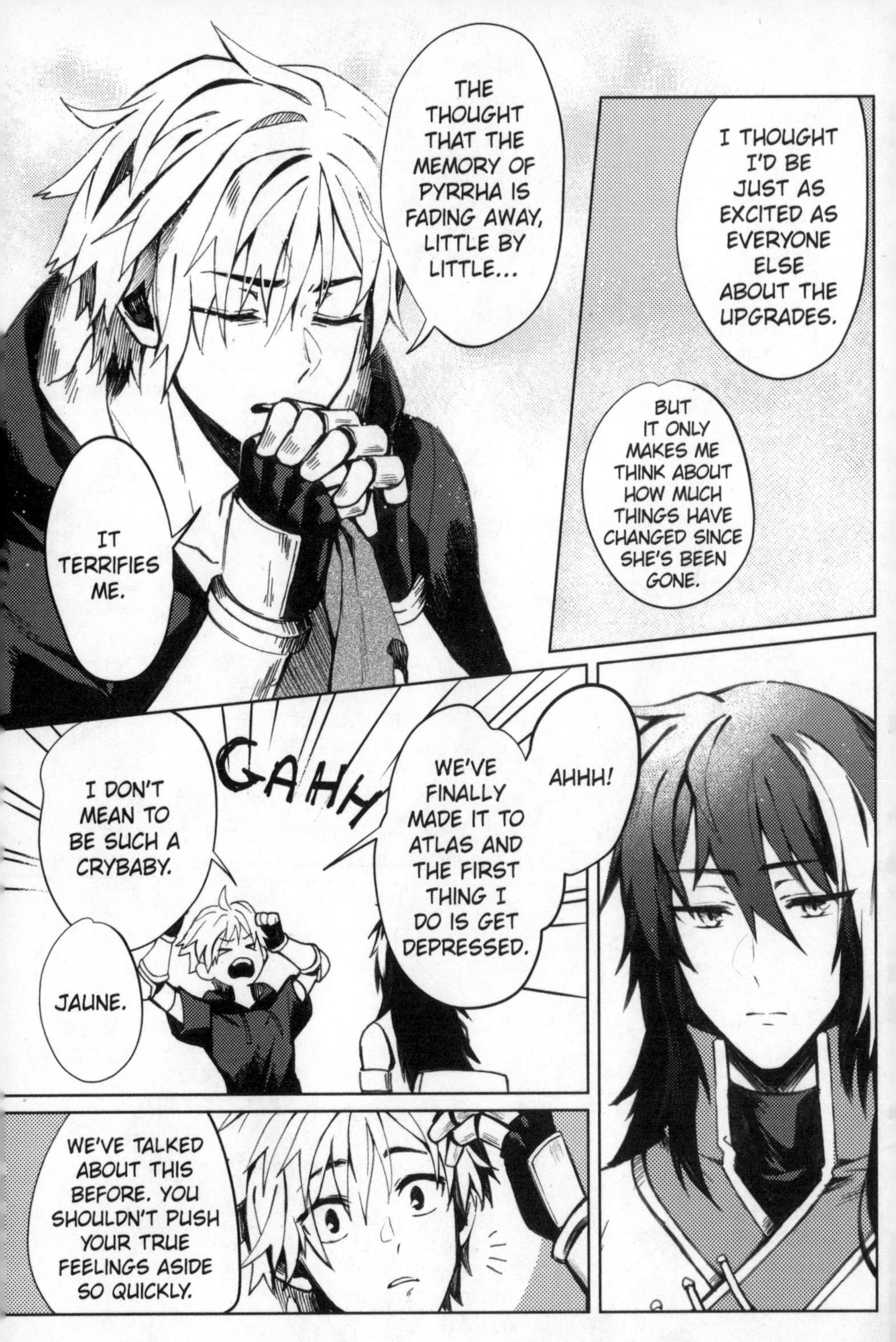
I THOUGHT I'D BE JUST AS EXCITED AS EVERYONE ELSE ABOUT THE UPGRADES.
BUT IT ONLY MAKES ME THINK ABOUT HOW MUCH THINGS HAVE CHANGED SINCE SHE'S BEEN GONE.
THE THOUGHT THAT THE MEMORY OF PYRRHA IS FADING AWAY, LITTLE BY LITTLE...
IT TERRIFIES ME.
AHHH!
GAHH
WE'VE FINALLY MADE IT TO ATLAS AND THE FIRST THING I DO IS GET DEPRESSED.
I DON'T MEAN TO BE SUCH A CRYBABY.
JAUNE.
WE'VE TALKED ABOUT THIS BEFORE. YOU SHOULDN'T PUSH YOUR TRUE FEELINGS ASIDE SO QUICKLY.

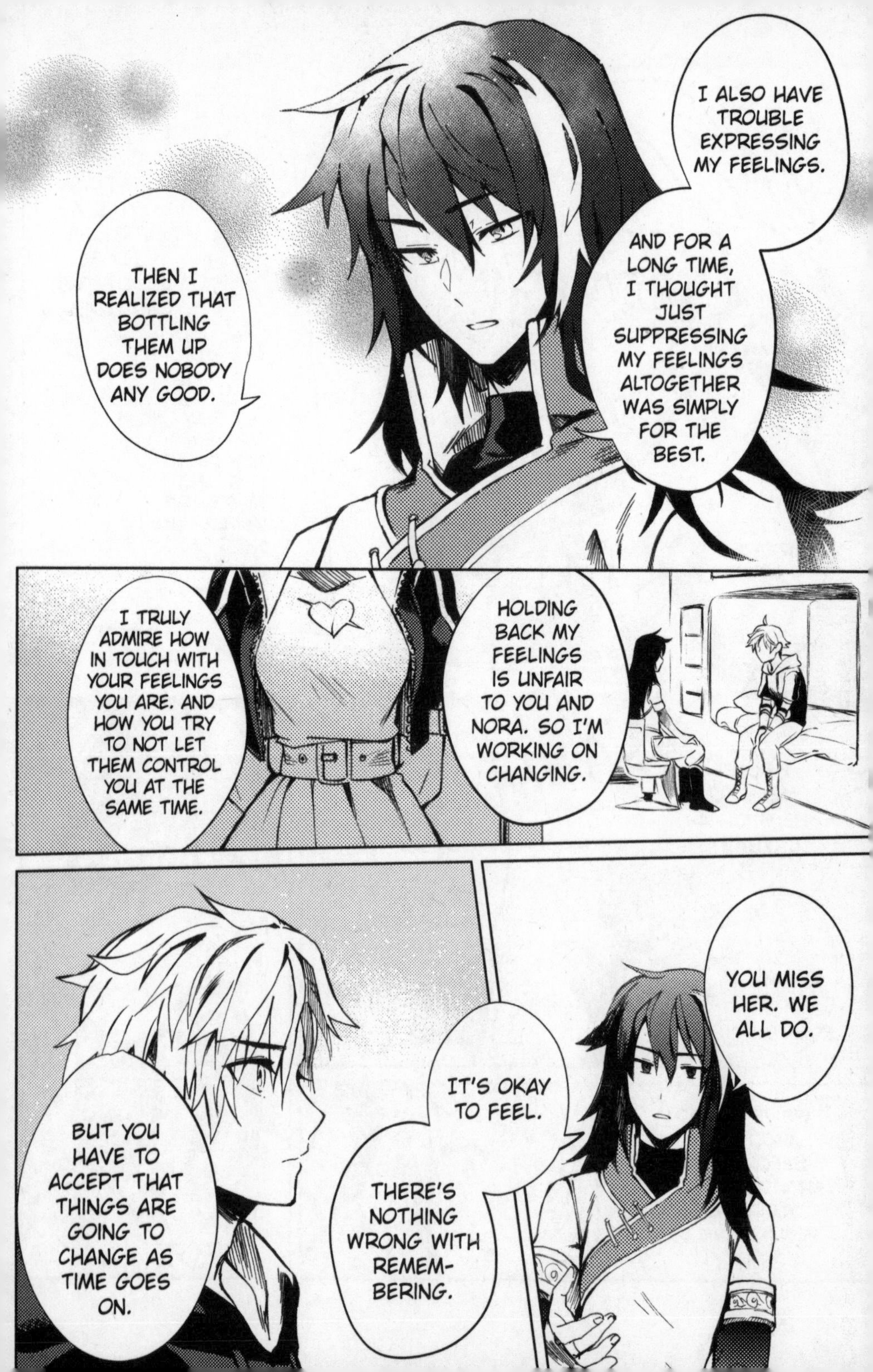
I ALSO HAVE TROUBLE EXPRESSING MY FEELINGS.
AND FOR A LONG TIME, I THOUGHT JUST SUPPRESSING MY FEELINGS ALTOGETHER WAS SIMPLY FOR THE BEST.
THEN I REALIZED THAT BOTTLING THEM UP DOES NOBODY ANY GOOD.
HOLDING BACK MY FEELINGS IS UNFAIR TO YOU AND NORA. SO I'M WORKING ON CHANGING.
I TRULY ADMIRE HOW IN TOUCH WITH YOUR FEELINGS YOU ARE. AND HOW YOU TRY TO NOT LET THEM CONTROL YOU AT THE SAME TIME.
YOU MISS HER. WE ALL DO.
IT'S OKAY TO FEEL.
THERE'S NOTHING WRONG WITH REMEM-BERING.
BUT YOU HAVE TO ACCEPT THAT THINGS ARE GOING TO CHANGE AS TIME GOES ON.

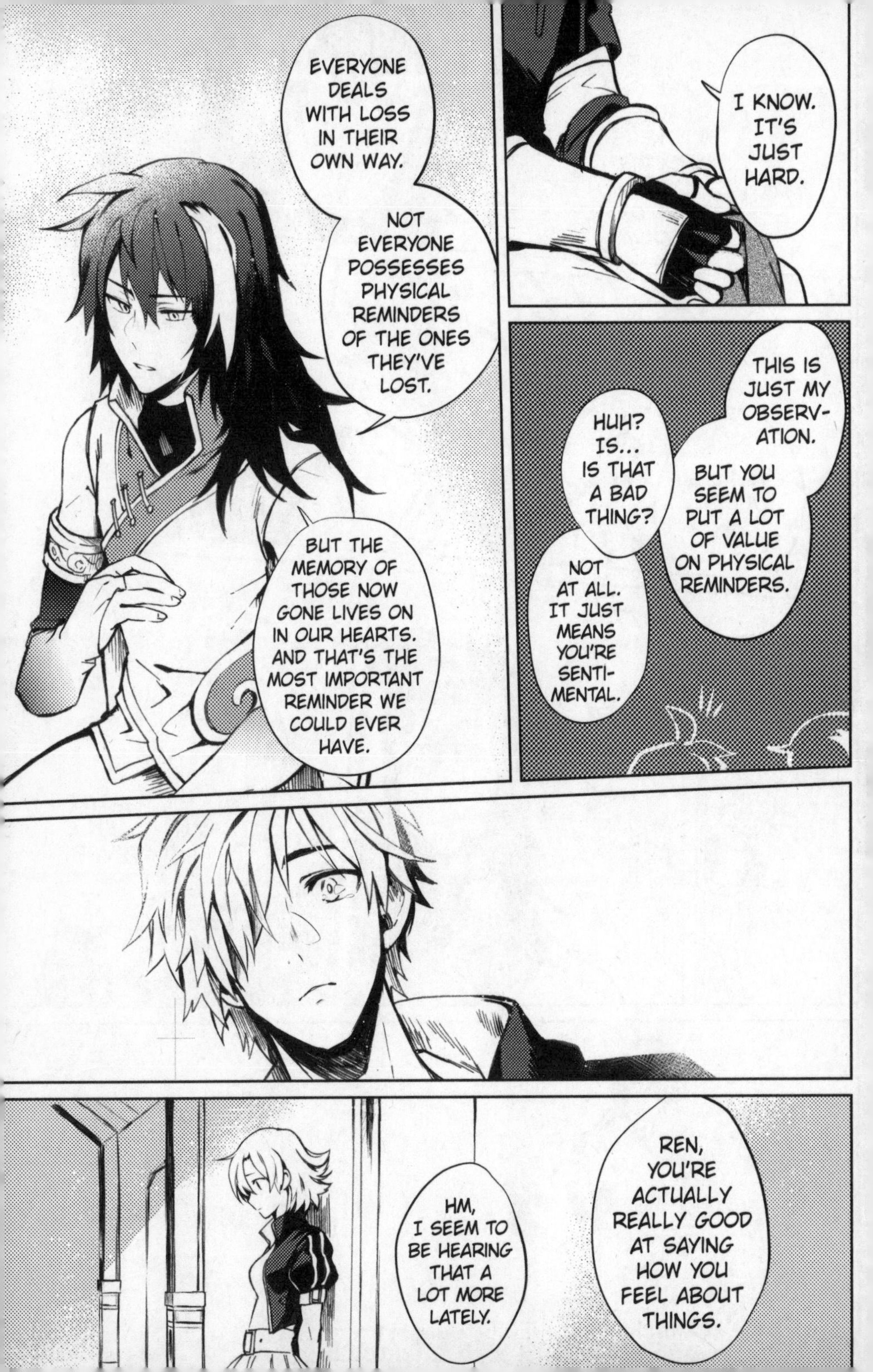
I KNOW. IT'S JUST HARD.
THIS IS JUST MY OBSERVATION.
BUT YOU SEEM TO PUT A LOT OF VALUE ON PHYSICAL REMINDERS.
HUH? IS... IS THAT A BAD THING?
NOT AT ALL. IT JUST MEANS YOU'RE SENTIMENTAL.
EVERYONE DEALS WITH LOSS IN THEIR OWN WAY.
NOT EVERYONE POSSESSES PHYSICAL REMINDERS OF THE ONES THEY'VE LOST.
BUT THE MEMORY OF THOSE NOW GONE LIVES ON IN OUR HEARTS. AND THAT'S THE MOST IMPORTANT REMINDER WE COULD EVER HAVE.
REN, YOU'RE ACTUALLY REALLY GOOD AT SAYING HOW YOU FEEL ABOUT THINGS.
HM, I SEEM TO BE HEARING THAT A LOT MORE LATELY.

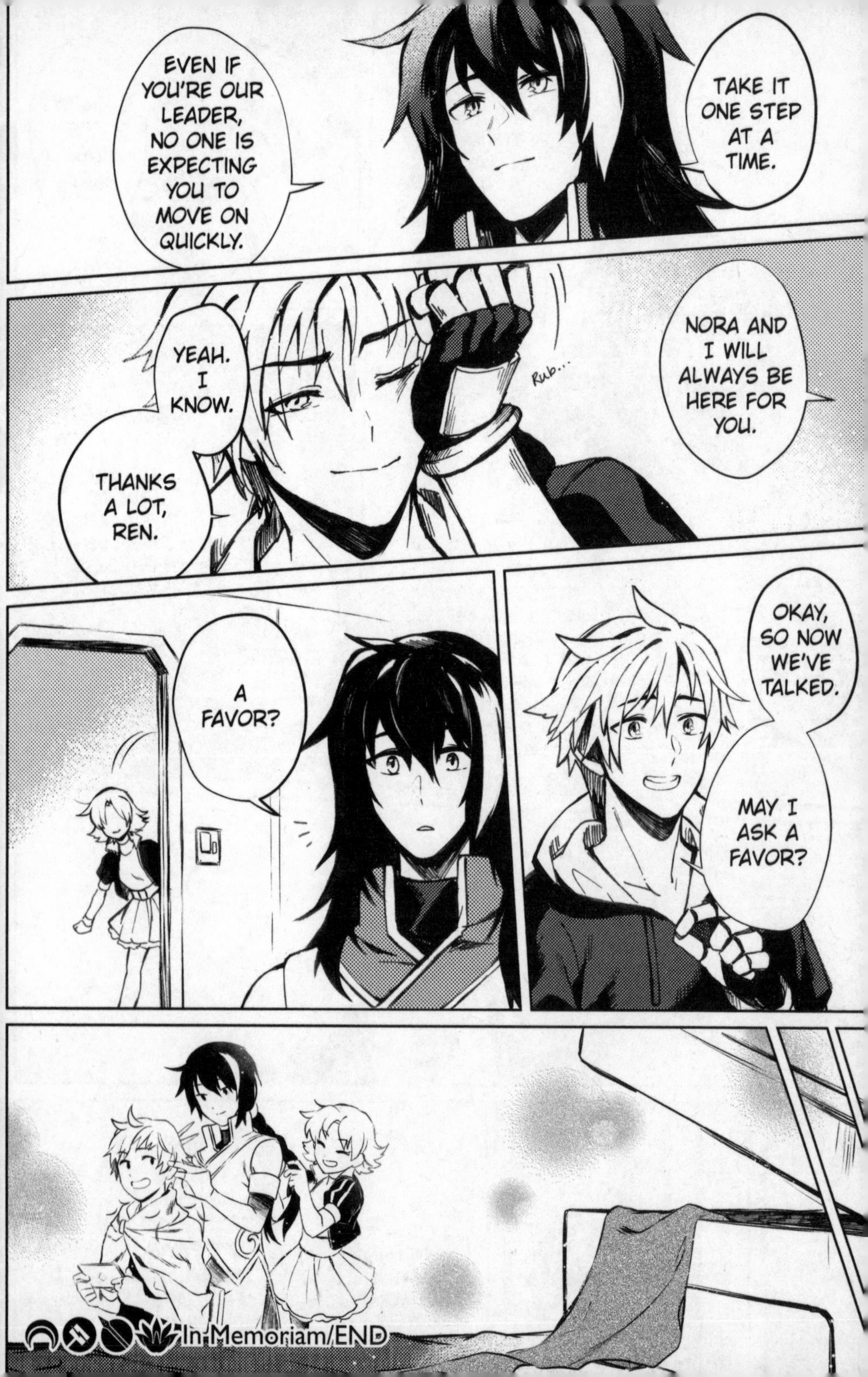
TAKE IT ONE STEP AT A TIME.
EVEN IF YOU'RE OUR LEADER, NO ONE IS EXPECTING YOU TO MOVE ON QUICKLY.
NORA AND I WILL ALWAYS BE HERE FOR YOU.
Rub...
YEAH. I KNOW.
THANKS A LOT, REN.
OKAY, SO NOW WE'VE TALKED.
MAY I ASK A FAVOR?
A FAVOR?
In Memoriam/END

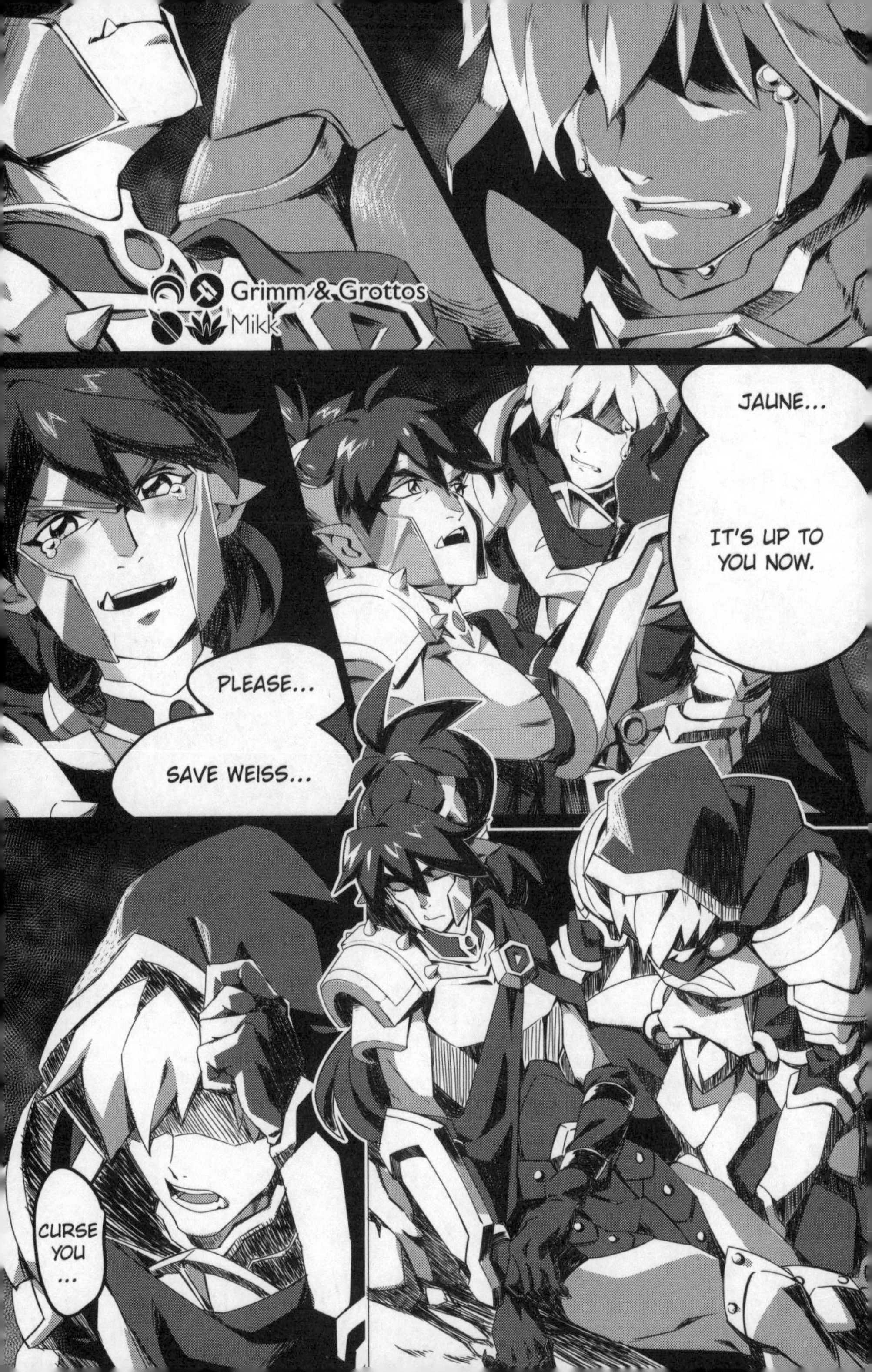
Grimm & Grottos
Mikk
JAUNE...
IT'S UP TO YOU NOW.
PLEASE...
SAVE WEISS...
CURSE YOU ...

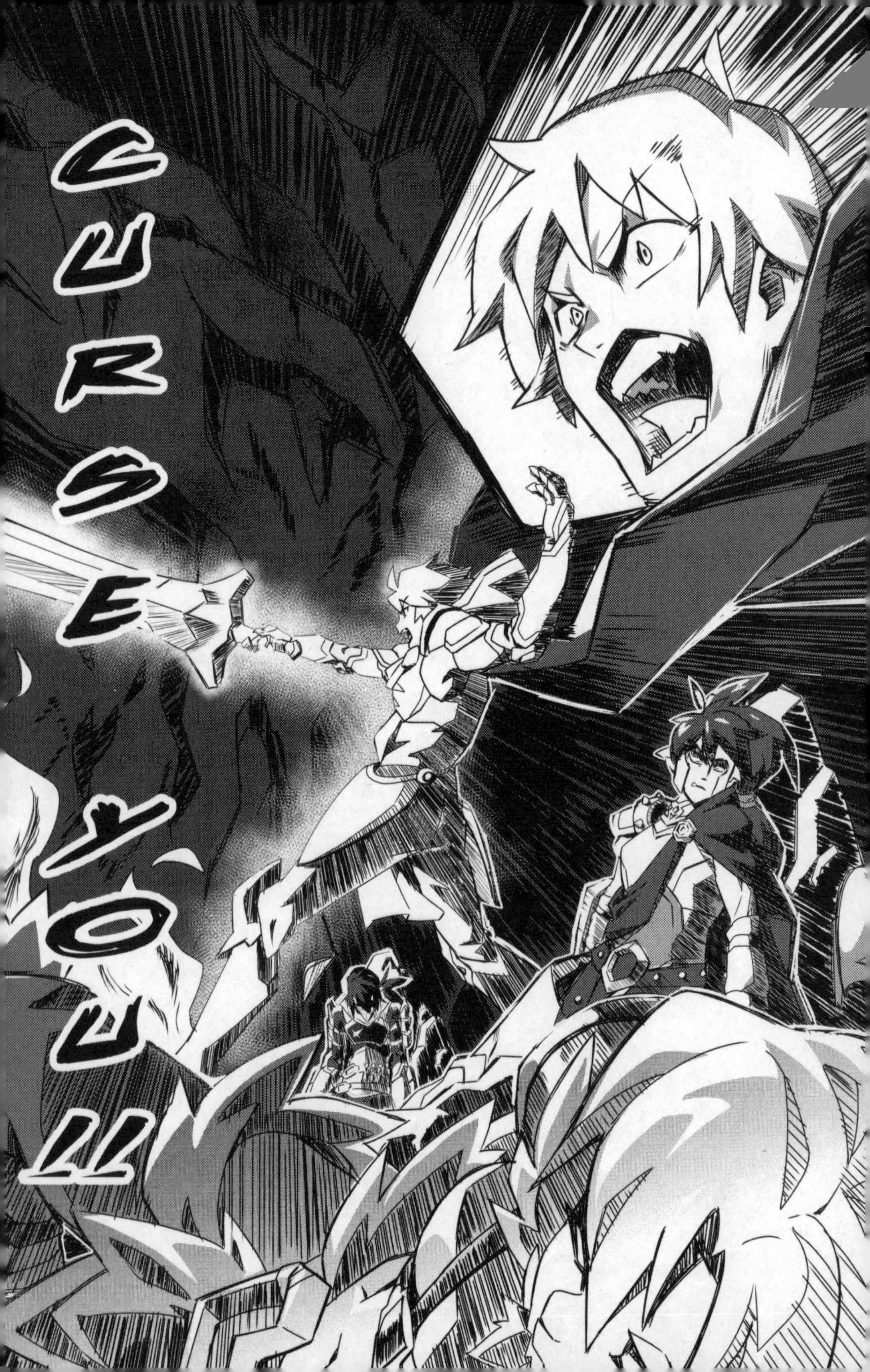
CURSE YOU!!

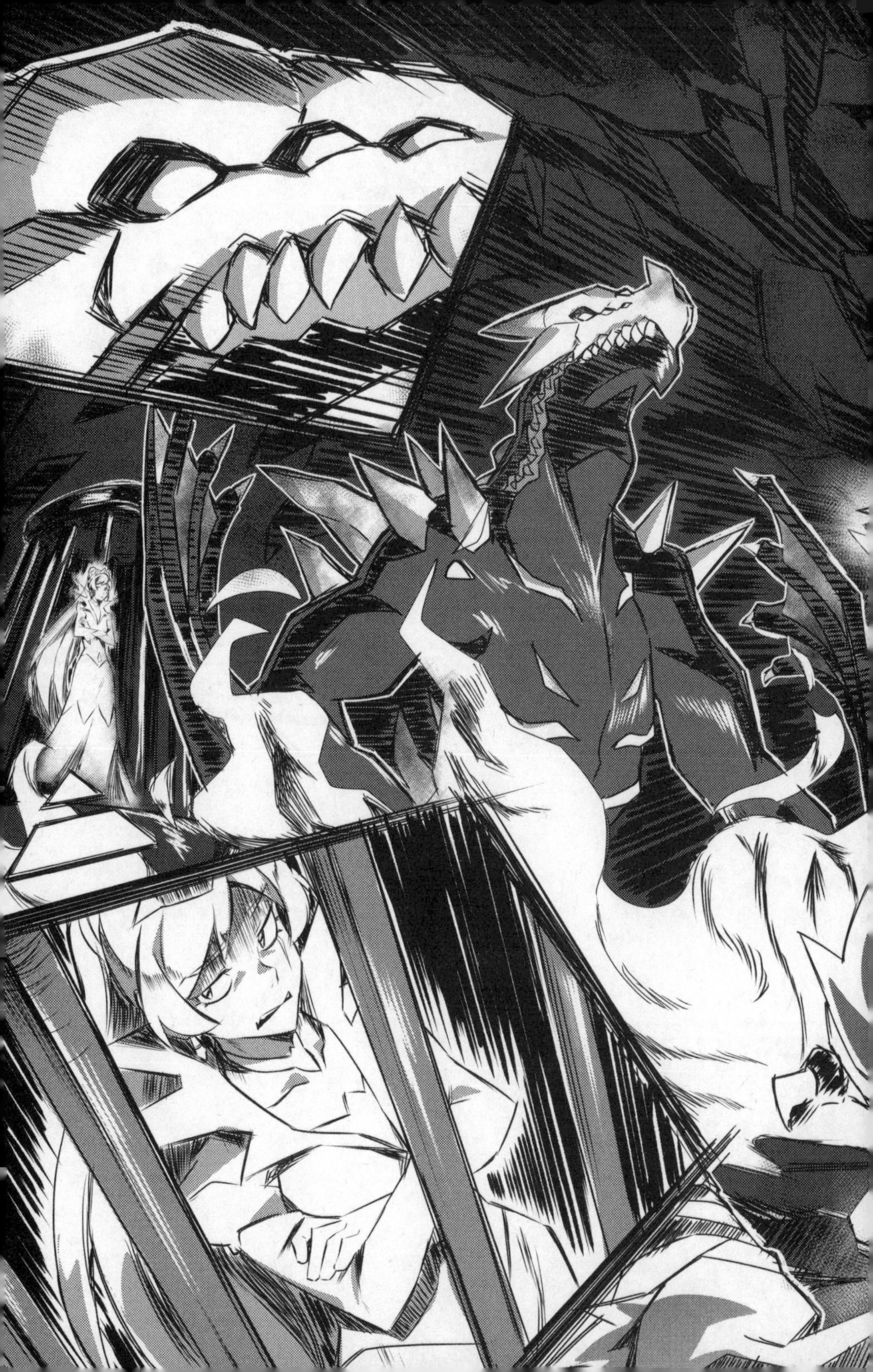

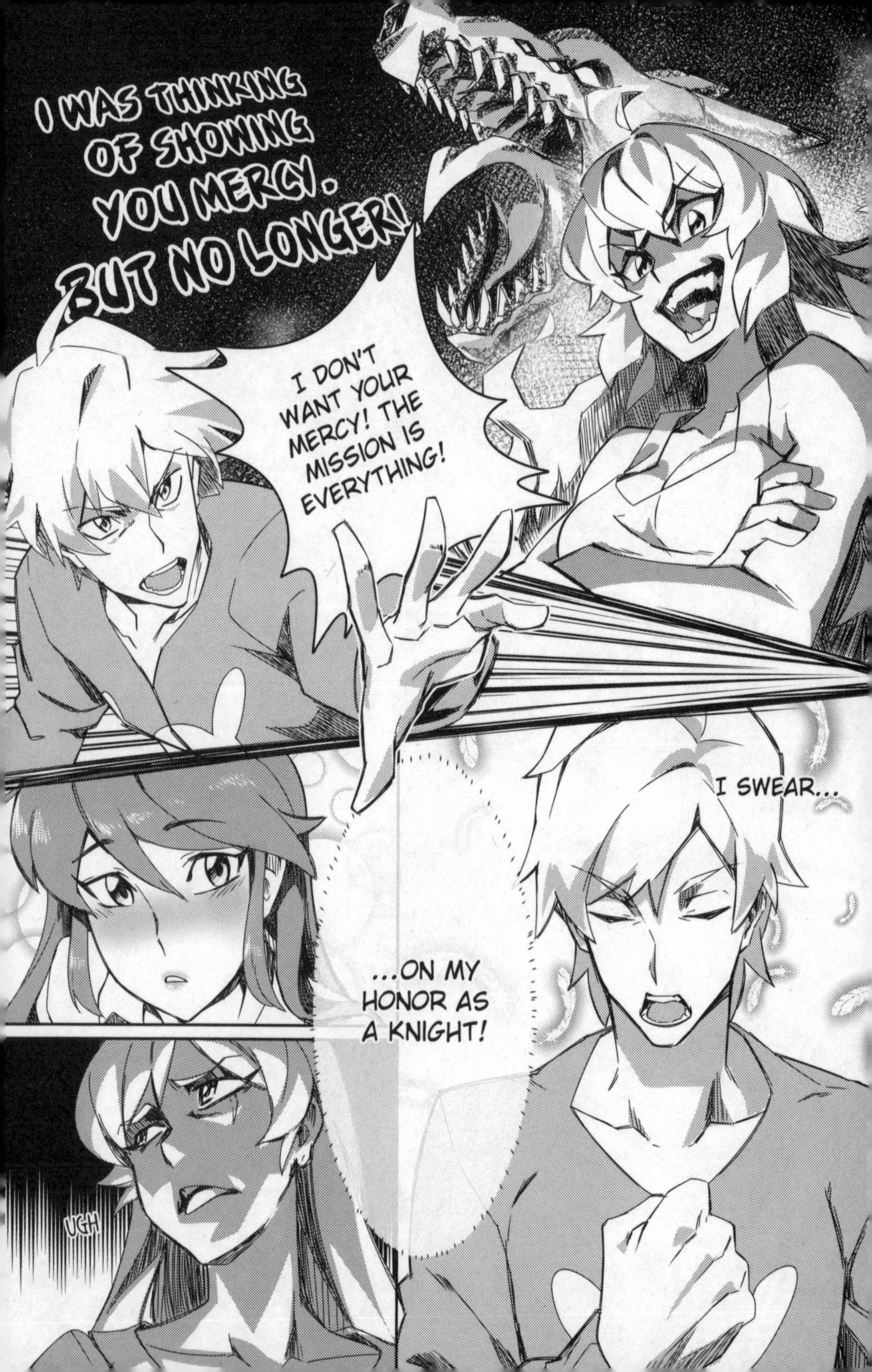
I WAS THINKING OF SHOWING YOU MERCY. BUT NO LONGER!
I DON'T WANT YOUR MERCY! THE MISSION IS EVERYTHING!
I SWEAR...
...ON MY HONOR AS A KNIGHT!
UGH

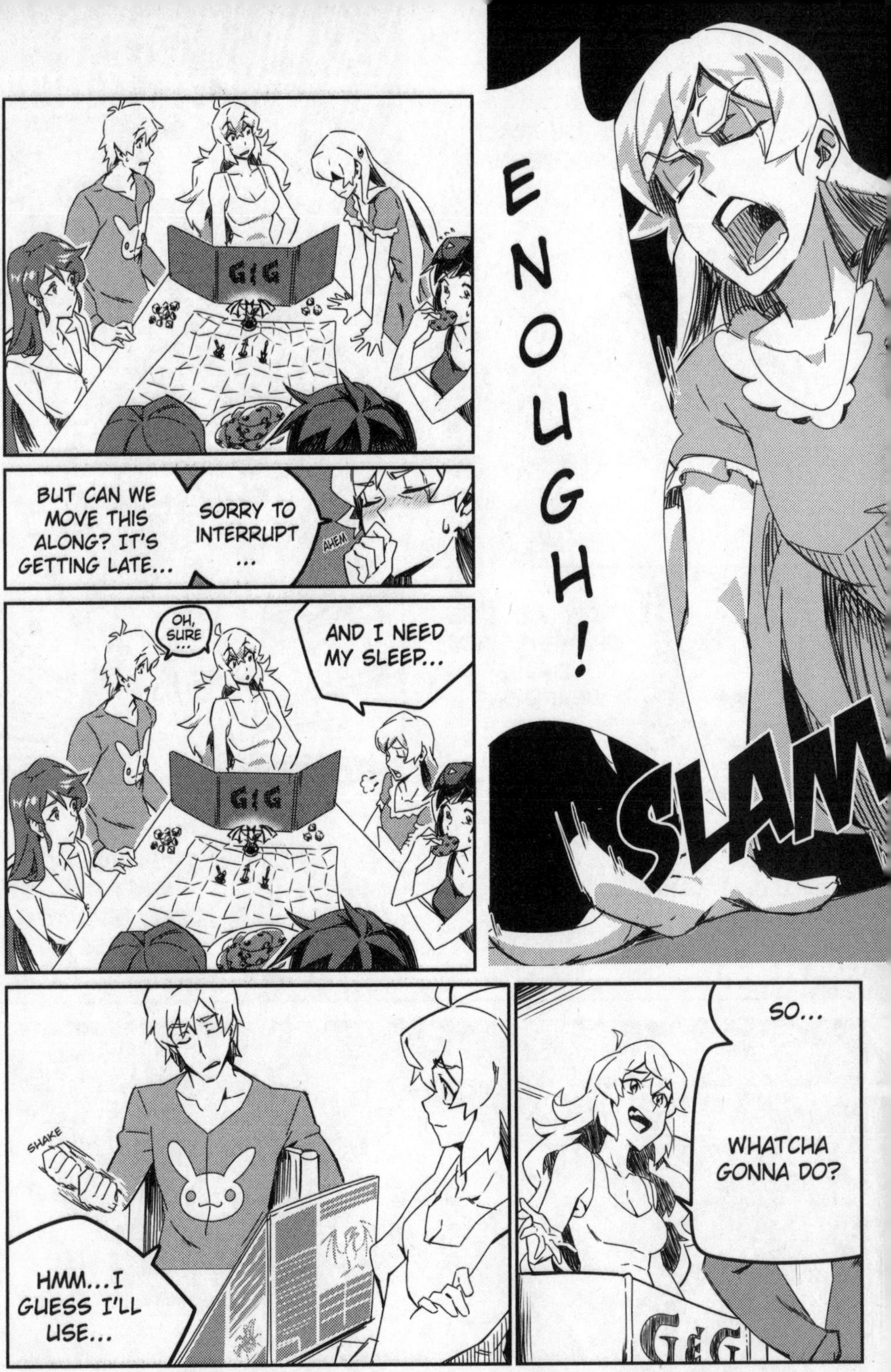
ENOUGH!
SLAM
AHEM
SORRY TO INTERRUPT...
BUT CAN WE MOVE THIS ALONG? IT'S GETTING LATE...
AND I NEED MY SLEEP...
OH, SURE...
SO...
WHATCHA GONNA DO?
SHAKE
HMM...I GUESS I'LL USE...

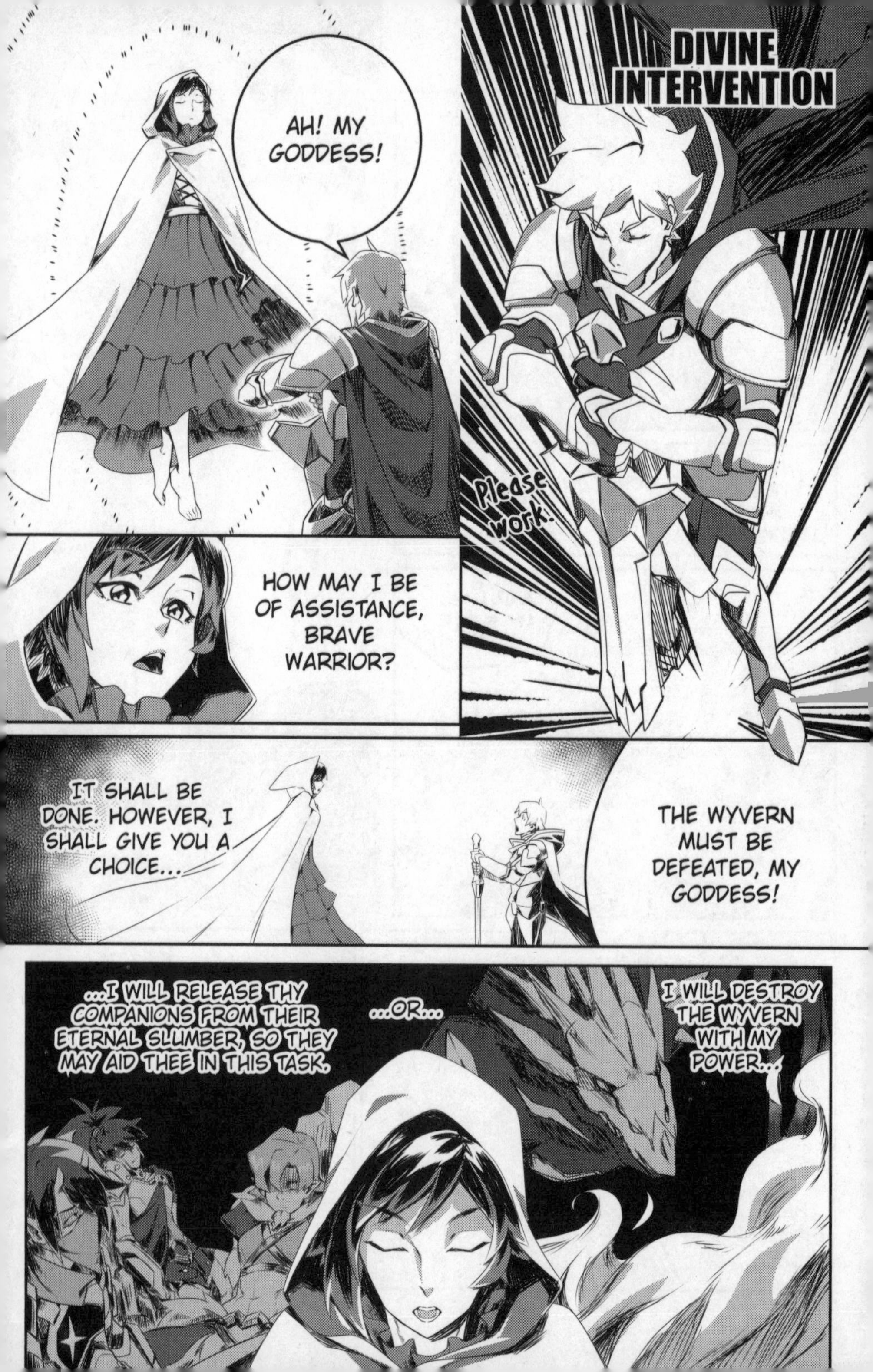
DIVINE INTERVENTION
Please work.
AH! MY GODDESS!
HOW MAY I BE OF ASSISTANCE, BRAVE WARRIOR?
THE WYVERN MUST BE DEFEATED, MY GODDESS!
IT SHALL BE DONE. HOWEVER, I SHALL GIVE YOU A CHOICE...
I WILL DESTROY THE WYVERN WITH MY POWER...
...OR...
...I WILL RELEASE THY COMPANIONS FROM THEIR ETERNAL SLUMBER, SO THEY MAY AID THEE IN THIS TASK.

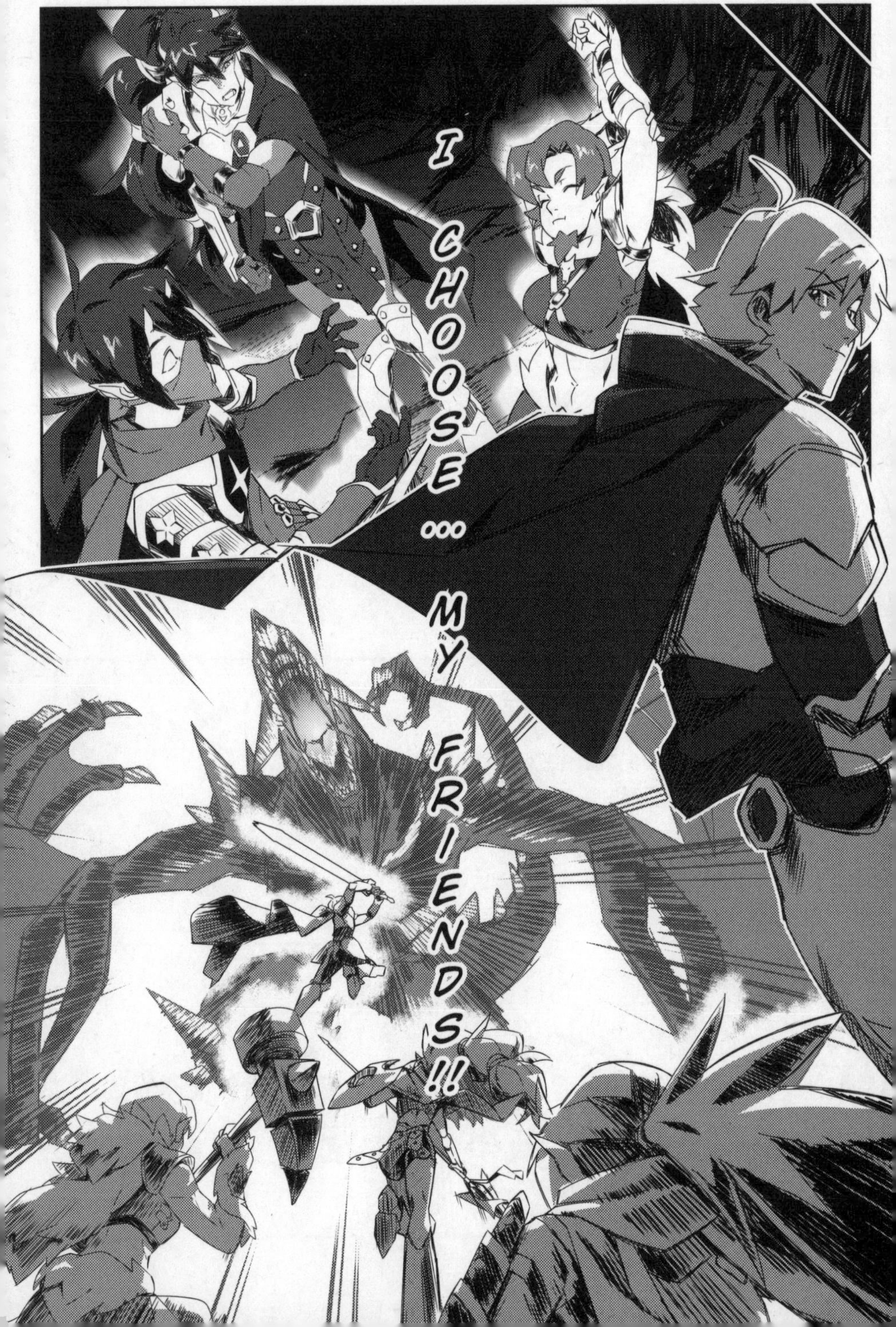
I CHOOSE... MY FRIENDS!!

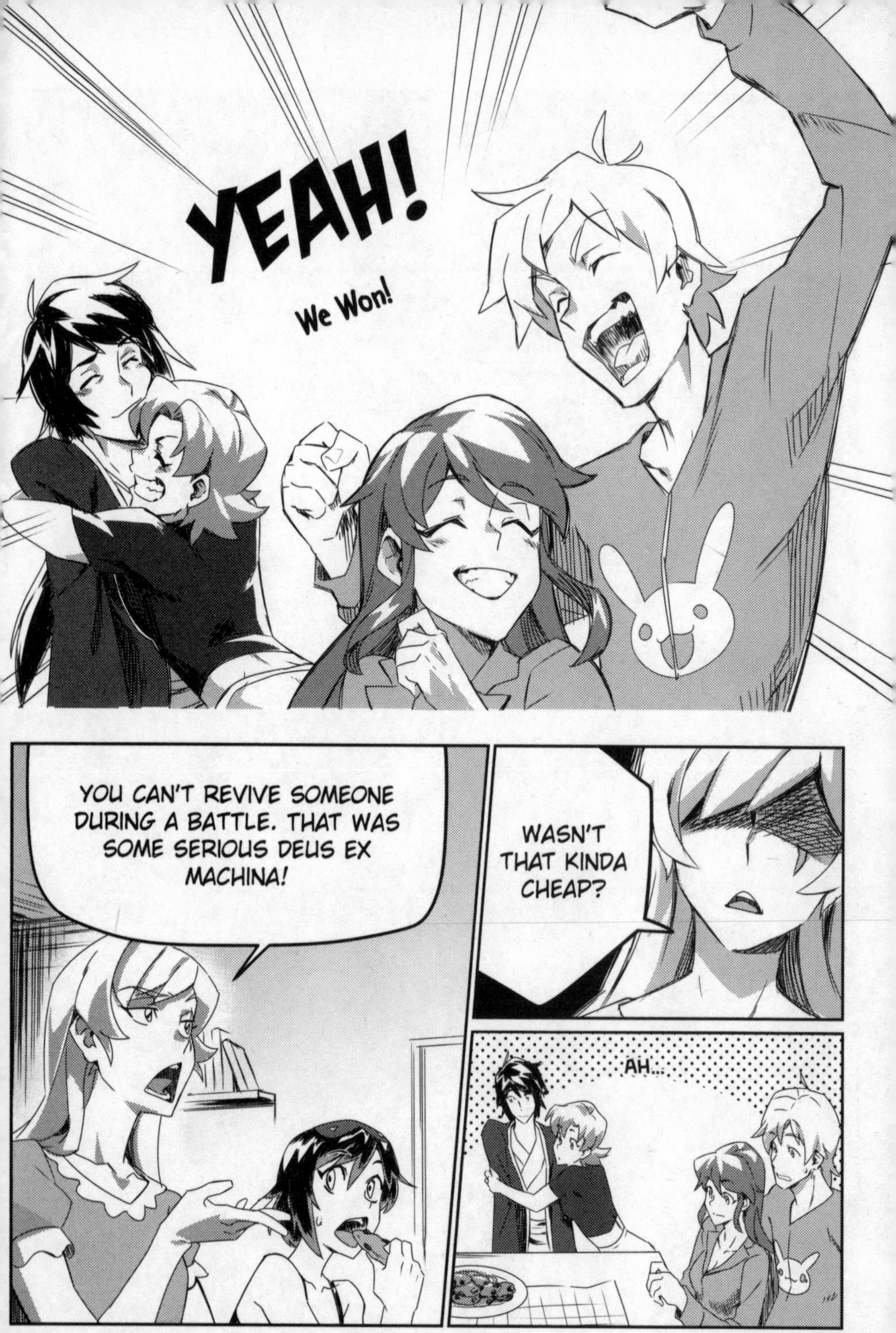
YEAH!
We Won!
WASN'T THAT KINDA CHEAP?
AH...
YOU CAN'T REVIVE SOMEONE DURING A BATTLE. THAT WAS SOME SERIOUS DEUS EX MACHINA!

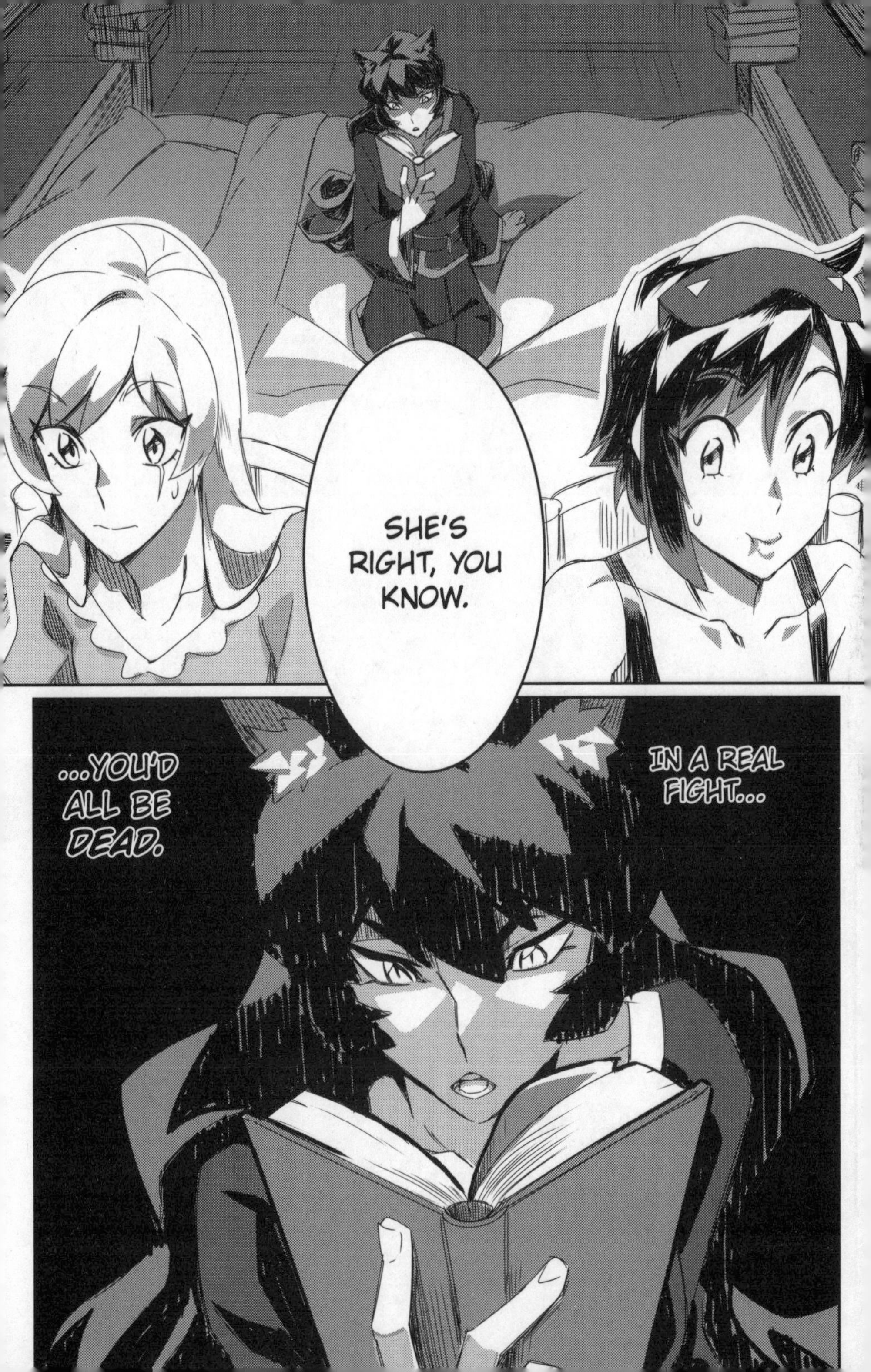
SHE'S RIGHT, YOU KNOW.
IN A REAL FIGHT...
...YOU'D ALL BE DEAD.

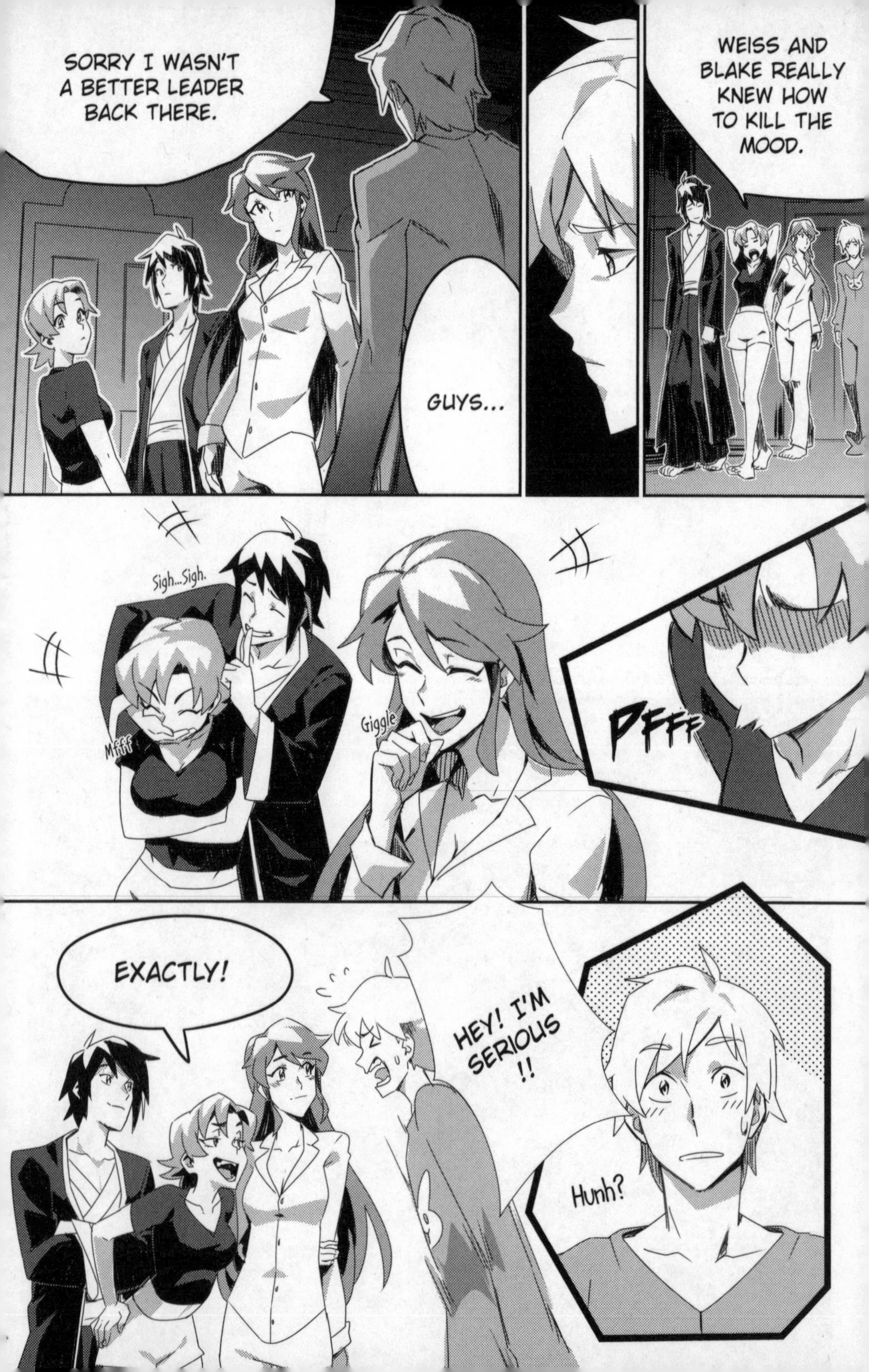
WEISS AND BLAKE REALLY KNEW HOW TO KILL THE MOOD.
SORRY I WASN'T A BETTER LEADER BACK THERE.
GUYS...
PFFF
Sigh...Sigh.
Giggle
Mfff
Hunh?
HEY! I'M SERIOUS !!
EXACTLY!

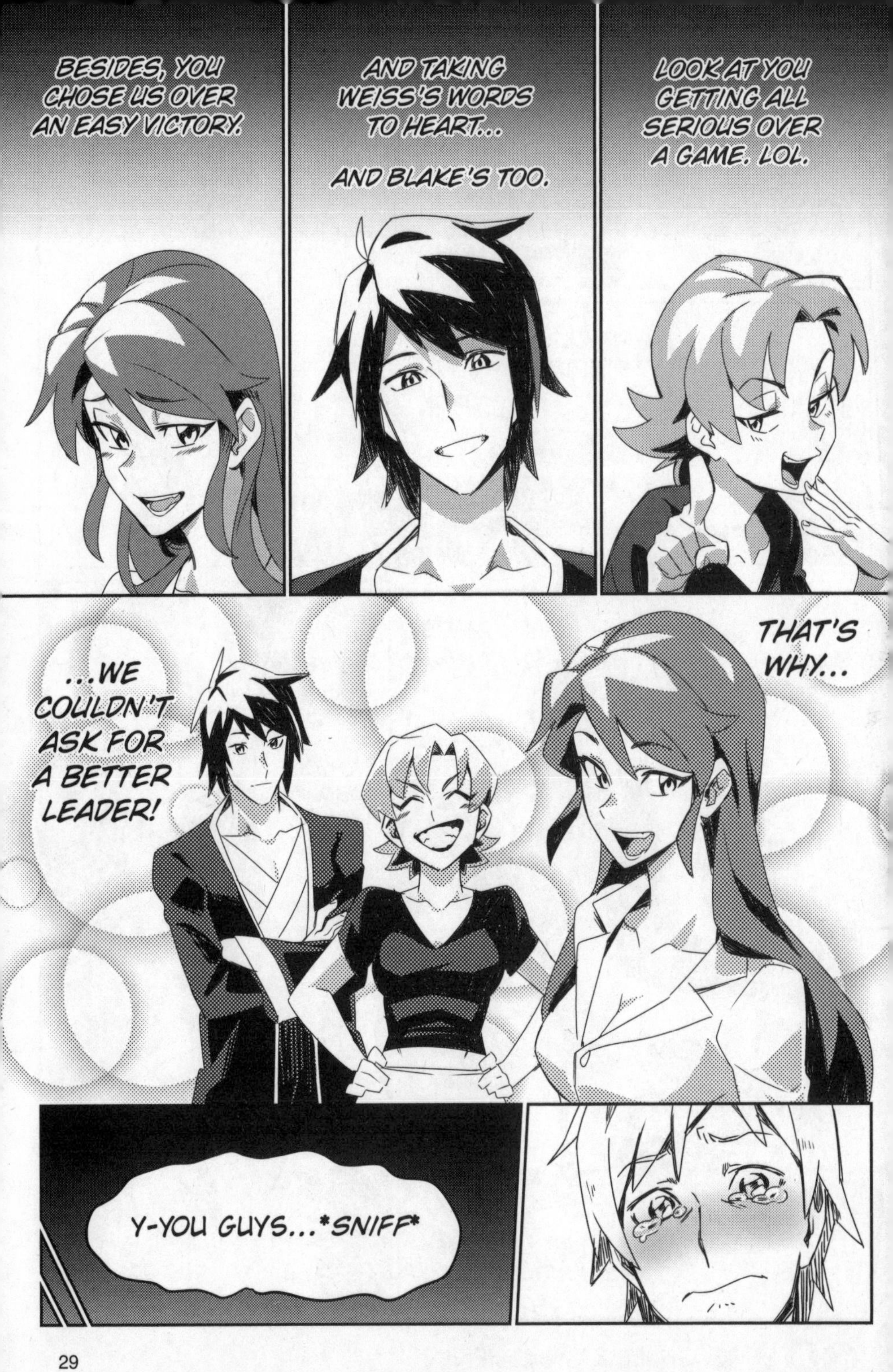
LOOK AT YOU GETTING ALL SERIOUS OVER A GAME. LOL.
AND TAKING WEISS'S WORDS TO HEART...
AND BLAKE'S TOO.
BESIDES, YOU CHOSE US OVER AN EASY VICTORY.
THAT'S WHY...
...WE COULDN'T ASK FOR A BETTER LEADER!
Y-YOU GUYS...*SNIFF*

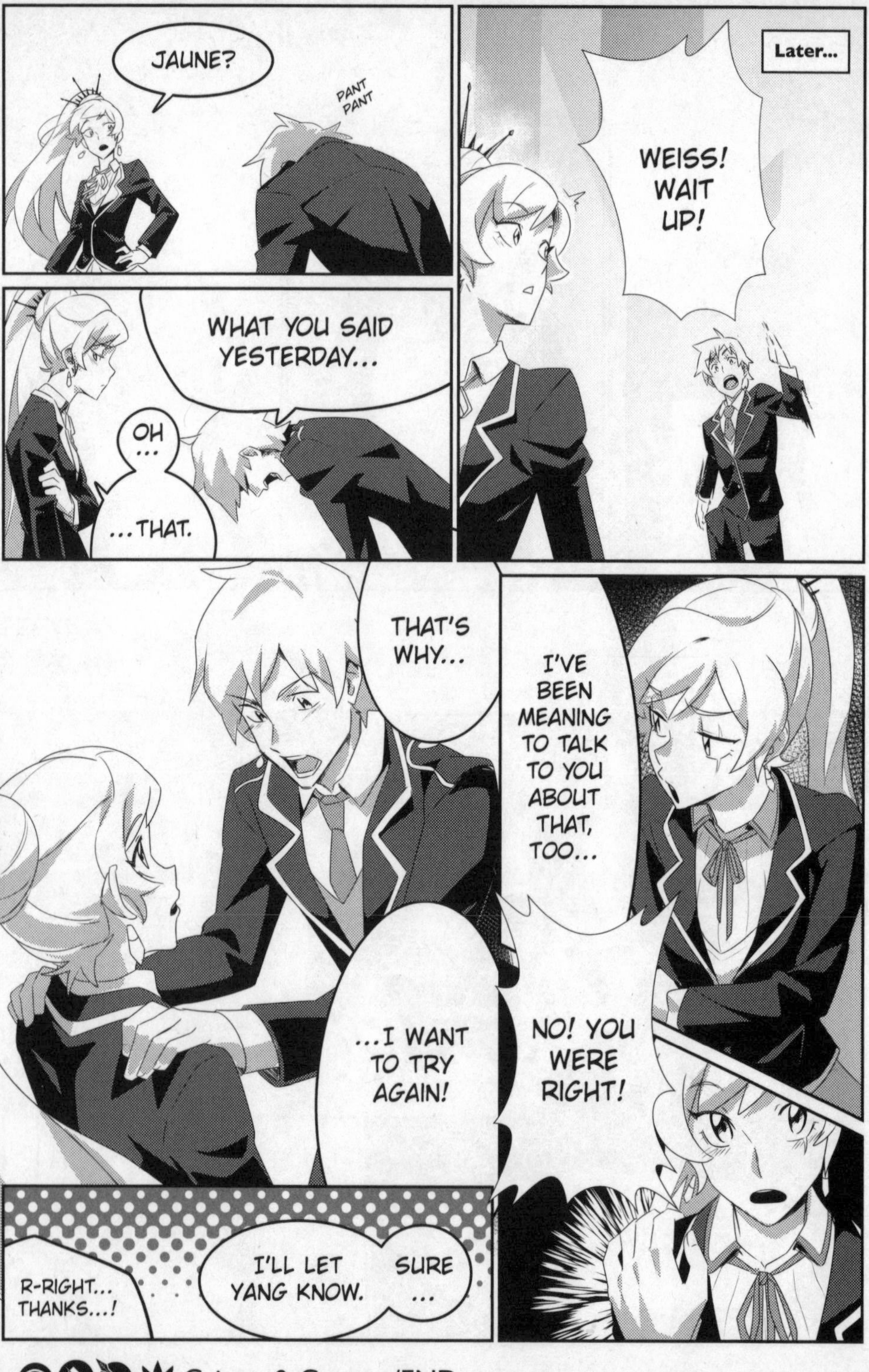
Later...
WEISS! WAIT UP!
JAUNE?
PANT PANT
WHAT YOU SAID YESTERDAY...
OH...
...THAT.
I'VE BEEN MEANING TO TALK TO YOU ABOUT THAT, TOO...
NO! YOU WERE RIGHT!
THAT'S WHY...
...I WANT TO TRY AGAIN!
SURE...
I'LL LET YANG KNOW.
R-RIGHT... THANKS...!

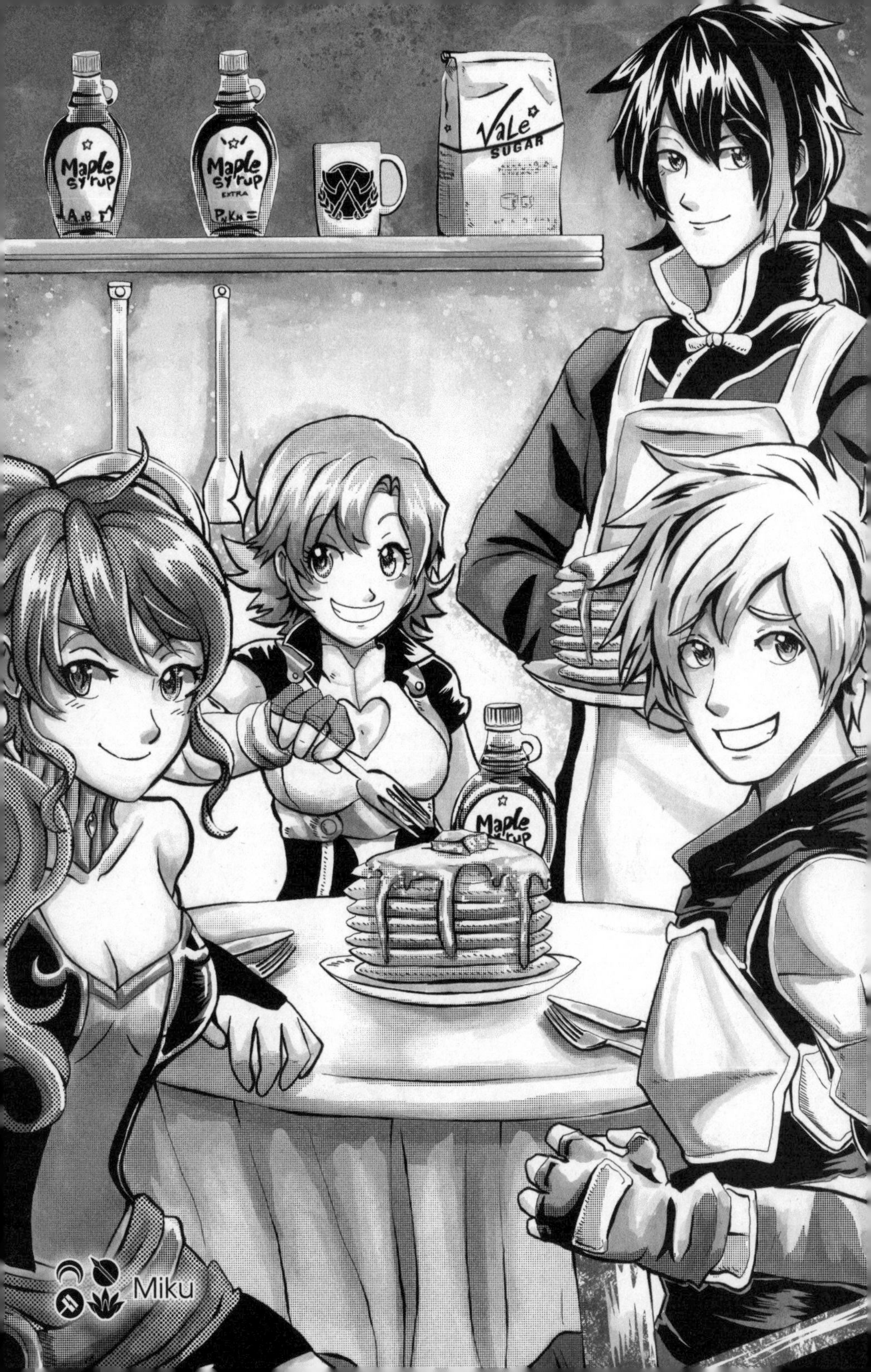
Maple syrup
Maple syrup
EXTRA
VaLe
SUGAR
Miku

RWBY
OFFICIAL MANGA ANTHOLOGY
Volume 5

Shine

Ecru

Beacon Days (JNPR)

mojojoj

Professor Pete

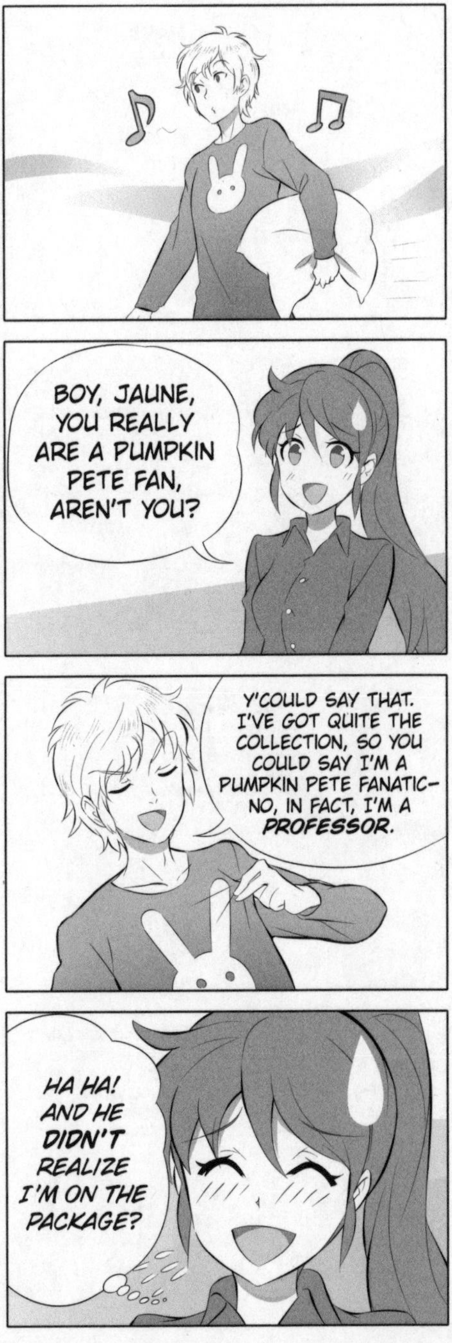

BOY, JAUNE, YOU REALLY ARE A PUMPKIN PETE FAN, AREN'T YOU?
Y'COULD SAY THAT. I'VE GOT QUITE THE COLLECTION, SO YOU COULD SAY I'M A PUMPKIN PETE FANATIC-NO, IN FACT, I'M A **PROFESSOR**.
*HA HA! AND HE **DIDN'T** REALIZE I'M ON THE PACKAGE?*

A Dangerous Girl

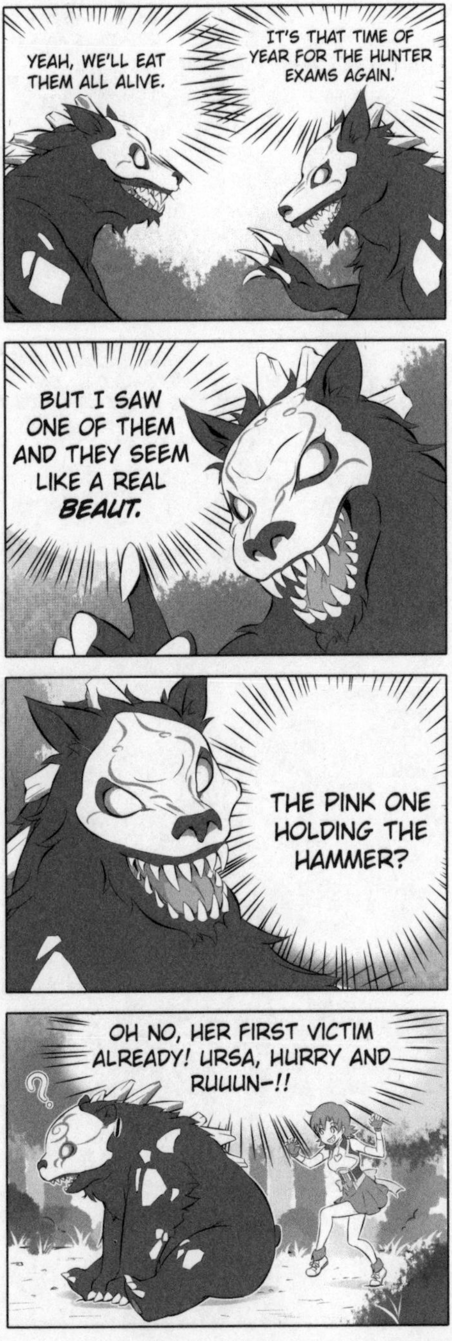

IT'S THAT TIME OF YEAR FOR THE HUNTER EXAMS AGAIN.
YEAH, WE'LL EAT THEM ALL ALIVE.
BUT I SAW ONE OF THEM AND THEY SEEM LIKE A REAL ***BEAUT.***
THE PINK ONE HOLDING THE HAMMER?
OH NO, HER FIRST VICTIM ALREADY! URSA, HURRY AND RUUUN-!!
?

Cat Bread

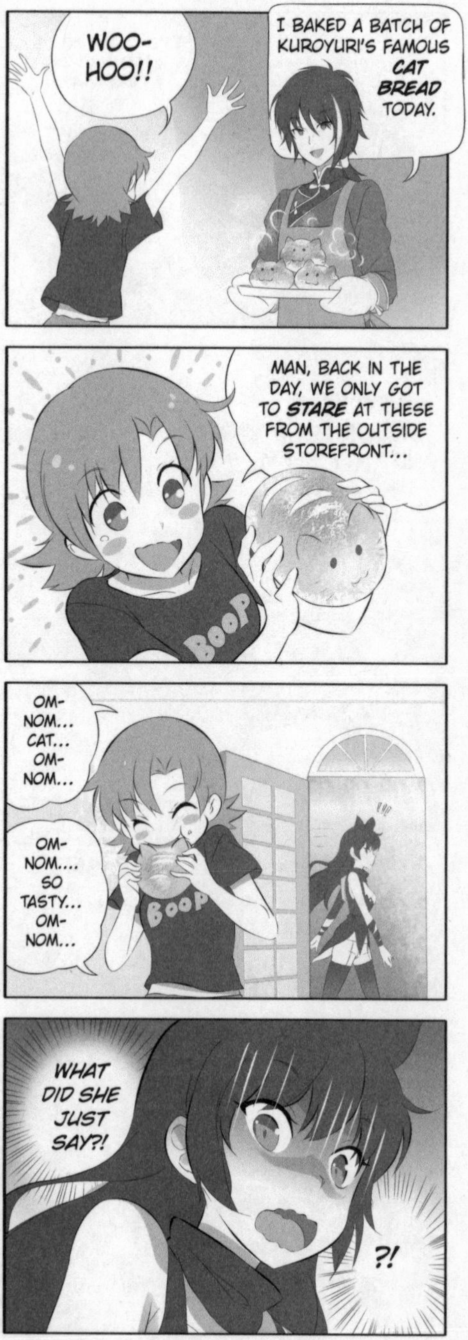
I BAKED A BATCH OF KUROYURI'S FAMOUS CAT BREAD TODAY.
WOO-HOO!!
MAN, BACK IN THE DAY, WE ONLY GOT TO STARE AT THESE FROM THE OUTSIDE STOREFRONT...
OM-NOM... CAT... OM-NOM...
OM-NOM.... SO TASTY... OM-NOM...
WHAT DID SHE JUST SAY?!
?!

The Great One

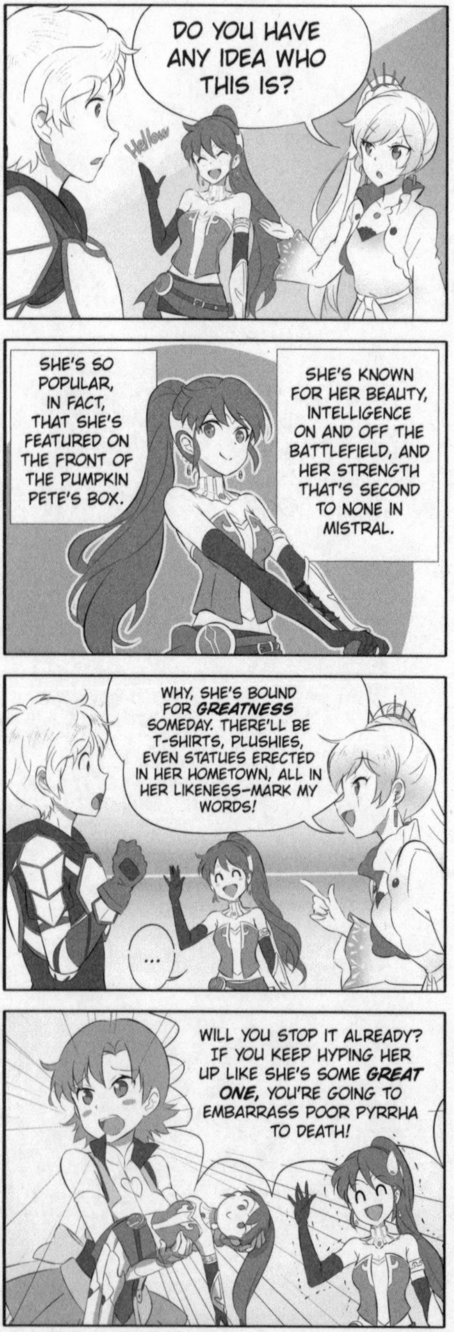
DO YOU HAVE ANY IDEA WHO THIS IS?
SHE'S KNOWN FOR HER BEAUTY, INTELLIGENCE ON AND OFF THE BATTLEFIELD, AND HER STRENGTH THAT'S SECOND TO NONE IN MISTRAL.
SHE'S SO POPULAR, IN FACT, THAT SHE'S FEATURED ON THE FRONT OF THE PUMPKIN PETE'S BOX.
WHY, SHE'S BOUND FOR GREATNESS SOMEDAY. THERE'LL BE T-SHIRTS, PLUSHIES, EVEN STATUES ERECTED IN HER HOMETOWN, ALL IN HER LIKENESS–MARK MY WORDS!
...
WILL YOU STOP IT ALREADY? IF YOU KEEP HYPING HER UP LIKE SHE'S SOME GREAT ONE, YOU'RE GOING TO EMBARRASS POOR PYRRHA TO DEATH!

Charades

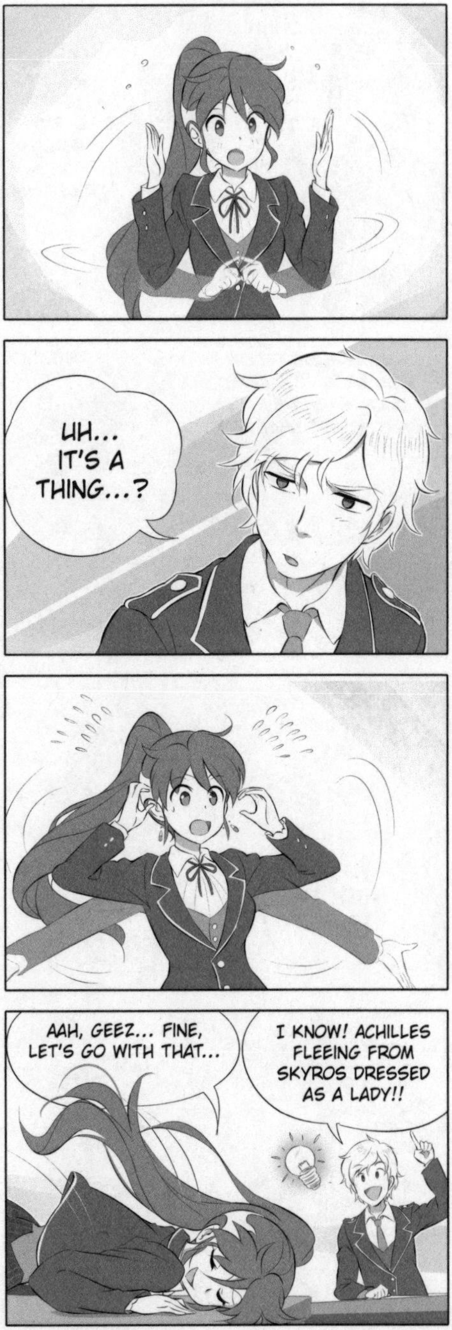
UH...
IT'S A
THING...?
I KNOW! ACHILLES FLEEING FROM SKYROS DRESSED AS A LADY!!
AAH, GEEZ... FINE, LET'S GO WITH THAT...

Your Name

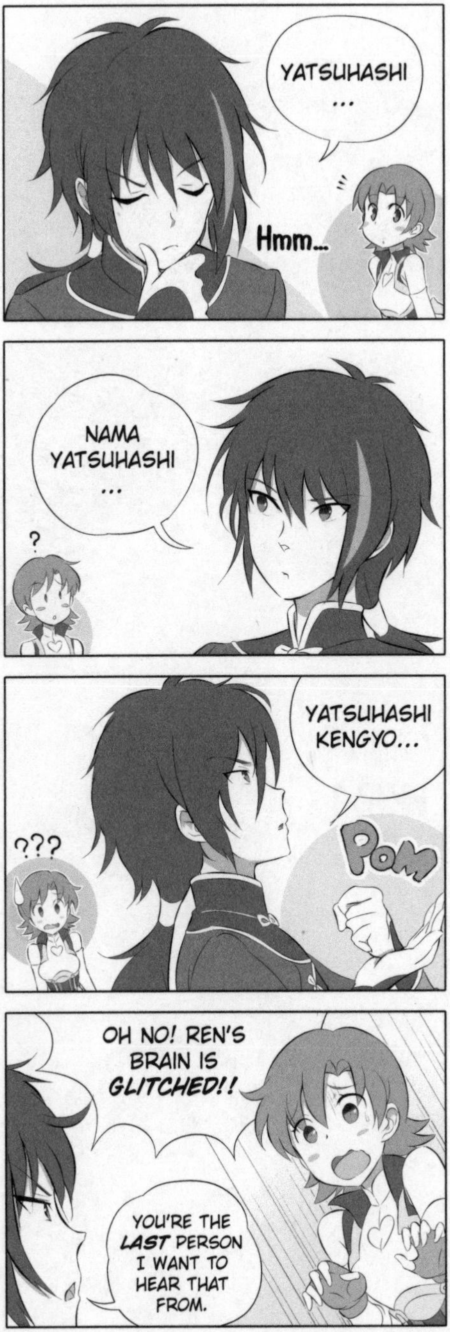
YATSUHASHI ...
Hmm...
NAMA YATSUHASHI ...
?
YATSUHASHI KENGYO...
POM
???
OH NO! REN'S BRAIN IS **GLITCHED!!**
YOU'RE THE **LAST** PERSON I WANT TO HEAR THAT FROM.

Beyond the Door

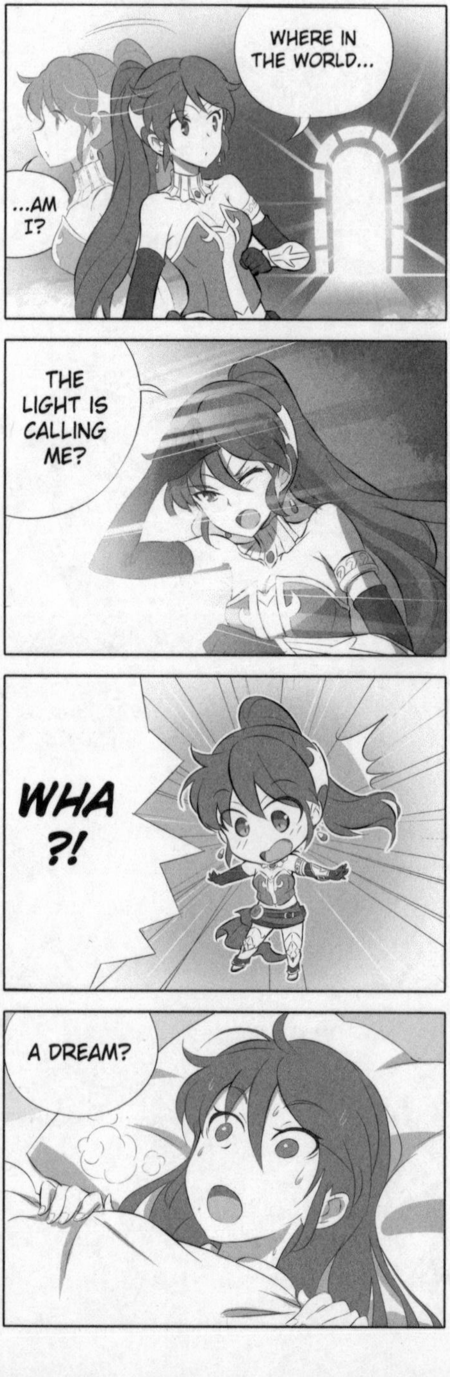
WHERE IN THE WORLD...
...AM I?
THE LIGHT IS CALLING ME?
WHA ?!
A DREAM?

Gun Kata

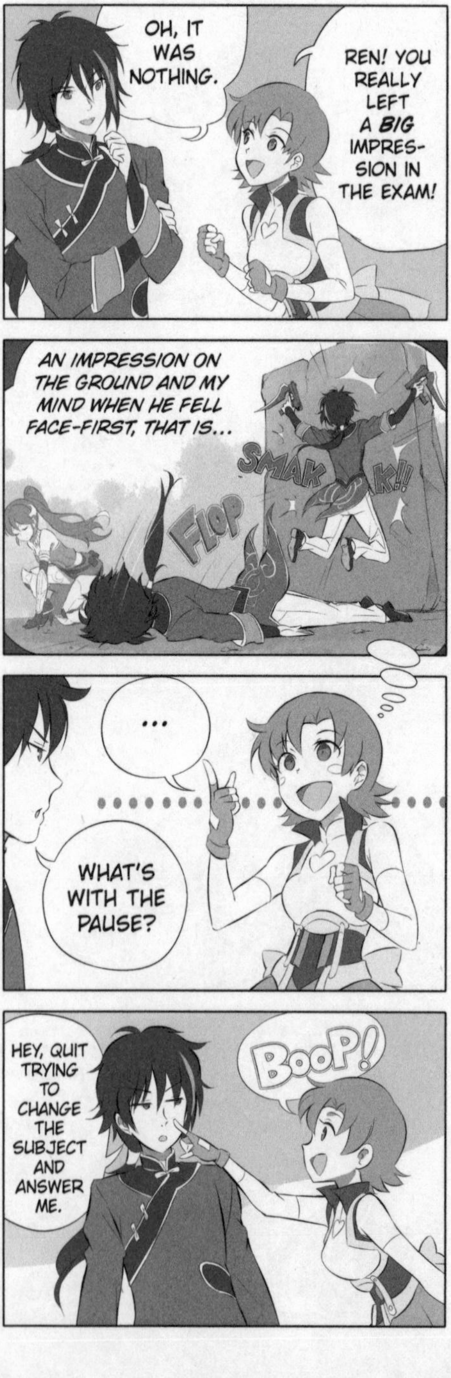
REN! YOU REALLY LEFT A *BIG* IMPRESSION IN THE EXAM!
OH, IT WAS NOTHING.
AN IMPRESSION ON THE GROUND AND MY MIND WHEN HE FELL FACE-FIRST, THAT IS...
SMAKK!!
FLOP
...
WHAT'S WITH THE PAUSE?
BOOP!
HEY, QUIT TRYING TO CHANGE THE SUBJECT AND ANSWER ME.

Be a Hero

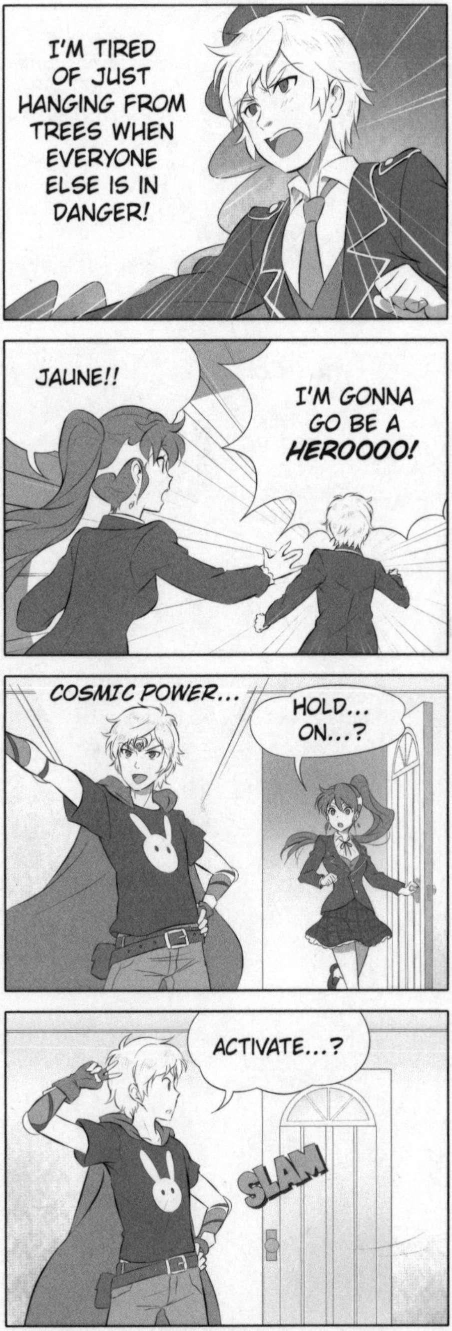
I'M TIRED OF JUST HANGING FROM TREES WHEN EVERYONE ELSE IS IN DANGER!
I'M GONNA GO BE A *HEROOOO!*
JAUNE!!
HOLD... ON...?
COSMIC POWER...
ACTIVATE...?
SLAM

Orleans Maiden

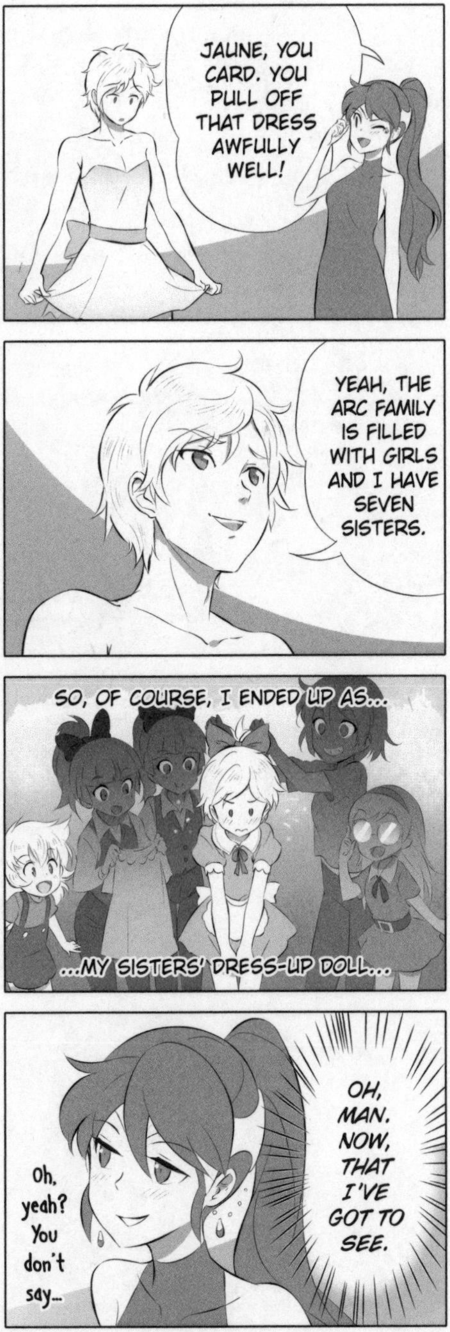
JAUNE, YOU CARD. YOU PULL OFF THAT DRESS AWFULLY WELL!
YEAH, THE ARC FAMILY IS FILLED WITH GIRLS AND I HAVE SEVEN SISTERS.
SO, OF COURSE, I ENDED UP AS...
...MY SISTERS' DRESS-UP DOLL...
OH, MAN. NOW, THAT I'VE GOT TO SEE.
Oh, yeah? You don't say...

Atrocious Treatment

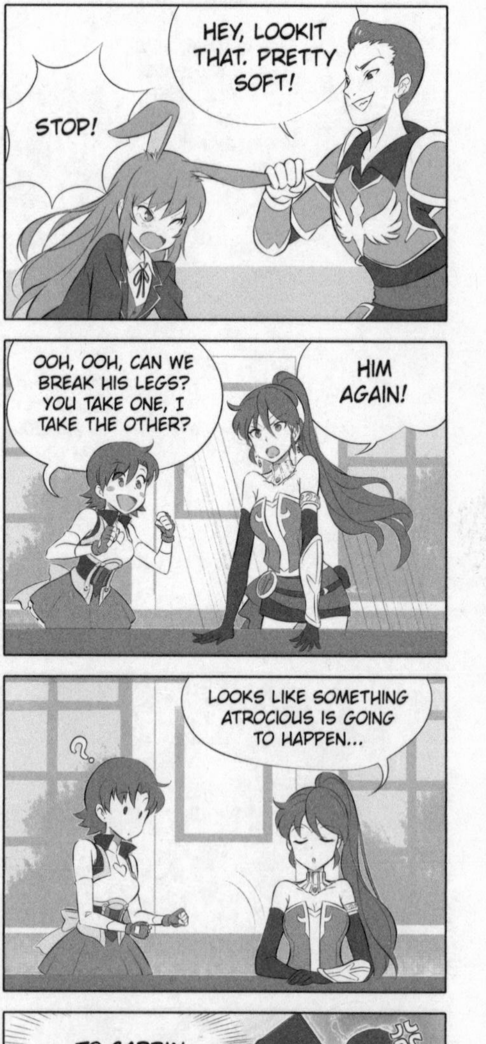
HEY, LOOKIT THAT. PRETTY SOFT!
STOP!
HIM AGAIN!
OOH, OOH, CAN WE BREAK HIS LEGS? YOU TAKE ONE, I TAKE THE OTHER?
LOOKS LIKE SOMETHING ATROCIOUS IS GOING TO HAPPEN...
...TO CARDIN.

Locker 636

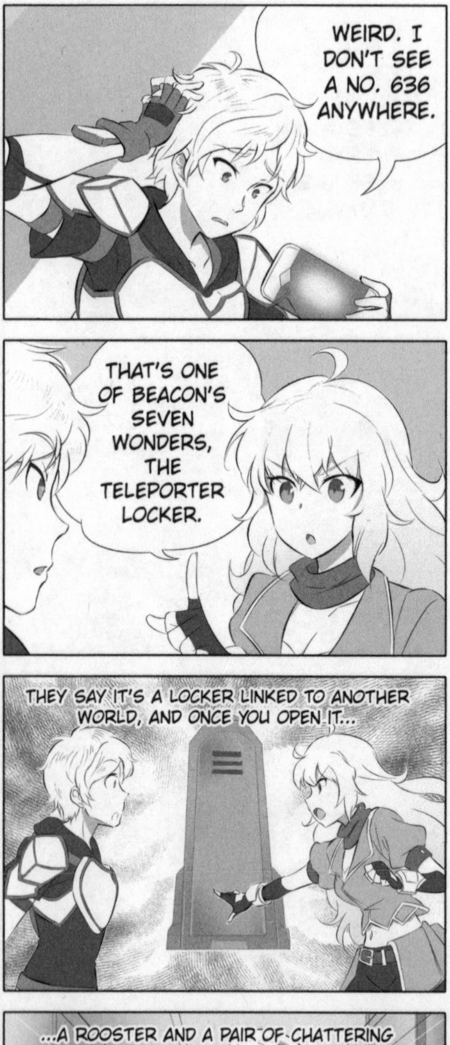
WEIRD. I DON'T SEE A NO. 636 ANYWHERE.
THAT'S ONE OF BEACON'S SEVEN WONDERS, THE TELEPORTER LOCKER.
THEY SAY IT'S A LOCKER LINKED TO ANOTHER WORLD, AND ONCE YOU OPEN IT...
...A ROOSTER AND A PAIR OF CHATTERING TEETH POPS OUT.
WHAT KIND OF WONDER IS THAT?!

Beacon Days (JNPR)/END

Cupid Relay

Mugupo

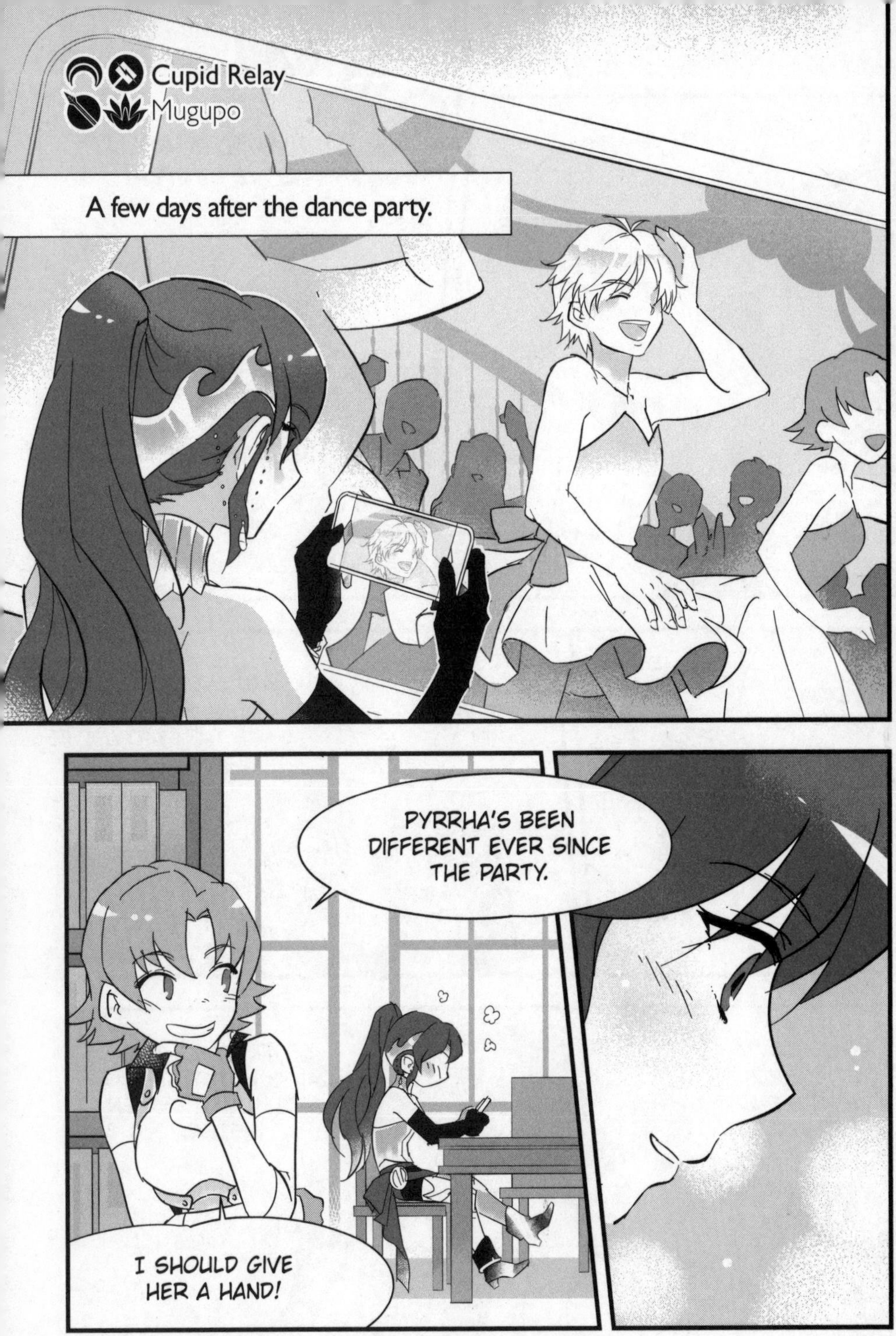
A few days after the dance party.
PYRRHA'S BEEN DIFFERENT EVER SINCE THE PARTY.
I SHOULD GIVE HER A HAND!

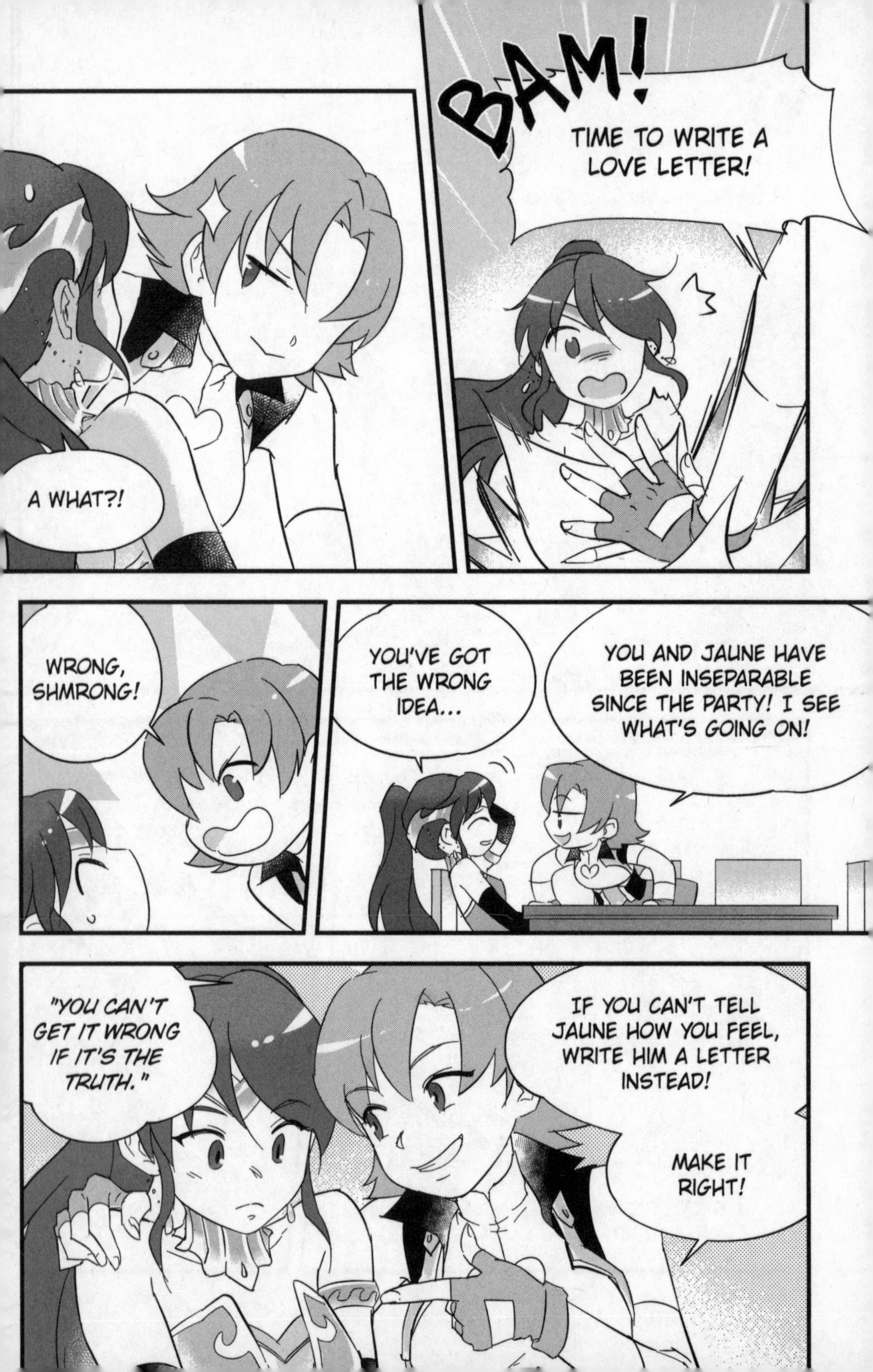
BAM!
TIME TO WRITE A LOVE LETTER!
A WHAT?!
YOU AND JAUNE HAVE BEEN INSEPARABLE SINCE THE PARTY! I SEE WHAT'S GOING ON!
YOU'VE GOT THE WRONG IDEA...
WRONG, SHMRONG!
IF YOU CAN'T TELL JAUNE HOW YOU FEEL, WRITE HIM A LETTER INSTEAD!
MAKE IT RIGHT!
"YOU CAN'T GET IT WRONG IF IT'S THE TRUTH."

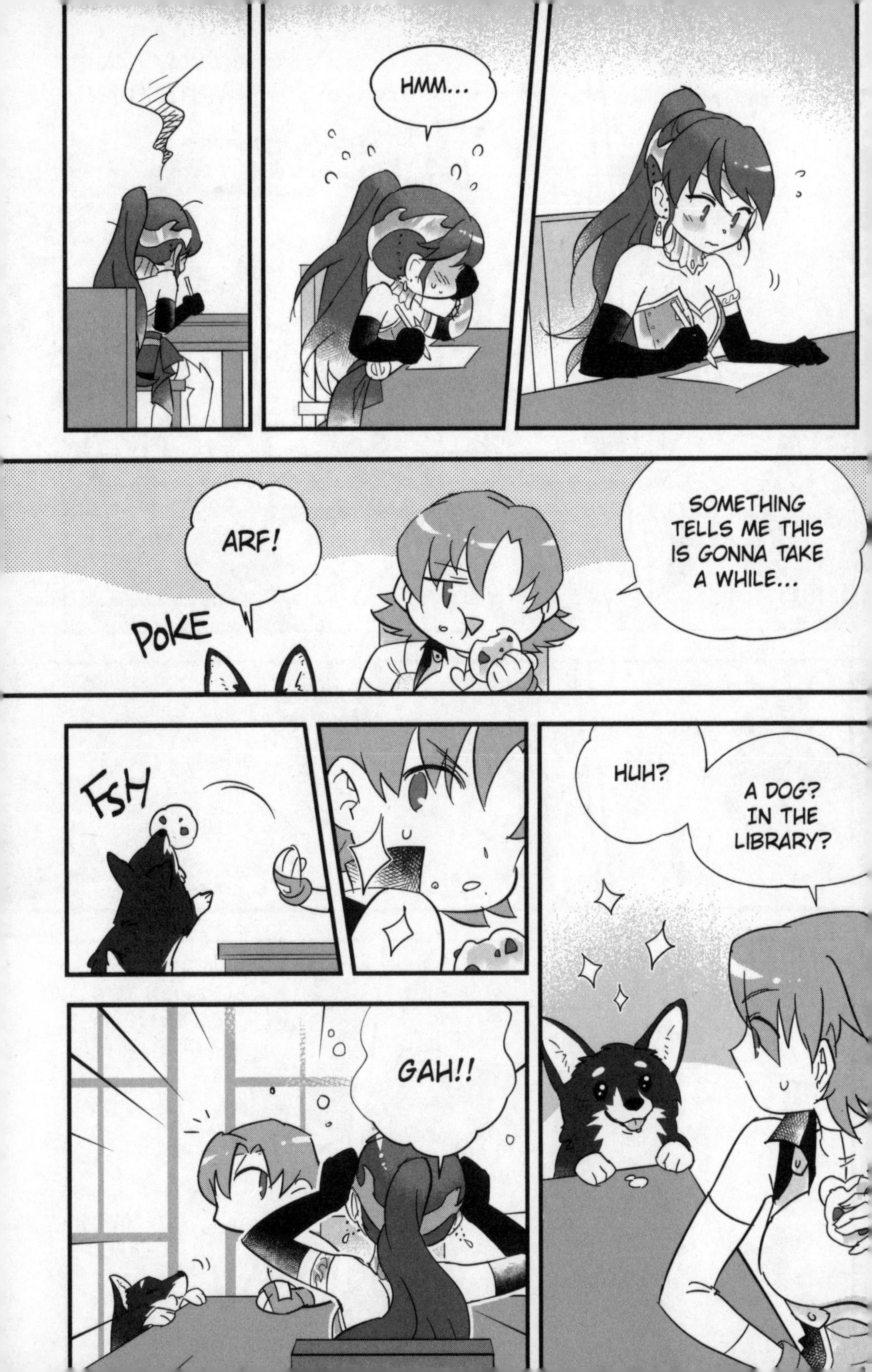
HMM...
SOMETHING TELLS ME THIS IS GONNA TAKE A WHILE...
ARF!
POKE
HUH?
A DOG? IN THE LIBRARY?
FSH
GAH!!

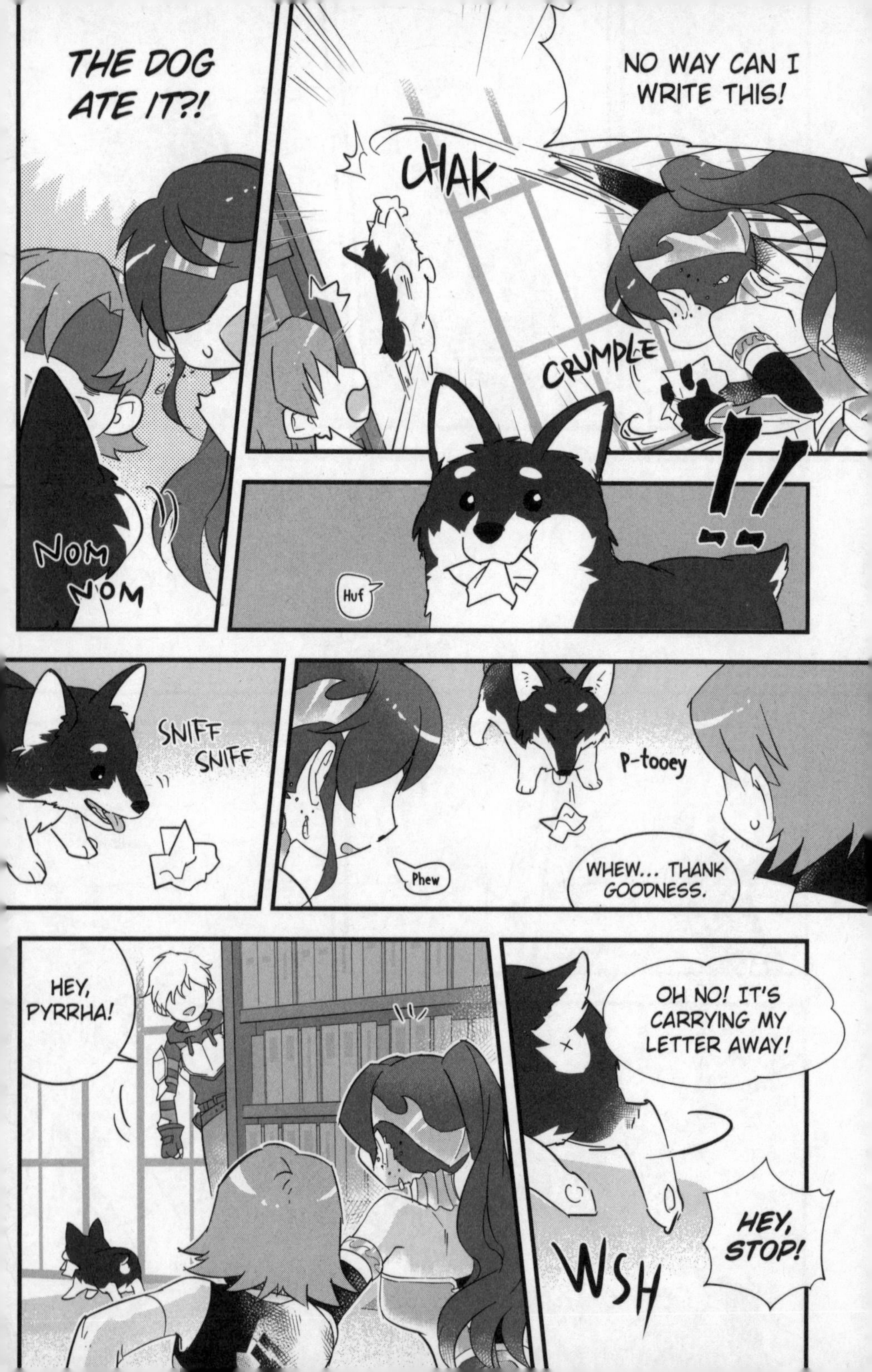
NO WAY CAN I WRITE THIS!
CHAK
CRUMPLE
Huf
THE DOG ATE IT?!
NOM NOM
p-tooey
Phew
WHEW... THANK GOODNESS.
SNIFF SNIFF
OH NO! IT'S CARRYING MY LETTER AWAY!
HEY, STOP!
WSH
HEY, PYRRHA!

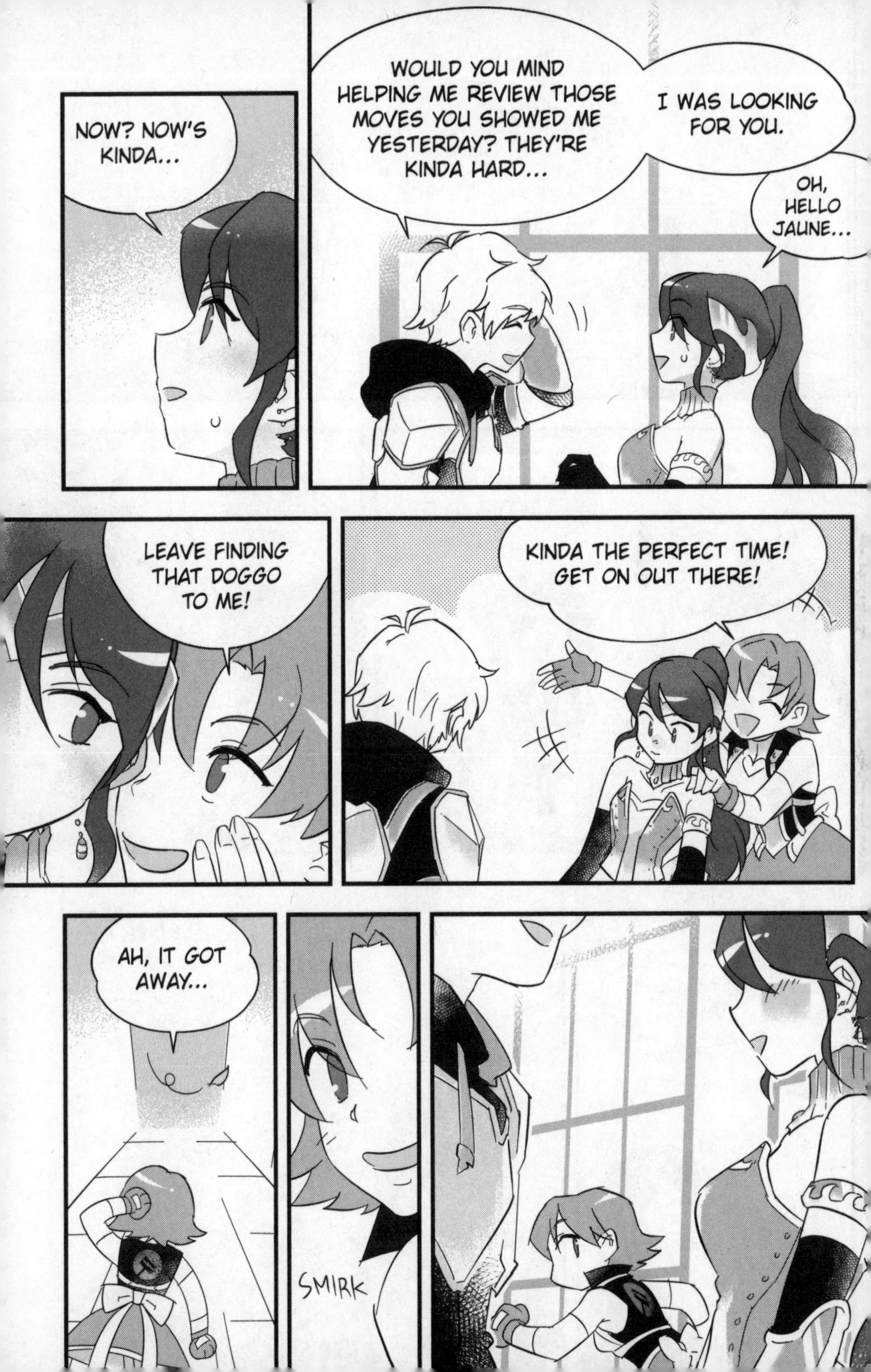
OH, HELLO JAUNE...
I WAS LOOKING FOR YOU.
WOULD YOU MIND HELPING ME REVIEW THOSE MOVES YOU SHOWED ME YESTERDAY? THEY'RE KINDA HARD...
NOW? NOW'S KINDA...
KINDA THE PERFECT TIME! GET ON OUT THERE!
LEAVE FINDING THAT DOGGO TO ME!
SMIRK
AH, IT GOT AWAY...

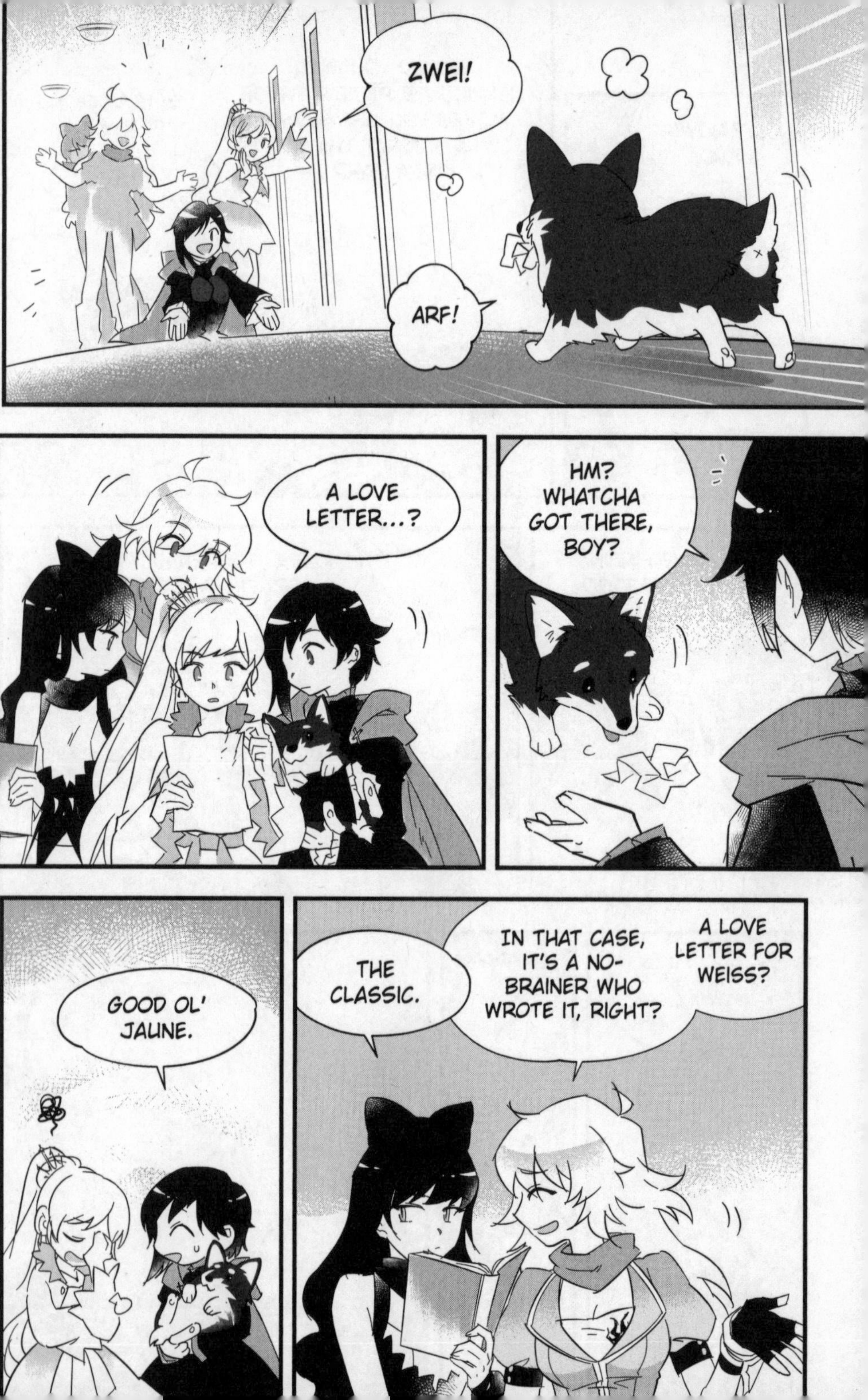
ZWEI!
ARF!
HM? WHATCHA GOT THERE, BOY?
A LOVE LETTER...?
A LOVE LETTER FOR WEISS?
IN THAT CASE, IT'S A NO-BRAINER WHO WROTE IT, RIGHT?
THE CLASSIC.
GOOD OL' JAUNE.

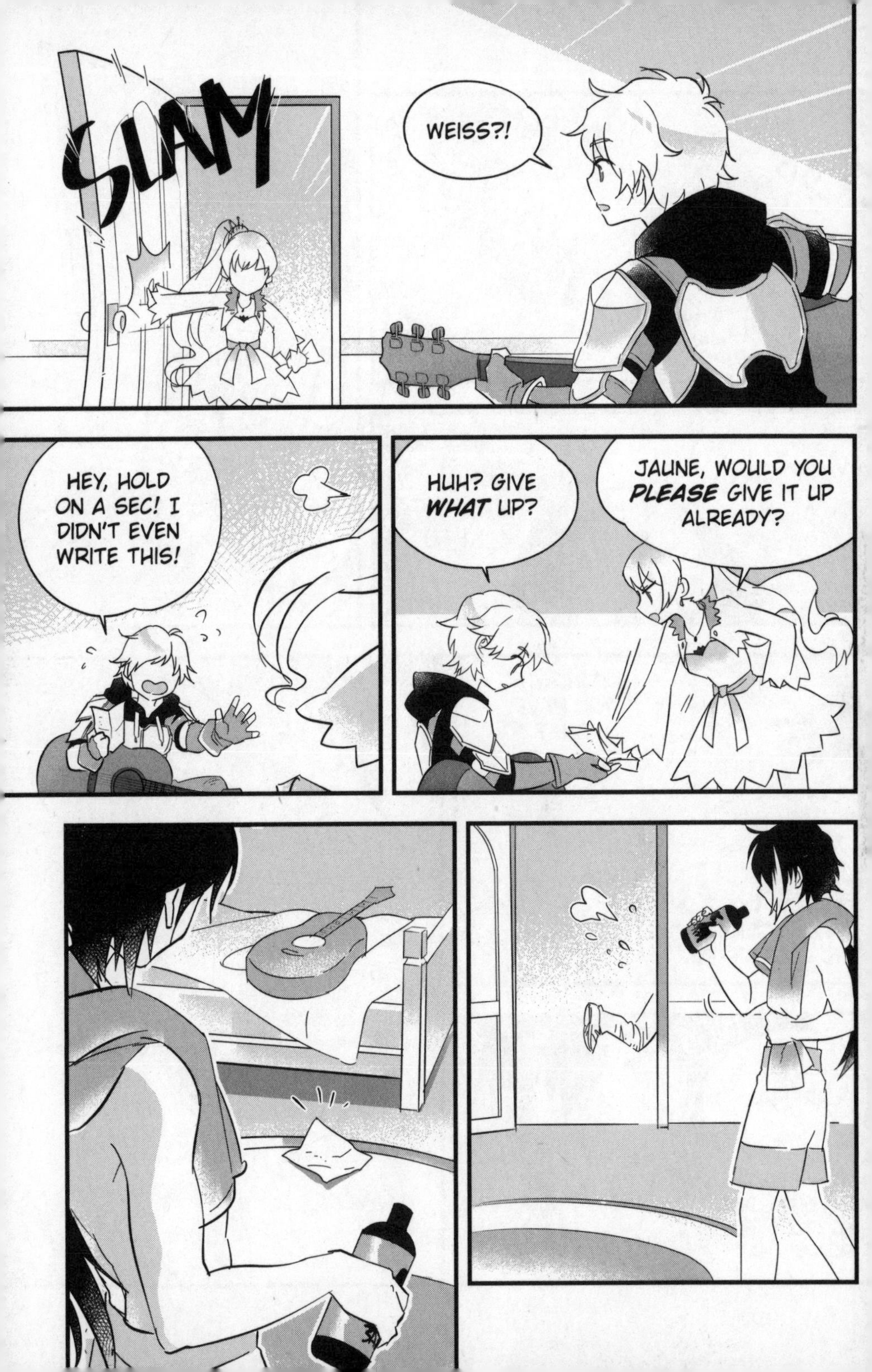
WEISS?!
SLAM
JAUNE, WOULD YOU PLEASE GIVE IT UP ALREADY?
HUH? GIVE WHAT UP?
HEY, HOLD ON A SEC! I DIDN'T EVEN WRITE THIS!

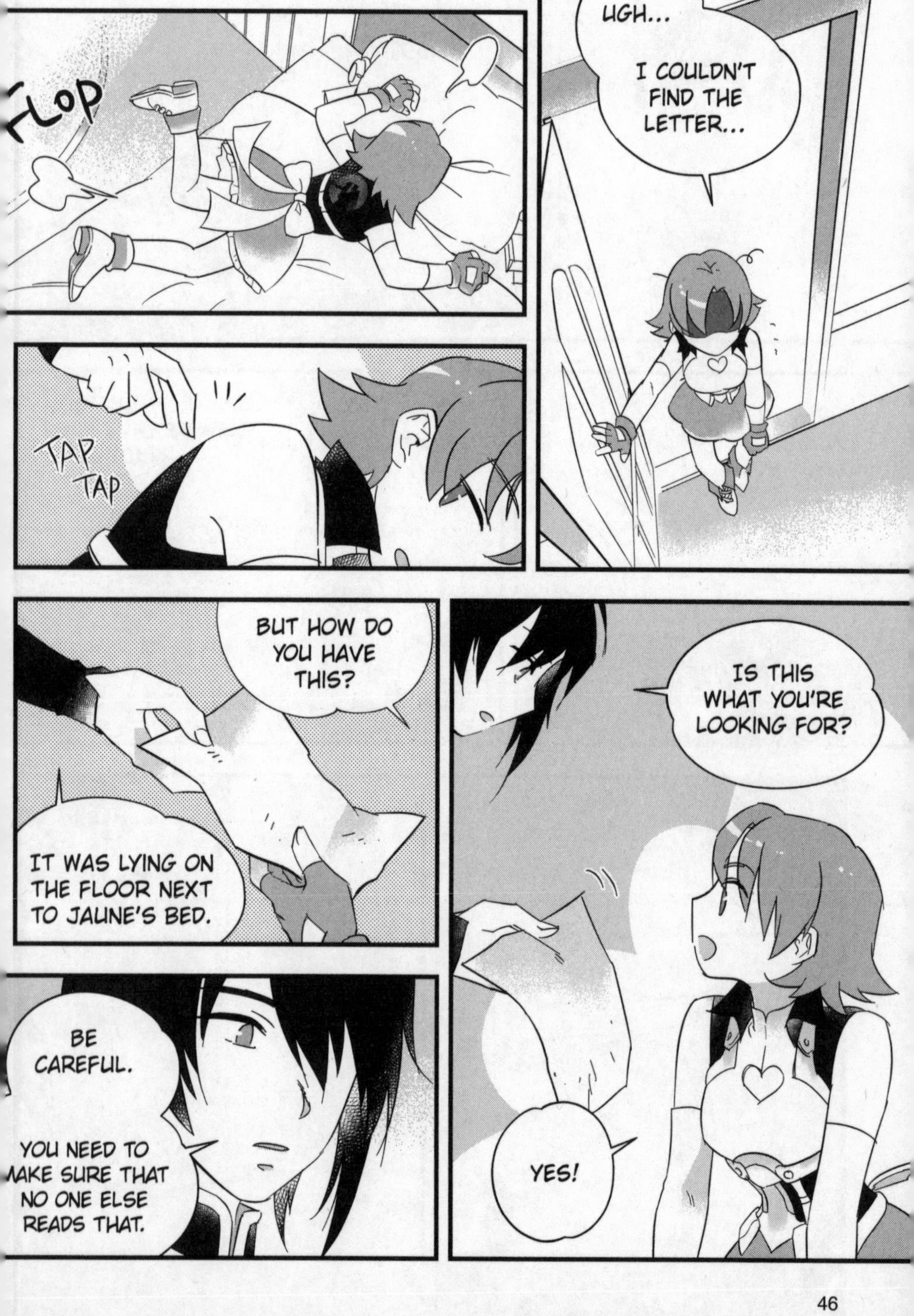
UGH...
I COULDN'T FIND THE LETTER...
FLOP
TAP TAP
IS THIS WHAT YOU'RE LOOKING FOR?
YES!
BUT HOW DO YOU HAVE THIS?
IT WAS LYING ON THE FLOOR NEXT TO JAUNE'S BED.
BE CAREFUL.
YOU NEED TO MAKE SURE THAT NO ONE ELSE READS THAT.

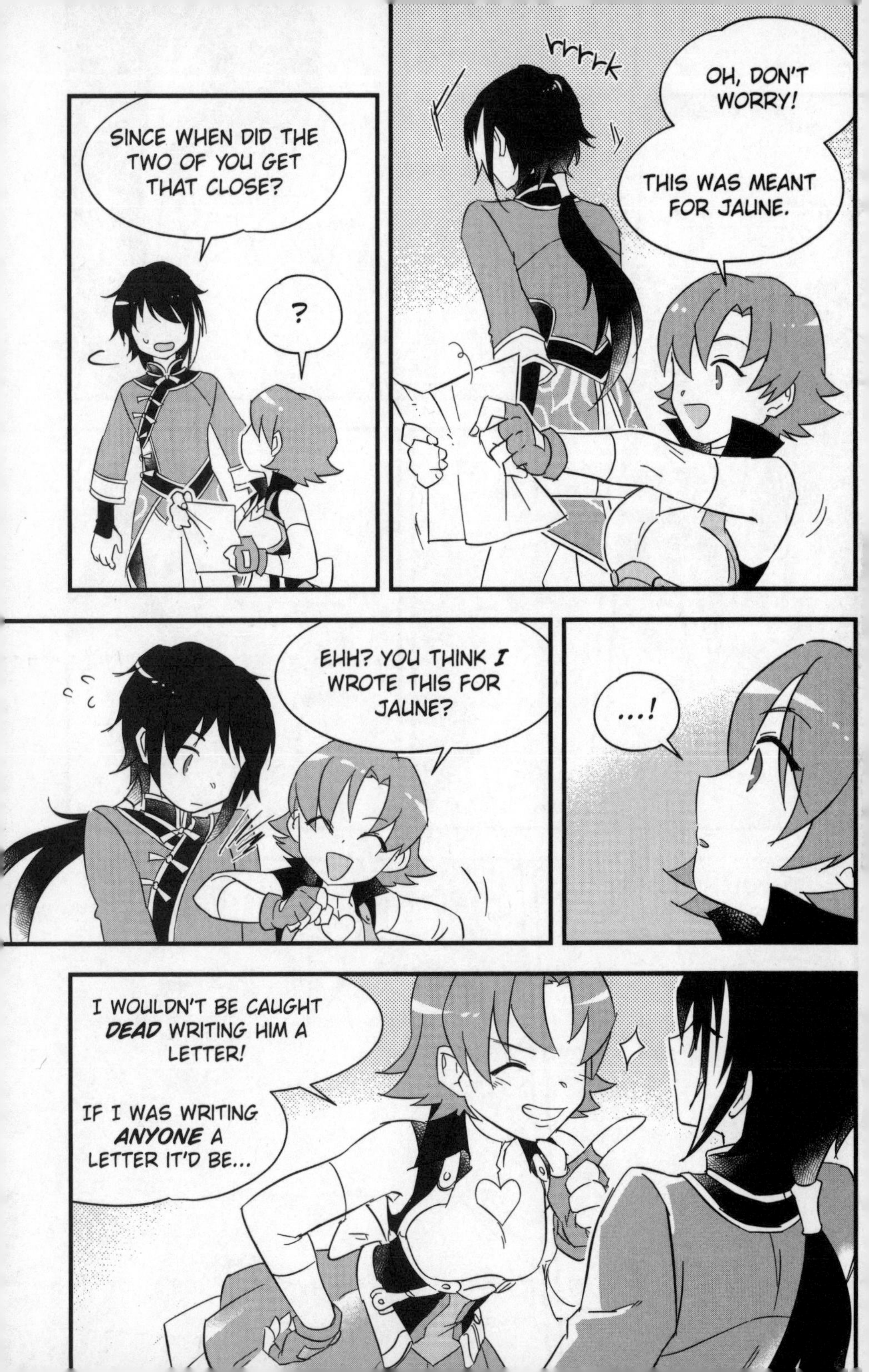
rrrrk
OH, DON'T WORRY!
THIS WAS MEANT FOR JAUNE.
SINCE WHEN DID THE TWO OF YOU GET THAT CLOSE?
?
...!
EHH? YOU THINK *I* WROTE THIS FOR JAUNE?
I WOULDN'T BE CAUGHT ***DEAD*** WRITING HIM A LETTER!
IF I WAS WRITING ***ANYONE*** A LETTER IT'D BE...

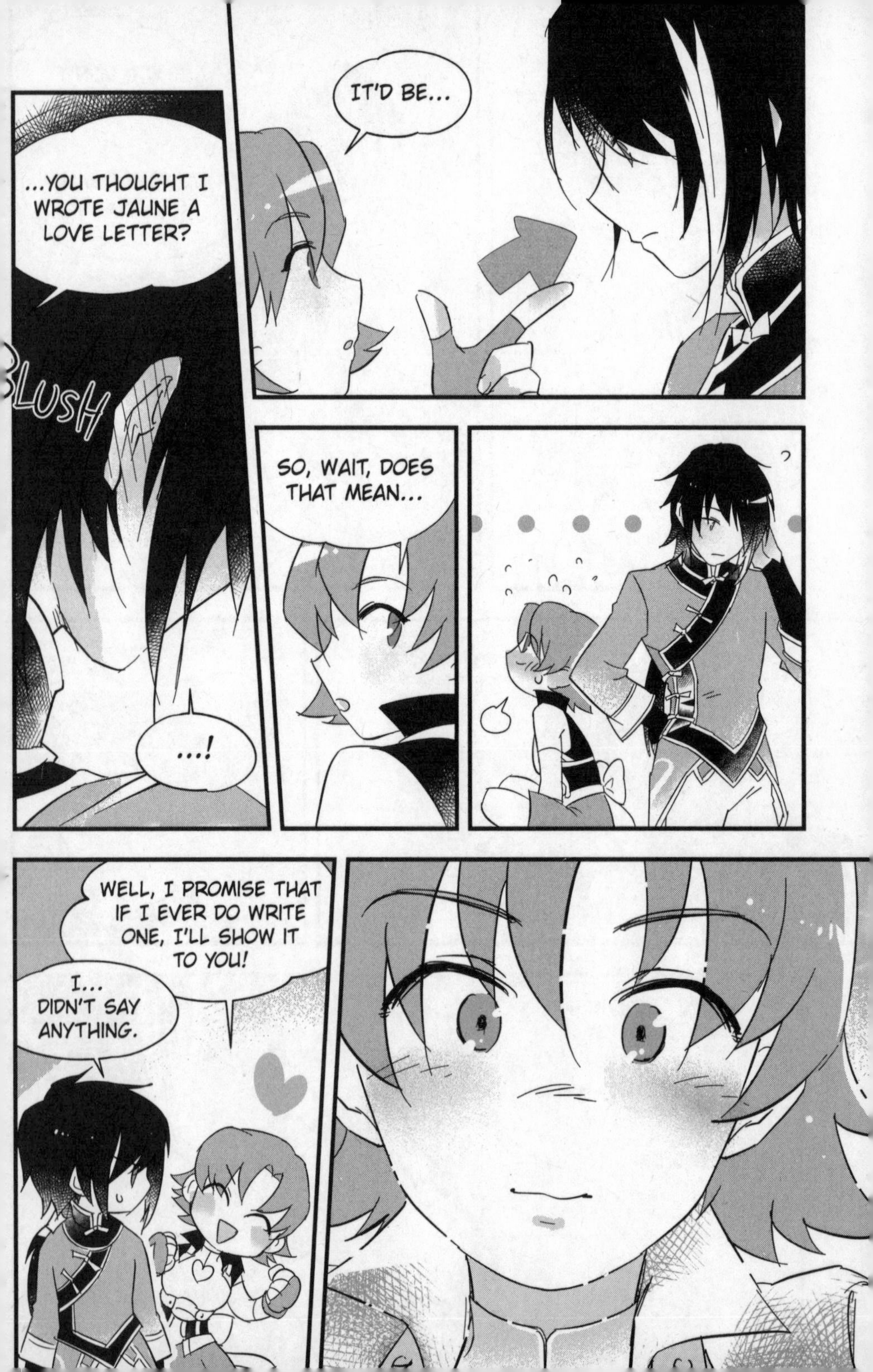
IT'D BE...
● ● ● ●
SO, WAIT, DOES THAT MEAN...
...YOU THOUGHT I WROTE JAUNE A LOVE LETTER?
BLUSH
...!
WELL, I PROMISE THAT IF I EVER DO WRITE ONE, I'LL SHOW IT TO YOU!
I... DIDN'T SAY ANYTHING.

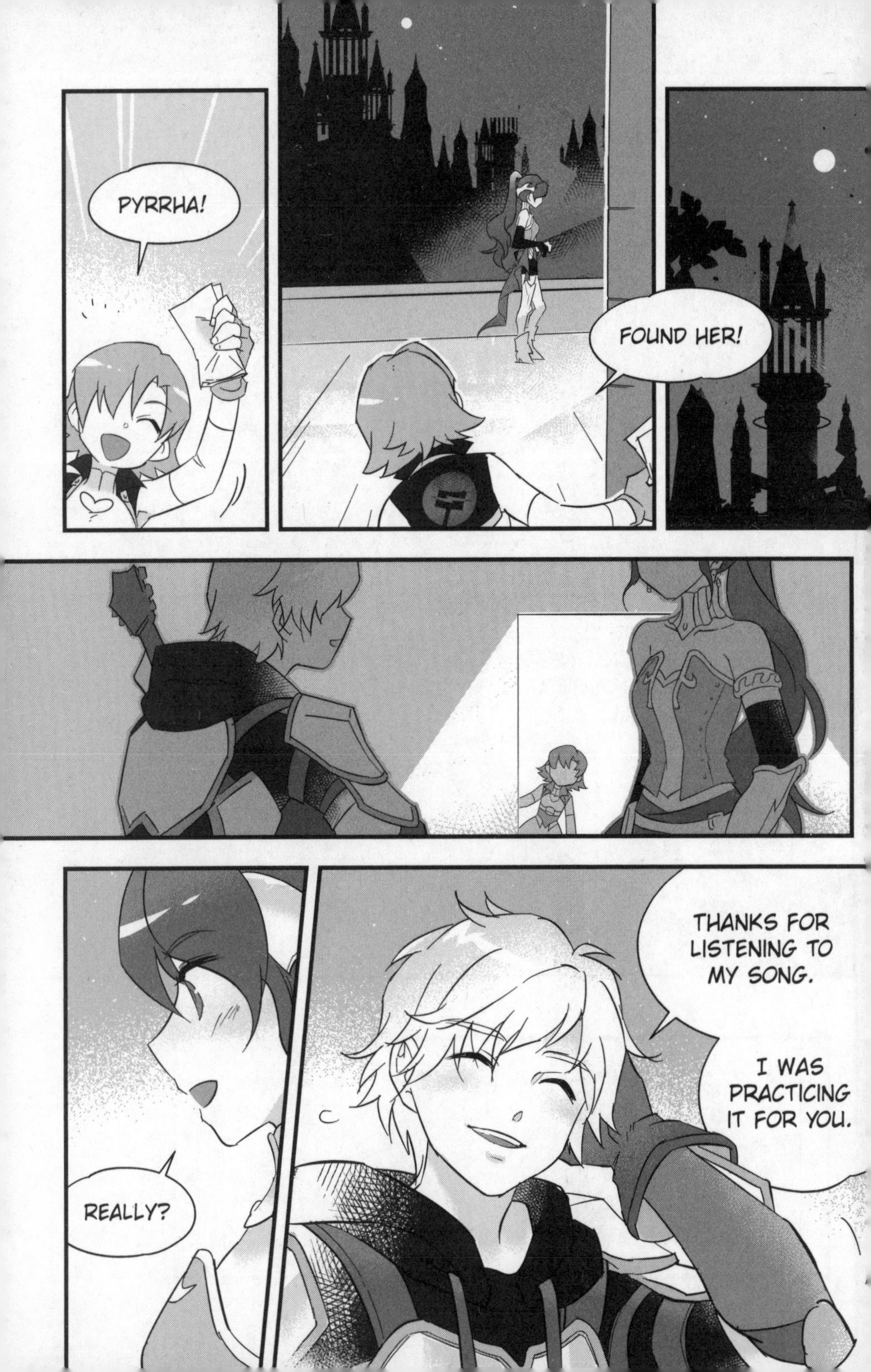
FOUND HER!
PYRRHA!
THANKS FOR LISTENING TO MY SONG.
I WAS PRACTICING IT FOR YOU.
REALLY?

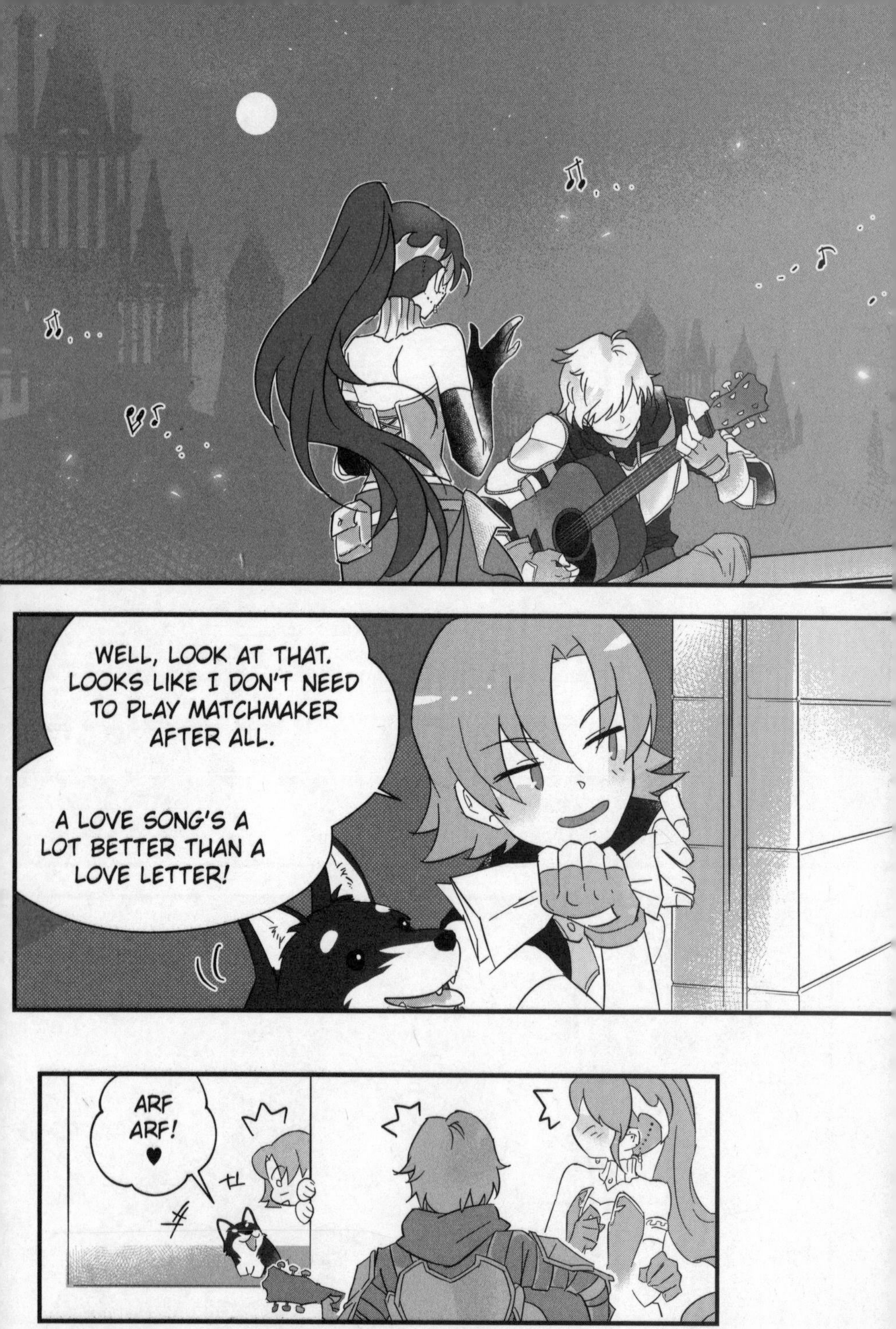
WELL, LOOK AT THAT. LOOKS LIKE I DON'T NEED TO PLAY MATCHMAKER AFTER ALL.
A LOVE SONG'S A LOT BETTER THAN A LOVE LETTER!
ARF ARF! ♥

Cupid Relay/END

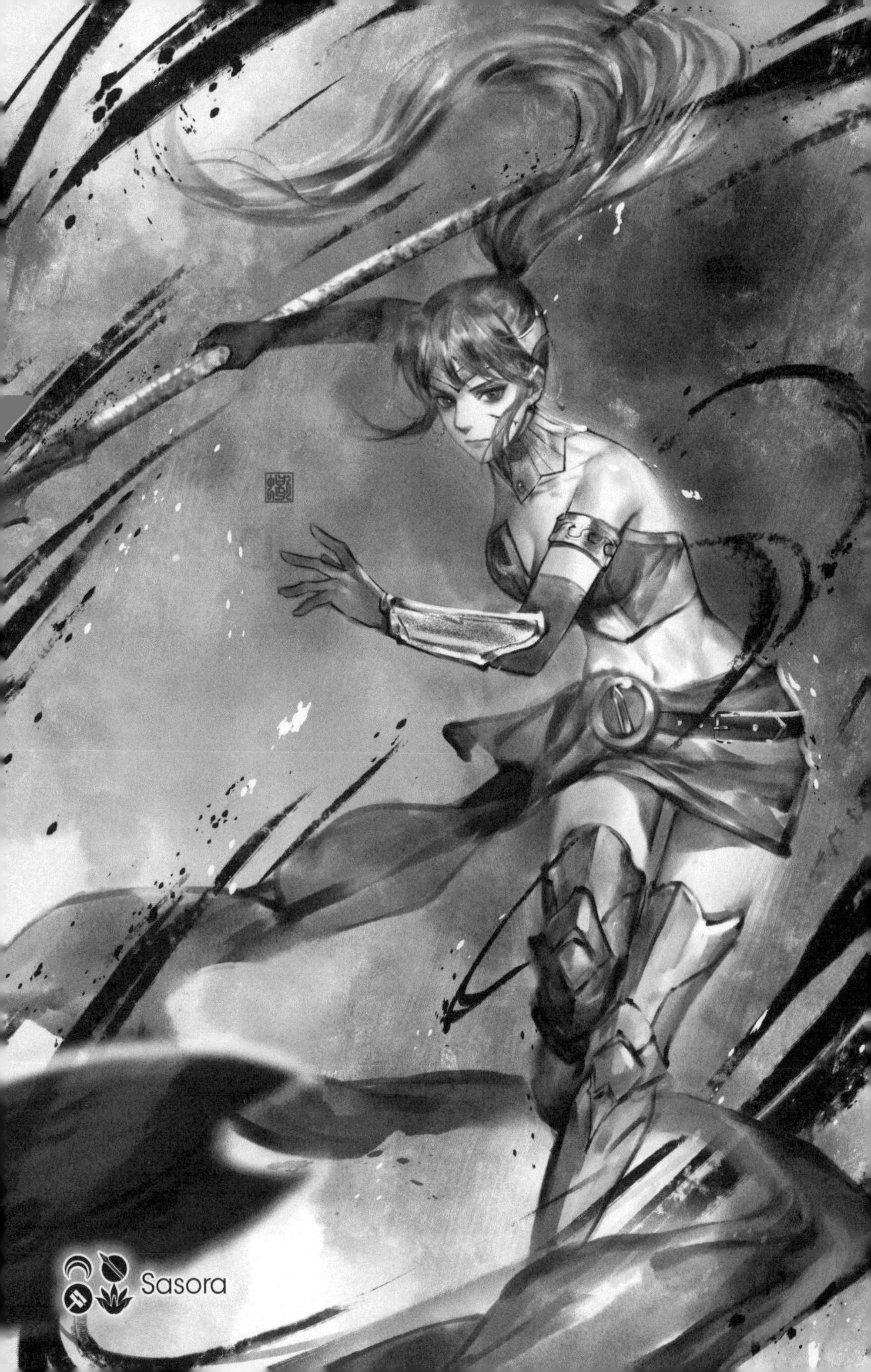
Sasora

RWBY
OFFICIAL MANGA ANTHOLOGY
Volume 5

Shine

Ecru

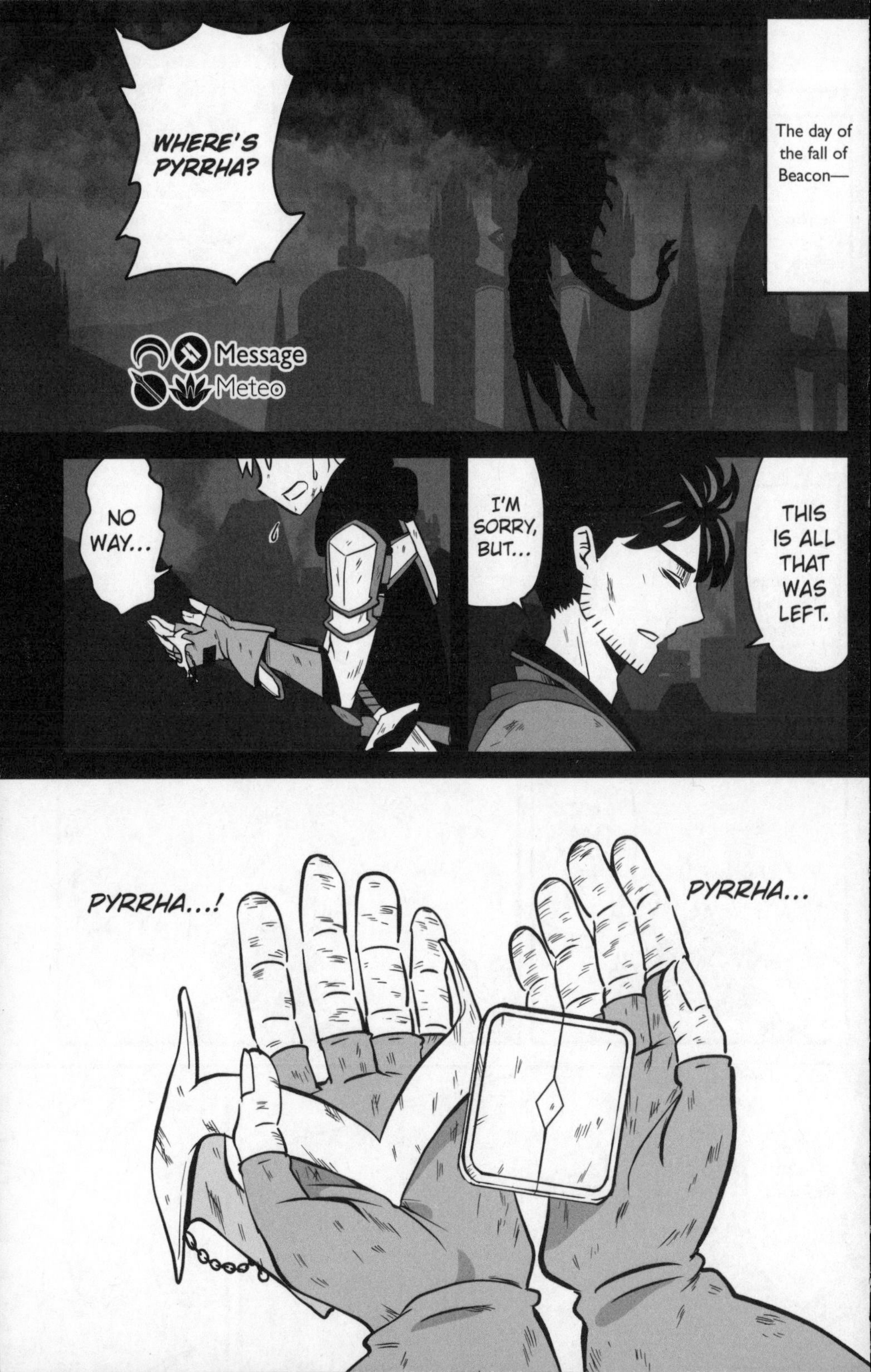

The day of the fall of Beacon—
WHERE'S PYRRHA?
Message
Meteo
I'M SORRY, BUT...
THIS IS ALL THAT WAS LEFT.
NO WAY...
PYRRHA...
PYRRHA...!

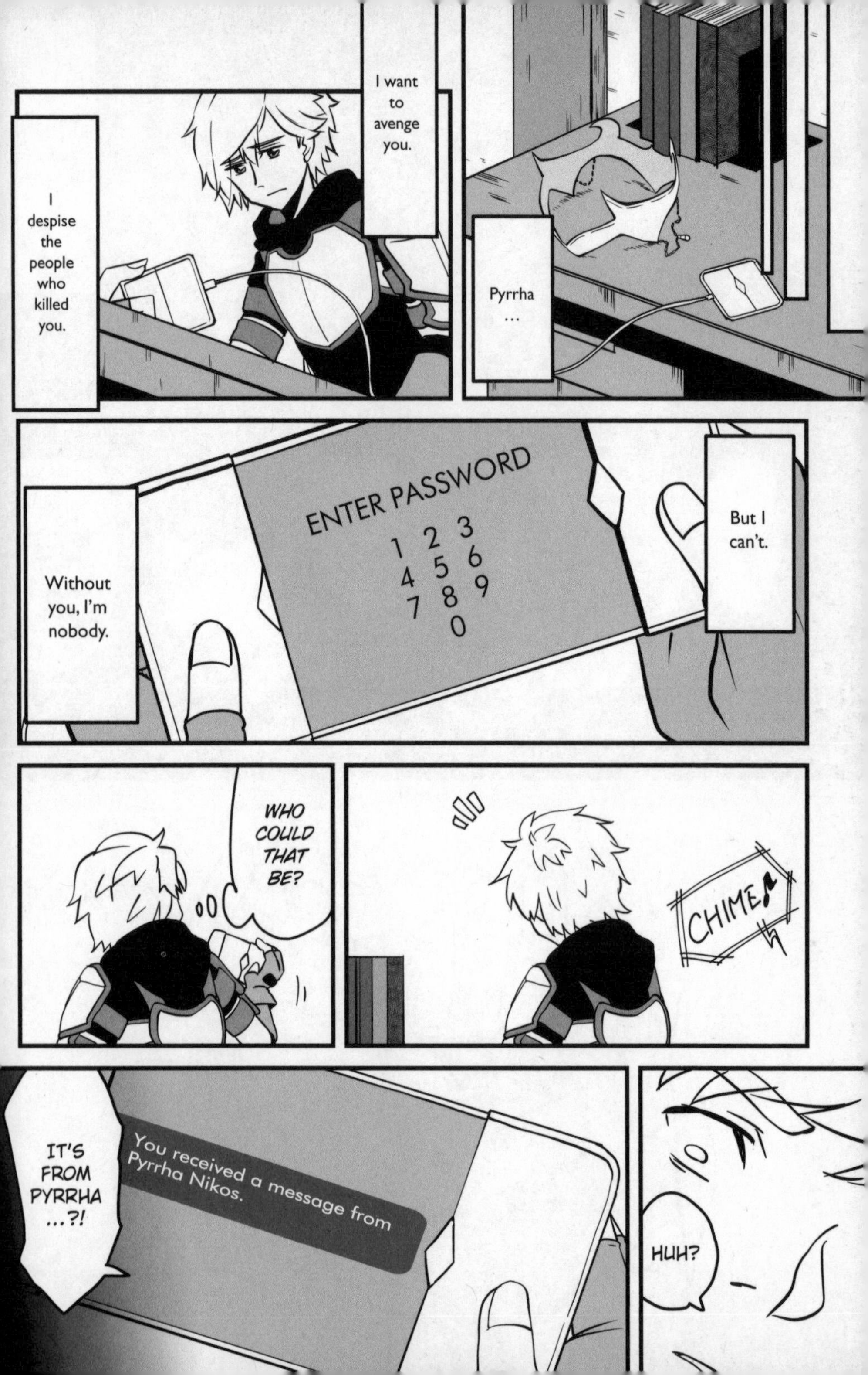

Pyrrha …
I want to avenge you.
I despise the people who killed you.
But I can't.
ENTER PASSWORD
1 2 3
4 5 6
7 8 9
0
Without you, I'm nobody.
CHIME
WHO COULD THAT BE?
HUH?
You received a message from Pyrrha Nikos.
IT'S FROM PYRRHA …?!

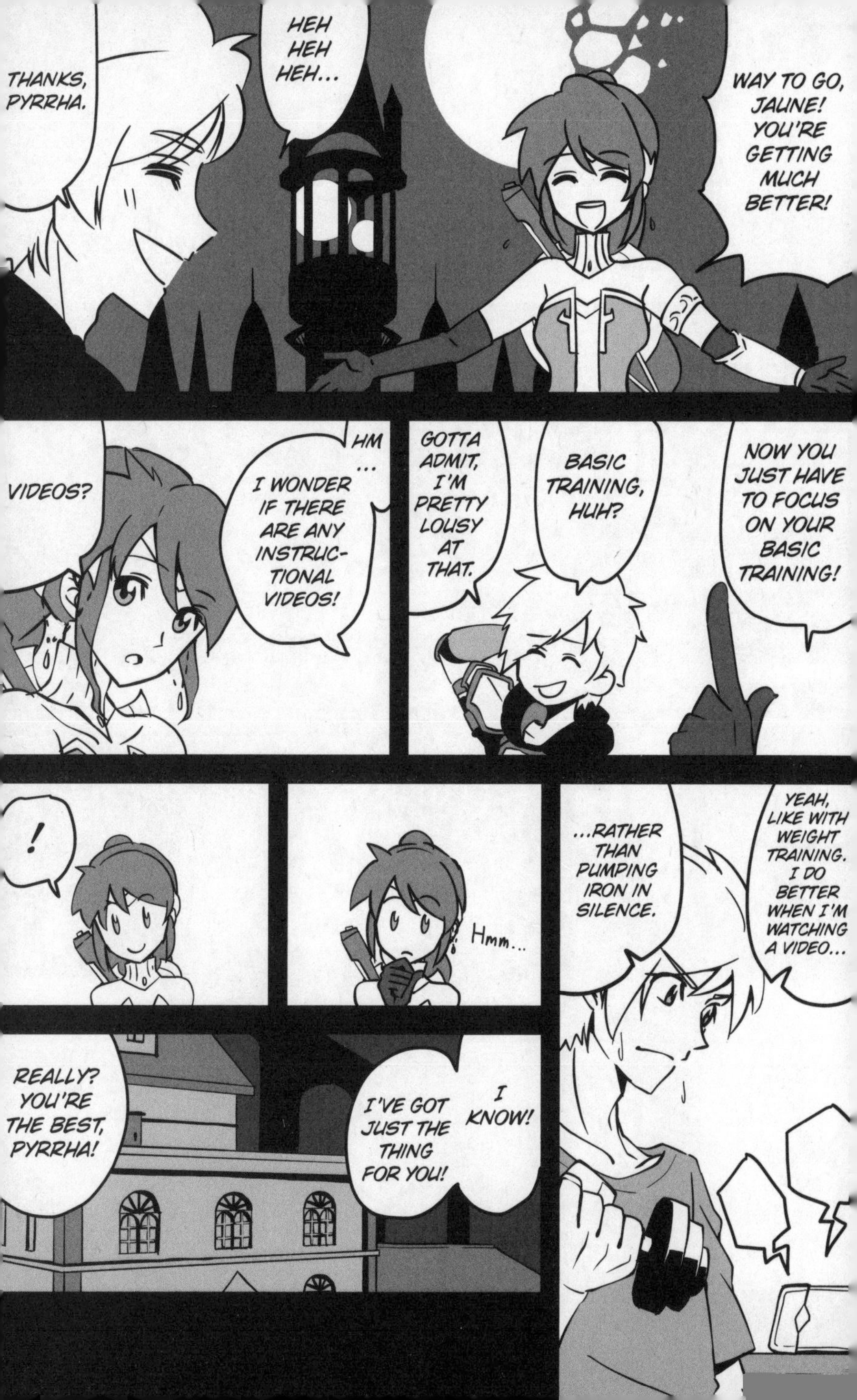
WAY TO GO, JAUNE! YOU'RE GETTING MUCH BETTER!
HEH HEH HEH...
THANKS, PYRRHA.
NOW YOU JUST HAVE TO FOCUS ON YOUR BASIC TRAINING!
BASIC TRAINING, HUH?
GOTTA ADMIT, I'M PRETTY LOUSY AT THAT.
HM ...
I WONDER IF THERE ARE ANY INSTRUCTIONAL VIDEOS!
VIDEOS?
YEAH, LIKE WITH WEIGHT TRAINING. I DO BETTER WHEN I'M WATCHING A VIDEO...
...RATHER THAN PUMPING IRON IN SILENCE.
Hmm...
!
I KNOW!
I'VE GOT JUST THE THING FOR YOU!
REALLY? YOU'RE THE BEST, PYRRHA!

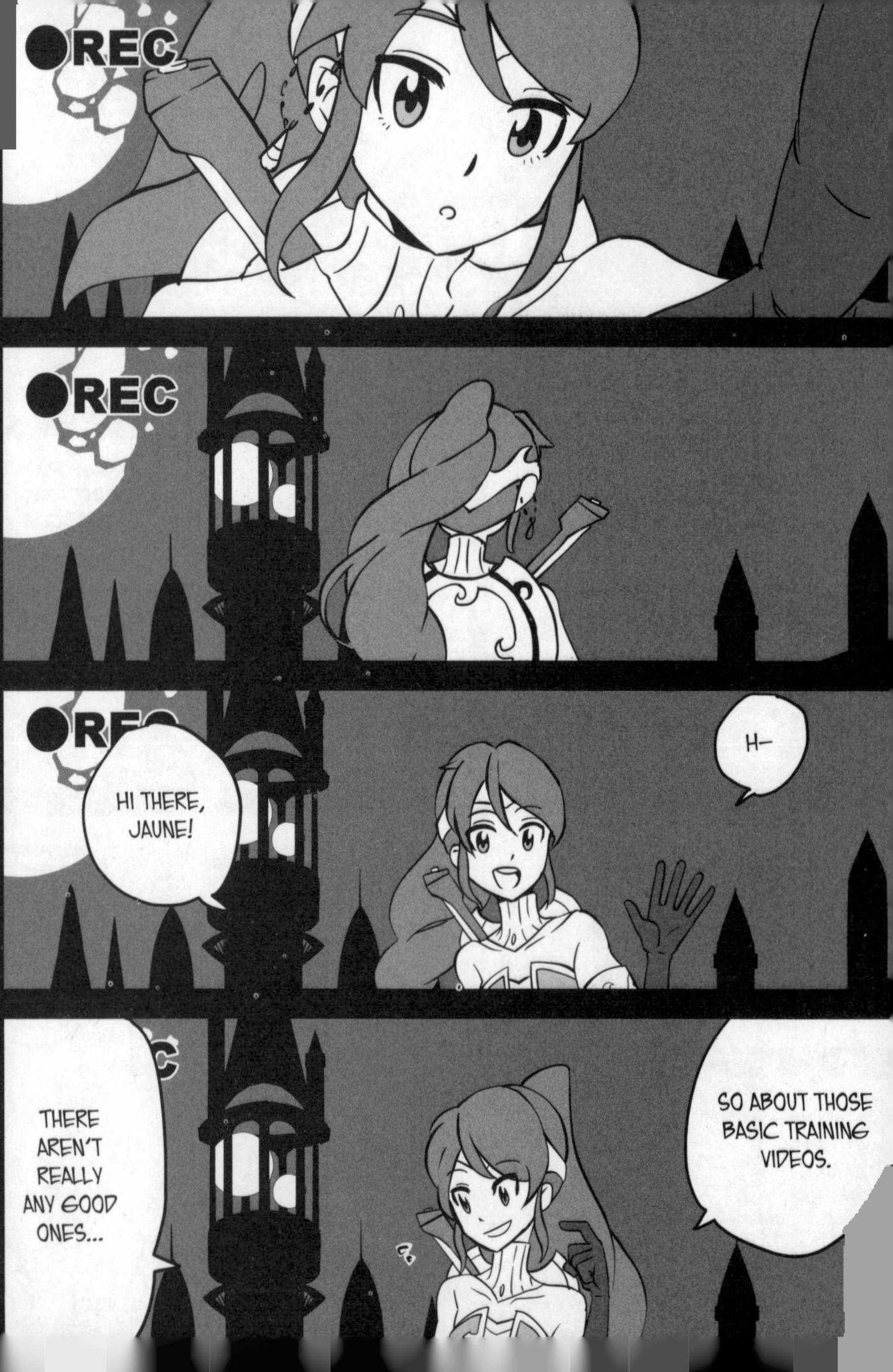
REC
REC
H—
HI THERE, JAUNE!
SO ABOUT THOSE BASIC TRAINING VIDEOS.
THERE AREN'T REALLY ANY GOOD ONES...

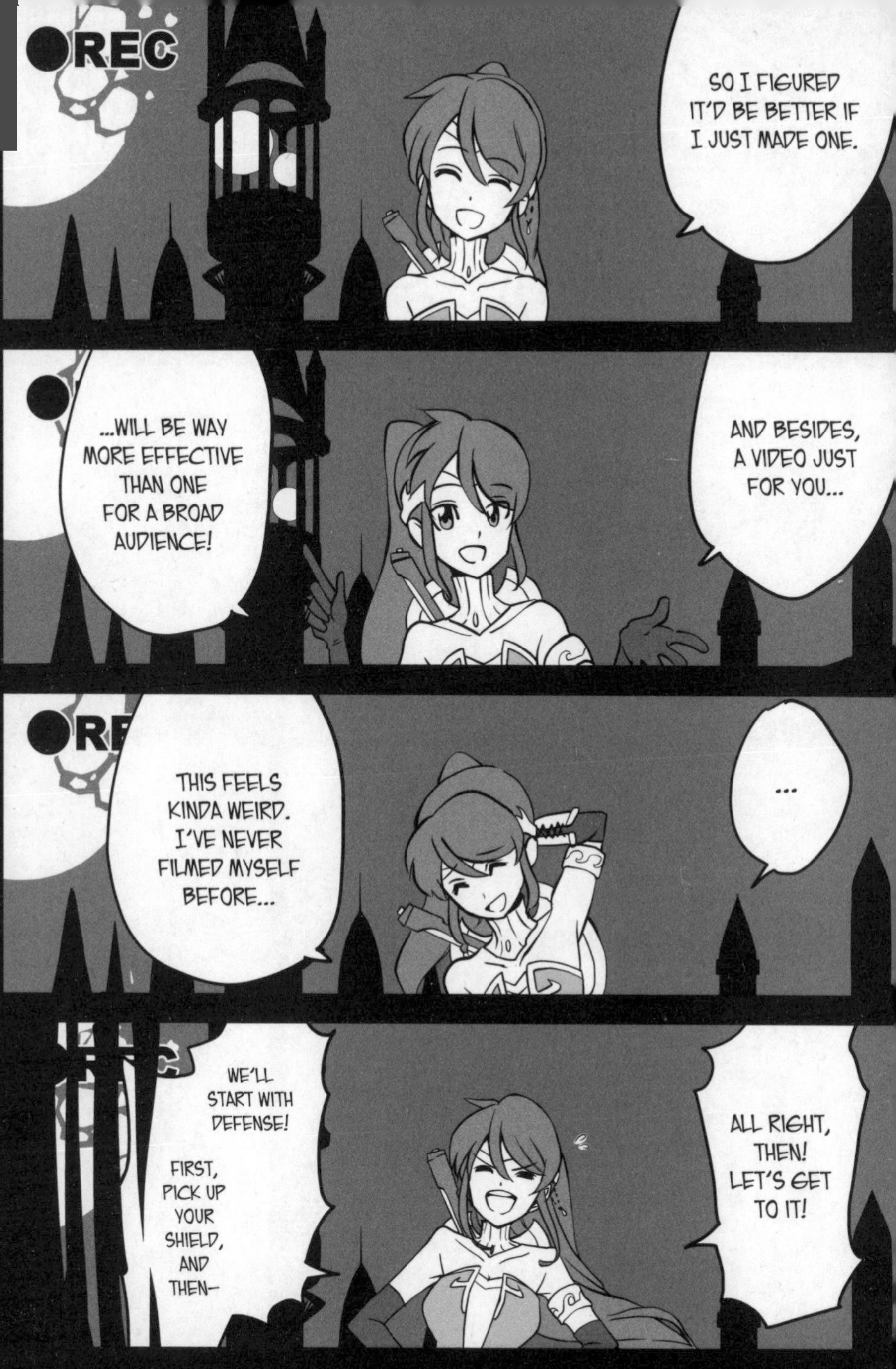
SO I FIGURED IT'D BE BETTER IF I JUST MADE ONE.
REC
AND BESIDES, A VIDEO JUST FOR YOU...
...WILL BE WAY MORE EFFECTIVE THAN ONE FOR A BROAD AUDIENCE!
...
THIS FEELS KINDA WEIRD. I'VE NEVER FILMED MYSELF BEFORE...
ALL RIGHT, THEN! LET'S GET TO IT!
WE'LL START WITH DEFENSE!
FIRST, PICK UP YOUR SHIELD, AND THEN—

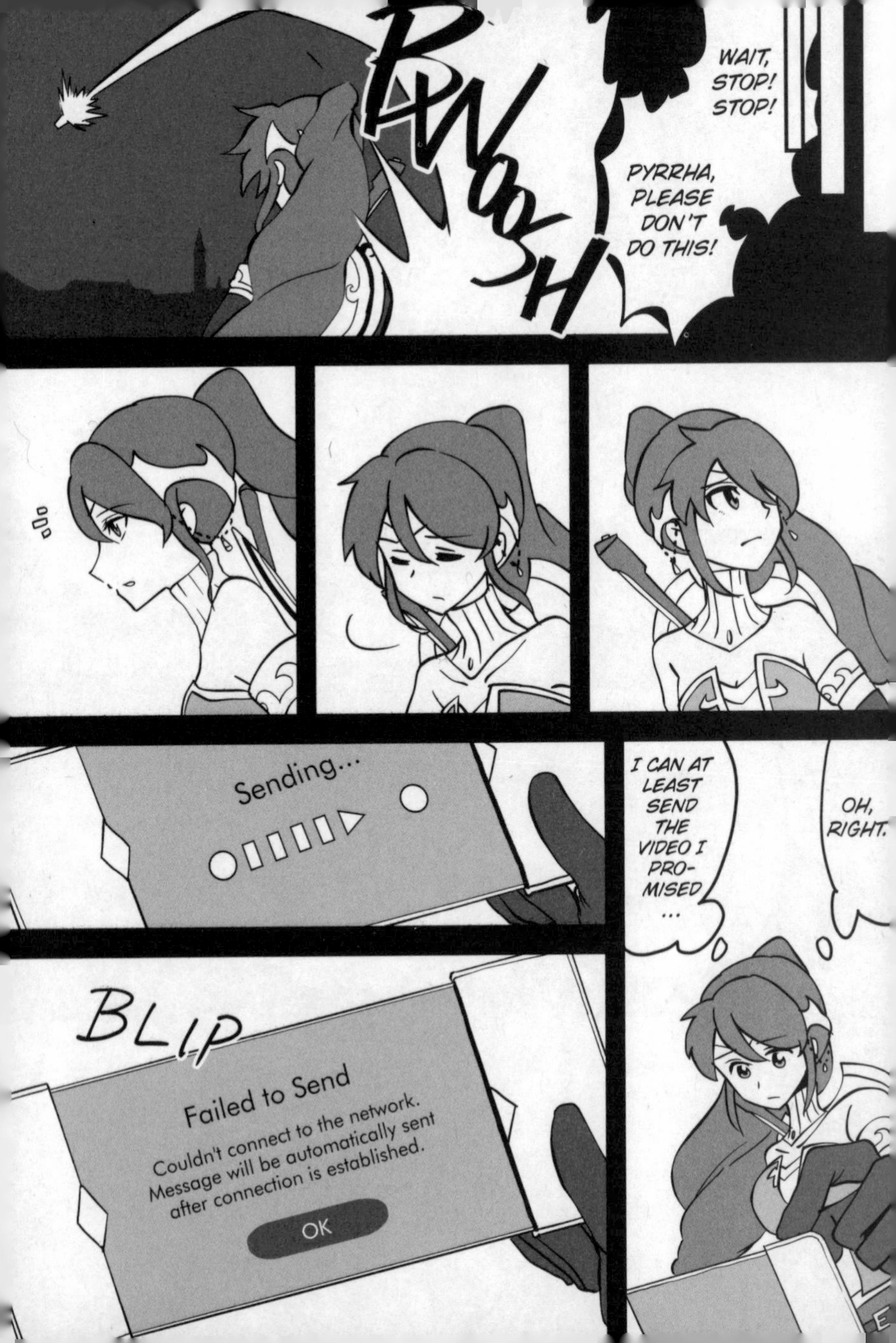
WAIT, STOP! STOP!
PYRRHA, PLEASE DON'T DO THIS!
PWOOSH
OH, RIGHT.
I CAN AT LEAST SEND THE VIDEO I PRO-MISED...
Sending...
BLIP
Failed to Send
Couldn't connect to the network. Message will be automatically sent after connection is established.
OK

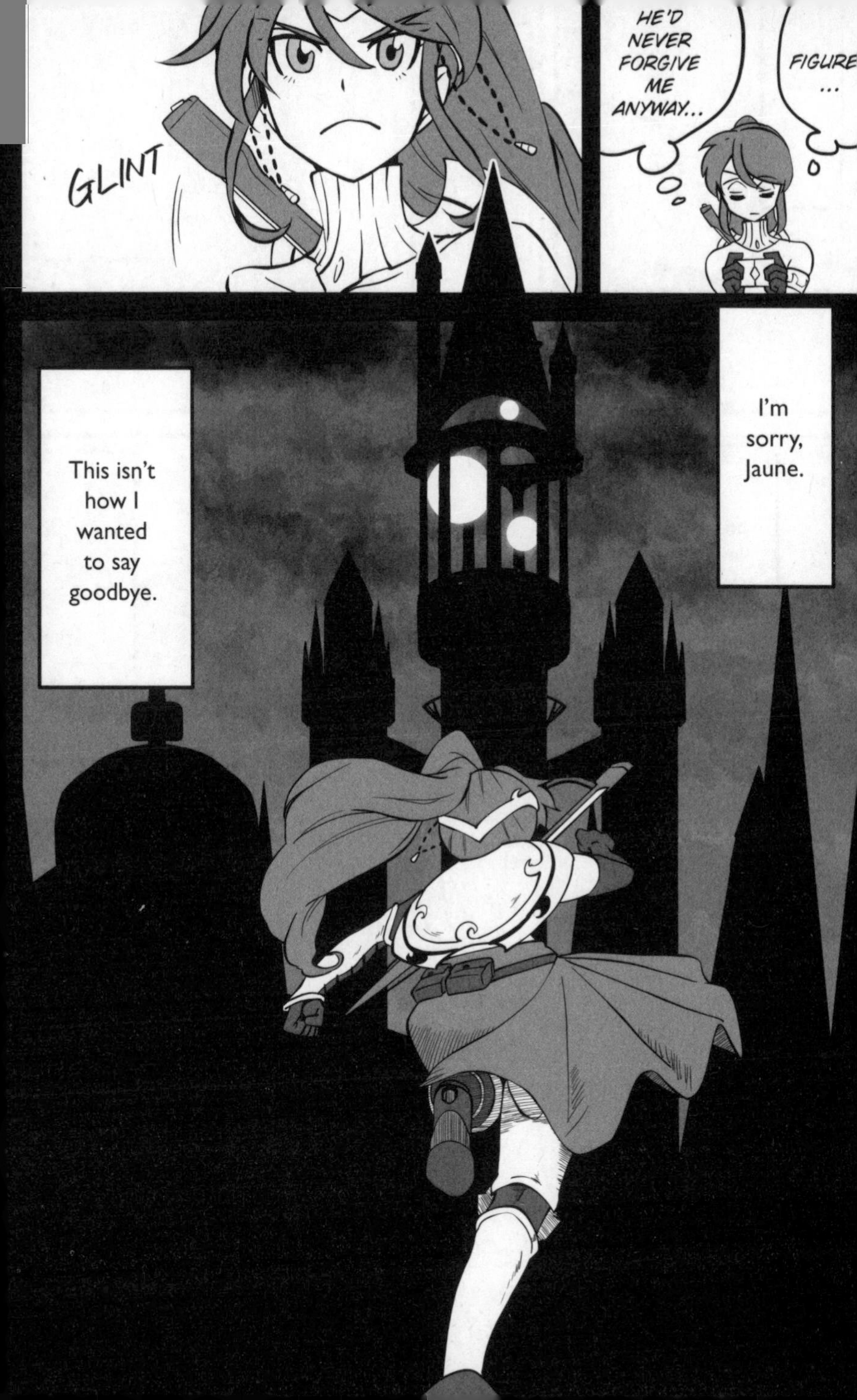
FIGURE ...
HE'D NEVER FORGIVE ME ANYWAY...
GLINT
I'm sorry, Jaune.
This isn't how I wanted to say goodbye.

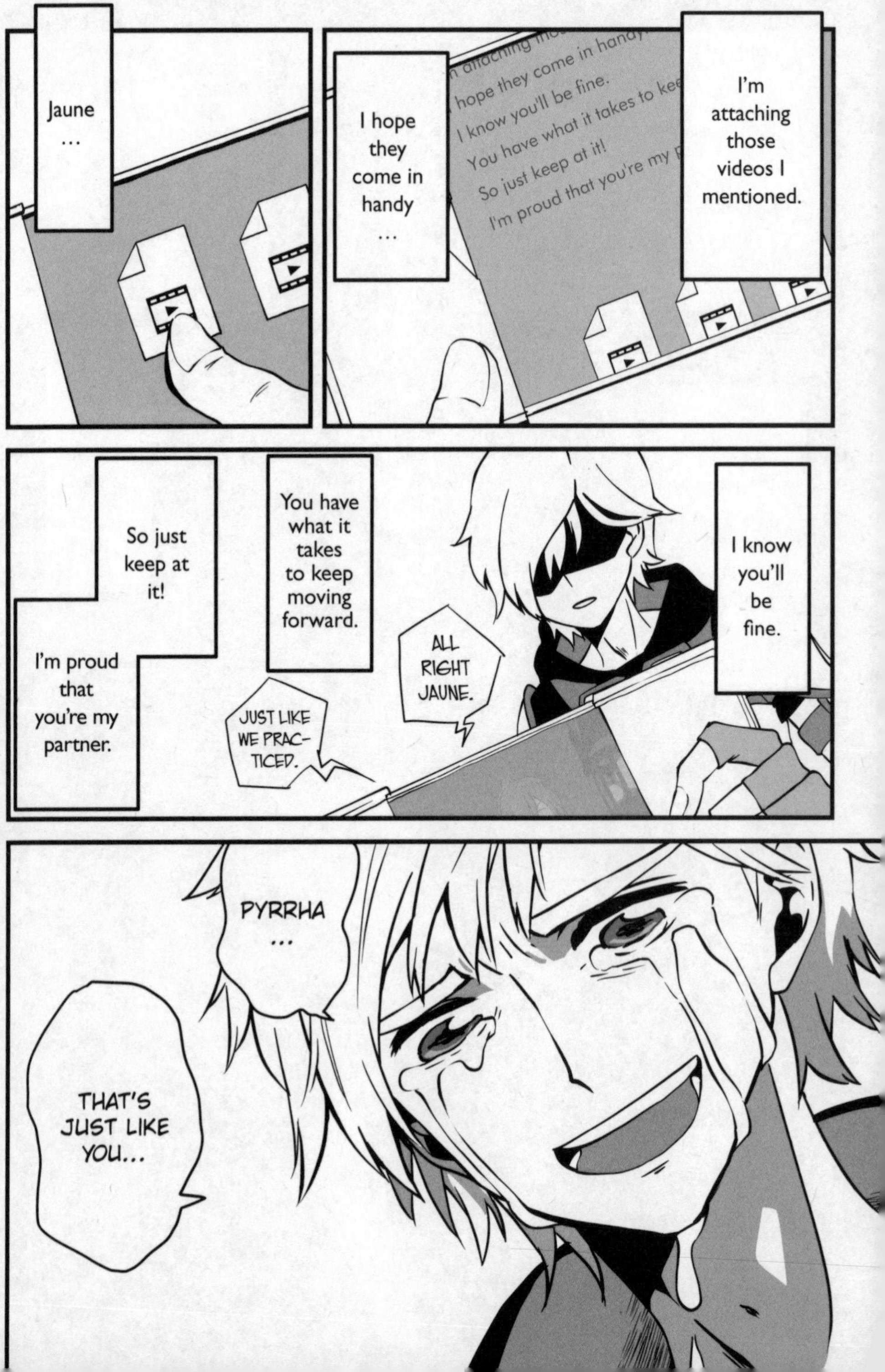
I'm attaching those videos I mentioned.
I know you'll be fine.
So just keep at it!
I hope they come in handy …
Jaune …
I know you'll be fine.
ALL RIGHT JAUNE.
You have what it takes to keep moving forward.
JUST LIKE WE PRACTICED.
So just keep at it!
I'm proud that you're my partner.
PYRRHA …
THAT'S JUST LIKE YOU…

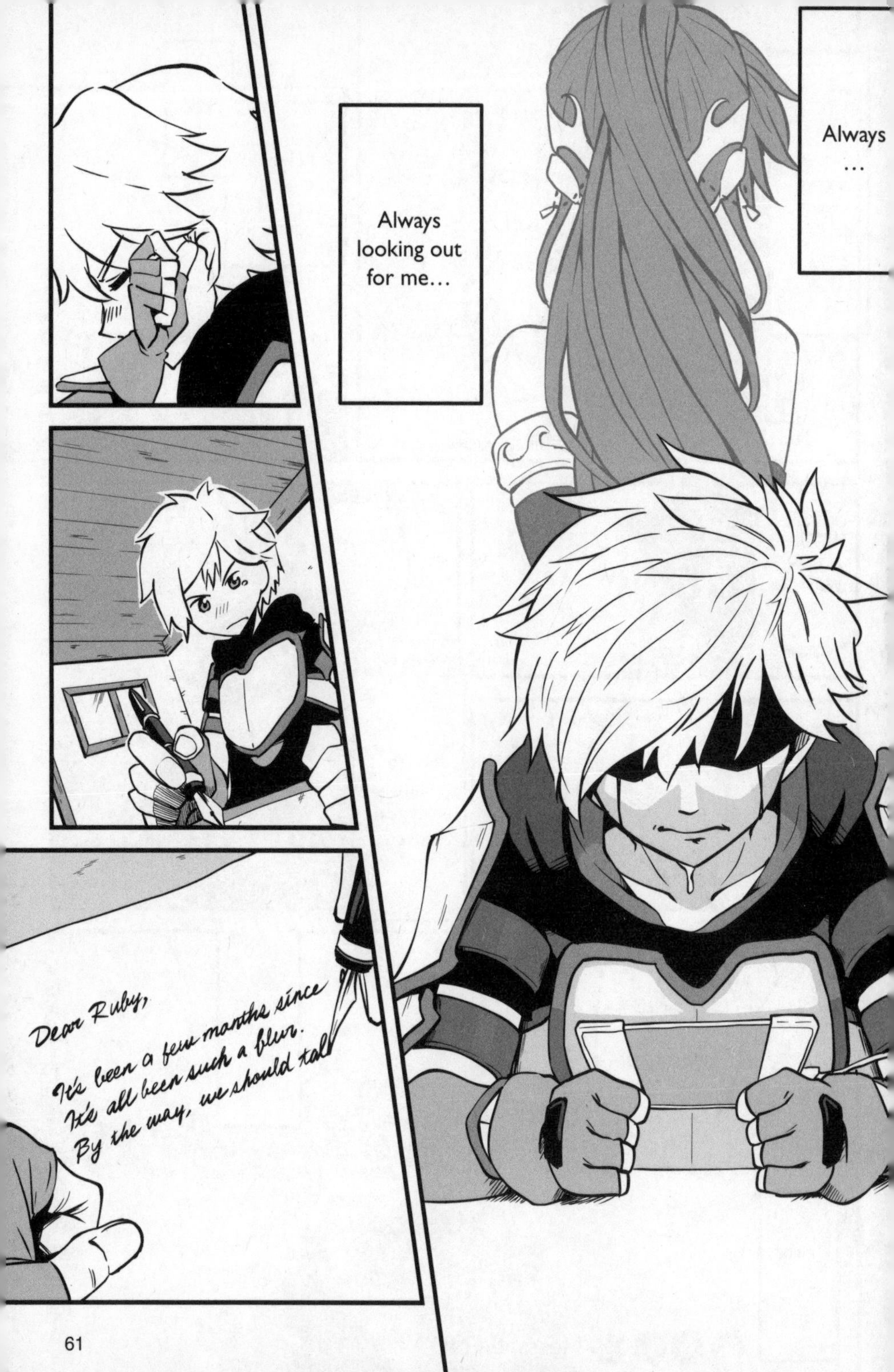
Always
…
Always looking out for me…
Dear Ruby,
It's been a few months since
It's all been such a blur.
By the way, we should tal

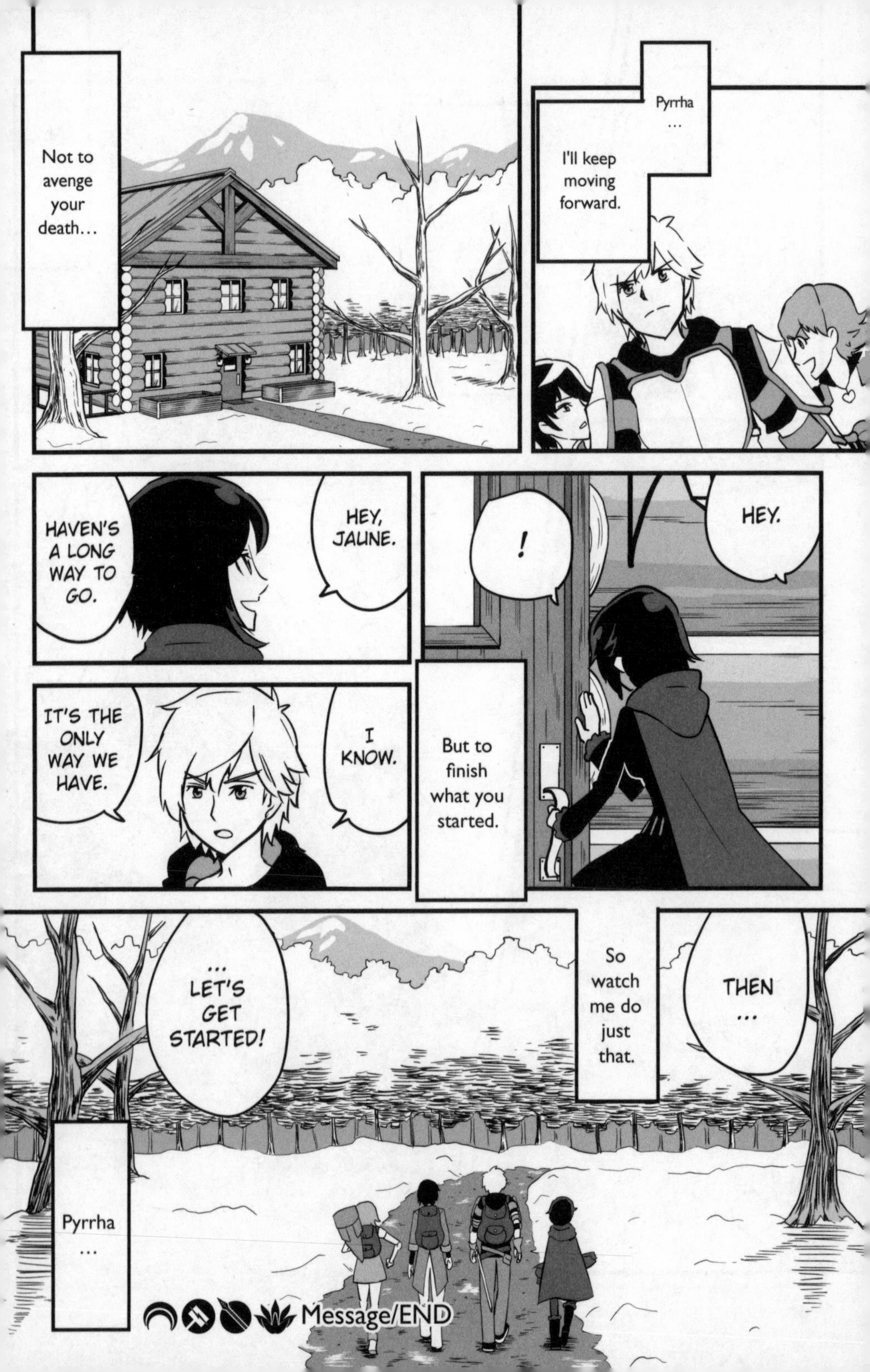
Pyrrha …
I'll keep moving forward.
Not to avenge your death…
HEY.
!
But to finish what you started.
HEY, JAUNE.
HAVEN'S A LONG WAY TO GO.
I KNOW.
IT'S THE ONLY WAY WE HAVE.
THEN …
So watch me do just that.
… LET'S GET STARTED!
Pyrrha …
Message/END

Dumb_JNPR.pdf

Eunnie

Pairs.png

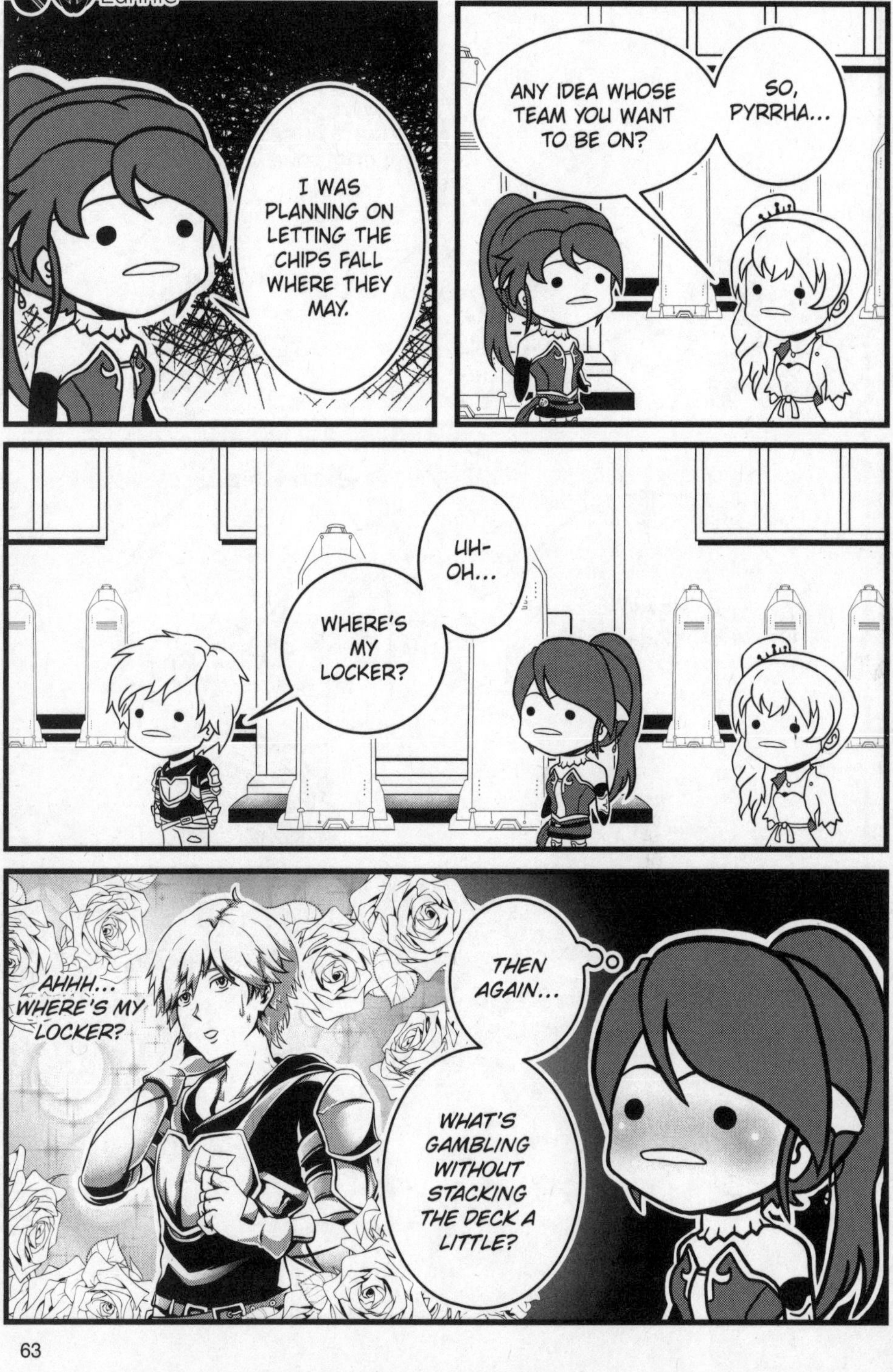
SO, PYRRHA...
ANY IDEA WHOSE TEAM YOU WANT TO BE ON?
I WAS PLANNING ON LETTING THE CHIPS FALL WHERE THEY MAY.
UH-OH...
WHERE'S MY LOCKER?
THEN AGAIN...
WHAT'S GAMBLING WITHOUT STACKING THE DECK A LITTLE?
AHHH... WHERE'S MY LOCKER?

Legs.png

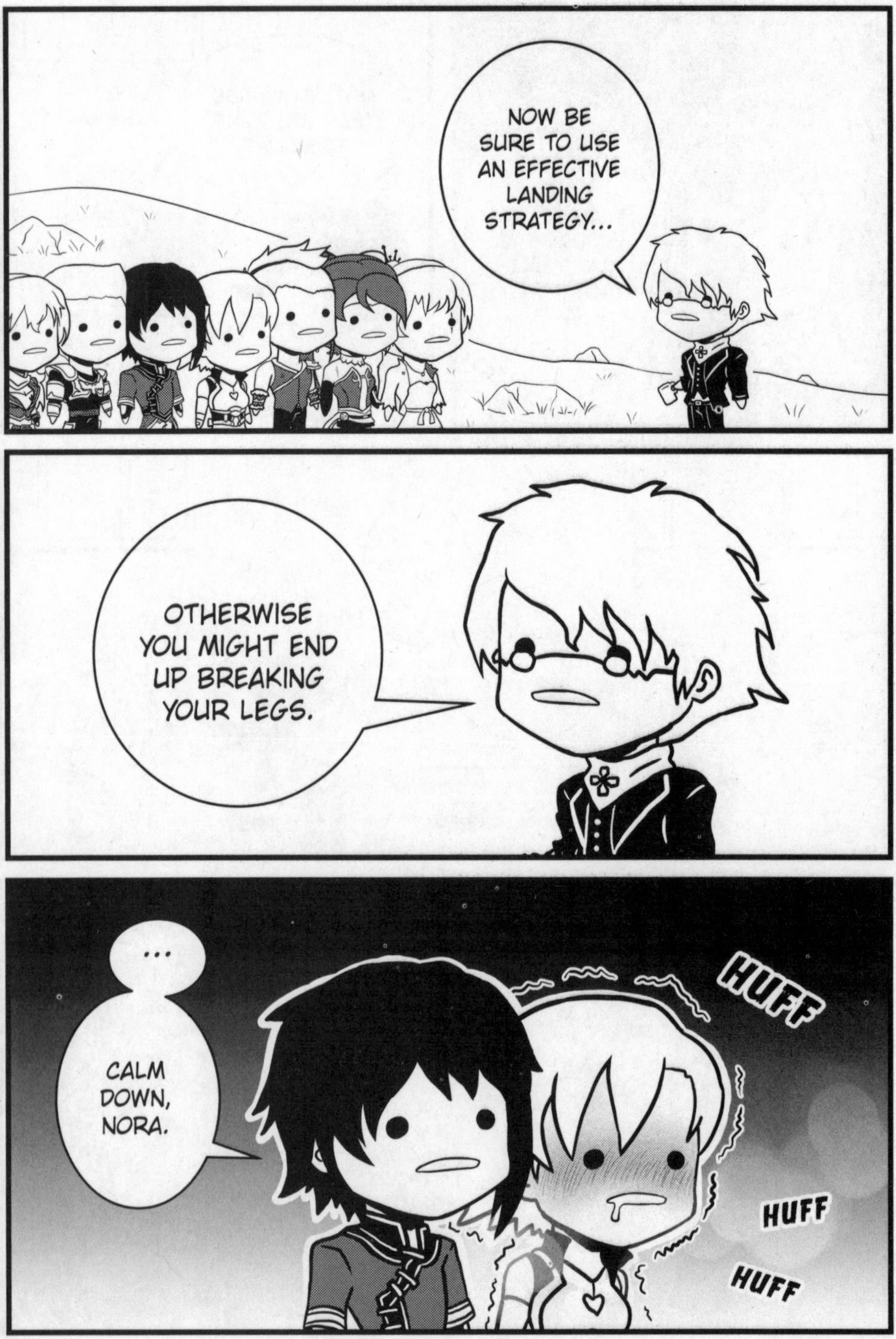
NOW BE SURE TO USE AN EFFECTIVE LANDING STRATEGY...
OTHERWISE YOU MIGHT END UP BREAKING YOUR LEGS.
HUFF
...
CALM DOWN, NORA.
HUFF
HUFF

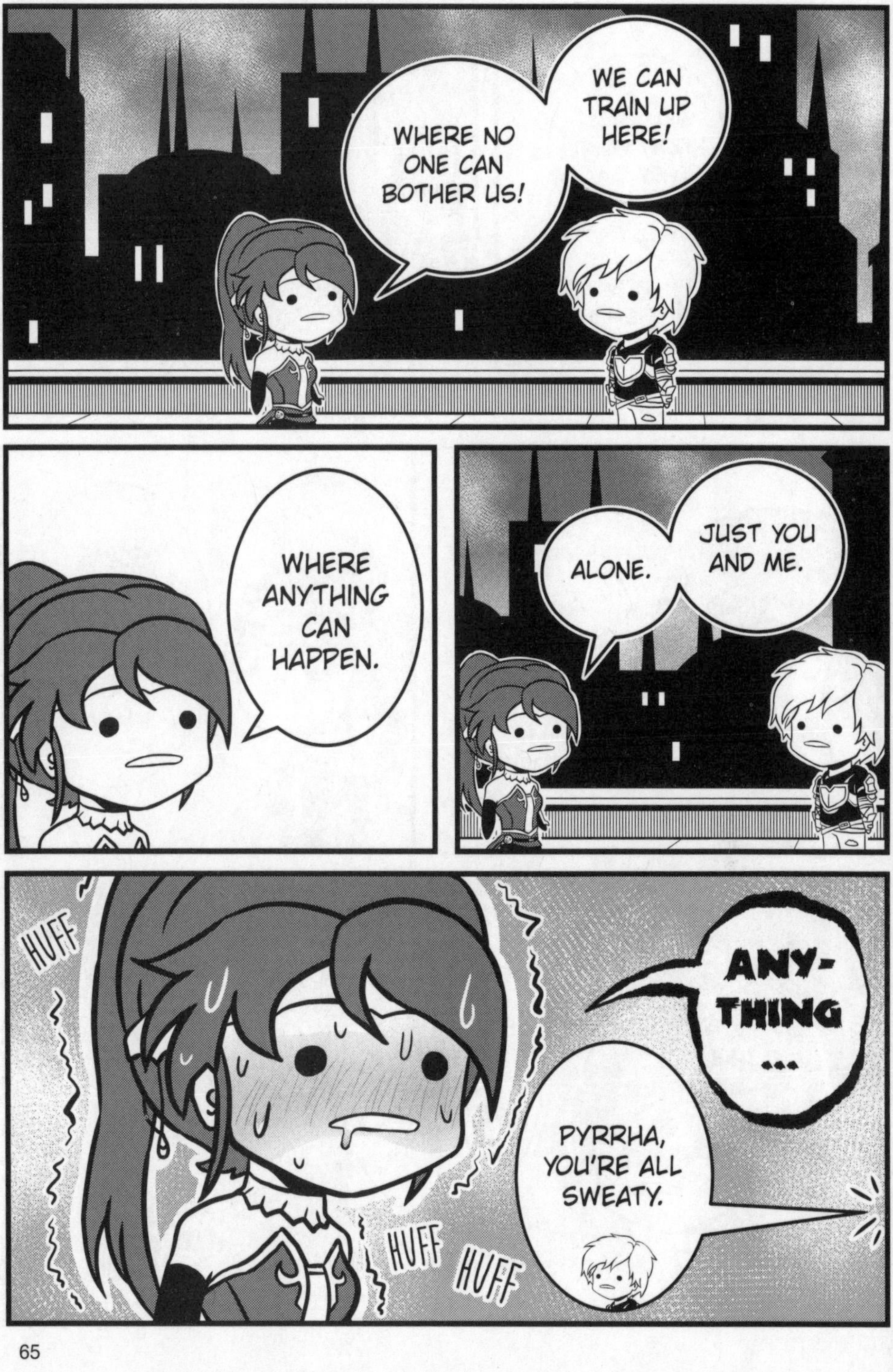
WE CAN TRAIN UP HERE!
WHERE NO ONE CAN BOTHER US!
JUST YOU AND ME.
ALONE.
WHERE ANYTHING CAN HAPPEN.
ANY-THING...
HUFF
PYRRHA, YOU'RE ALL SWEATY.
HUFF
HUFF

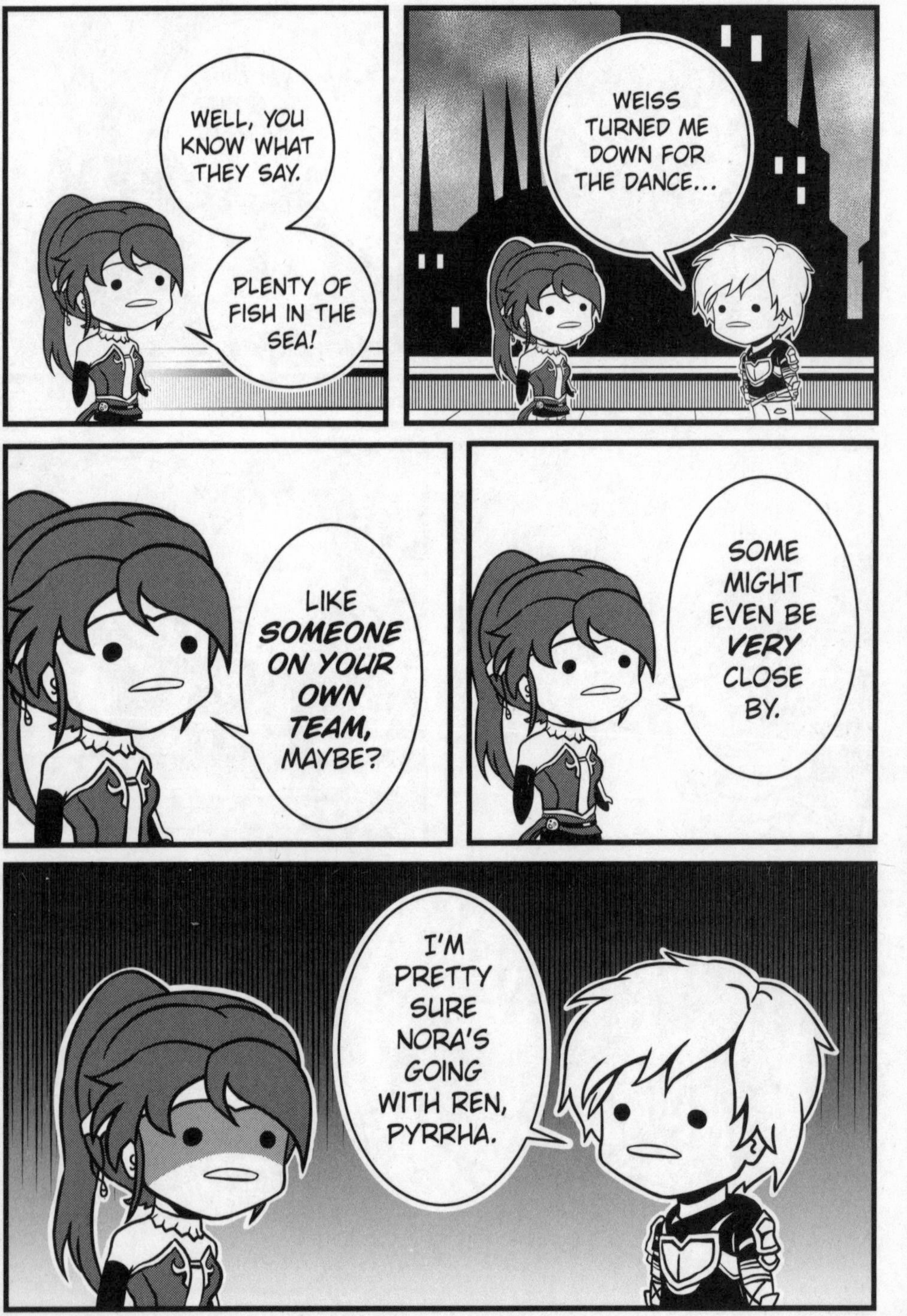
WEISS TURNED ME DOWN FOR THE DANCE...
WELL, YOU KNOW WHAT THEY SAY.
PLENTY OF FISH IN THE SEA!
SOME MIGHT EVEN BE **VERY** CLOSE BY.
LIKE **SOMEONE ON YOUR OWN TEAM,** MAYBE?
I'M PRETTY SURE NORA'S GOING WITH REN, PYRRHA.

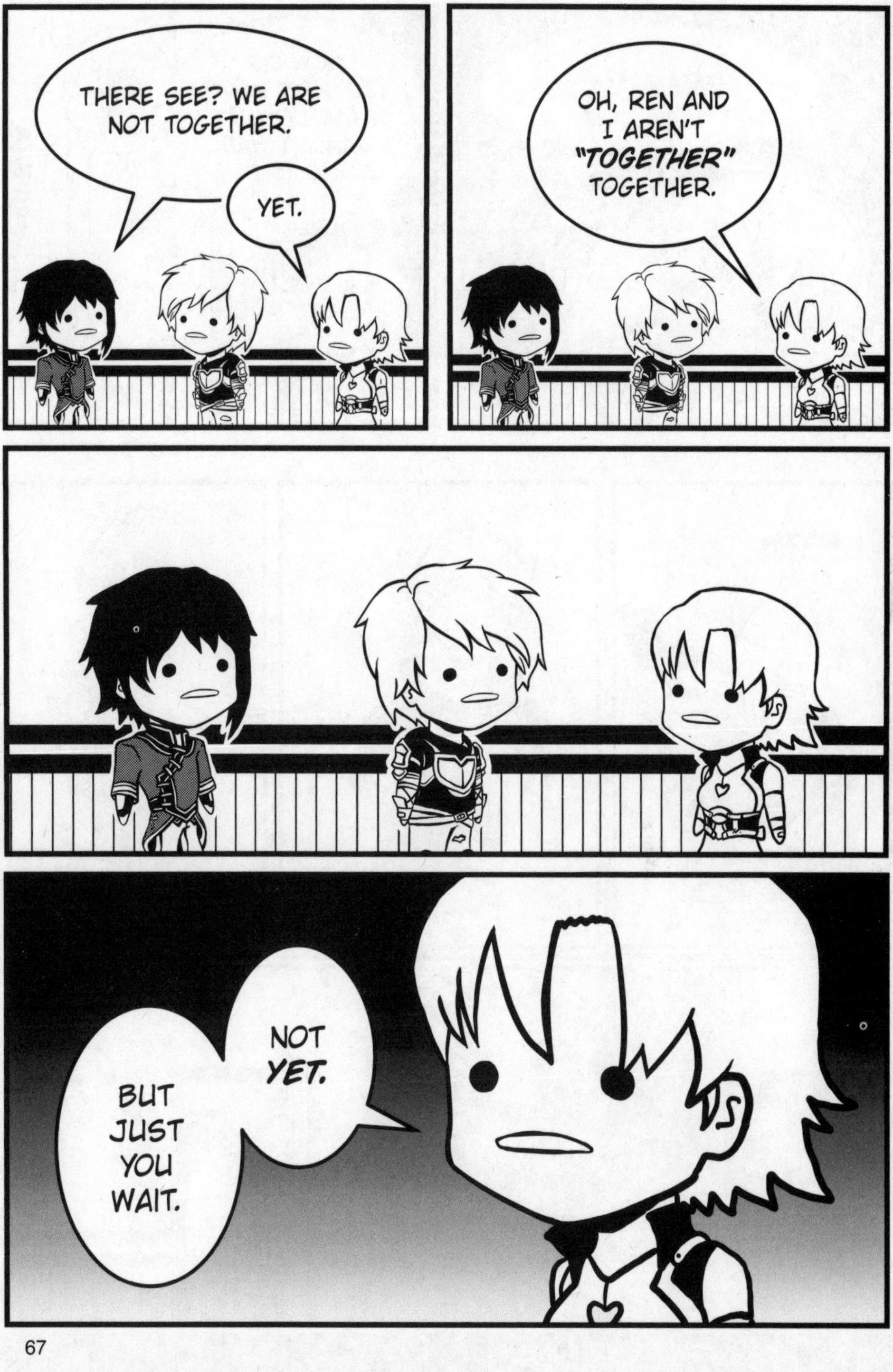
OH, REN AND I AREN'T "*TOGETHER*" TOGETHER.
THERE SEE? WE ARE NOT TOGETHER.
YET.
NOT *YET.*
BUT JUST YOU WAIT.

Dance.png

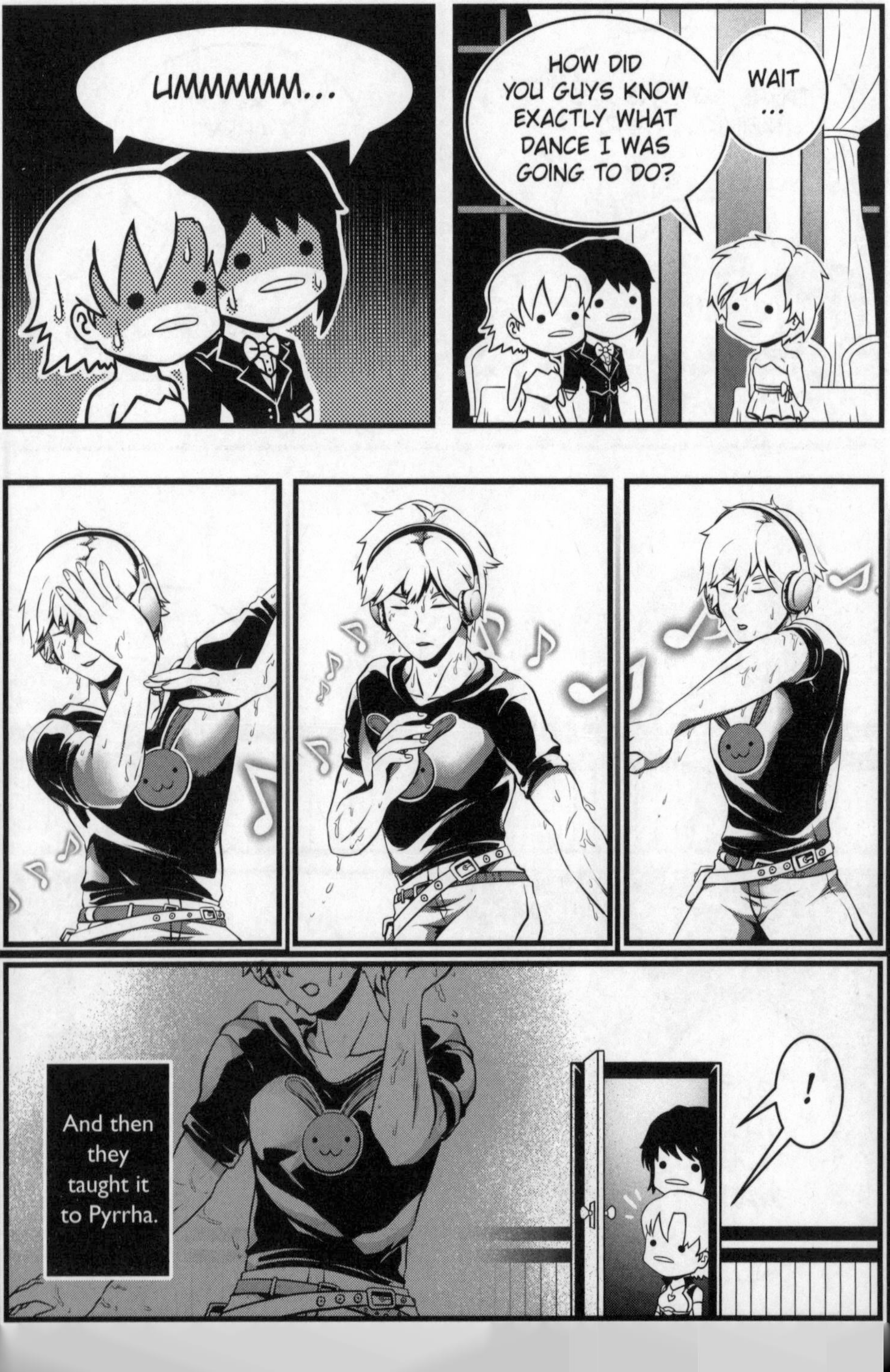
HOW DID YOU GUYS KNOW EXACTLY WHAT DANCE I WAS GOING TO DO?
WAIT ...
UMMMMMM...
!
And then they taught it to Pyrrha.

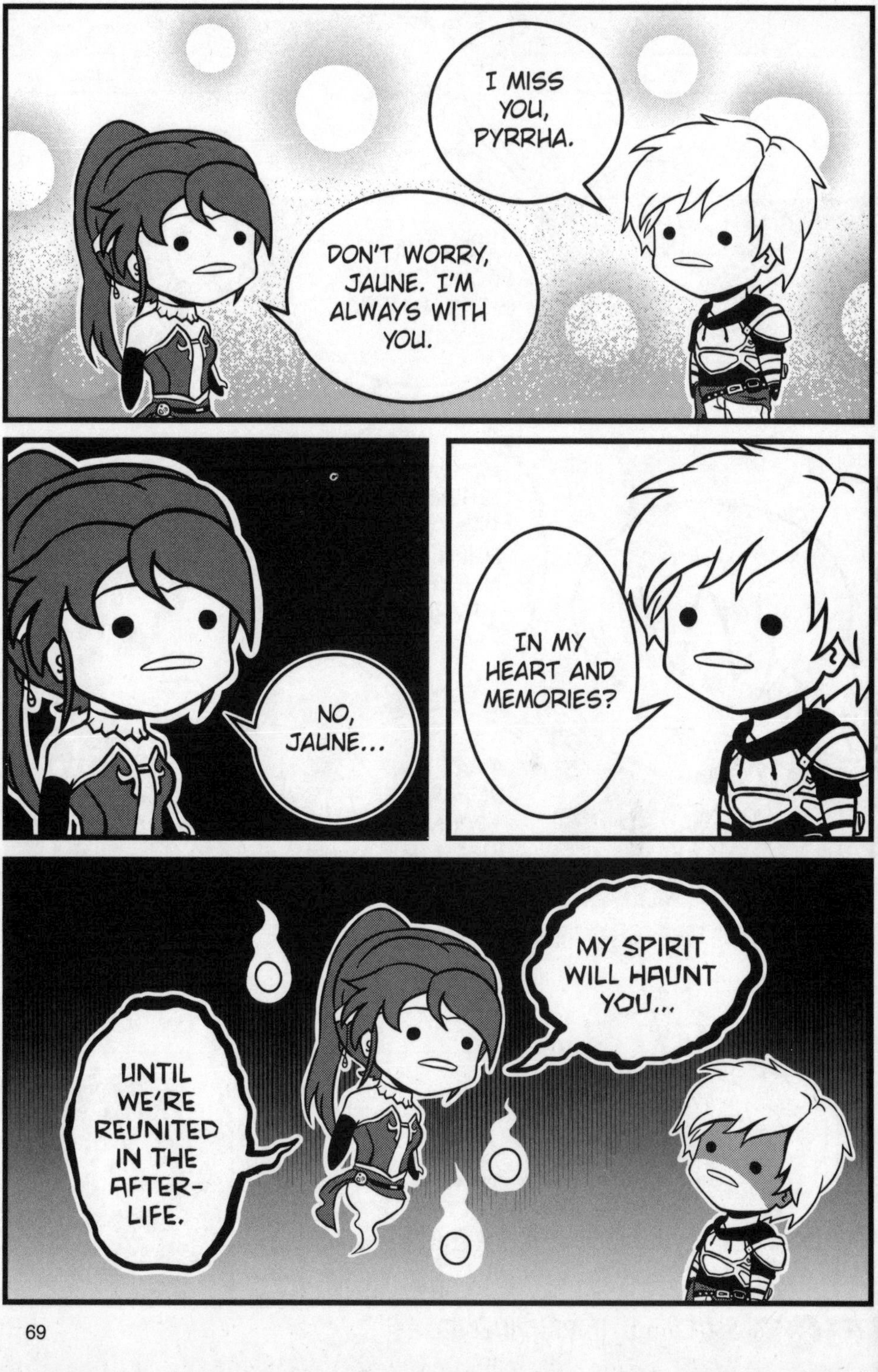
I MISS YOU, PYRRHA.
DON'T WORRY, JAUNE. I'M ALWAYS WITH YOU.
IN MY HEART AND MEMORIES?
NO, JAUNE...
MY SPIRIT WILL HAUNT YOU...
UNTIL WE'RE REUNITED IN THE AFTER-LIFE.

Renora02.png

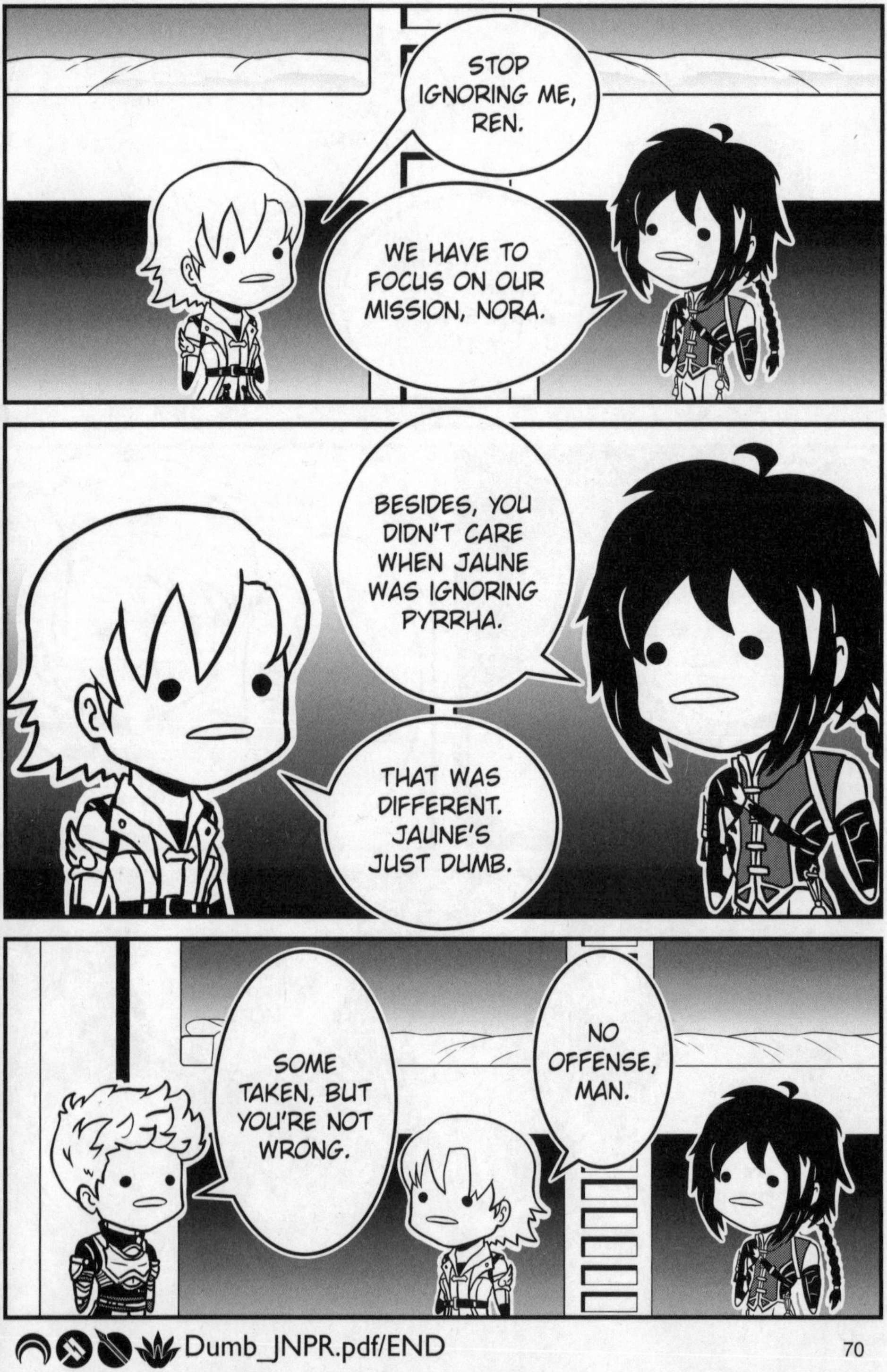
STOP IGNORING ME, REN.
WE HAVE TO FOCUS ON OUR MISSION, NORA.
BESIDES, YOU DIDN'T CARE WHEN JAUNE WAS IGNORING PYRRHA.
THAT WAS DIFFERENT. JAUNE'S JUST DUMB.
NO OFFENSE, MAN.
SOME TAKEN, BUT YOU'RE NOT WRONG.

Dumb_JNPR.pdf/END

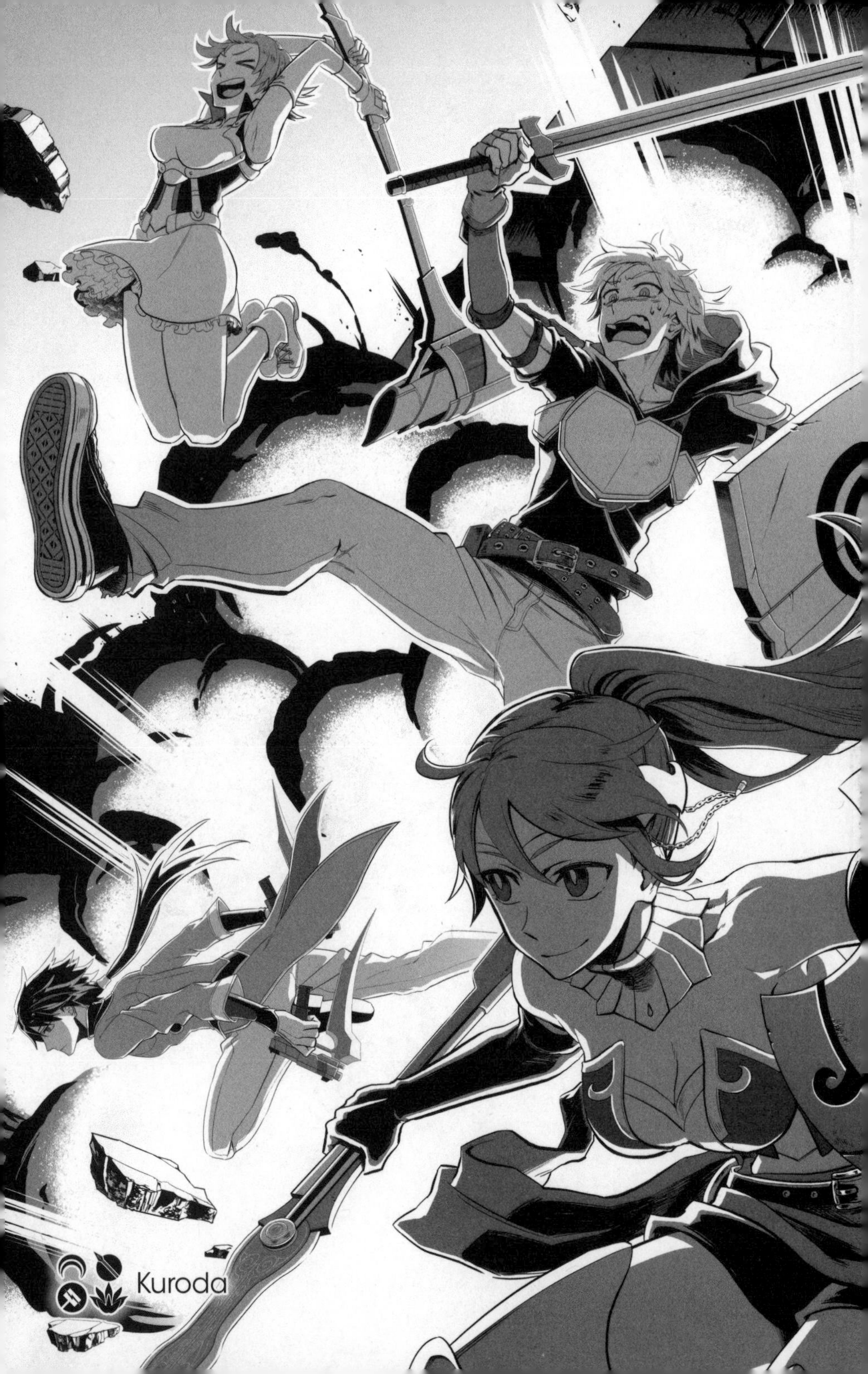
Kuroda

RWBY
OFFICIAL MANGA ANTHOLOGY
Volume 5

Shine

Ecru

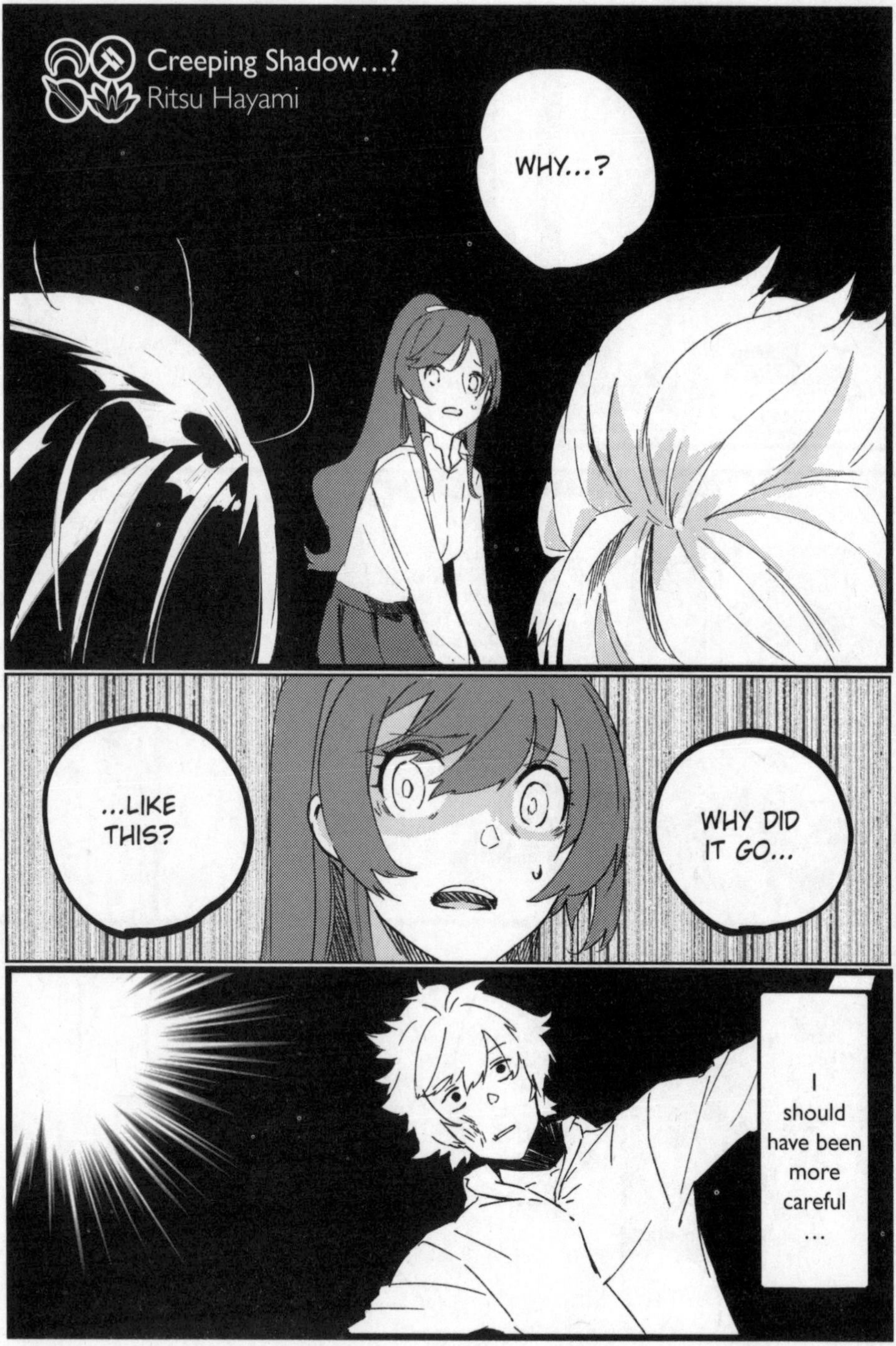
Creeping Shadow…?
Ritsu Hayami
WHY...?
WHY DID IT GO...
...LIKE THIS?
I should have been more careful ...

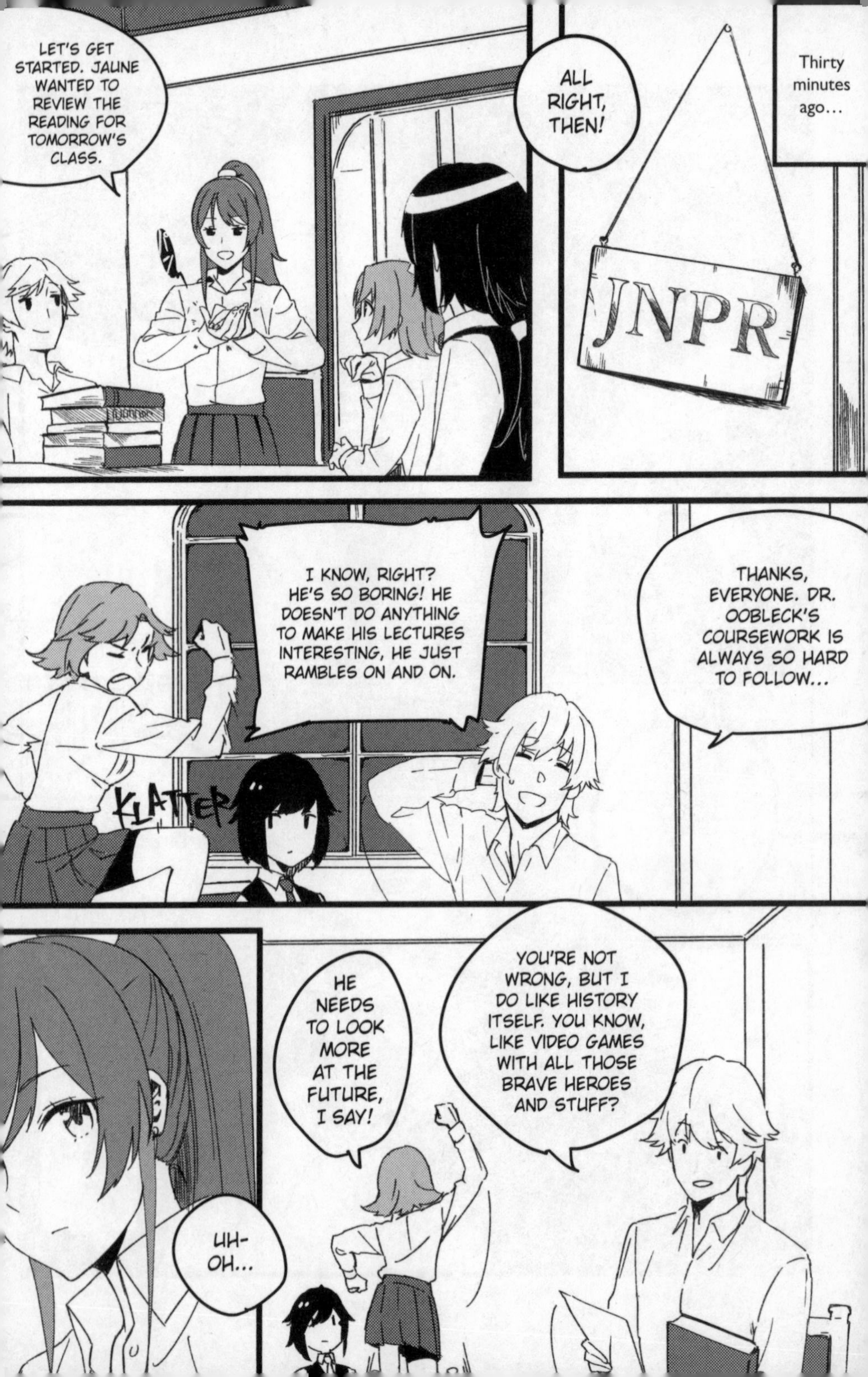
Thirty minutes ago...
JNPR
ALL RIGHT, THEN!
LET'S GET STARTED. JAUNE WANTED TO REVIEW THE READING FOR TOMORROW'S CLASS.
THANKS, EVERYONE. DR. OOBLECK'S COURSEWORK IS ALWAYS SO HARD TO FOLLOW...
I KNOW, RIGHT? HE'S SO BORING! HE DOESN'T DO ANYTHING TO MAKE HIS LECTURES INTERESTING, HE JUST RAMBLES ON AND ON.
KLATTER
YOU'RE NOT WRONG, BUT I DO LIKE HISTORY ITSELF. YOU KNOW, LIKE VIDEO GAMES WITH ALL THOSE BRAVE HEROES AND STUFF?
HE NEEDS TO LOOK MORE AT THE FUTURE, I SAY!
UH-OH...

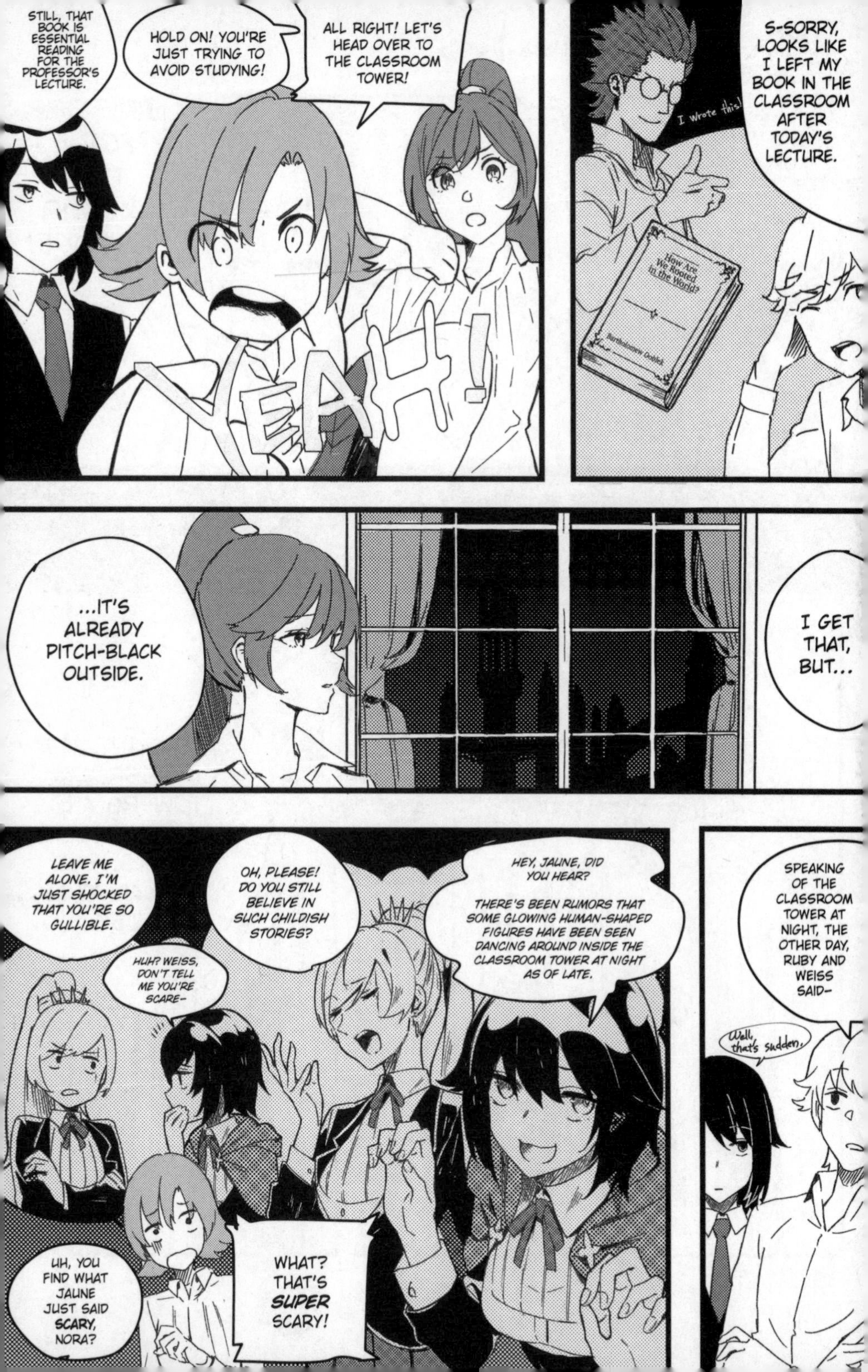
S-SORRY, LOOKS LIKE I LEFT MY BOOK IN THE CLASSROOM AFTER TODAY'S LECTURE.
I wrote this!
How Are We Rooted in the World?
ALL RIGHT! LET'S HEAD OVER TO THE CLASSROOM TOWER!
HOLD ON! YOU'RE JUST TRYING TO AVOID STUDYING!
STILL, THAT BOOK IS ESSENTIAL READING FOR THE PROFESSOR'S LECTURE.
YEAH!
I GET THAT, BUT...
...IT'S ALREADY PITCH-BLACK OUTSIDE.
SPEAKING OF THE CLASSROOM TOWER AT NIGHT, THE OTHER DAY, RUBY AND WEISS SAID-
Well, that's sudden.
HEY, JAUNE, DID YOU HEAR?
THERE'S BEEN RUMORS THAT SOME GLOWING HUMAN-SHAPED FIGURES HAVE BEEN SEEN DANCING AROUND INSIDE THE CLASSROOM TOWER AT NIGHT AS OF LATE.
OH, PLEASE! DO YOU STILL BELIEVE IN SUCH CHILDISH STORIES?
LEAVE ME ALONE. I'M JUST SHOCKED THAT YOU'RE SO GULLIBLE.
HUH? WEISS, DON'T TELL ME YOU'RE SCARE-
WHAT? THAT'S SUPER SCARY!
UH, YOU FIND WHAT JAUNE JUST SAID SCARY, NORA?

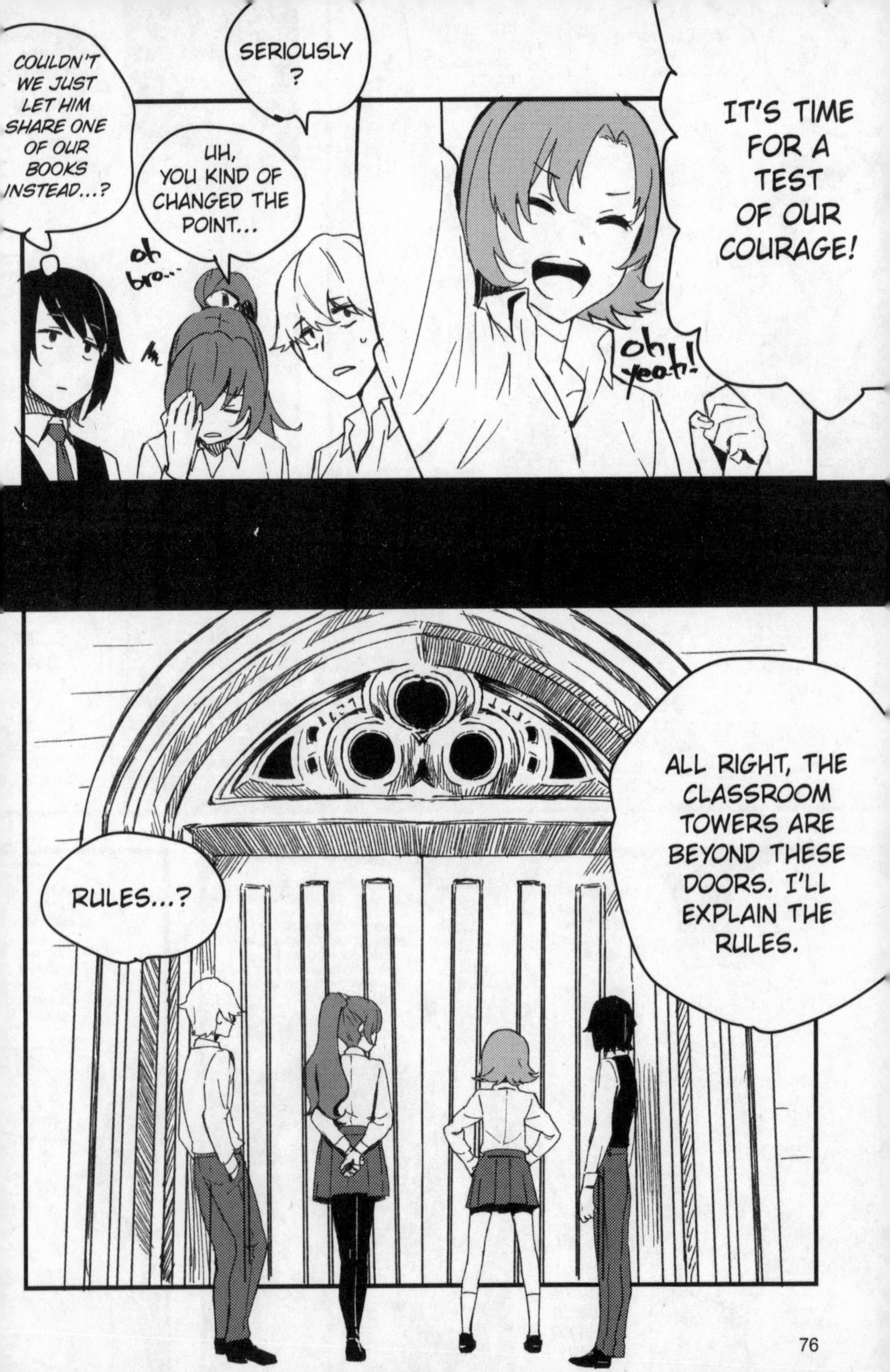
IT'S TIME FOR A TEST OF OUR COURAGE!
oh yeah!
SERIOUSLY?
COULDN'T WE JUST LET HIM SHARE ONE OF OUR BOOKS INSTEAD...?
UH, YOU KIND OF CHANGED THE POINT...
oh bro...
ALL RIGHT, THE CLASSROOM TOWERS ARE BEYOND THESE DOORS. I'LL EXPLAIN THE RULES.
RULES...?

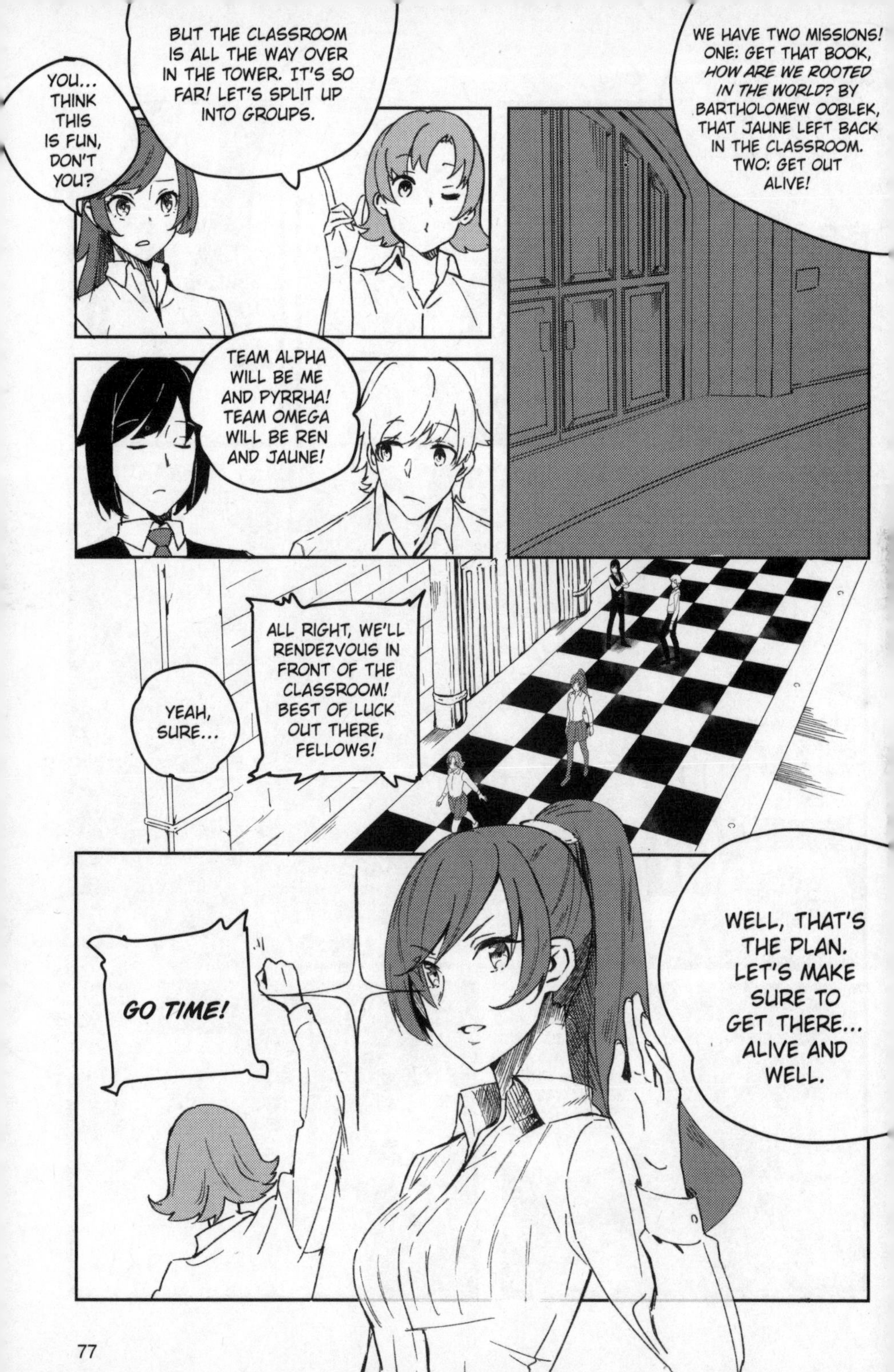
WE HAVE TWO MISSIONS! ONE: GET THAT BOOK, HOW ARE WE ROOTED IN THE WORLD? BY BARTHOLOMEW OOBLEK, THAT JAUNE LEFT BACK IN THE CLASSROOM. TWO: GET OUT ALIVE!
BUT THE CLASSROOM IS ALL THE WAY OVER IN THE TOWER. IT'S SO FAR! LET'S SPLIT UP INTO GROUPS.
YOU... THINK THIS IS FUN, DON'T YOU?
TEAM ALPHA WILL BE ME AND PYRRHA! TEAM OMEGA WILL BE REN AND JAUNE!
ALL RIGHT, WE'LL RENDEZVOUS IN FRONT OF THE CLASSROOM! BEST OF LUCK OUT THERE, FELLOWS!
YEAH, SURE...
WELL, THAT'S THE PLAN. LET'S MAKE SURE TO GET THERE... ALIVE AND WELL.
GO TIME!

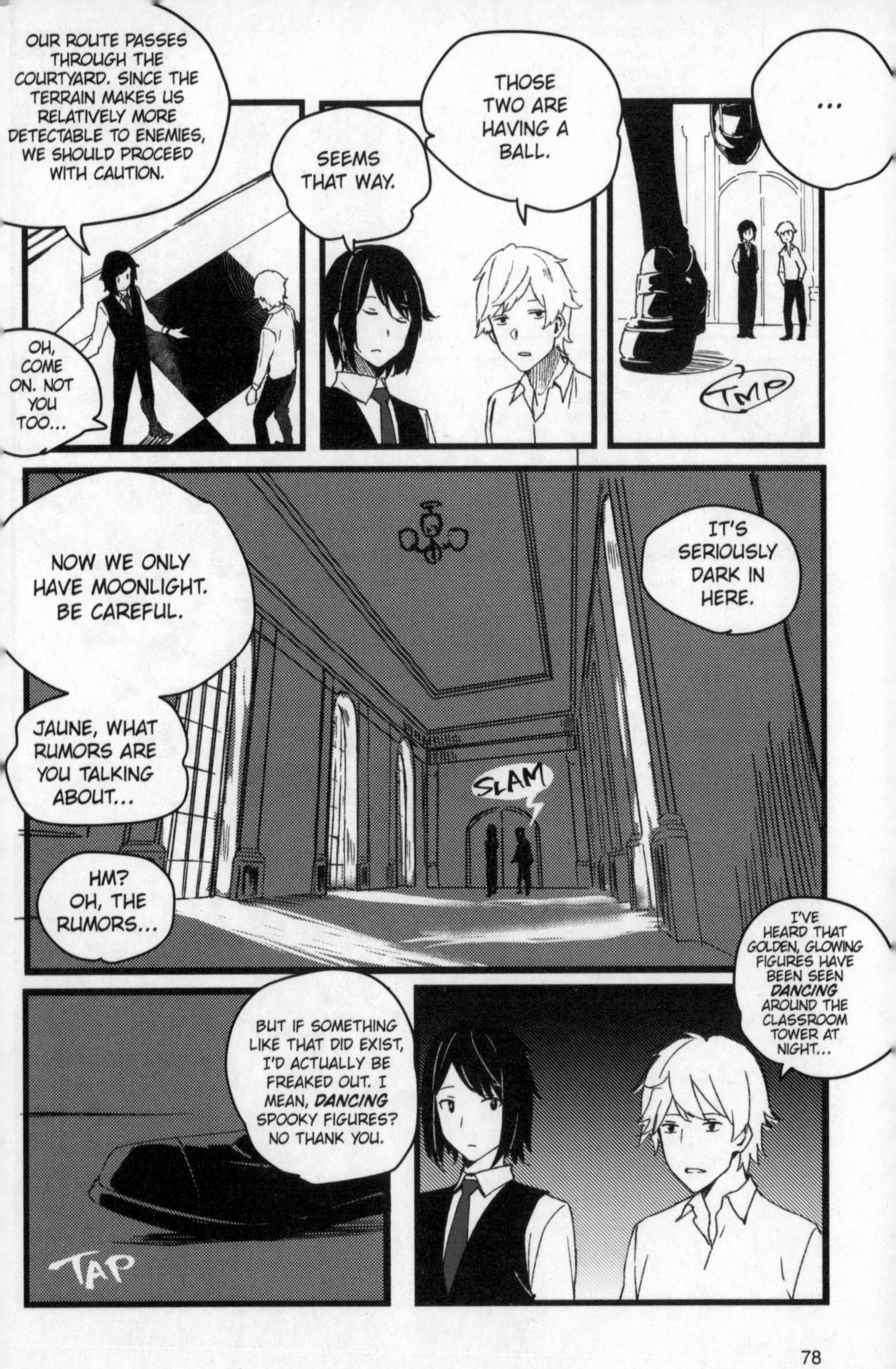
...
TMP
THOSE TWO ARE HAVING A BALL.
SEEMS THAT WAY.
OUR ROUTE PASSES THROUGH THE COURTYARD. SINCE THE TERRAIN MAKES US RELATIVELY MORE DETECTABLE TO ENEMIES, WE SHOULD PROCEED WITH CAUTION.
OH, COME ON. NOT YOU TOO...
IT'S SERIOUSLY DARK IN HERE.
NOW WE ONLY HAVE MOONLIGHT. BE CAREFUL.
SLAM
JAUNE, WHAT RUMORS ARE YOU TALKING ABOUT...
HM? OH, THE RUMORS...
I'VE HEARD THAT GOLDEN, GLOWING FIGURES HAVE BEEN SEEN DANCING AROUND THE CLASSROOM TOWER AT NIGHT...
BUT IF SOMETHING LIKE THAT DID EXIST, I'D ACTUALLY BE FREAKED OUT. I MEAN, DANCING SPOOKY FIGURES? NO THANK YOU.
TAP

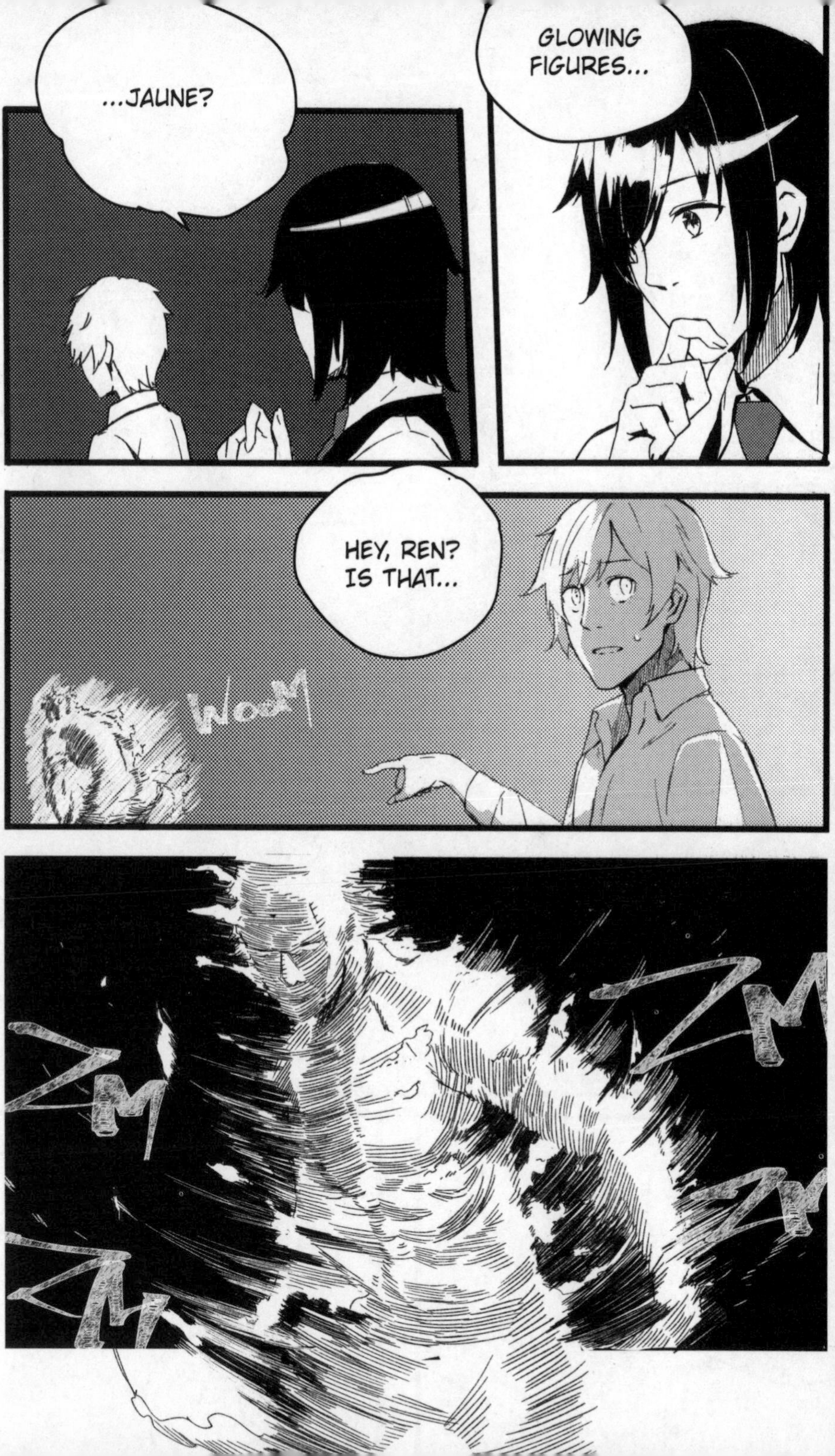
GLOWING FIGURES...
...JAUNE?
HEY, REN? IS THAT...
WOOM
ZM
ZM
ZM
ZM

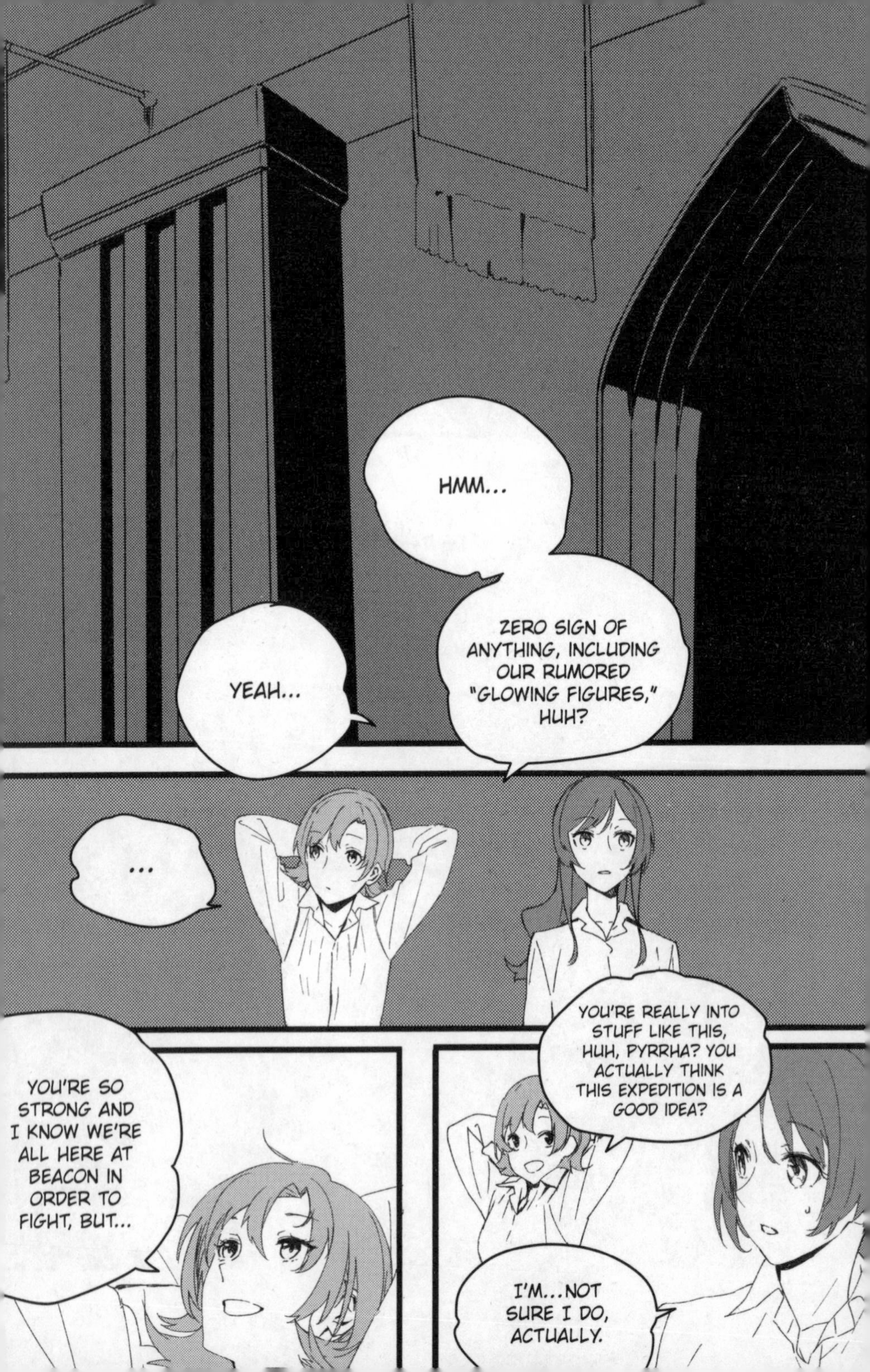
HMM...
ZERO SIGN OF ANYTHING, INCLUDING OUR RUMORED "GLOWING FIGURES," HUH?
YEAH...
...
YOU'RE REALLY INTO STUFF LIKE THIS, HUH, PYRRHA? YOU ACTUALLY THINK THIS EXPEDITION IS A GOOD IDEA?
I'M...NOT SURE I DO, ACTUALLY.
YOU'RE SO STRONG AND I KNOW WE'RE ALL HERE AT BEACON IN ORDER TO FIGHT, BUT...

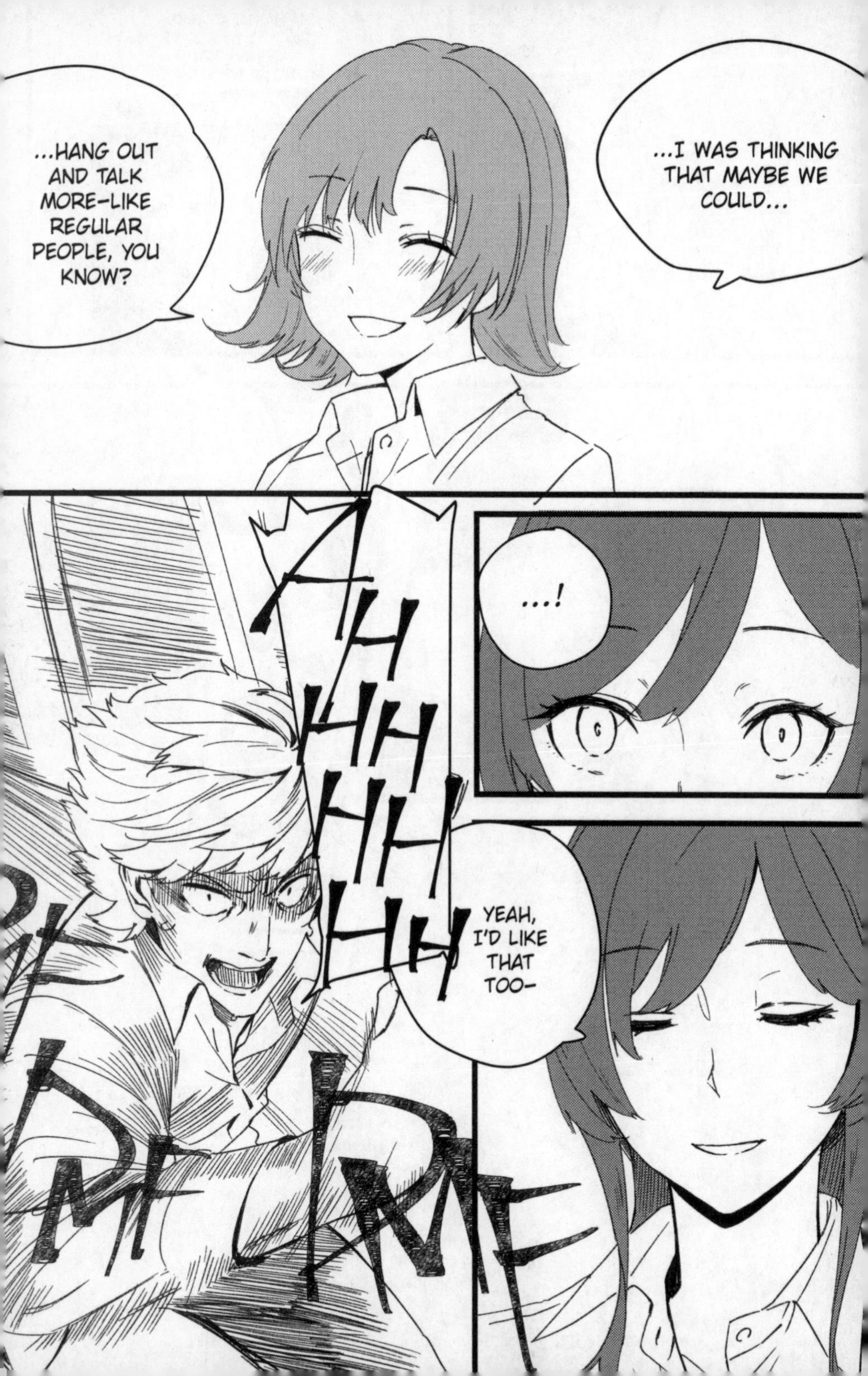
...I WAS THINKING THAT MAYBE WE COULD...
...HANG OUT AND TALK MORE—LIKE REGULAR PEOPLE, YOU KNOW?
...!
YEAH, I'D LIKE THAT TOO—

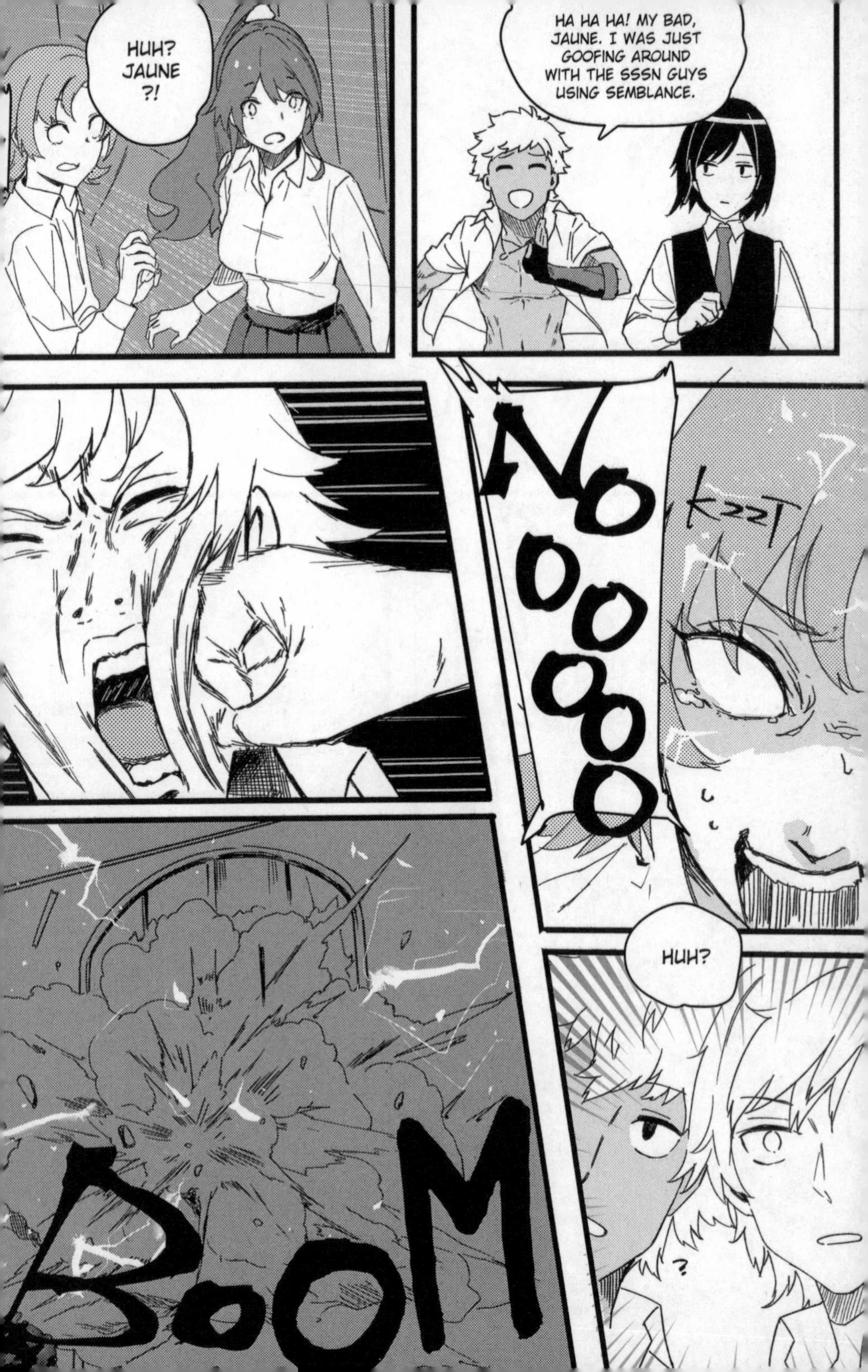
HA HA HA! MY BAD, JAUNE. I WAS JUST GOOFING AROUND WITH THE SSSN GUYS USING SEMBLANCE.
HUH? JAUNE ?!
NOOOOOO
KZZT
HUH?
BOOM

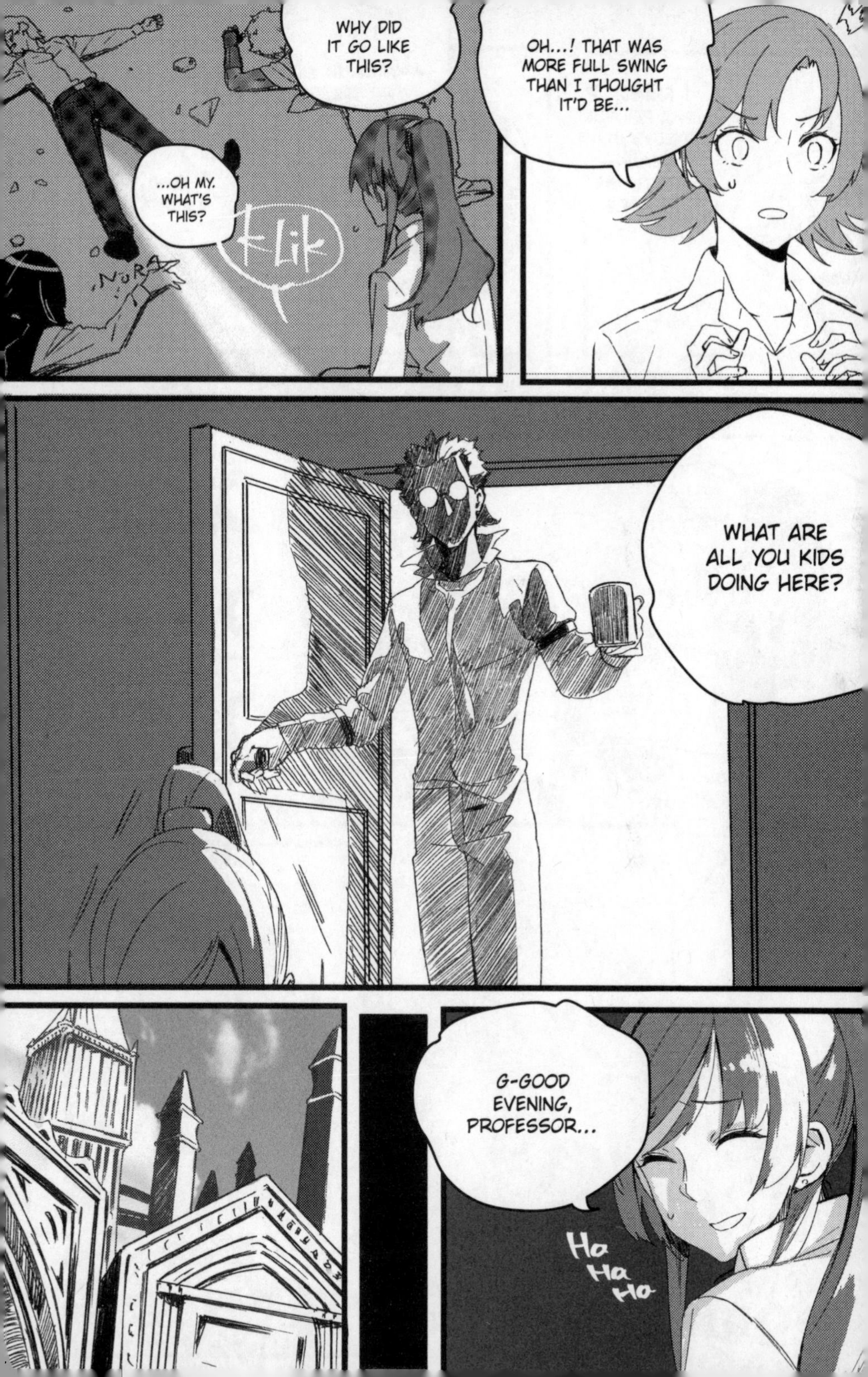
OH...! THAT WAS MORE FULL SWING THAN I THOUGHT IT'D BE...
WHY DID IT GO LIKE THIS?
...OH MY. WHAT'S THIS?
KLIK
NURA
WHAT ARE ALL YOU KIDS DOING HERE?
G-GOOD EVENING, PROFESSOR...
Ha Ha Ha

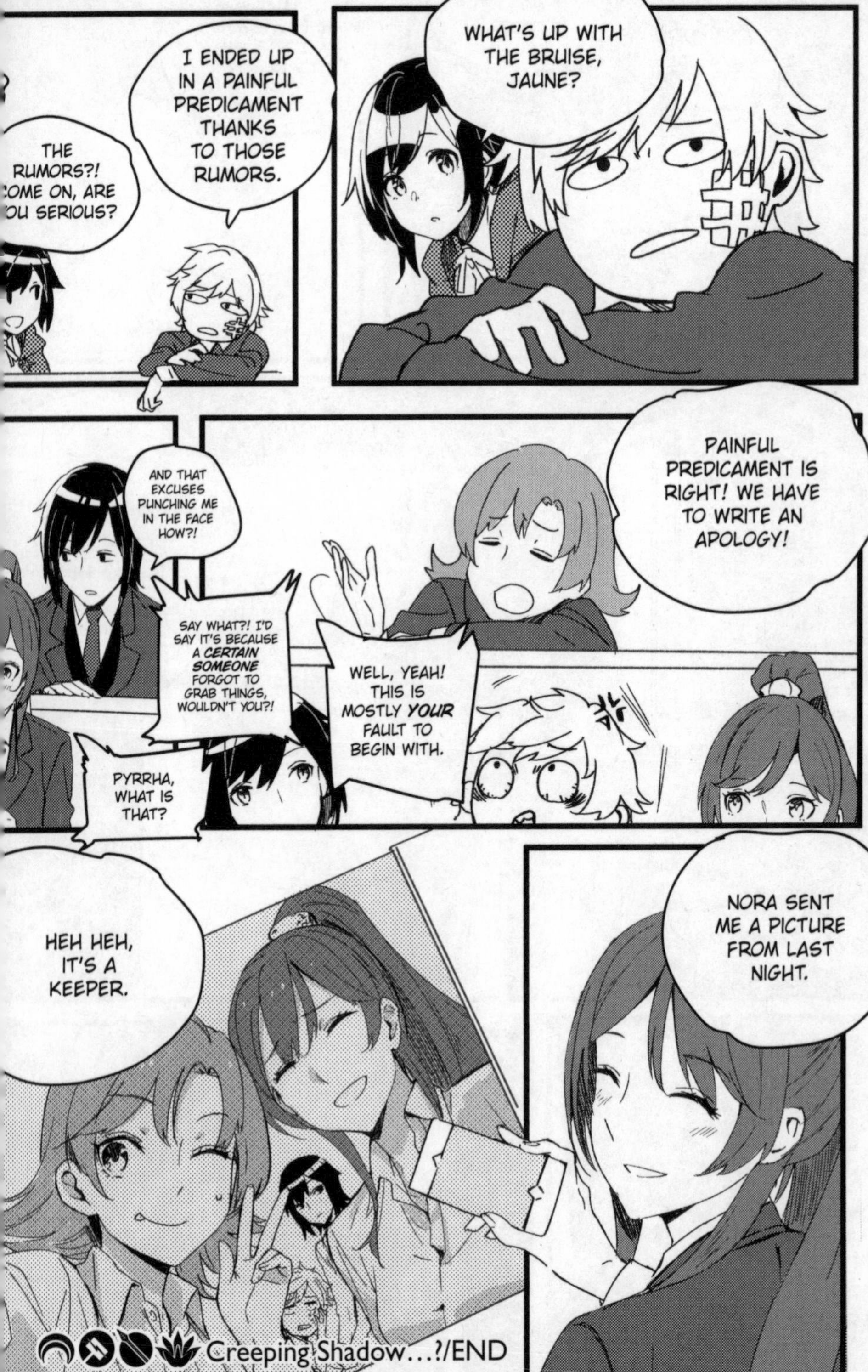
WHAT'S UP WITH THE BRUISE, JAUNE?
I ENDED UP IN A PAINFUL PREDICAMENT THANKS TO THOSE RUMORS.
THE RUMORS?! OME ON, ARE OU SERIOUS?
PAINFUL PREDICAMENT IS RIGHT! WE HAVE TO WRITE AN APOLOGY!
WELL, YEAH! THIS IS MOSTLY *YOUR* FAULT TO BEGIN WITH.
SAY WHAT?! I'D SAY IT'S BECAUSE A ***CERTAIN SOMEONE*** FORGOT TO GRAB THINGS, WOULDN'T YOU?!
AND THAT EXCUSES PUNCHING ME IN THE FACE HOW?!
PYRRHA, WHAT IS THAT?
NORA SENT ME A PICTURE FROM LAST NIGHT.
HEH HEH, IT'S A KEEPER.
Creeping Shadow…?/END

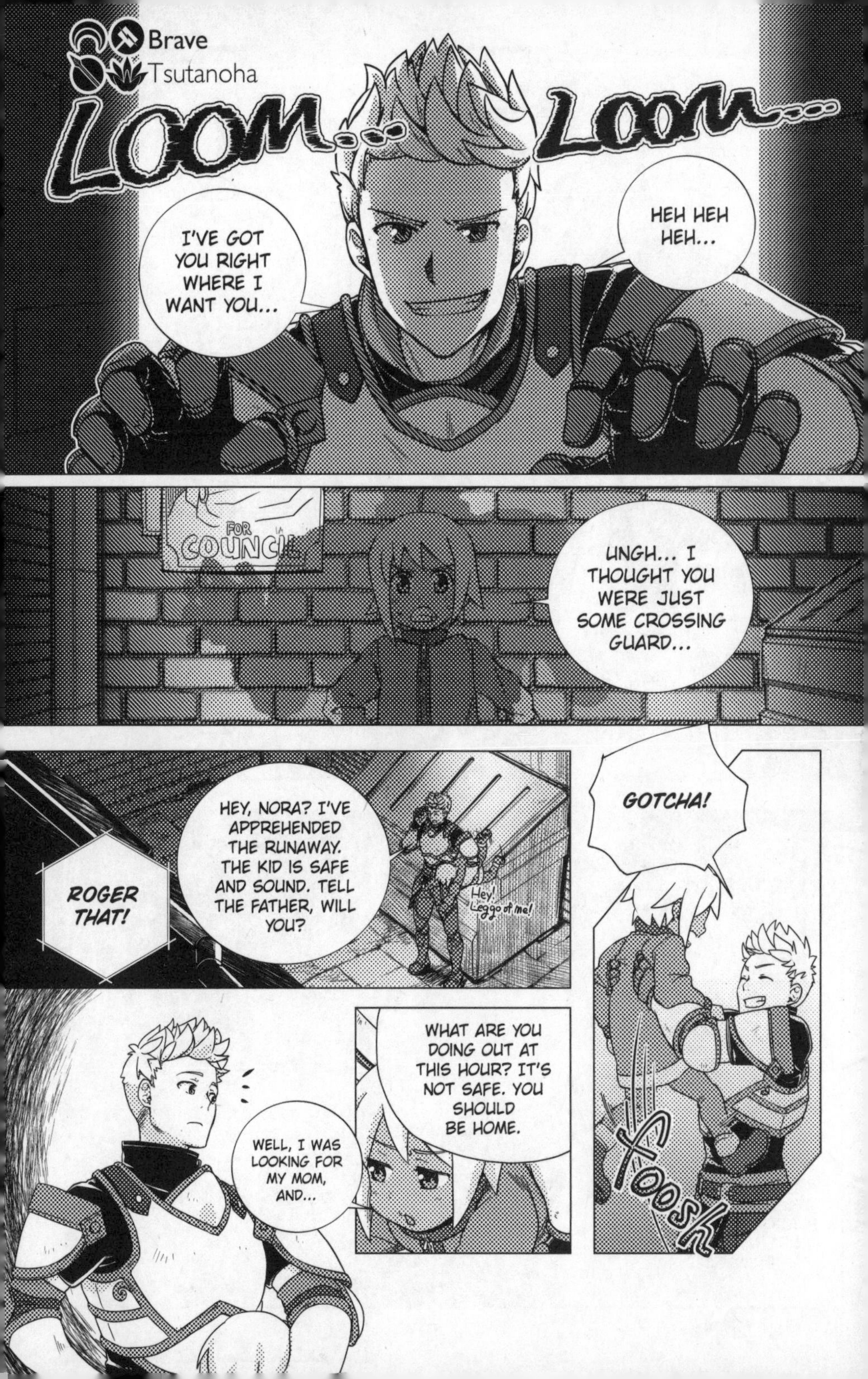
Brave
Tsutanoha
LOOM... LOOM...
I'VE GOT YOU RIGHT WHERE I WANT YOU...
HEH HEH HEH...
FOR COUNCIL
UNGH... I THOUGHT YOU WERE JUST SOME CROSSING GUARD...
GOTCHA!
FOOSH
HEY, NORA? I'VE APPREHENDED THE RUNAWAY. THE KID IS SAFE AND SOUND. TELL THE FATHER, WILL YOU?
Hey! Leggo of me!
ROGER THAT!
WHAT ARE YOU DOING OUT AT THIS HOUR? IT'S NOT SAFE. YOU SHOULD BE HOME.
WELL, I WAS LOOKING FOR MY MOM, AND...

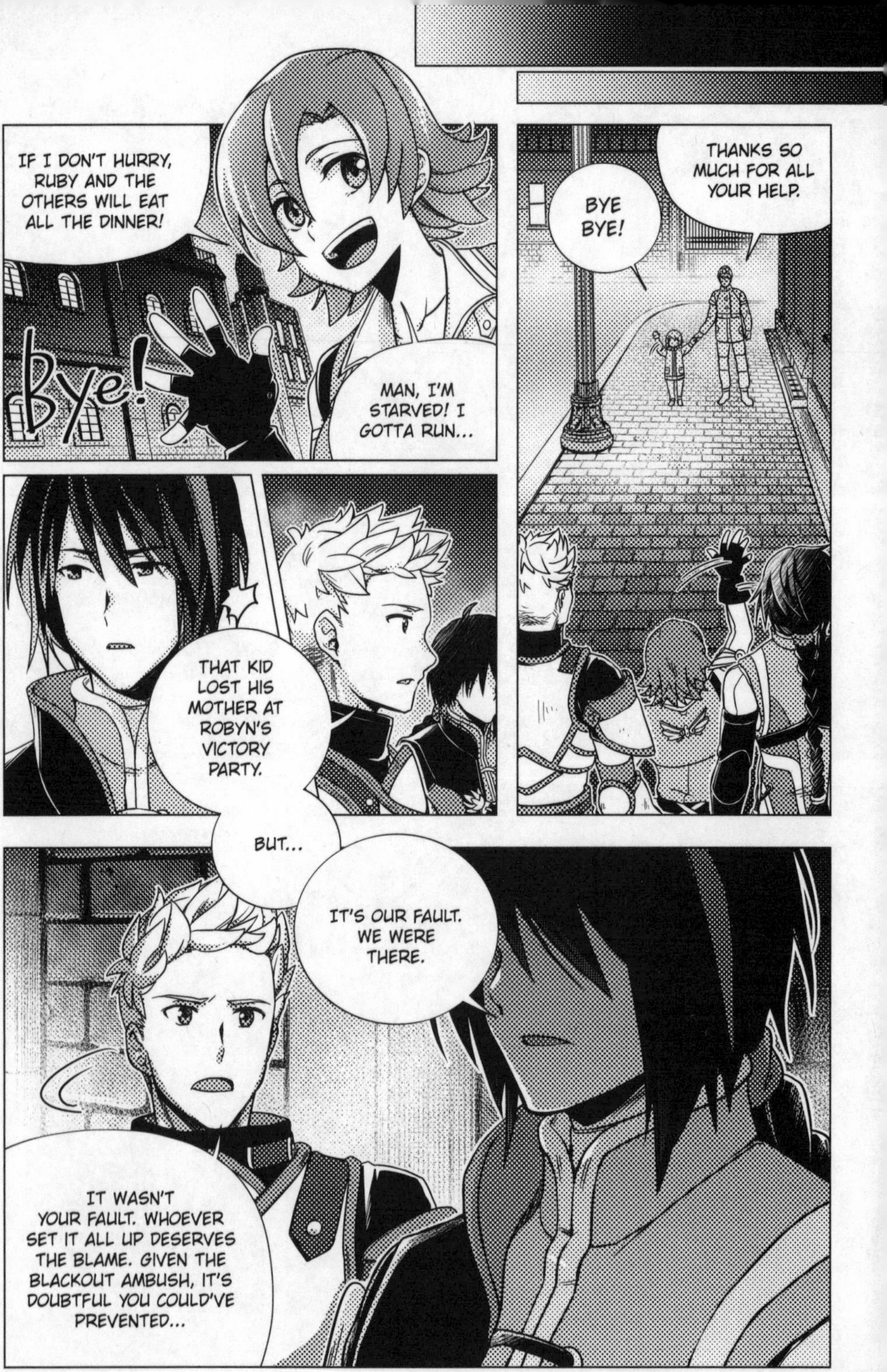
THANKS SO MUCH FOR ALL YOUR HELP.
BYE BYE!
MAN, I'M STARVED! I GOTTA RUN...
IF I DON'T HURRY, RUBY AND THE OTHERS WILL EAT ALL THE DINNER!
Bye!
THAT KID LOST HIS MOTHER AT ROBYN'S VICTORY PARTY.
BUT...
IT'S OUR FAULT. WE WERE THERE.
IT WASN'T YOUR FAULT. WHOEVER SET IT ALL UP DESERVES THE BLAME. GIVEN THE BLACKOUT AMBUSH, IT'S DOUBTFUL YOU COULD'VE PREVENTED...

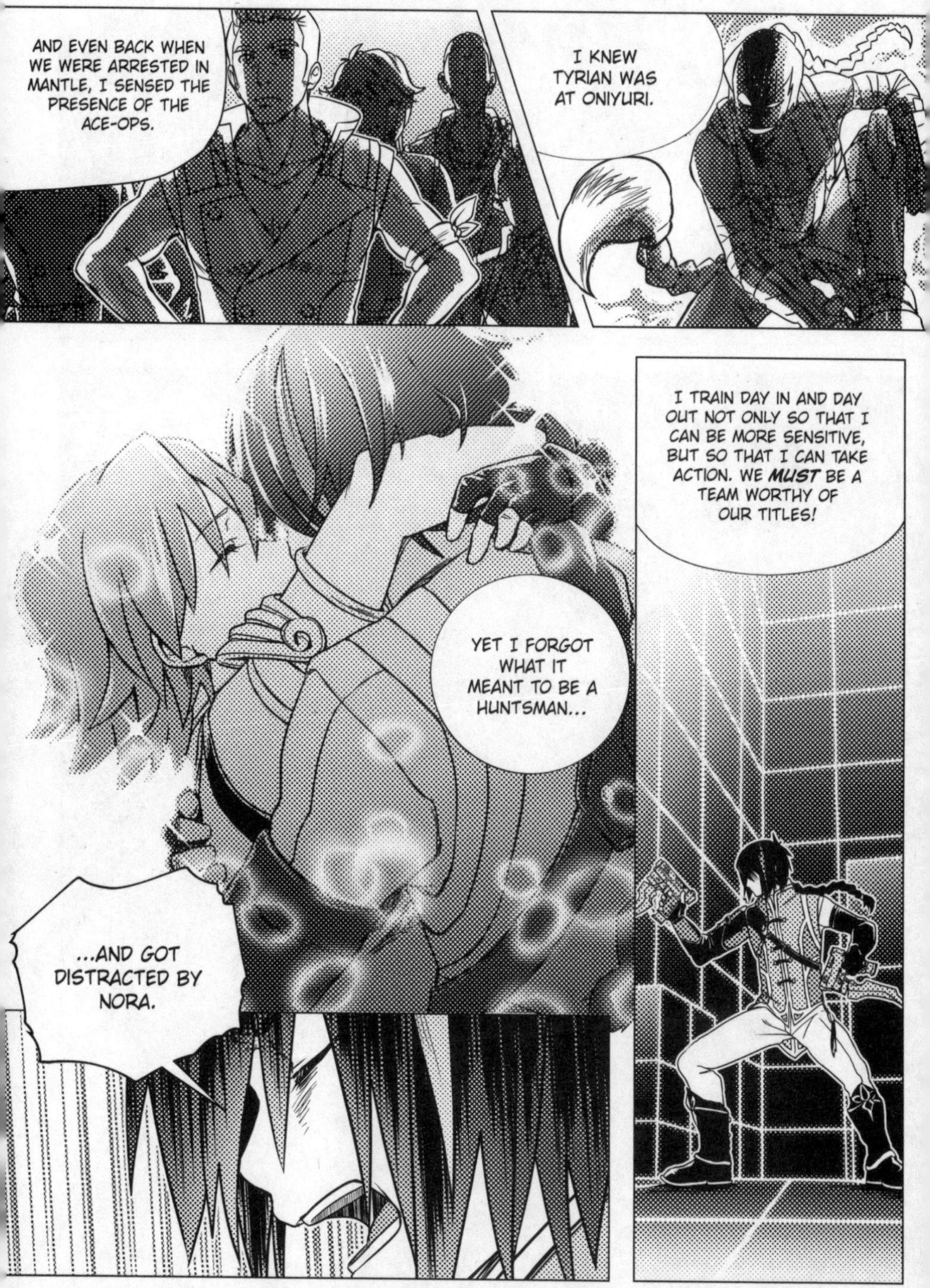
I KNEW TYRIAN WAS AT ONIYURI.
AND EVEN BACK WHEN WE WERE ARRESTED IN MANTLE, I SENSED THE PRESENCE OF THE ACE-OPS.
I TRAIN DAY IN AND DAY OUT NOT ONLY SO THAT I CAN BE MORE SENSITIVE, BUT SO THAT I CAN TAKE ACTION. WE *MUST* BE A TEAM WORTHY OF OUR TITLES!
YET I FORGOT WHAT IT MEANT TO BE A HUNTSMAN...
...AND GOT DISTRACTED BY NORA.

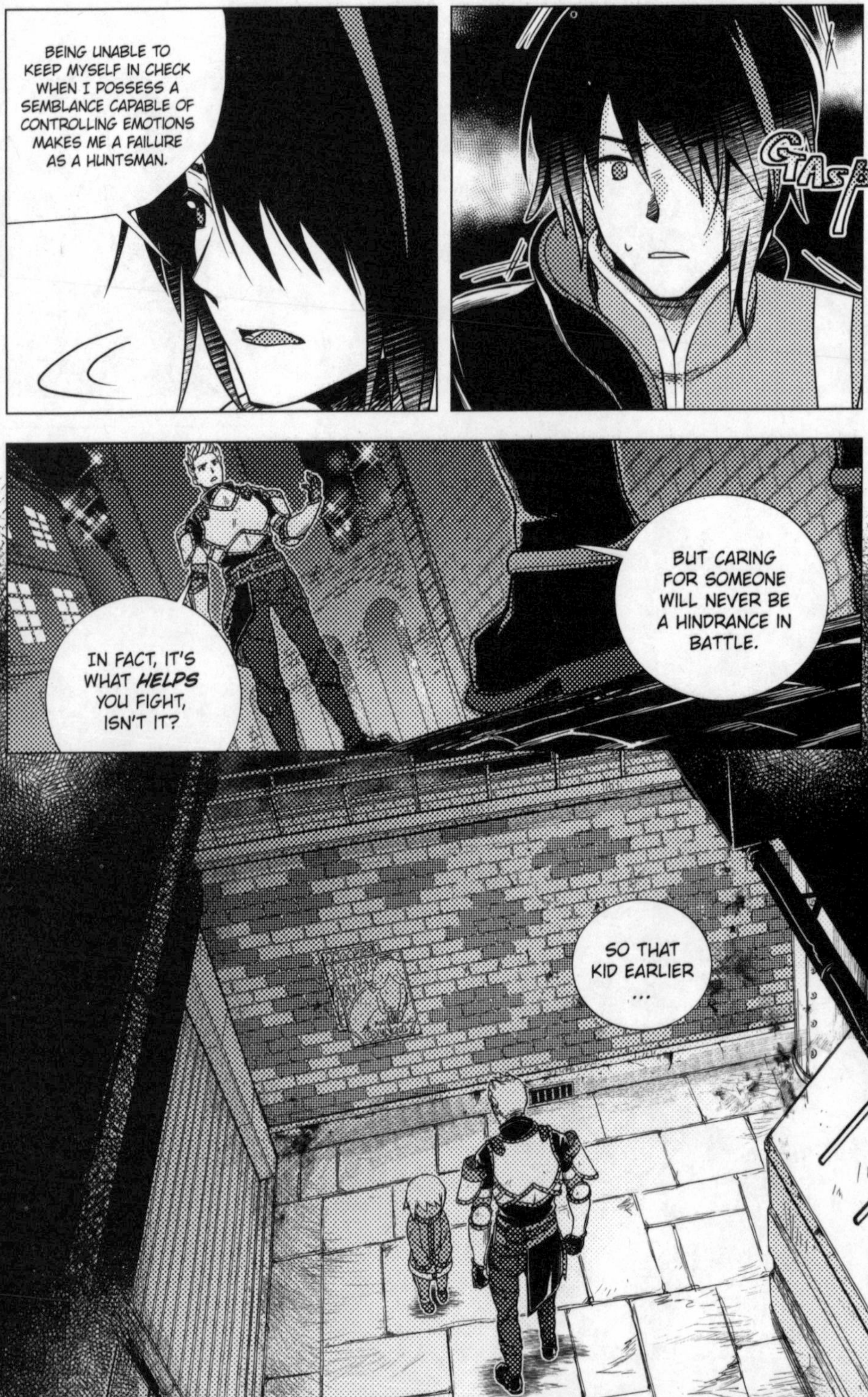
GASP
BEING UNABLE TO KEEP MYSELF IN CHECK WHEN I POSSESS A SEMBLANCE CAPABLE OF CONTROLLING EMOTIONS MAKES ME A FAILURE AS A HUNTSMAN.
BUT CARING FOR SOMEONE WILL NEVER BE A HINDRANCE IN BATTLE.
IN FACT, IT'S WHAT **HELPS** YOU FIGHT, ISN'T IT?
SO THAT KID EARLIER ...

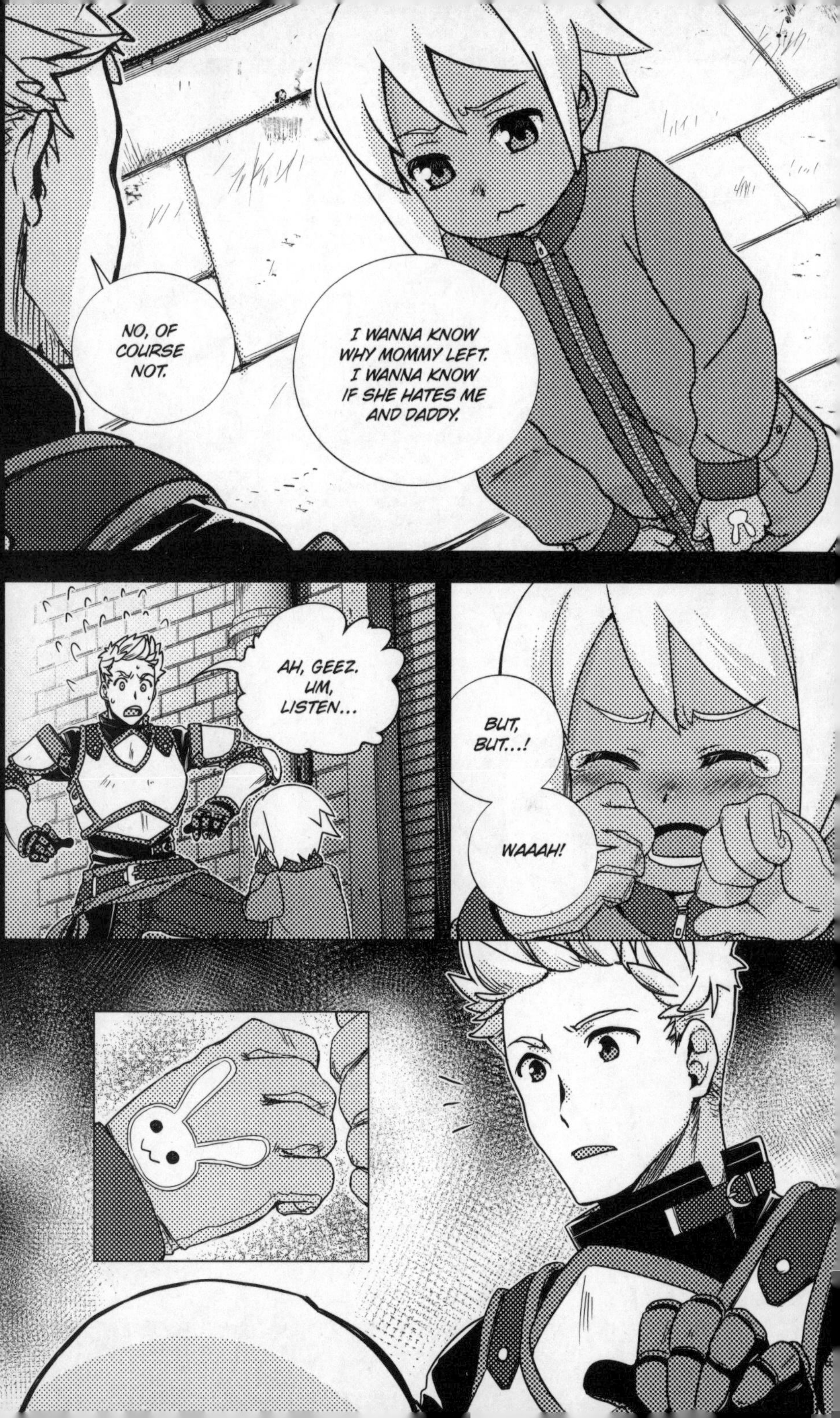
I WANNA KNOW WHY MOMMY LEFT. I WANNA KNOW IF SHE HATES ME AND DADDY.
NO, OF COURSE NOT.
BUT, BUT...!
WAAAH!
AH, GEEZ. UM, LISTEN...

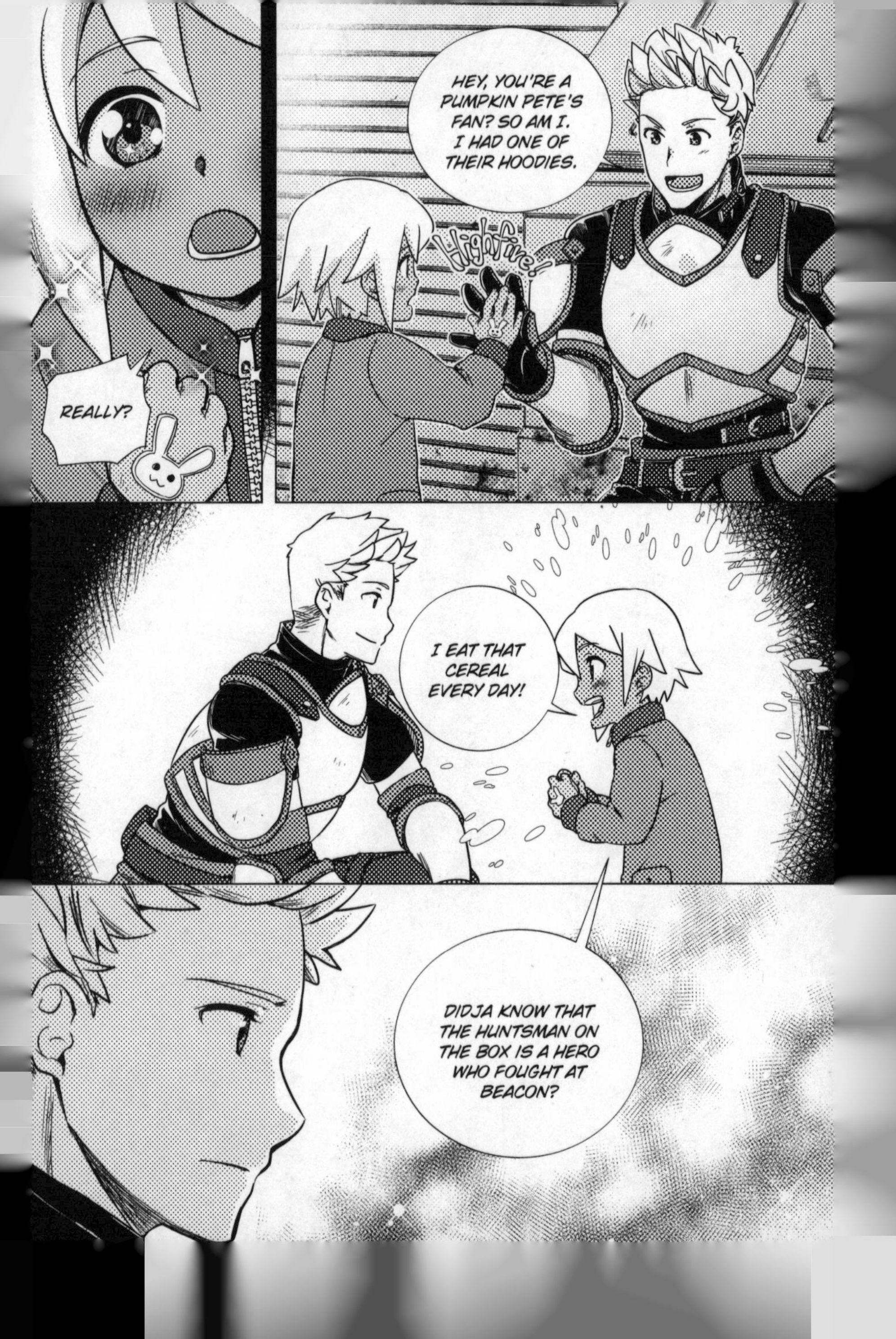
HEY, YOU'RE A PUMPKIN PETE'S FAN? SO AM I. I HAD ONE OF THEIR HOODIES.
High five!
REALLY?
I EAT THAT CEREAL EVERY DAY!
DIDJA KNOW THAT THE HUNTSMAN ON THE BOX IS A HERO WHO FOUGHT AT BEACON?

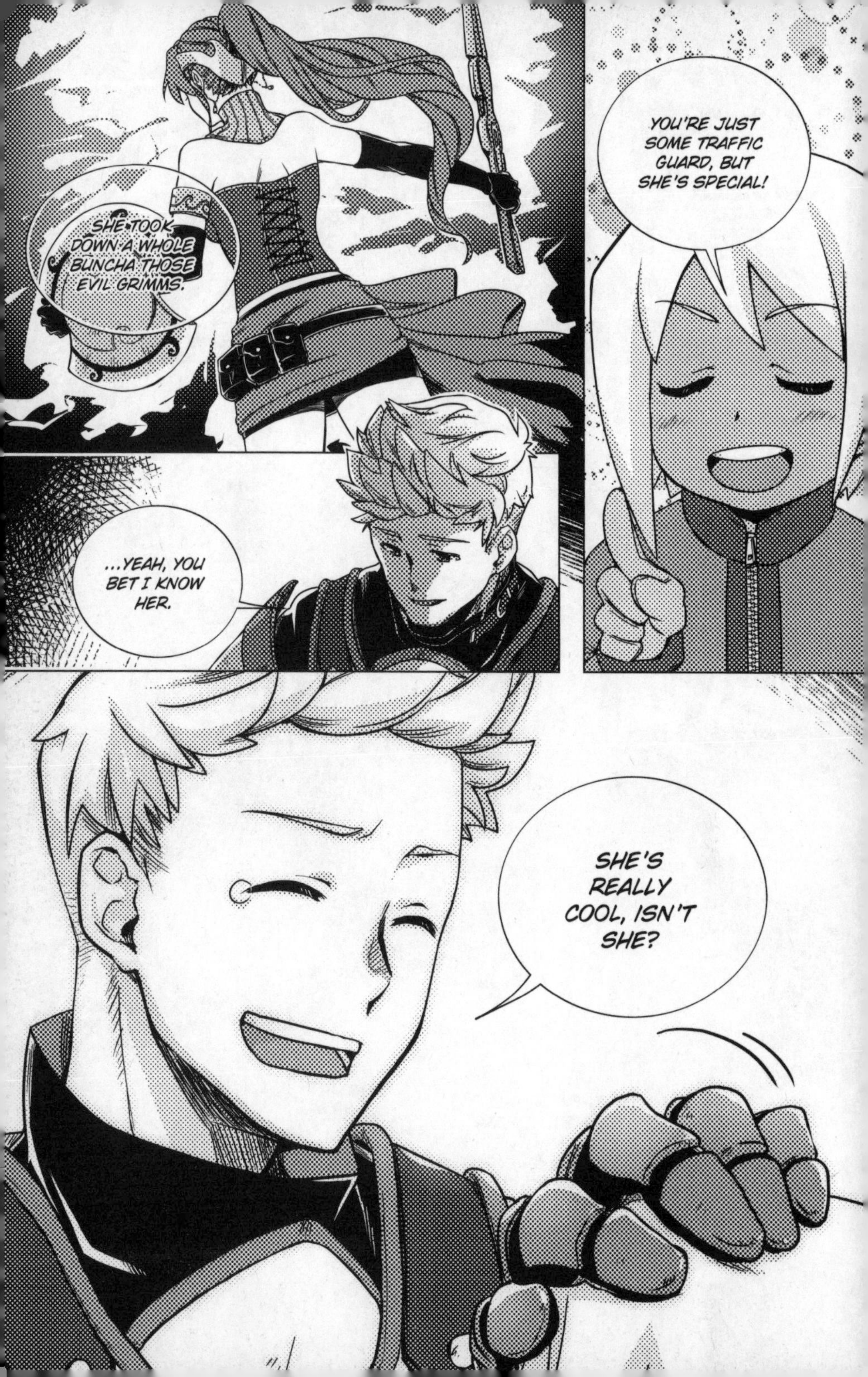
YOU'RE JUST SOME TRAFFIC GUARD, BUT SHE'S SPECIAL!
SHE TOOK DOWN A WHOLE BUNCHA THOSE EVIL GRIMMS.
...YEAH, YOU BET I KNOW HER.
SHE'S REALLY COOL, ISN'T SHE?

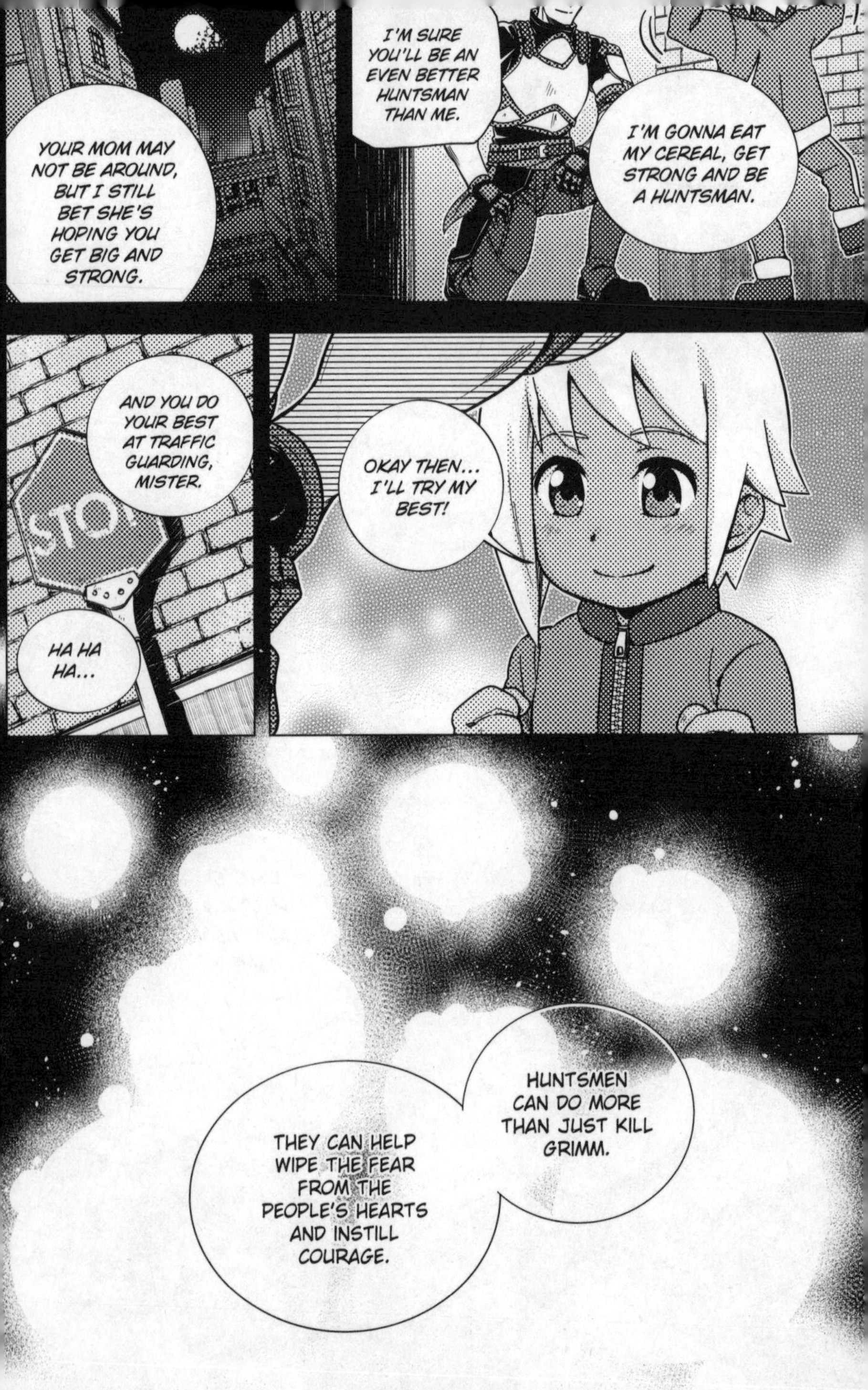
YOUR MOM MAY NOT BE AROUND, BUT I STILL BET SHE'S HOPING YOU GET BIG AND STRONG.
I'M SURE YOU'LL BE AN EVEN BETTER HUNTSMAN THAN ME.
I'M GONNA EAT MY CEREAL, GET STRONG AND BE A HUNTSMAN.
AND YOU DO YOUR BEST AT TRAFFIC GUARDING, MISTER.
STOP
HA HA HA...
OKAY THEN... I'LL TRY MY BEST!
HUNTSMEN CAN DO MORE THAN JUST KILL GRIMM.
THEY CAN HELP WIPE THE FEAR FROM THE PEOPLE'S HEARTS AND INSTILL COURAGE.

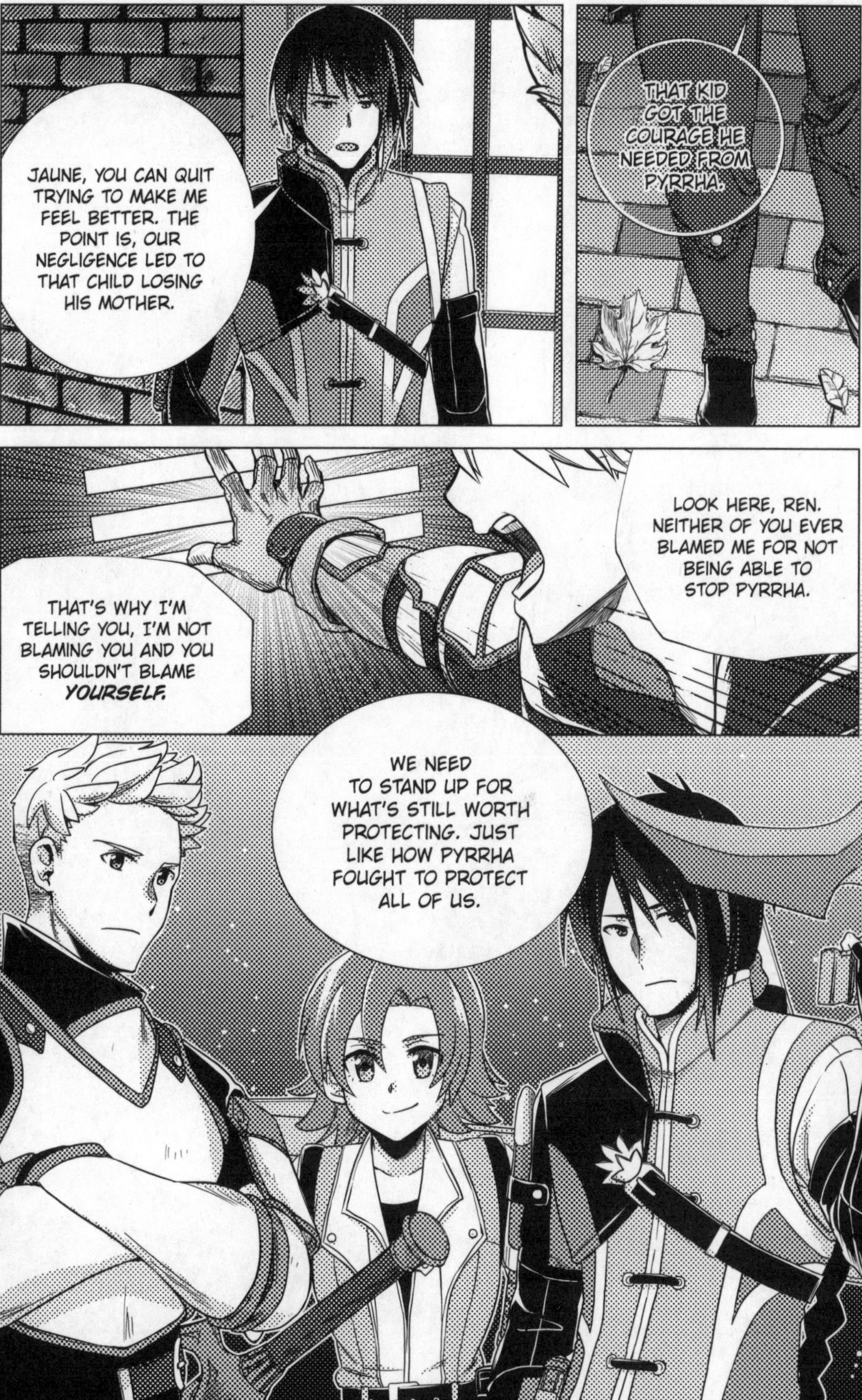
THAT KID GOT THE COURAGE HE NEEDED FROM PYRRHA.
JAUNE, YOU CAN QUIT TRYING TO MAKE ME FEEL BETTER. THE POINT IS, OUR NEGLIGENCE LED TO THAT CHILD LOSING HIS MOTHER.
LOOK HERE, REN. NEITHER OF YOU EVER BLAMED ME FOR NOT BEING ABLE TO STOP PYRRHA.
THAT'S WHY I'M TELLING YOU, I'M NOT BLAMING YOU AND YOU SHOULDN'T BLAME *YOURSELF.*
WE NEED TO STAND UP FOR WHAT'S STILL WORTH PROTECTING. JUST LIKE HOW PYRRHA FOUGHT TO PROTECT ALL OF US.

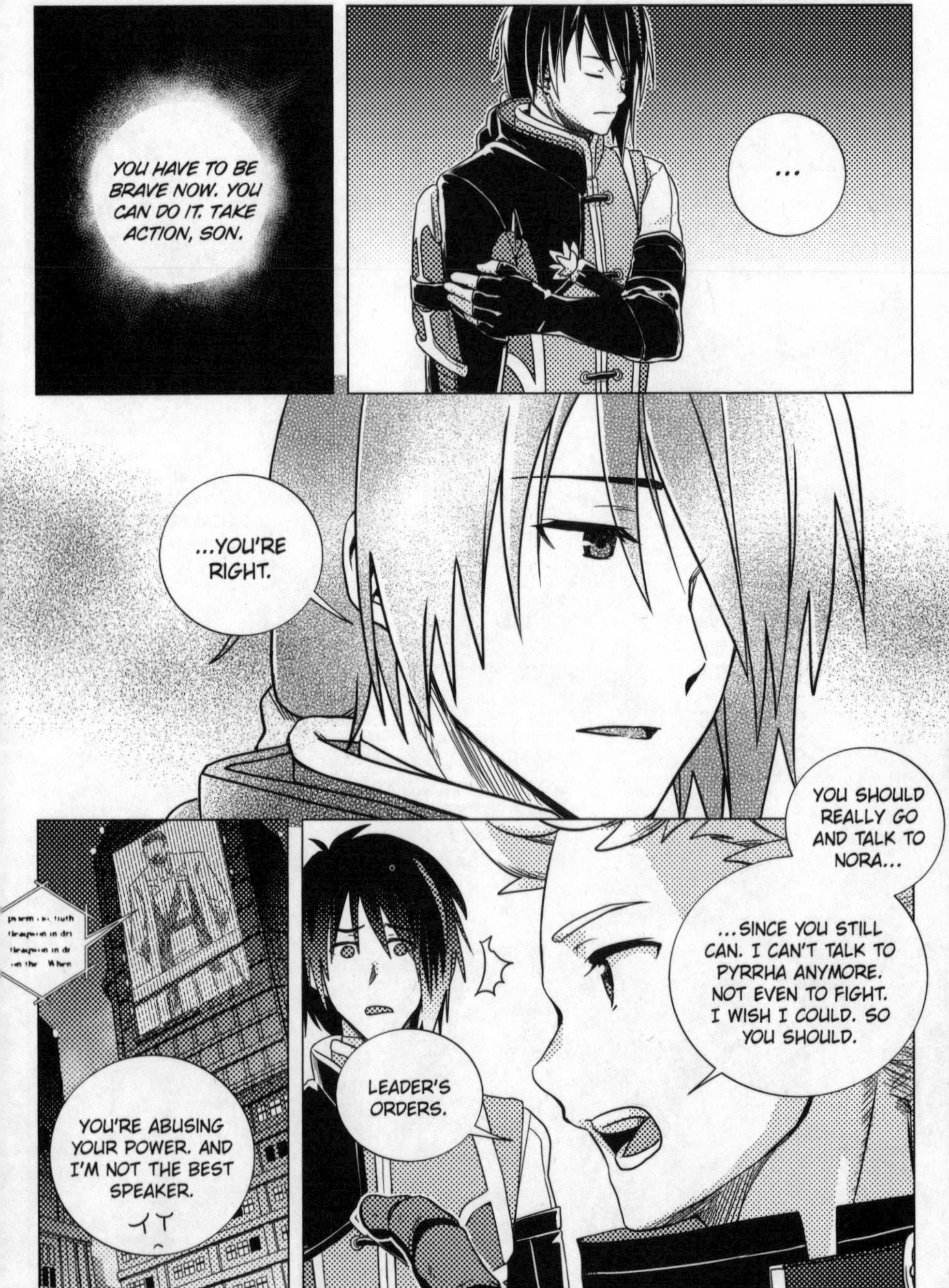
...
YOU HAVE TO BE BRAVE NOW. YOU CAN DO IT. TAKE ACTION, SON.
...YOU'RE RIGHT.
YOU SHOULD REALLY GO AND TALK TO NORA...
...SINCE YOU STILL CAN. I CAN'T TALK TO PYRRHA ANYMORE. NOT EVEN TO FIGHT. I WISH I COULD. SO YOU SHOULD.
LEADER'S ORDERS.
YOU'RE ABUSING YOUR POWER. AND I'M NOT THE BEST SPEAKER.

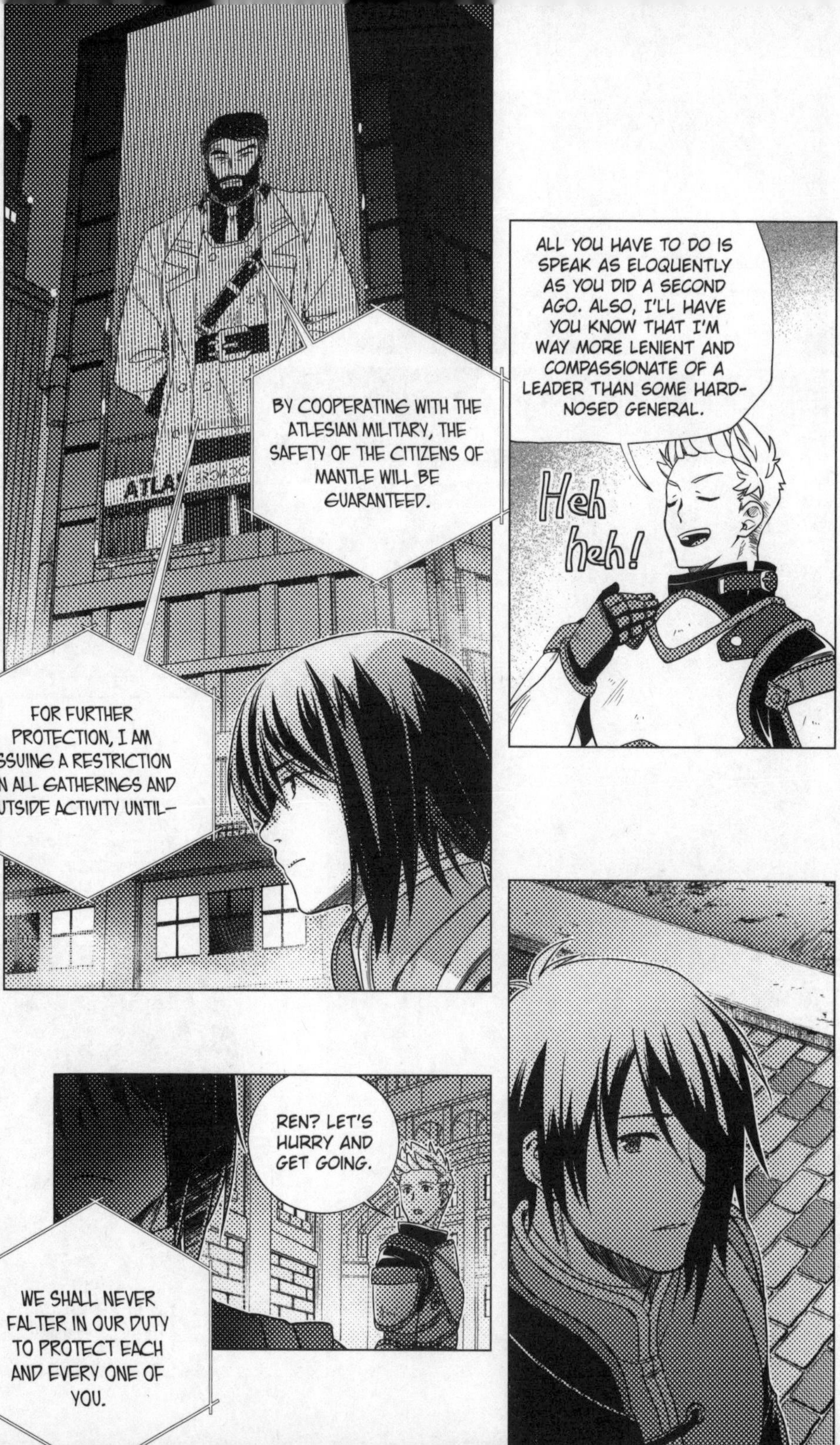
ALL YOU HAVE TO DO IS SPEAK AS ELOQUENTLY AS YOU DID A SECOND AGO. ALSO, I'LL HAVE YOU KNOW THAT I'M WAY MORE LENIENT AND COMPASSIONATE OF A LEADER THAN SOME HARD-NOSED GENERAL.
Heh heh!
BY COOPERATING WITH THE ATLESIAN MILITARY, THE SAFETY OF THE CITIZENS OF MANTLE WILL BE GUARANTEED.
FOR FURTHER PROTECTION, I AM ISSUING A RESTRICTION ON ALL GATHERINGS AND OUTSIDE ACTIVITY UNTIL—
REN? LET'S HURRY AND GET GOING.
WE SHALL NEVER FALTER IN OUR DUTY TO PROTECT EACH AND EVERY ONE OF YOU.

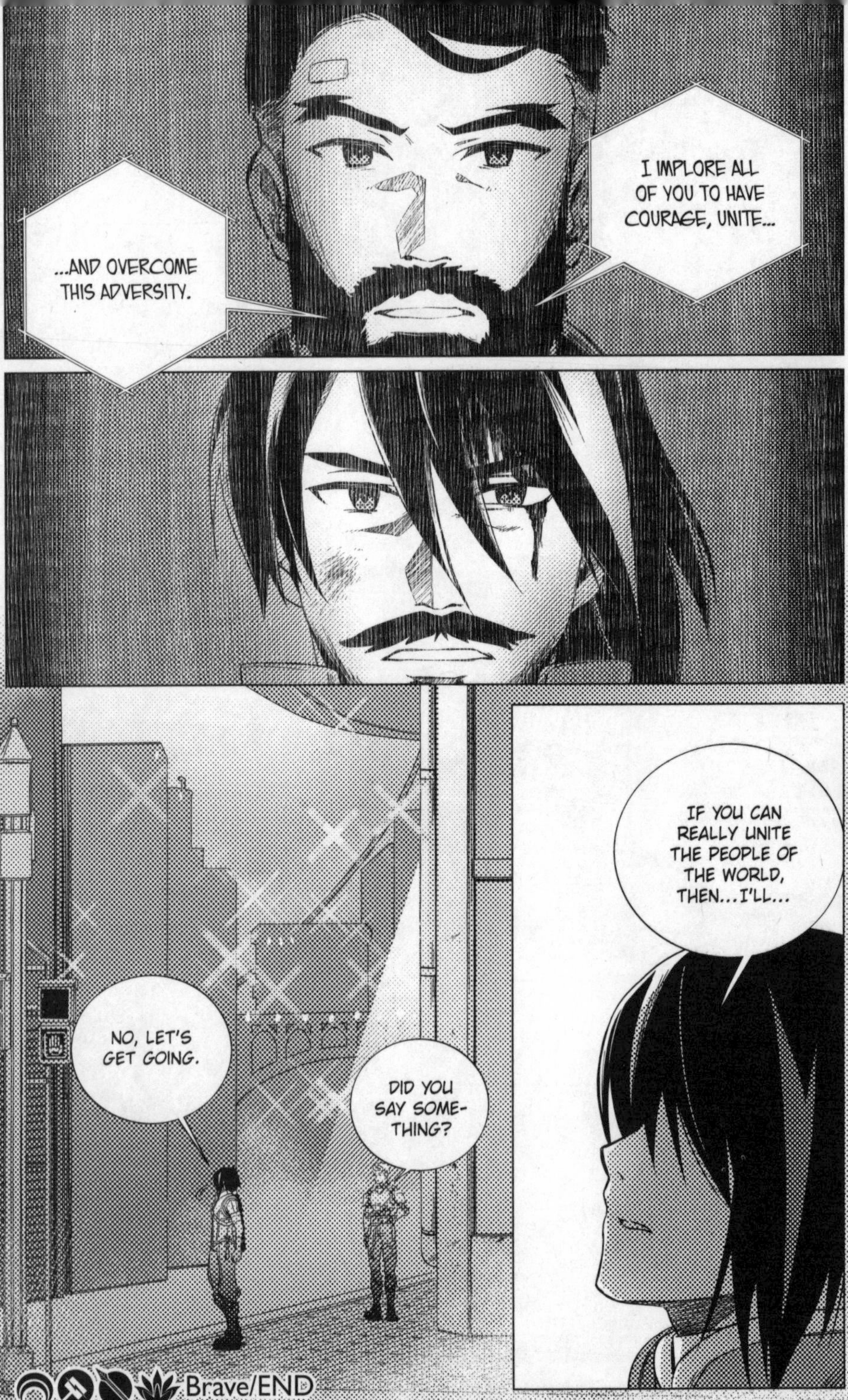
I IMPLORE ALL OF YOU TO HAVE COURAGE, UNITE...
...AND OVERCOME THIS ADVERSITY.
IF YOU CAN REALLY UNITE THE PEOPLE OF THE WORLD, THEN...I'LL...
DID YOU SAY SOME-THING?
NO, LET'S GET GOING.
Brave/END

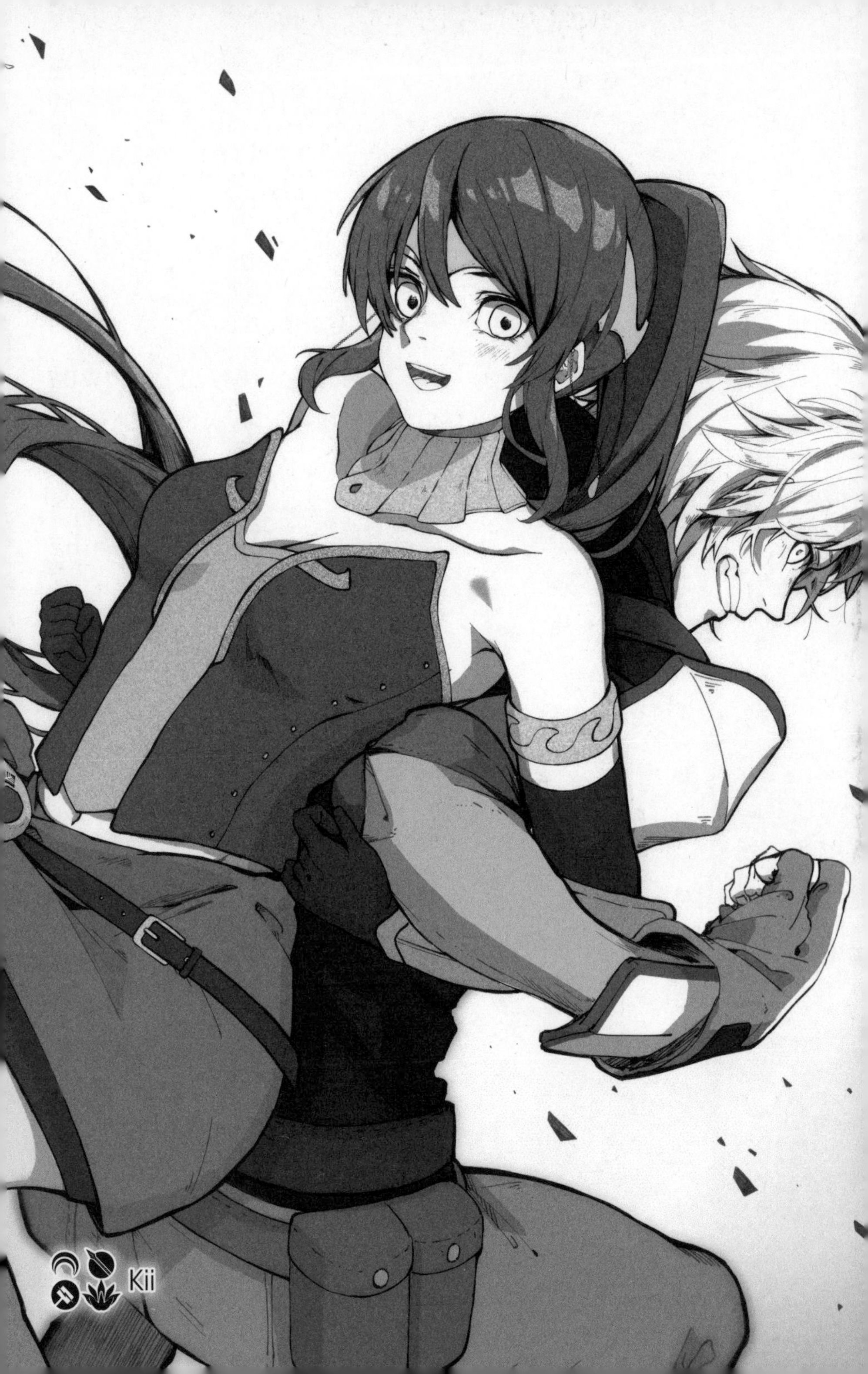
Kii

RWBY

OFFICIAL MANGA ANTHOLOGY

Volume 5

Shine

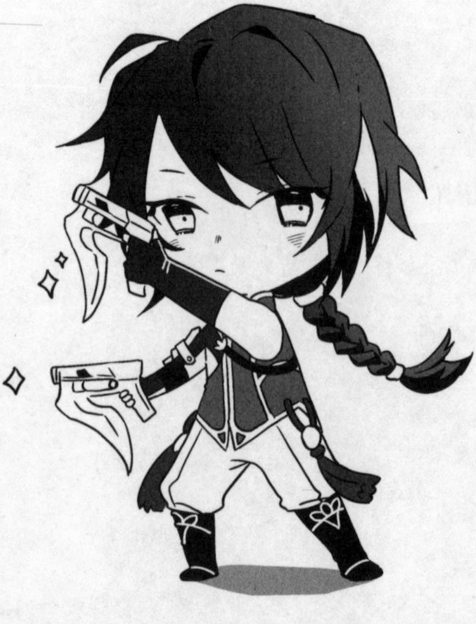

Ecru

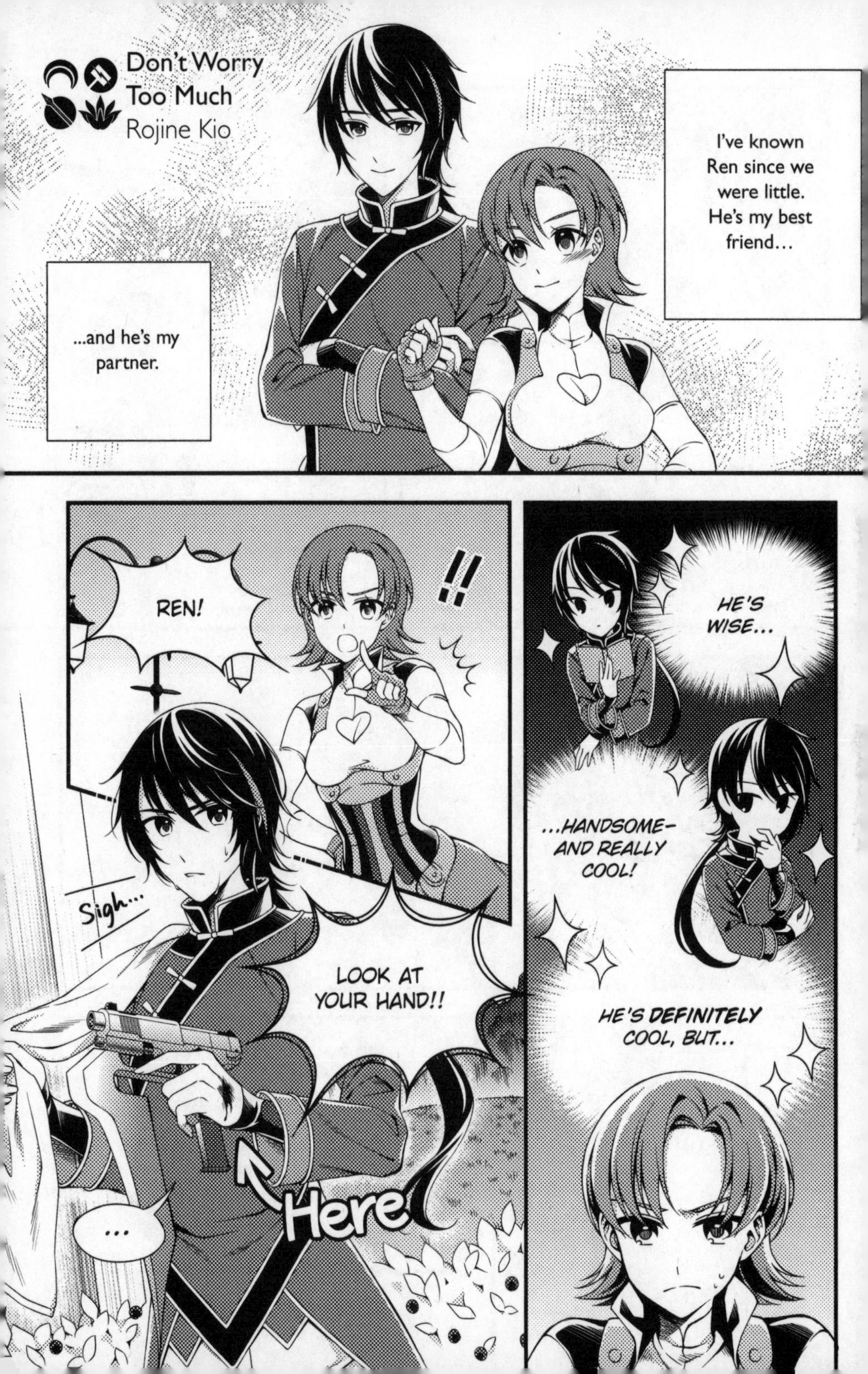

Don't Worry Too Much
Rojine Kio
I've known Ren since we were little. He's my best friend...
...and he's my partner.
HE'S WISE...
...HANDSOME- AND REALLY COOL!
HE'S DEFINITELY COOL, BUT...
!!
REN!
Sigh...
LOOK AT YOUR HAND!!
Here
...

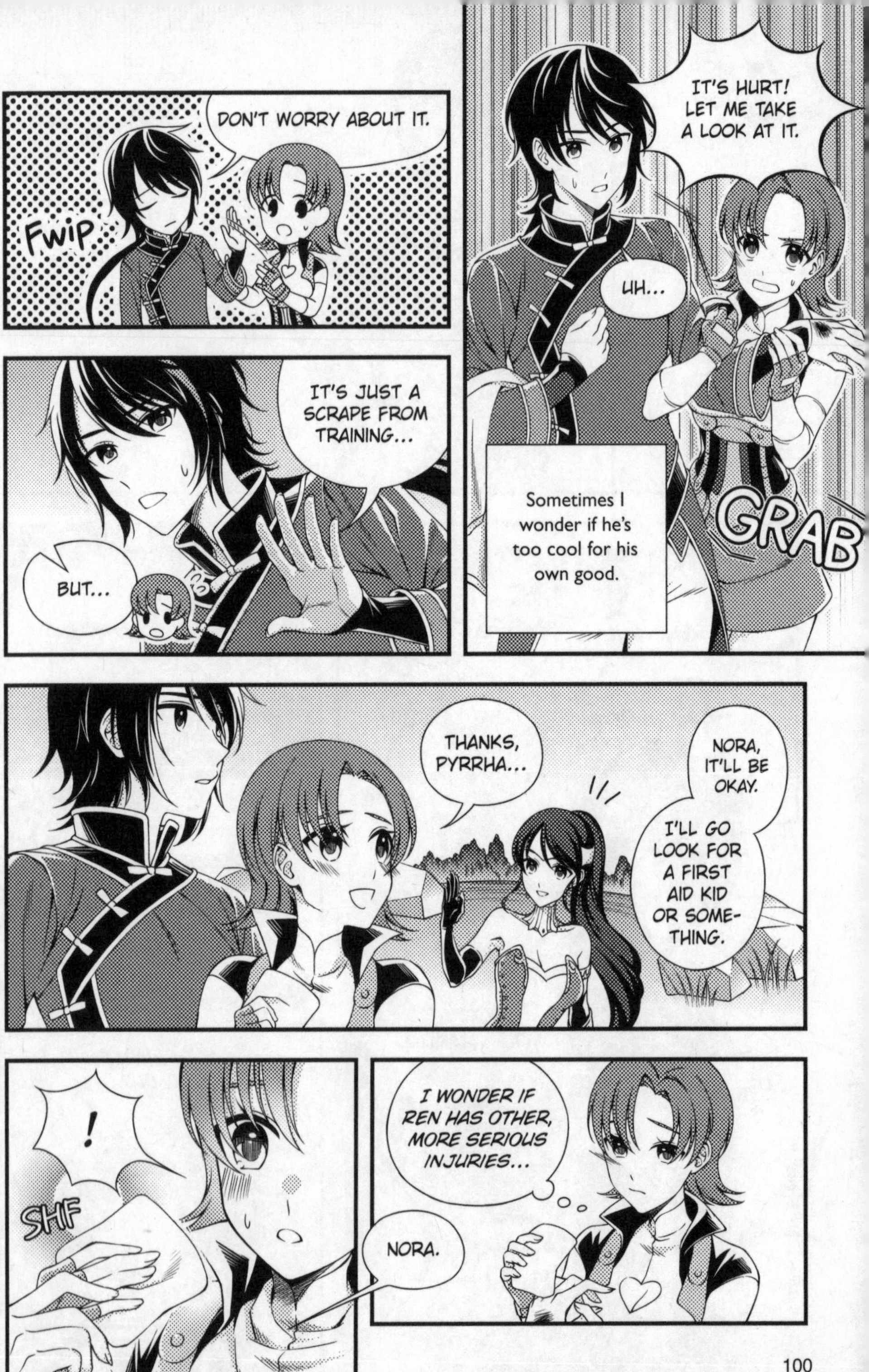
IT'S HURT! LET ME TAKE A LOOK AT IT.
UH...
GRAB
Sometimes I wonder if he's too cool for his own good.
DON'T WORRY ABOUT IT.
FWIP
IT'S JUST A SCRAPE FROM TRAINING...
BUT...
NORA, IT'LL BE OKAY.
I'LL GO LOOK FOR A FIRST AID KID OR SOME-THING.
THANKS, PYRRHA...
I WONDER IF REN HAS OTHER, MORE SERIOUS INJURIES...
!
SHIF
NORA.

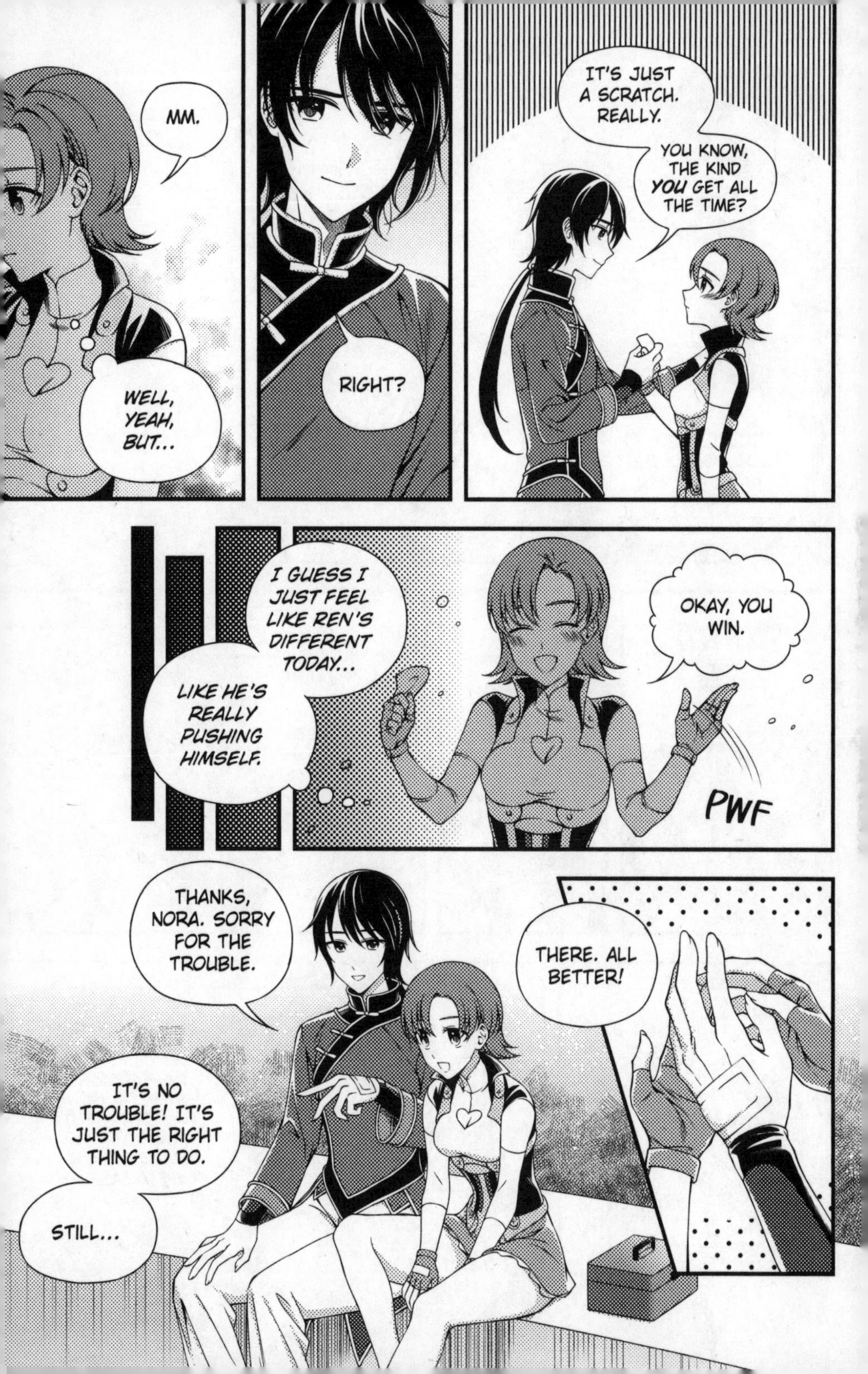
IT'S JUST A SCRATCH. REALLY.
YOU KNOW, THE KIND *YOU* GET ALL THE TIME?
RIGHT?
MM.
WELL, YEAH, BUT...
OKAY, YOU WIN.
PWF
I GUESS I JUST FEEL LIKE REN'S DIFFERENT TODAY...
LIKE HE'S REALLY PUSHING HIMSELF.
THERE. ALL BETTER!
THANKS, NORA. SORRY FOR THE TROUBLE.
IT'S NO TROUBLE! IT'S JUST THE RIGHT THING TO DO.
STILL...

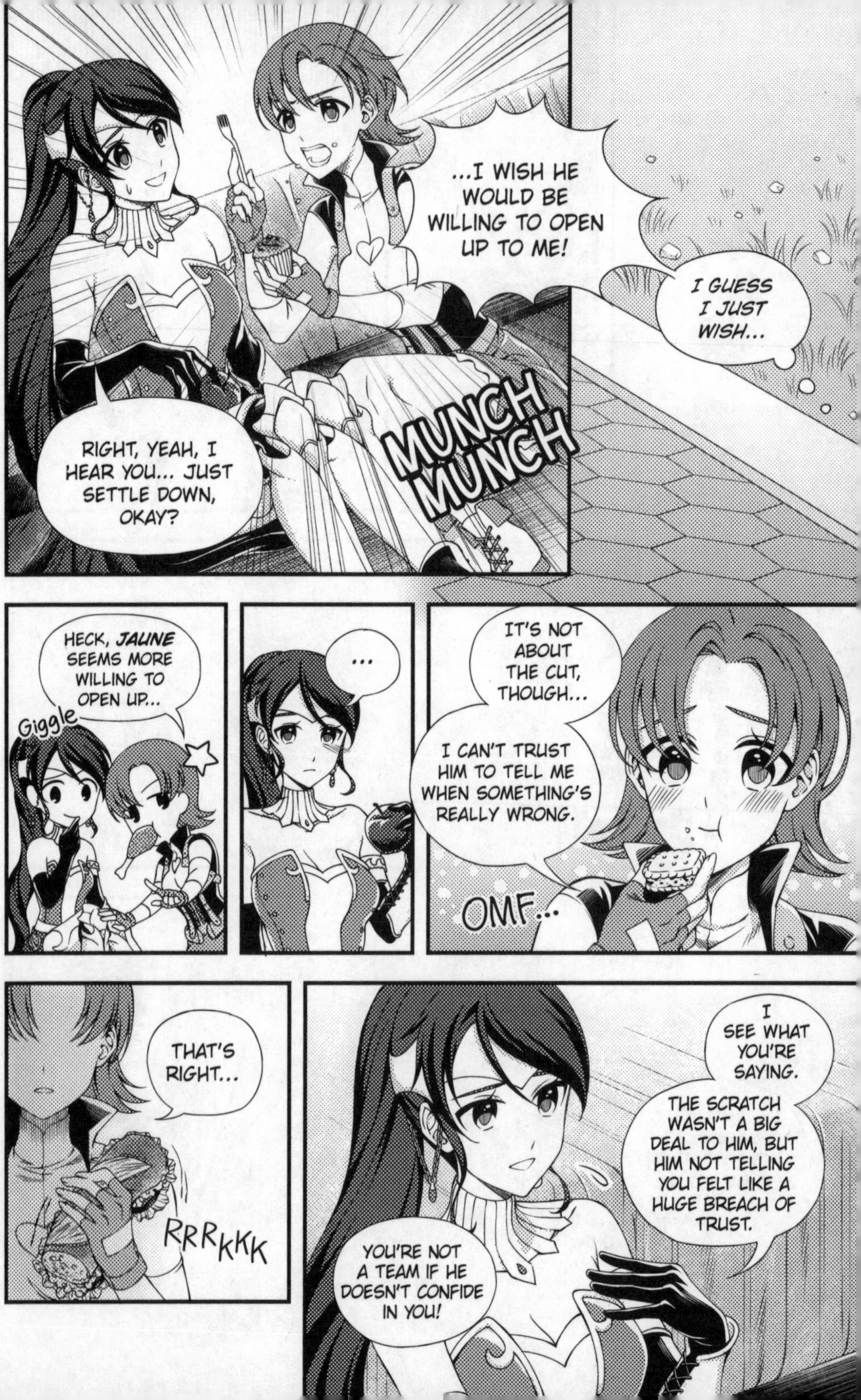
I GUESS I JUST WISH...
...I WISH HE WOULD BE WILLING TO OPEN UP TO ME!
RIGHT, YEAH, I HEAR YOU... JUST SETTLE DOWN, OKAY?
MUNCH MUNCH
IT'S NOT ABOUT THE CUT, THOUGH...
I CAN'T TRUST HIM TO TELL ME WHEN SOMETHING'S REALLY WRONG.
OMF...
...
HECK, *JAUNE* SEEMS MORE WILLING TO OPEN UP...
Giggle
I SEE WHAT YOU'RE SAYING.
THE SCRATCH WASN'T A BIG DEAL TO HIM, BUT HIM NOT TELLING YOU FELT LIKE A HUGE BREACH OF TRUST.
YOU'RE NOT A TEAM IF HE DOESN'T CONFIDE IN YOU!
THAT'S RIGHT...
RRRKKK

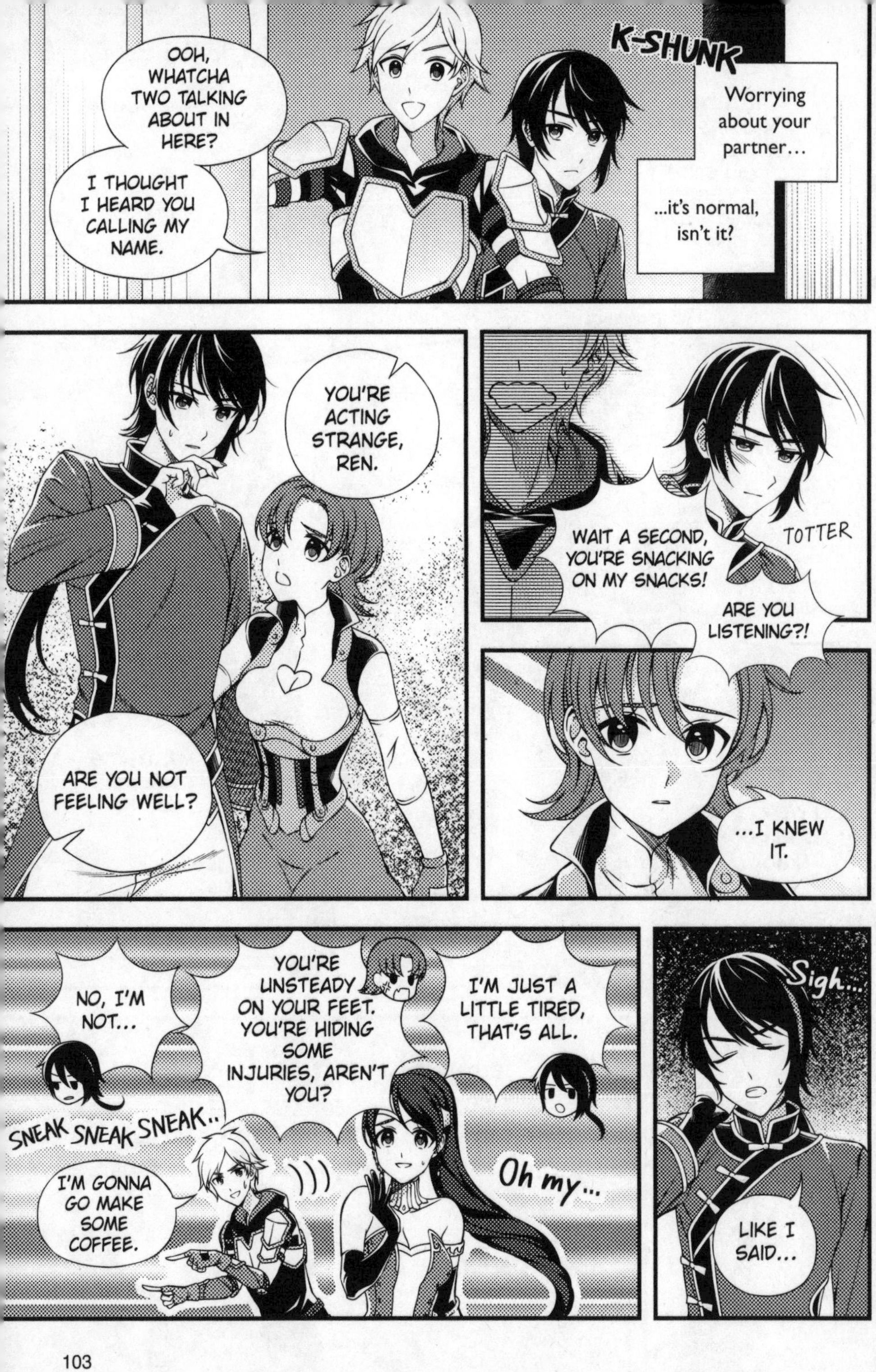
K-SHUNK
Worrying about your partner…
...it's normal, isn't it?
OOH, WHATCHA TWO TALKING ABOUT IN HERE?
I THOUGHT I HEARD YOU CALLING MY NAME.
WAIT A SECOND, YOU'RE SNACKING ON MY SNACKS!
TOTTER
ARE YOU LISTENING?!
...I KNEW IT.
YOU'RE ACTING STRANGE, REN.
ARE YOU NOT FEELING WELL?
Sigh...
LIKE I SAID...
I'M JUST A LITTLE TIRED, THAT'S ALL.
YOU'RE UNSTEADY ON YOUR FEET. YOU'RE HIDING SOME INJURIES, AREN'T YOU?
NO, I'M NOT...
Oh my...
SNEAK SNEAK SNEAK..
I'M GONNA GO MAKE SOME COFFEE.

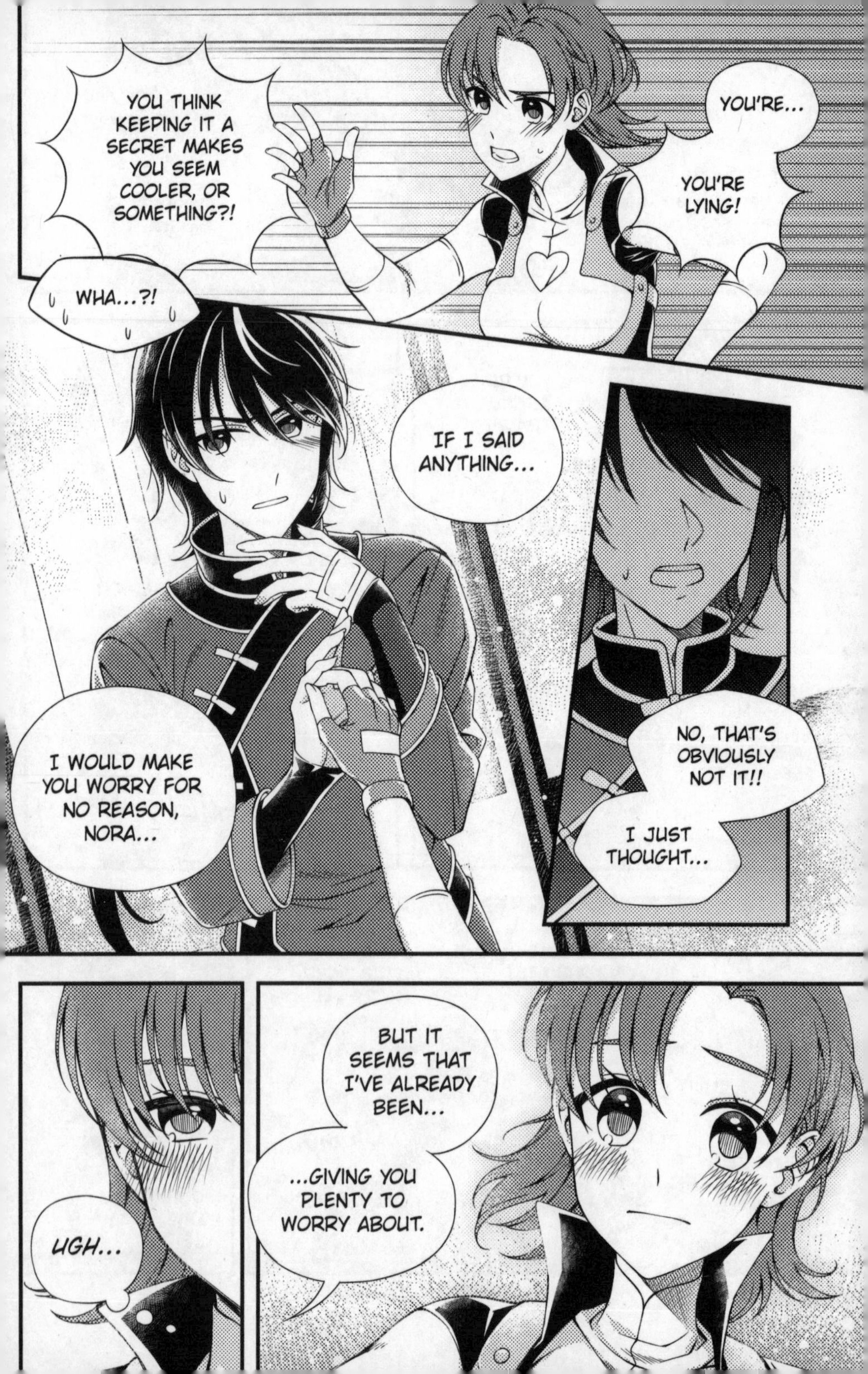
YOU'RE...
YOU'RE LYING!
YOU THINK KEEPING IT A SECRET MAKES YOU SEEM COOLER, OR SOMETHING?!
WHA...?!
IF I SAID ANYTHING...
I WOULD MAKE YOU WORRY FOR NO REASON, NORA...
NO, THAT'S OBVIOUSLY NOT IT!!
I JUST THOUGHT...
BUT IT SEEMS THAT I'VE ALREADY BEEN...
...GIVING YOU PLENTY TO WORRY ABOUT.
UGH...

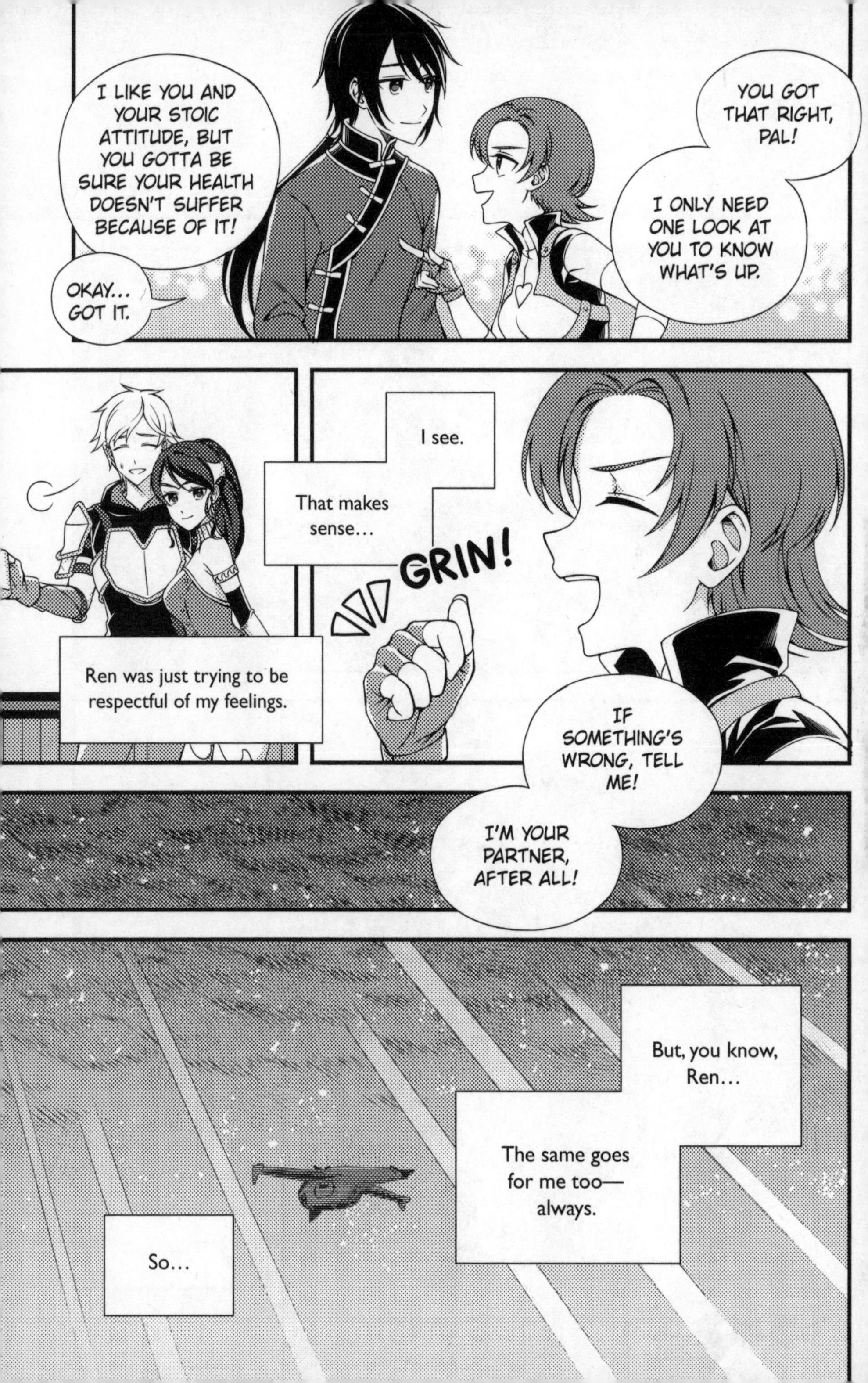
YOU GOT THAT RIGHT, PAL!
I LIKE YOU AND YOUR STOIC ATTITUDE, BUT YOU GOTTA BE SURE YOUR HEALTH DOESN'T SUFFER BECAUSE OF IT!
I ONLY NEED ONE LOOK AT YOU TO KNOW WHAT'S UP.
OKAY... GOT IT.
I see.
That makes sense...
GRIN!
IF SOMETHING'S WRONG, TELL ME!
I'M YOUR PARTNER, AFTER ALL!
Ren was just trying to be respectful of my feelings.
But, you know, Ren...
The same goes for me too—always.
So...

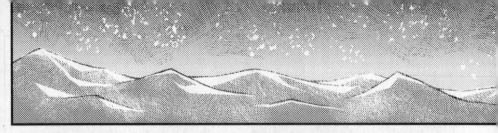

I AM HERE FOR YOU...

...WHENEVER YOU NEED ME.

 Don't Worry Too Much/END

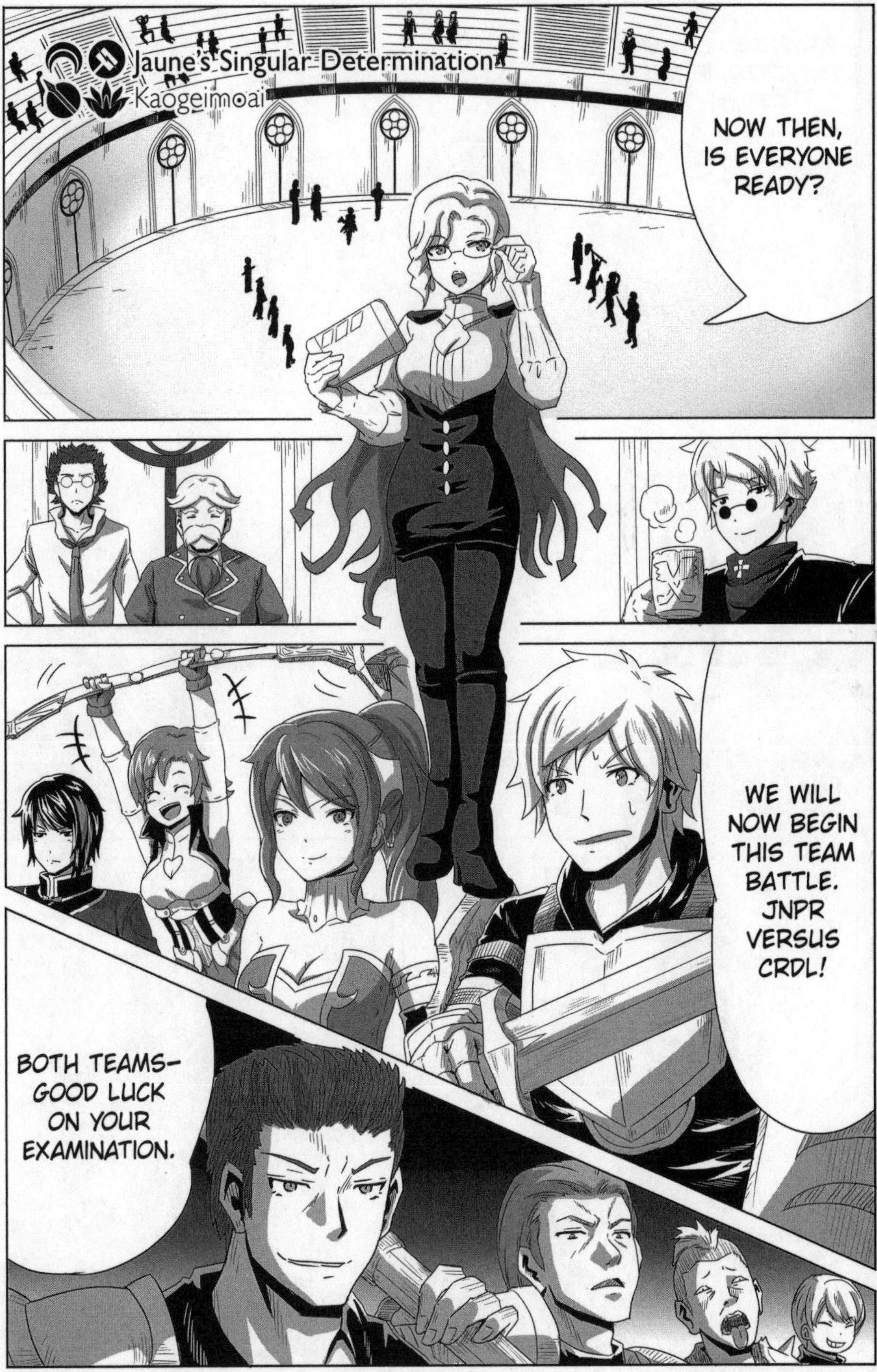
Jaune's Singular Determination
Kaogeimoai
NOW THEN, IS EVERYONE READY?
WE WILL NOW BEGIN THIS TEAM BATTLE. JNPR VERSUS CRDL!
BOTH TEAMS- GOOD LUCK ON YOUR EXAMINATION.

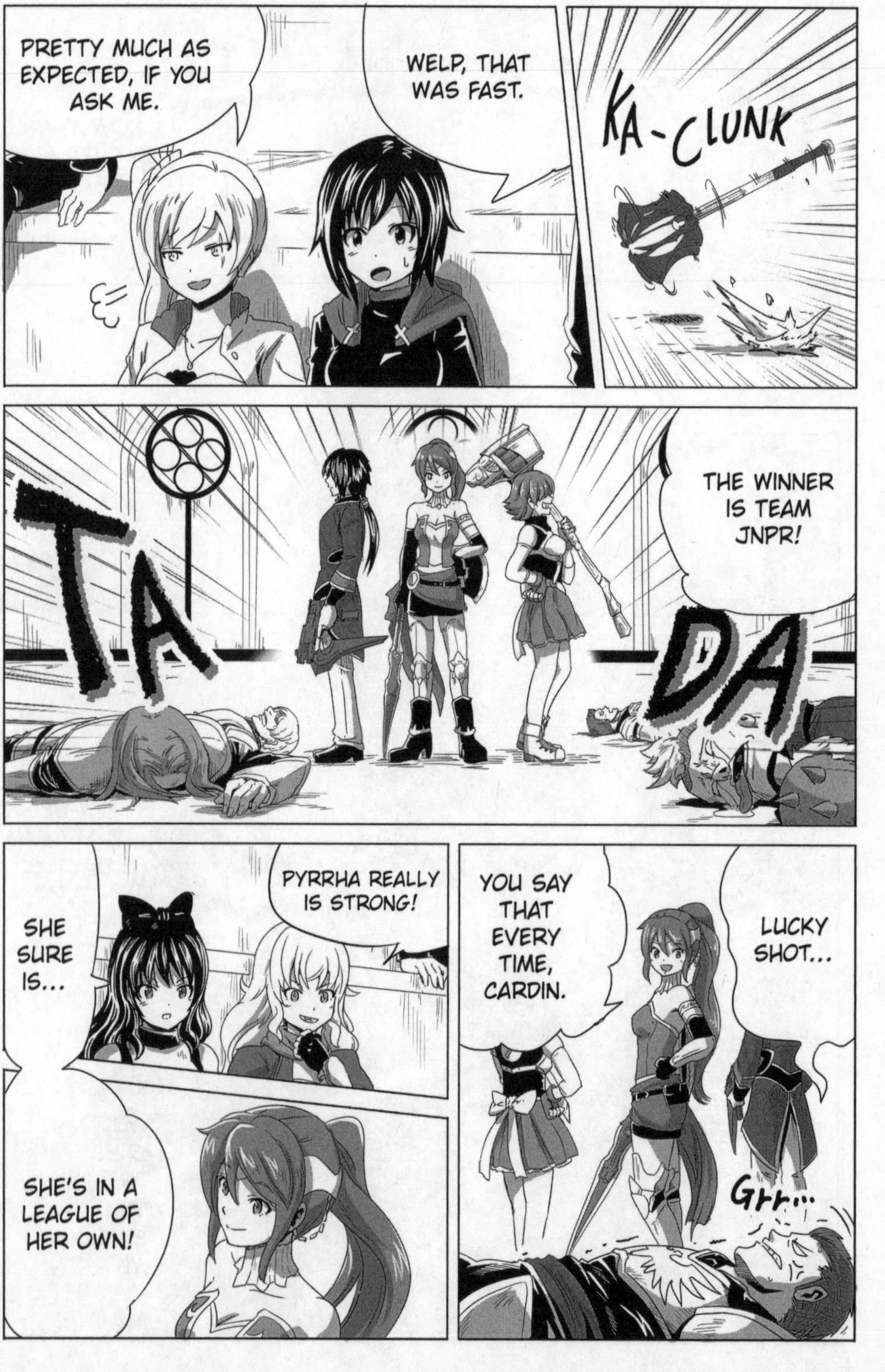
KA-CLUNK
WELP, THAT WAS FAST.
PRETTY MUCH AS EXPECTED, IF YOU ASK ME.
THE WINNER IS TEAM JNPR!
TA
DA
LUCKY SHOT...
YOU SAY THAT EVERY TIME, CARDIN.
Grr...
PYRRHA REALLY IS STRONG!
SHE SURE IS...
SHE'S IN A LEAGUE OF HER OWN!

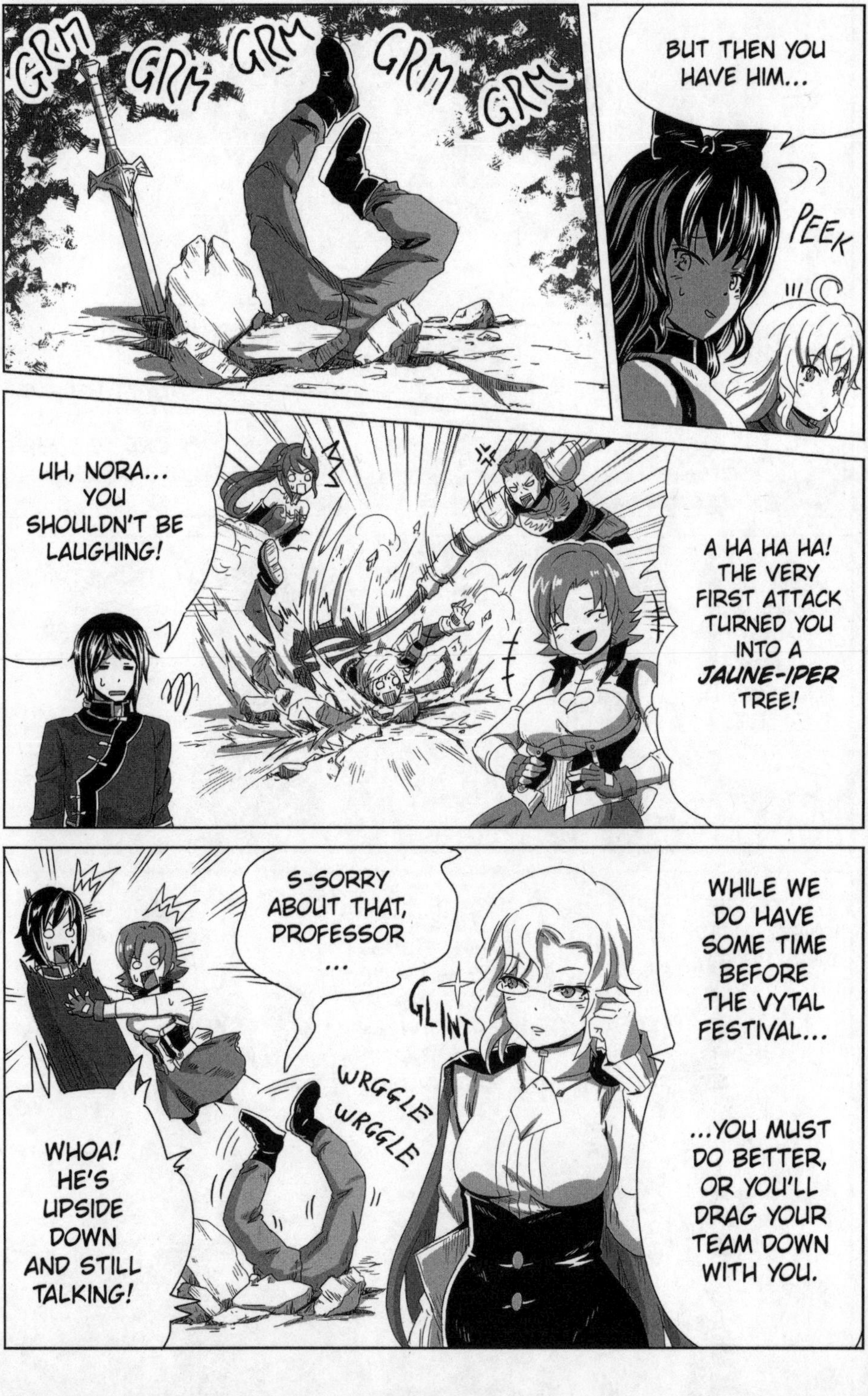
BUT THEN YOU HAVE HIM...
PEEK
GRM GRM GRM GRM GRM
A HA HA HA! THE VERY FIRST ATTACK TURNED YOU INTO A *JAUNE-IPER* TREE!
UH, NORA... YOU SHOULDN'T BE LAUGHING!
WHILE WE DO HAVE SOME TIME BEFORE THE VYTAL FESTIVAL...
...YOU MUST DO BETTER, OR YOU'LL DRAG YOUR TEAM DOWN WITH YOU.
GLINT
S-SORRY ABOUT THAT, PROFESSOR ...
WRGGLE WRGGLE
WHOA! HE'S UPSIDE DOWN AND STILL TALKING!

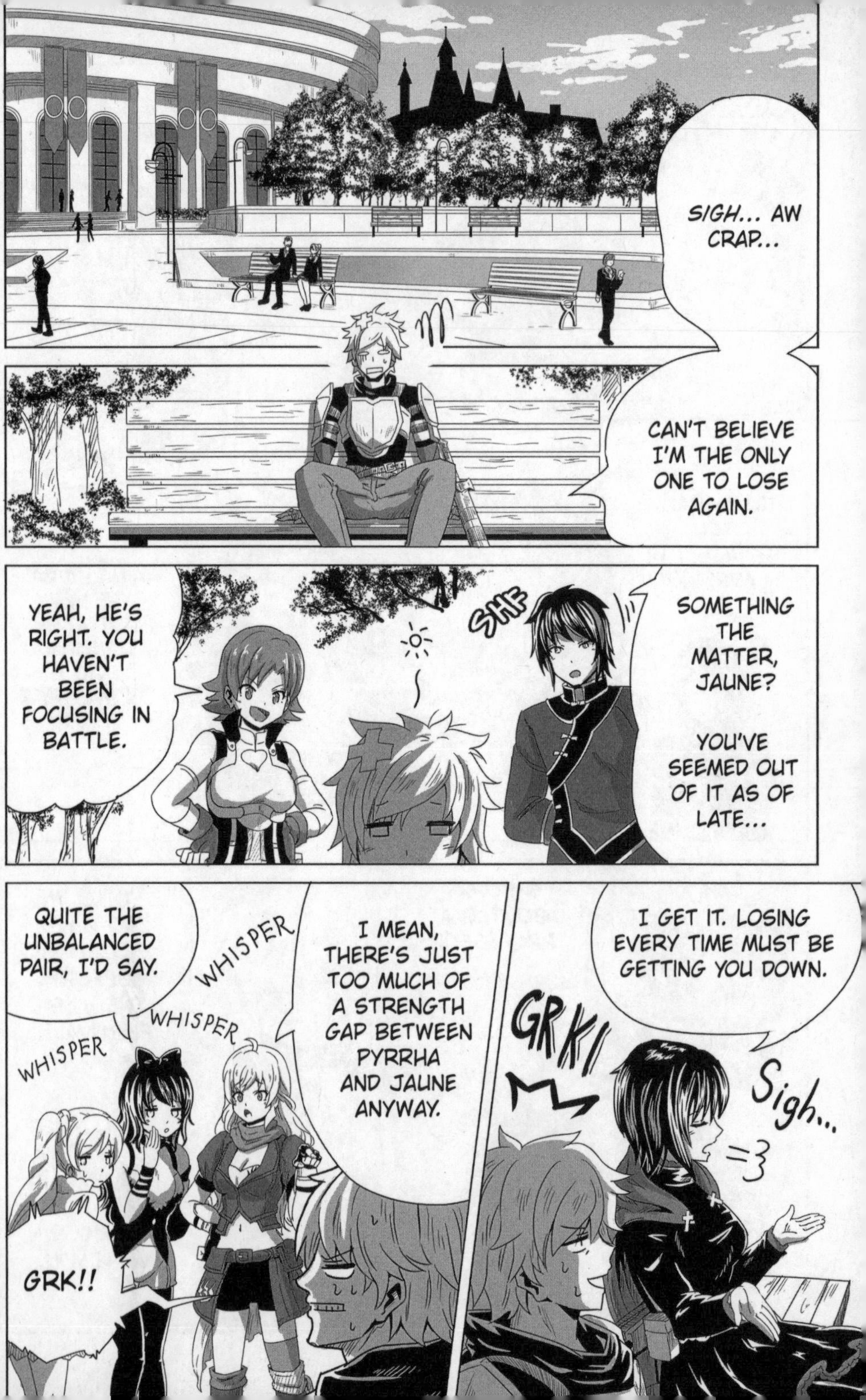
SIGH... AW CRAP...
CAN'T BELIEVE I'M THE ONLY ONE TO LOSE AGAIN.
SOMETHING THE MATTER, JAUNE?
YOU'VE SEEMED OUT OF IT AS OF LATE...
SHF
YEAH, HE'S RIGHT. YOU HAVEN'T BEEN FOCUSING IN BATTLE.
I GET IT. LOSING EVERY TIME MUST BE GETTING YOU DOWN.
GRK!
Sigh...
I MEAN, THERE'S JUST TOO MUCH OF A STRENGTH GAP BETWEEN PYRRHA AND JAUNE ANYWAY.
WHISPER
WHISPER
WHISPER
QUITE THE UNBALANCED PAIR, I'D SAY.
GRK!!

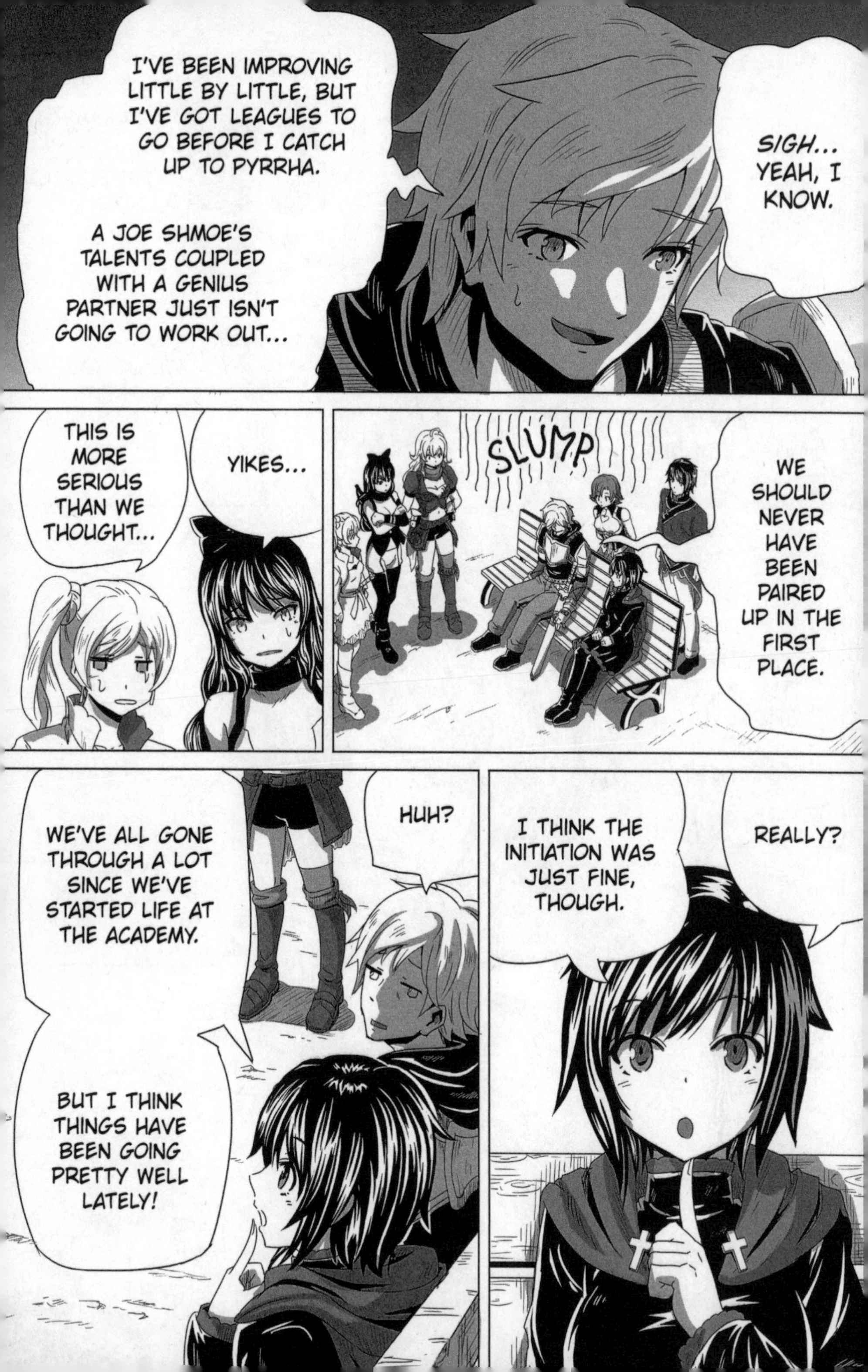
SIGH... YEAH, I KNOW.
I'VE BEEN IMPROVING LITTLE BY LITTLE, BUT I'VE GOT LEAGUES TO GO BEFORE I CATCH UP TO PYRRHA.
A JOE SHMOE'S TALENTS COUPLED WITH A GENIUS PARTNER JUST ISN'T GOING TO WORK OUT...
WE SHOULD NEVER HAVE BEEN PAIRED UP IN THE FIRST PLACE.
SLUMP
YIKES...
THIS IS MORE SERIOUS THAN WE THOUGHT...
REALLY?
I THINK THE INITIATION WAS JUST FINE, THOUGH.
HUH?
WE'VE ALL GONE THROUGH A LOT SINCE WE'VE STARTED LIFE AT THE ACADEMY.
BUT I THINK THINGS HAVE BEEN GOING PRETTY WELL LATELY!

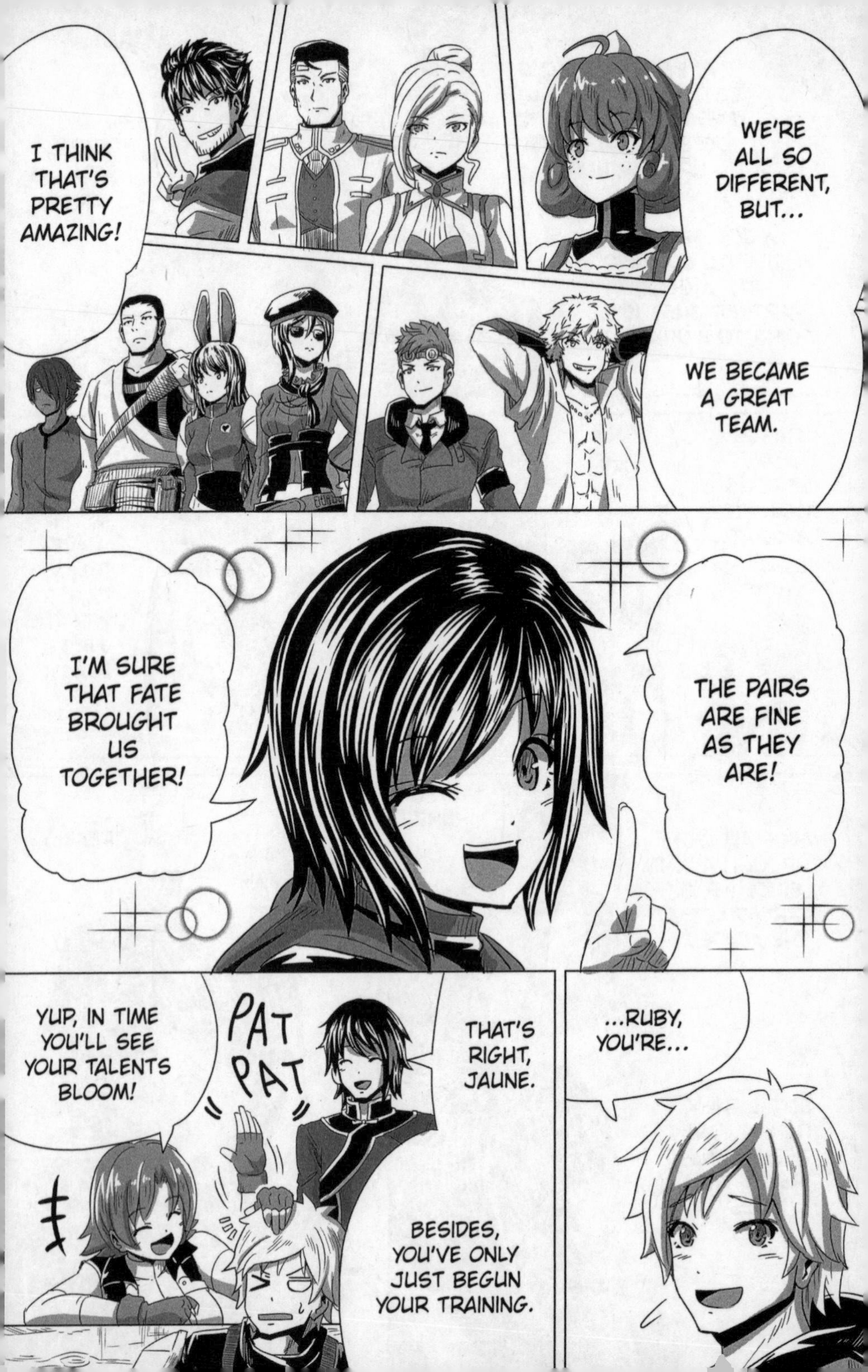
WE'RE ALL SO DIFFERENT, BUT...
WE BECAME A GREAT TEAM.
I THINK THAT'S PRETTY AMAZING!
THE PAIRS ARE FINE AS THEY ARE!
I'M SURE THAT FATE BROUGHT US TOGETHER!
...RUBY, YOU'RE...
THAT'S RIGHT, JAUNE.
PAT PAT
YUP, IN TIME YOU'LL SEE YOUR TALENTS BLOOM!
BESIDES, YOU'VE ONLY JUST BEGUN YOUR TRAINING.

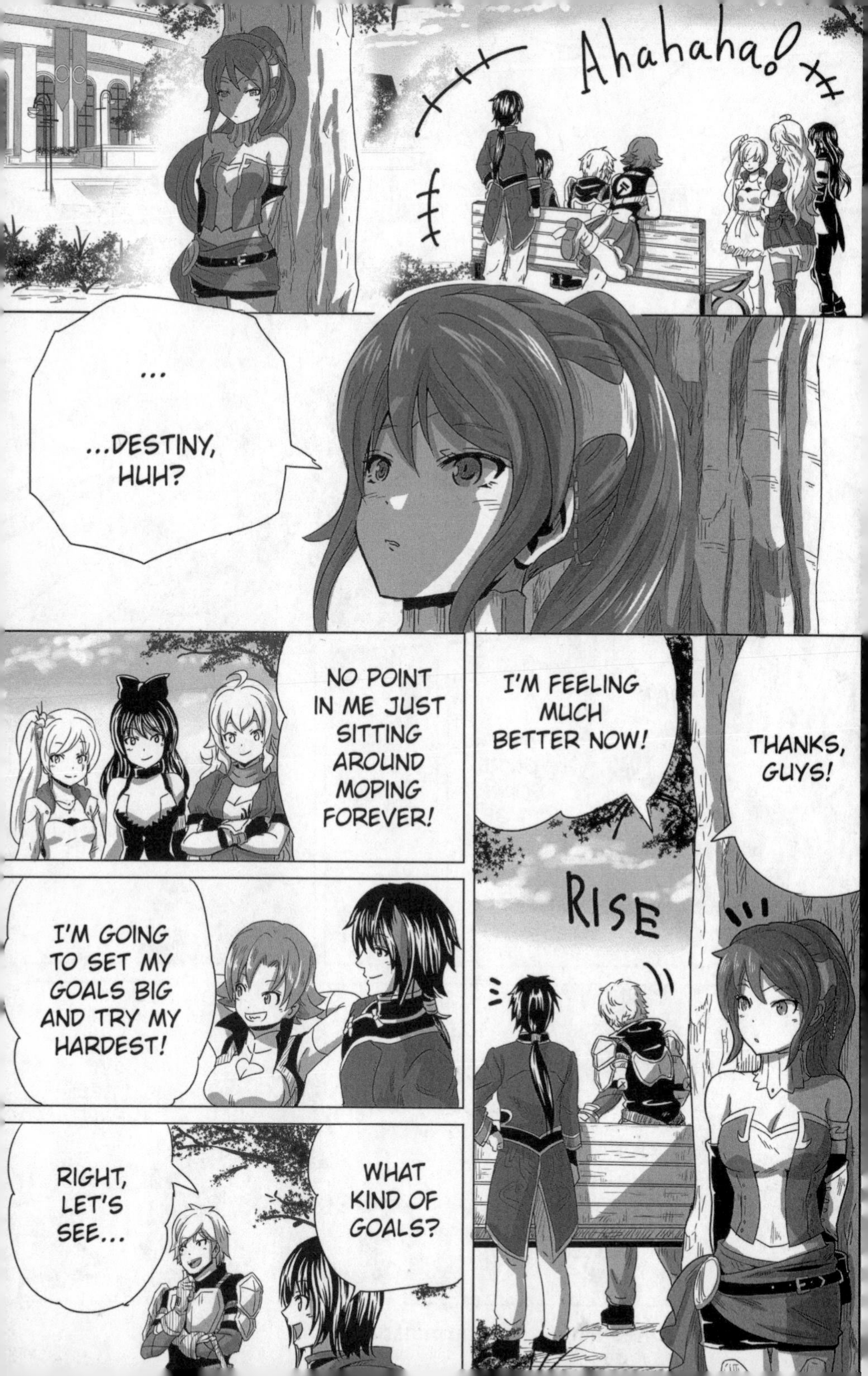
Ahahaha!
...
...DESTINY, HUH?
I'M FEELING MUCH BETTER NOW!
THANKS, GUYS!
RISE
NO POINT IN ME JUST SITTING AROUND MOPING FOREVER!
I'M GOING TO SET MY GOALS BIG AND TRY MY HARDEST!
WHAT KIND OF GOALS?
RIGHT, LET'S SEE...

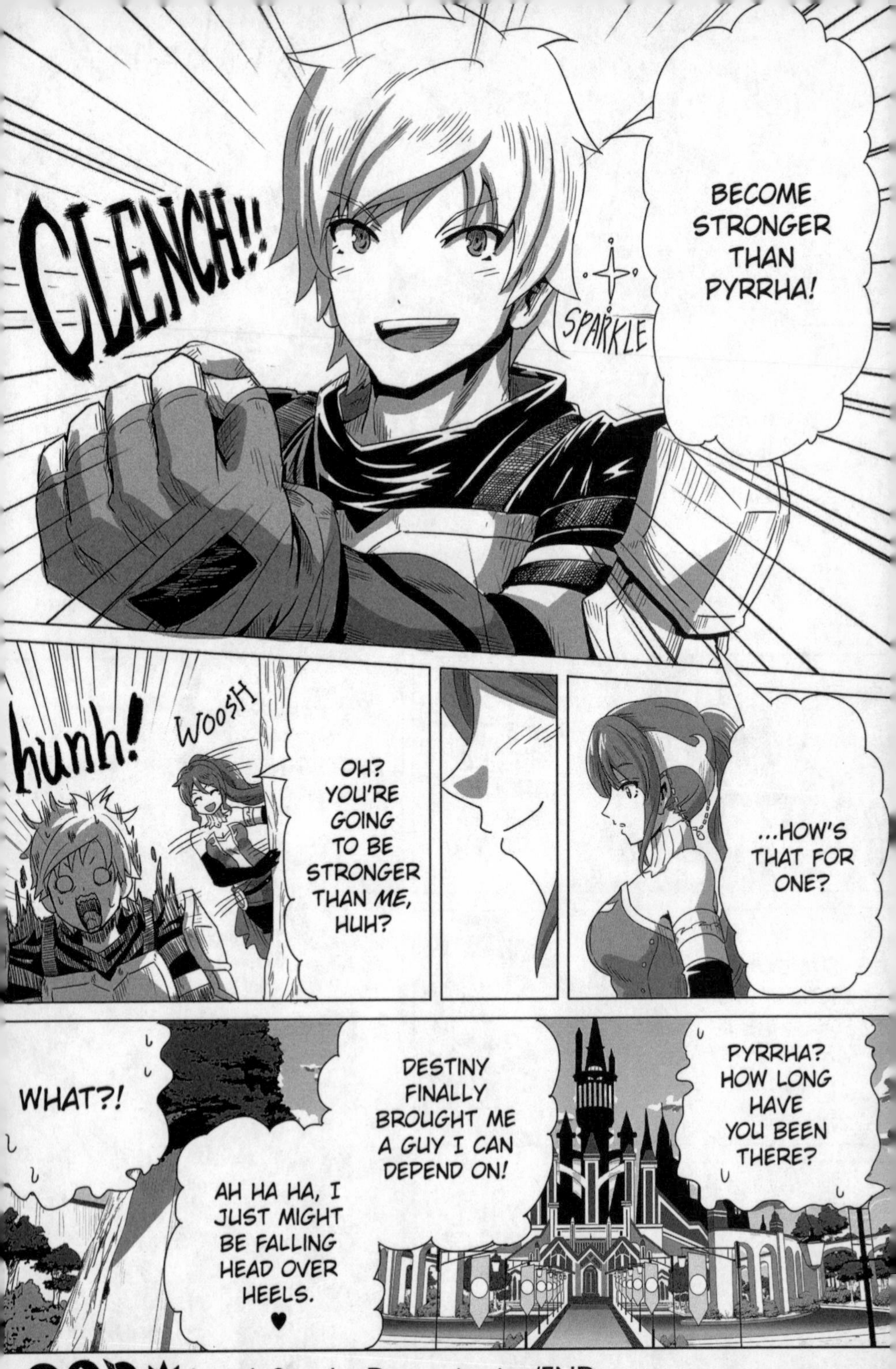
BECOME STRONGER THAN PYRRHA!
SPARKLE
CLENCH!!
...HOW'S THAT FOR ONE?
OH? YOU'RE GOING TO BE STRONGER THAN ME, HUH?
WOOSH
hunh!
PYRRHA? HOW LONG HAVE YOU BEEN THERE?
DESTINY FINALLY BROUGHT ME A GUY I CAN DEPEND ON!
AH HA HA, I JUST MIGHT BE FALLING HEAD OVER HEELS. ♥
WHAT?!

Jaune's Singular Determination/END

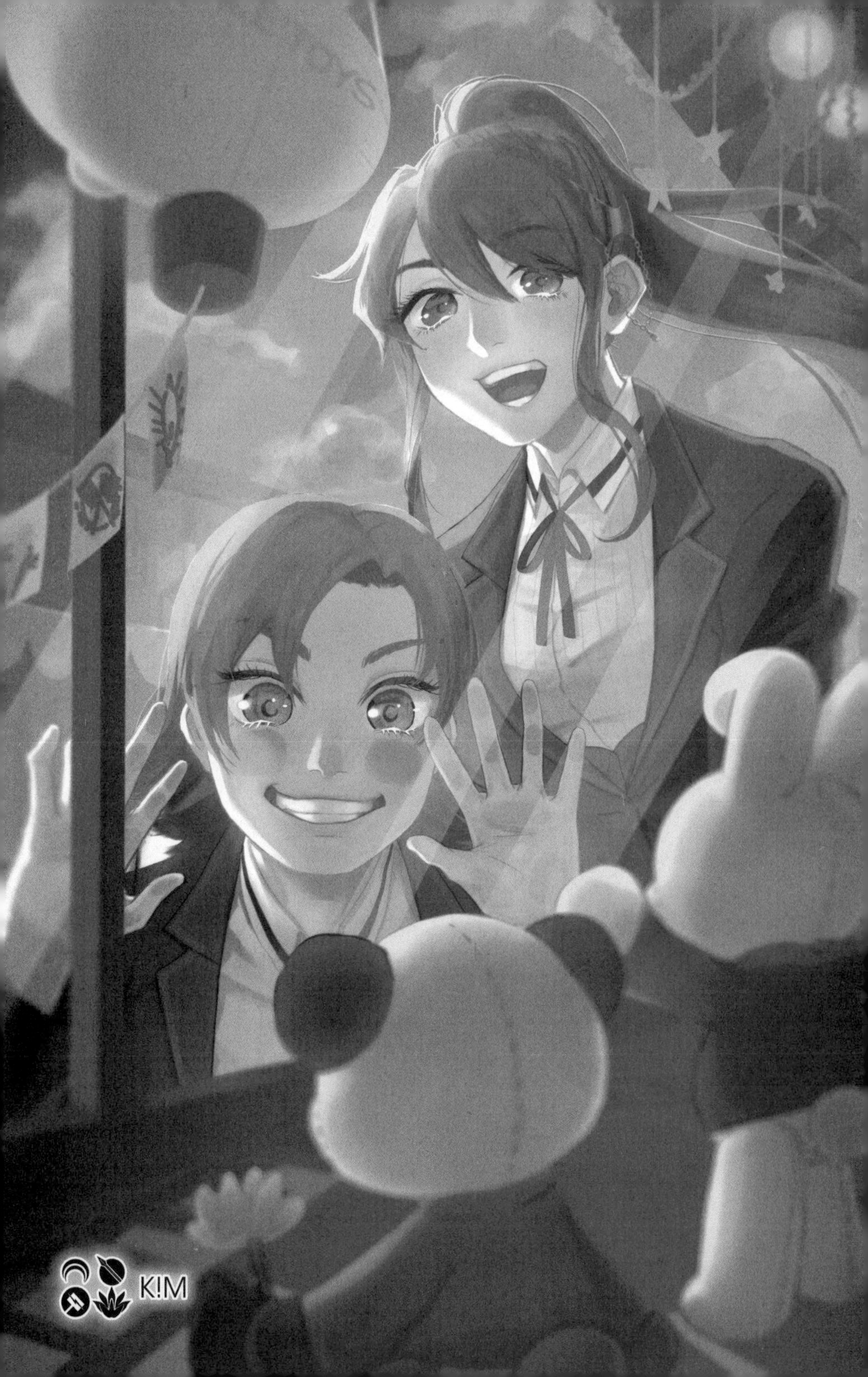
K!M

RWBY
OFFICIAL MANGA ANTHOLOGY
Volume 5

Shine

Ecru

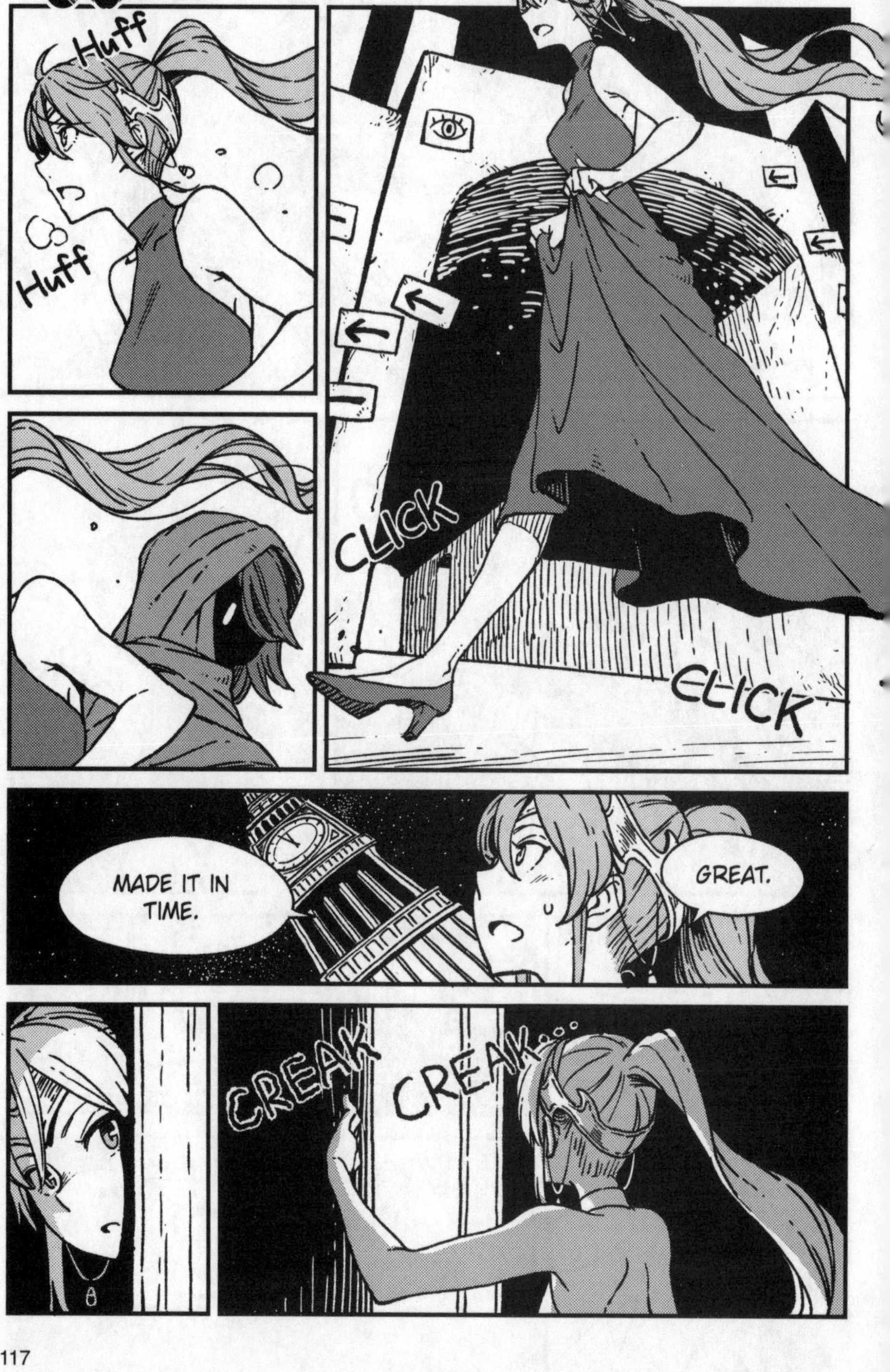
CLICK
CLICK
Huff
Huff
GREAT.
MADE IT IN TIME.
CREAK
CREAK...

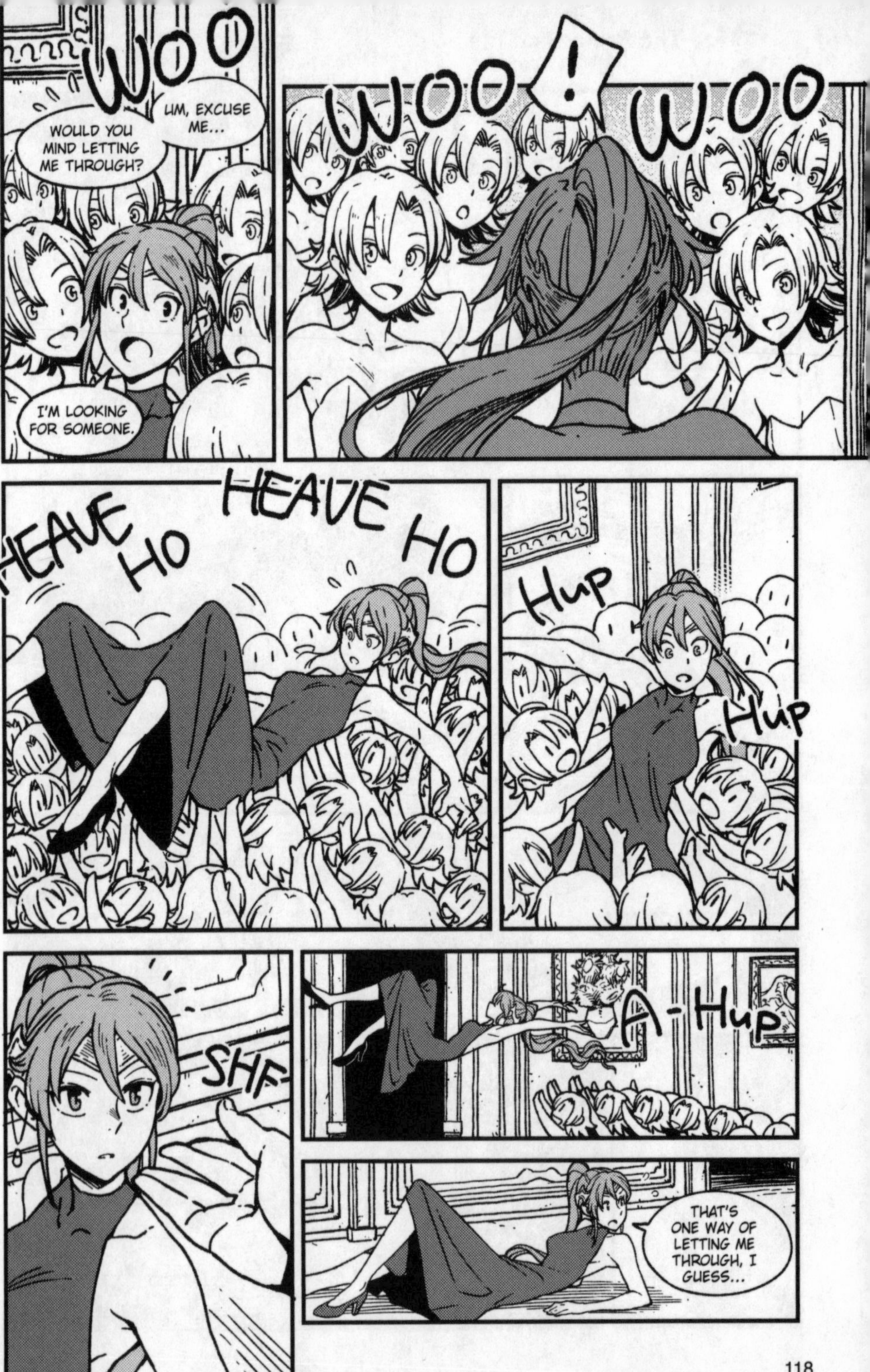

WOO
!
WOO
WOO
UM, EXCUSE ME...
WOULD YOU MIND LETTING ME THROUGH?
I'M LOOKING FOR SOMEONE.
Hup
Hup
HEAVE HO
HEAVE HO
A-Hup
THAT'S ONE WAY OF LETTING ME THROUGH, I GUESS...
SHF

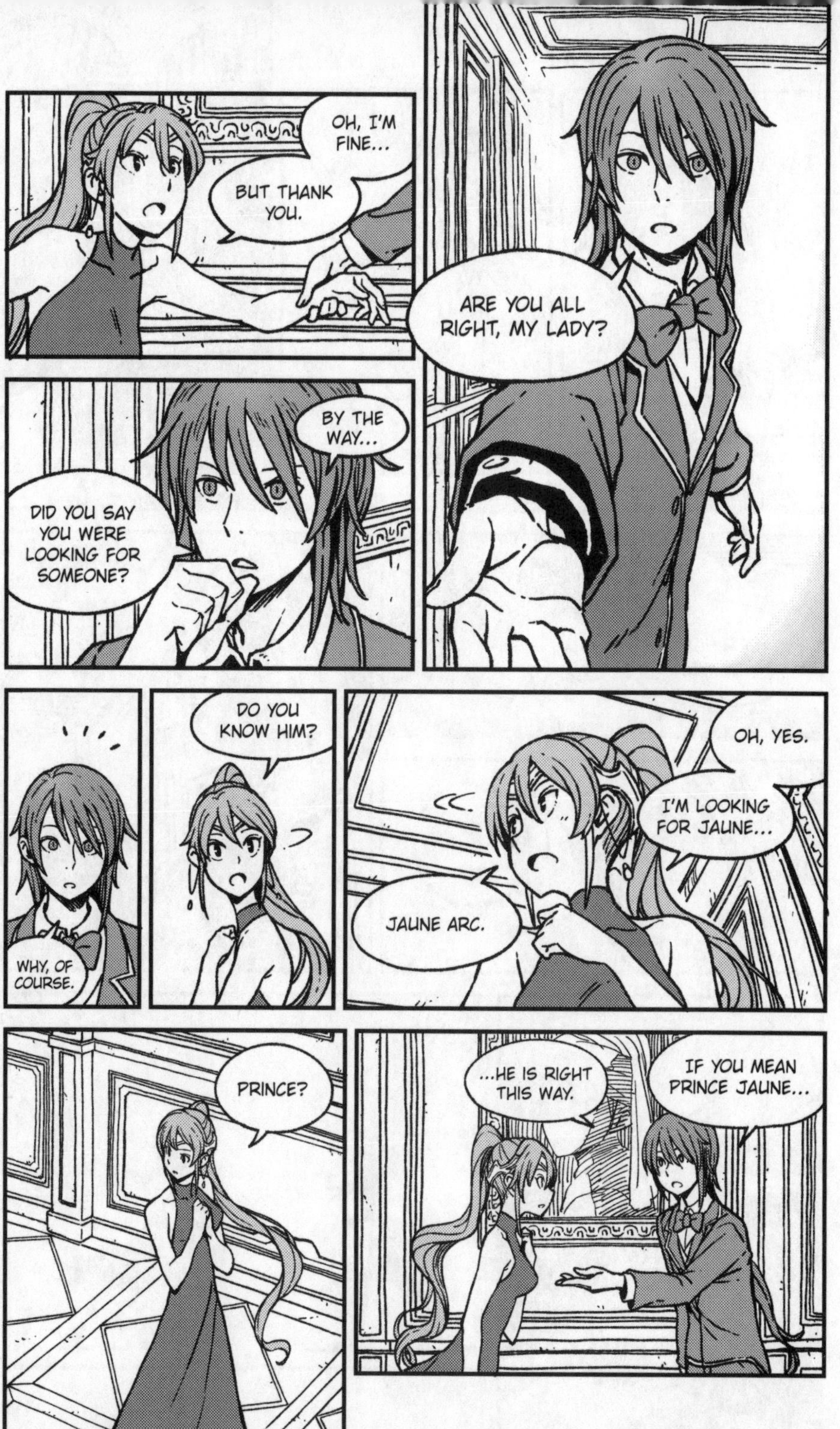
ARE YOU ALL RIGHT, MY LADY?
OH, I'M FINE...
BUT THANK YOU.
BY THE WAY...
DID YOU SAY YOU WERE LOOKING FOR SOMEONE?
OH, YES.
I'M LOOKING FOR JAUNE...
JAUNE ARC.
DO YOU KNOW HIM?
WHY, OF COURSE.
IF YOU MEAN PRINCE JAUNE...
...HE IS RIGHT THIS WAY.
PRINCE?

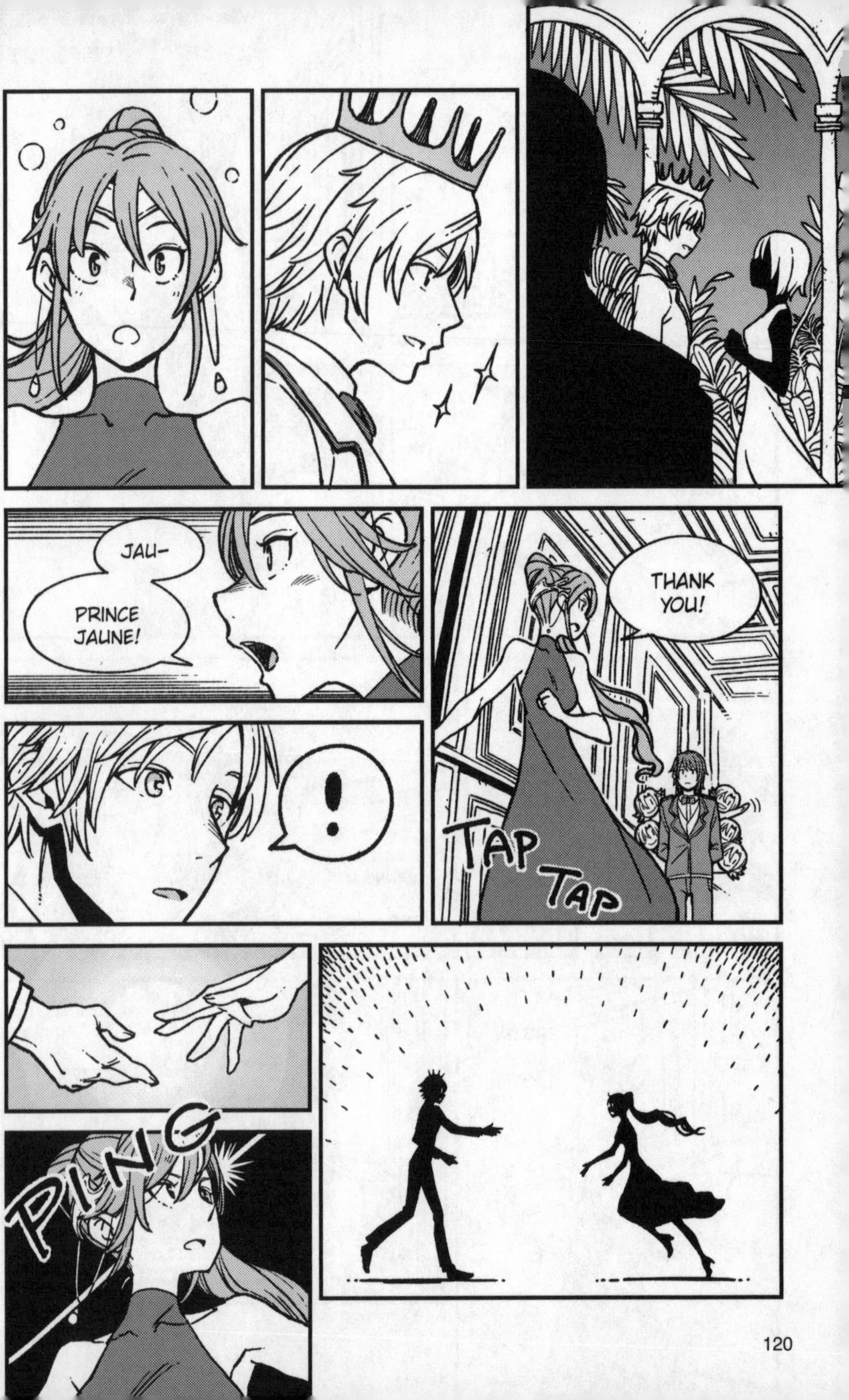
THANK YOU!
TAP TAP
JAU-
PRINCE JAUNE!
!
PING

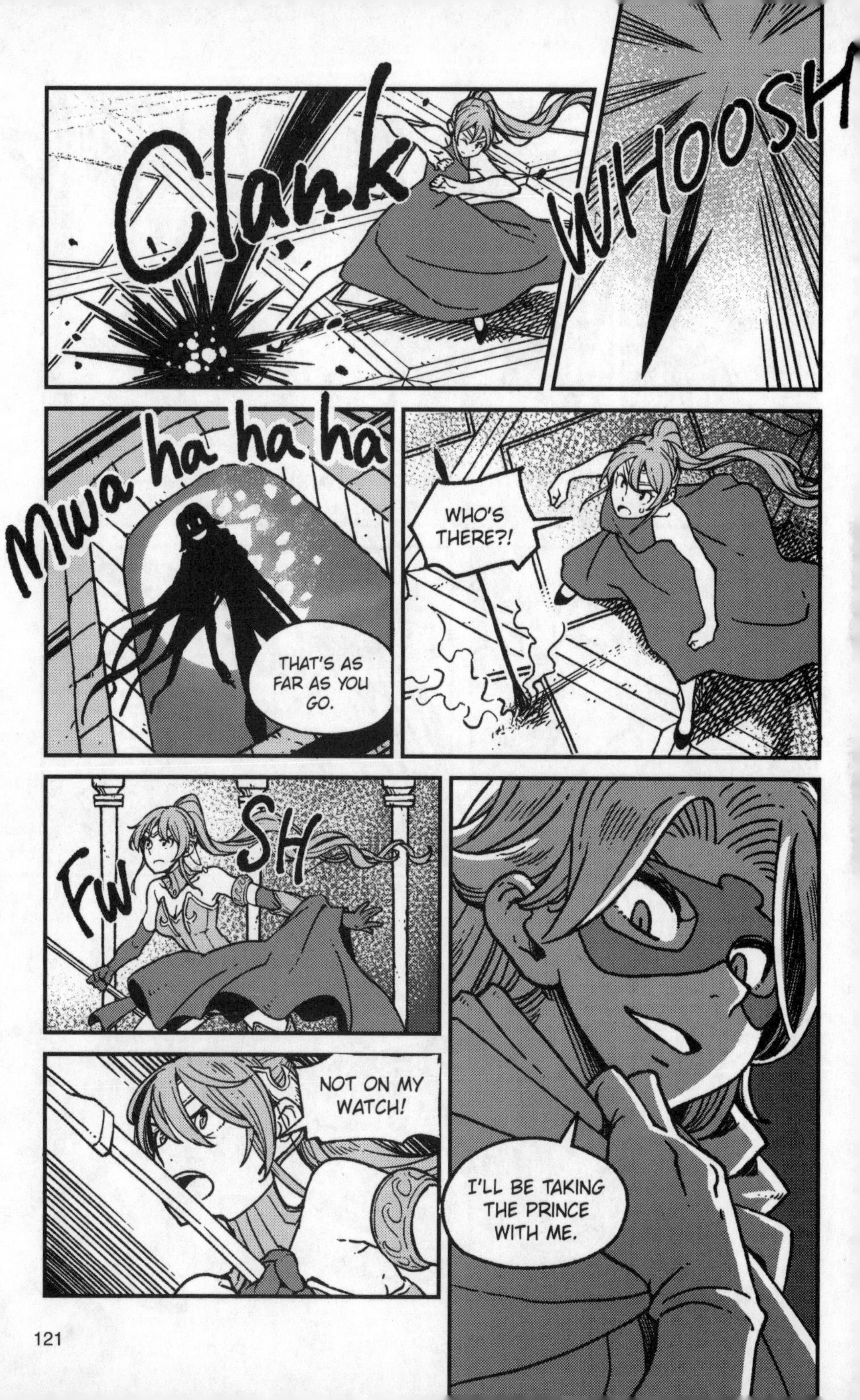
WHOOSH
Clank
WHO'S THERE?!
Mwa ha ha ha
THAT'S AS FAR AS YOU GO.
I'LL BE TAKING THE PRINCE WITH ME.
FwSH
NOT ON MY WATCH!

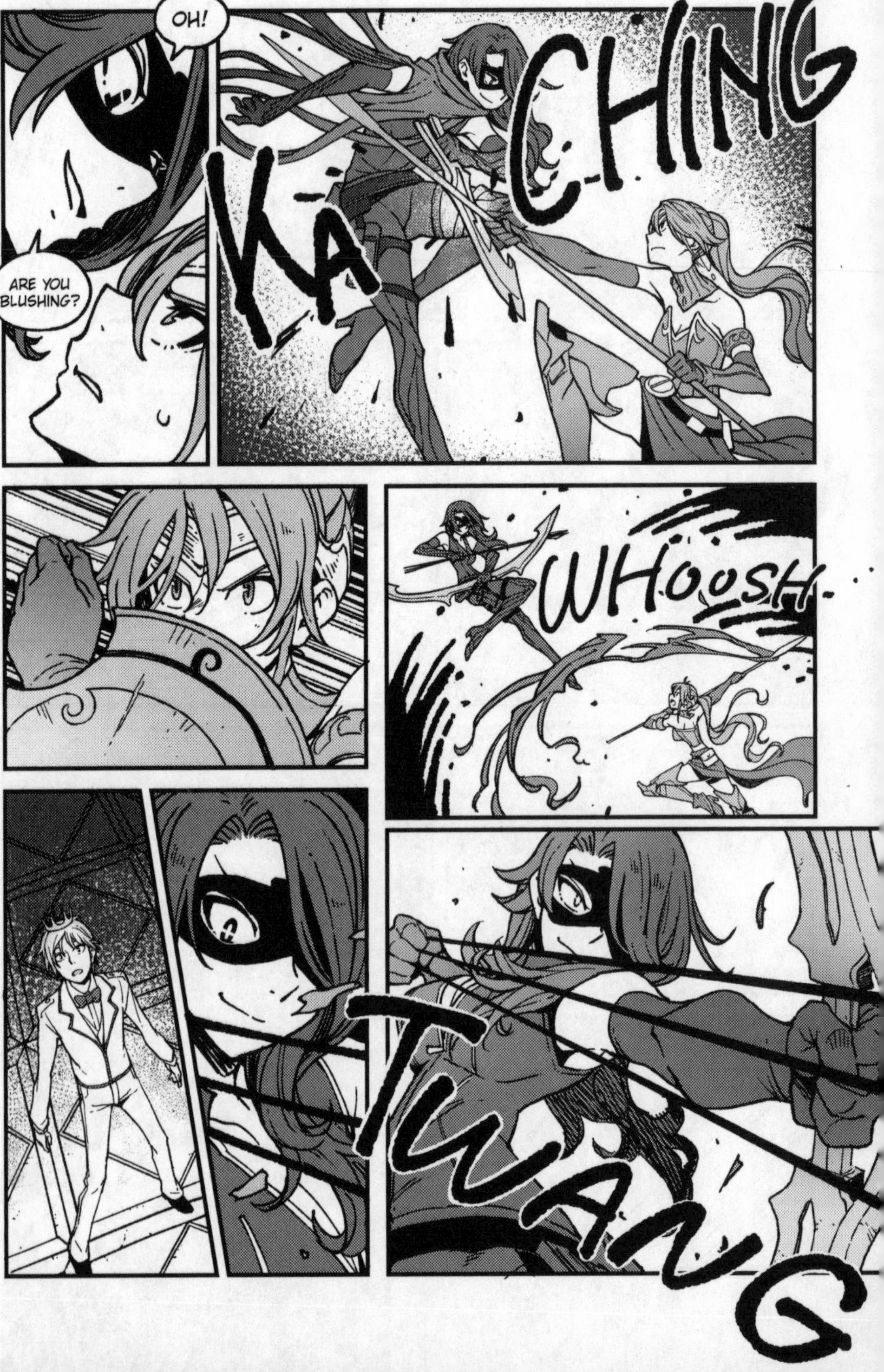
KA CHING
OH!
ARE YOU BLUSHING?
WHOOSH
TWANG

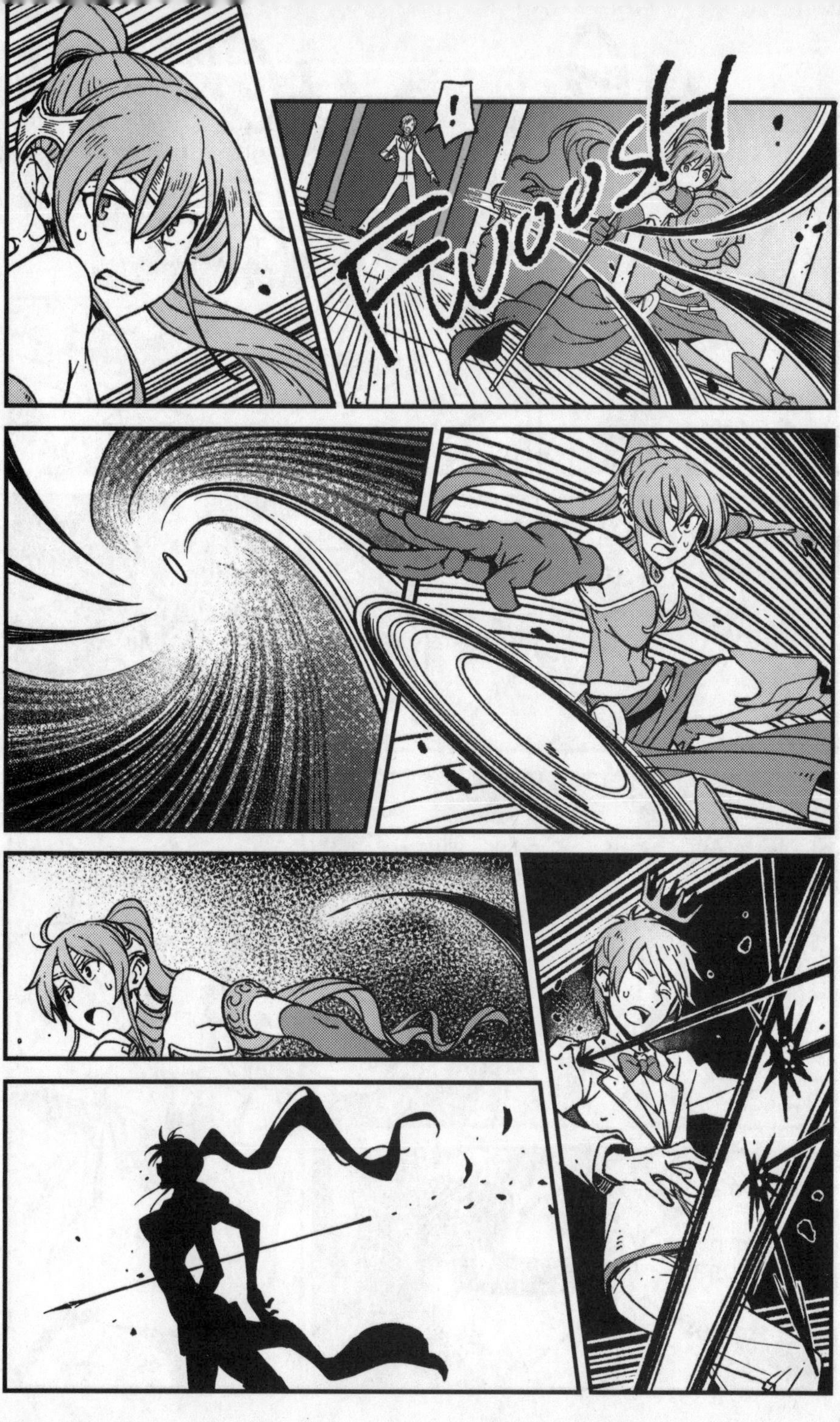
!
FWOOSH

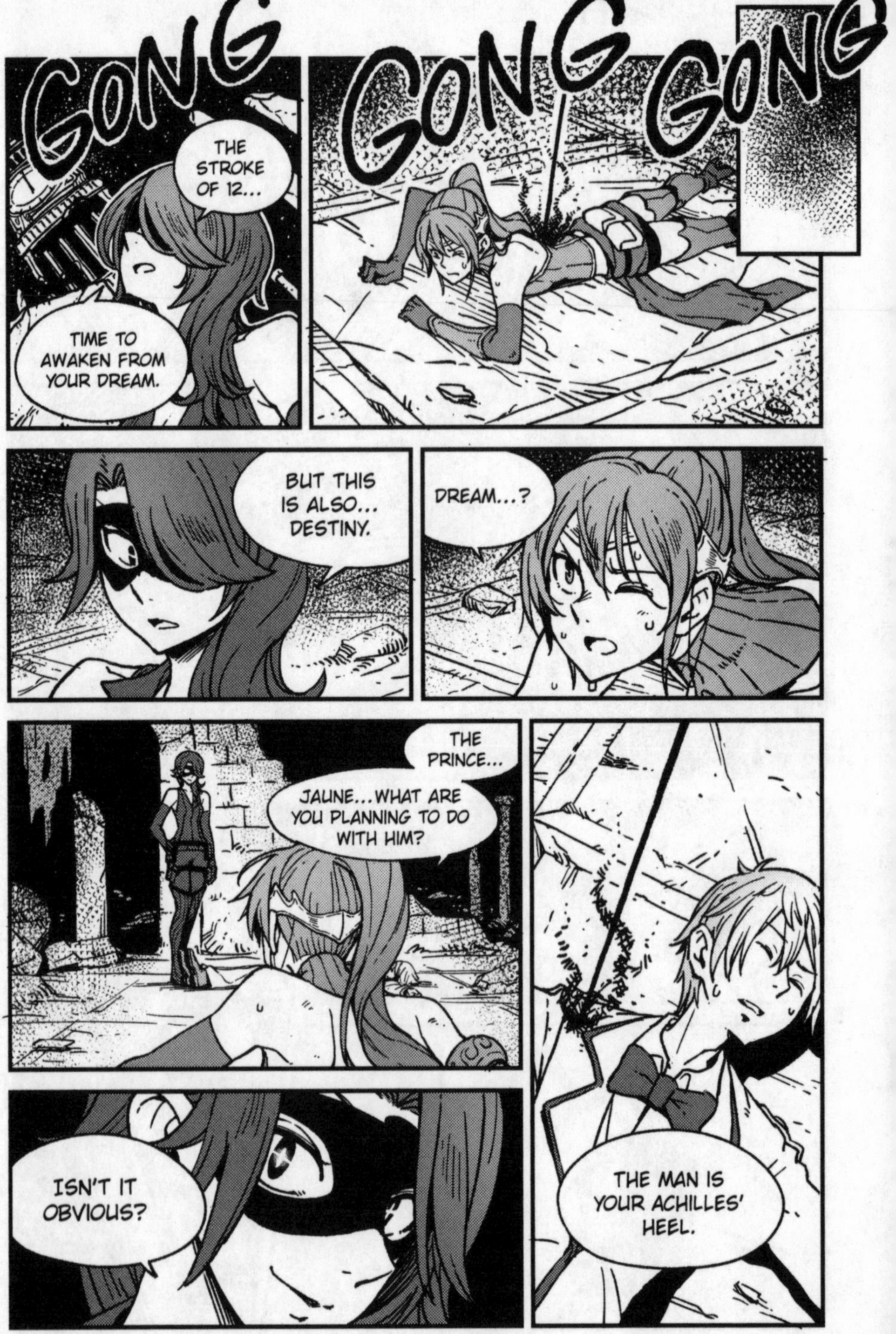
GONG
GONG
GONG
THE STROKE OF 12...
TIME TO AWAKEN FROM YOUR DREAM.
DREAM...?
BUT THIS IS ALSO... DESTINY.
THE MAN IS YOUR ACHILLES' HEEL.
THE PRINCE...
JAUNE...WHAT ARE YOU PLANNING TO DO WITH HIM?
ISN'T IT OBVIOUS?

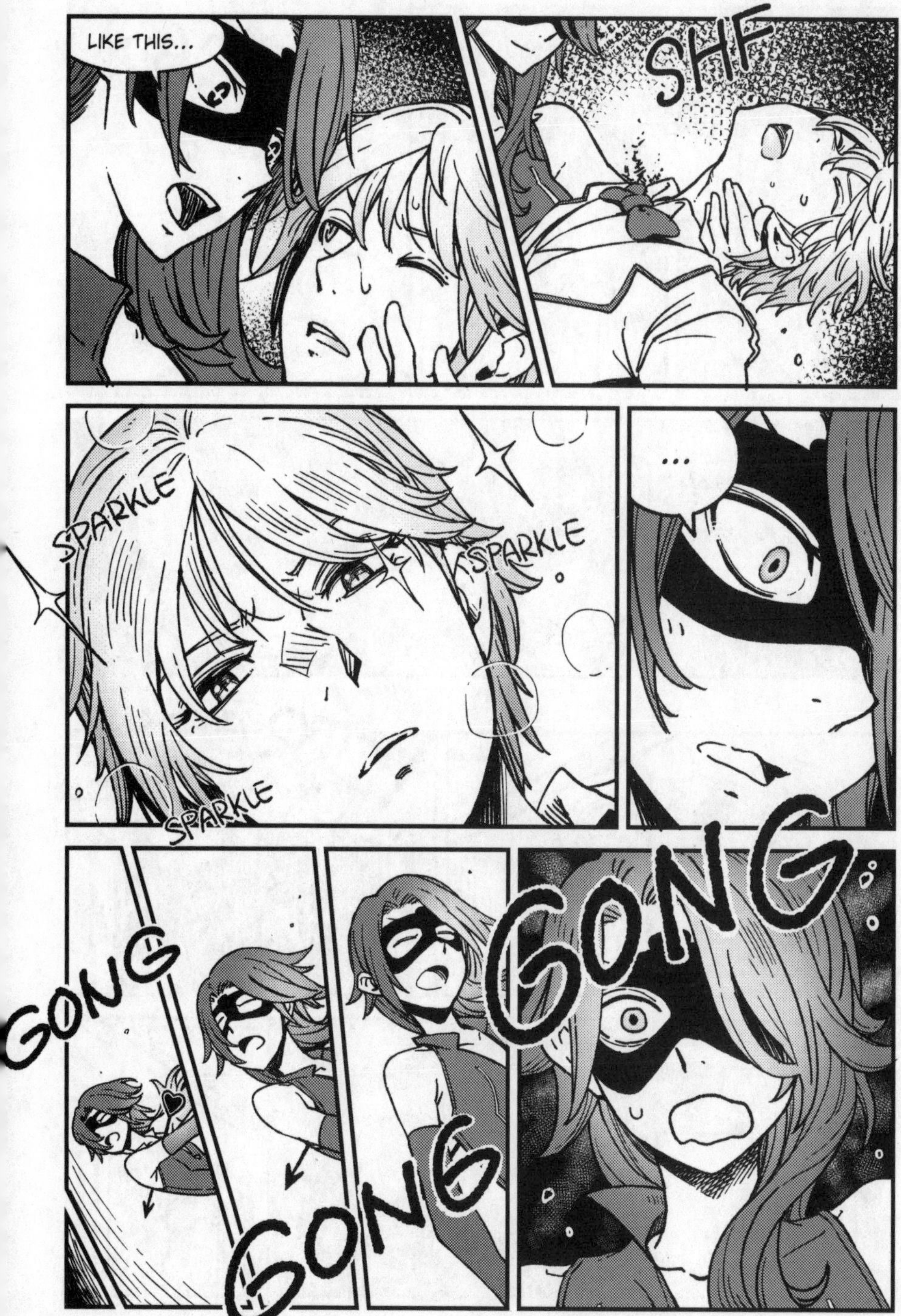
SHF
LIKE THIS...
...
SPARKLE
SPARKLE
SPARKLE
GONG
GONG
GONG

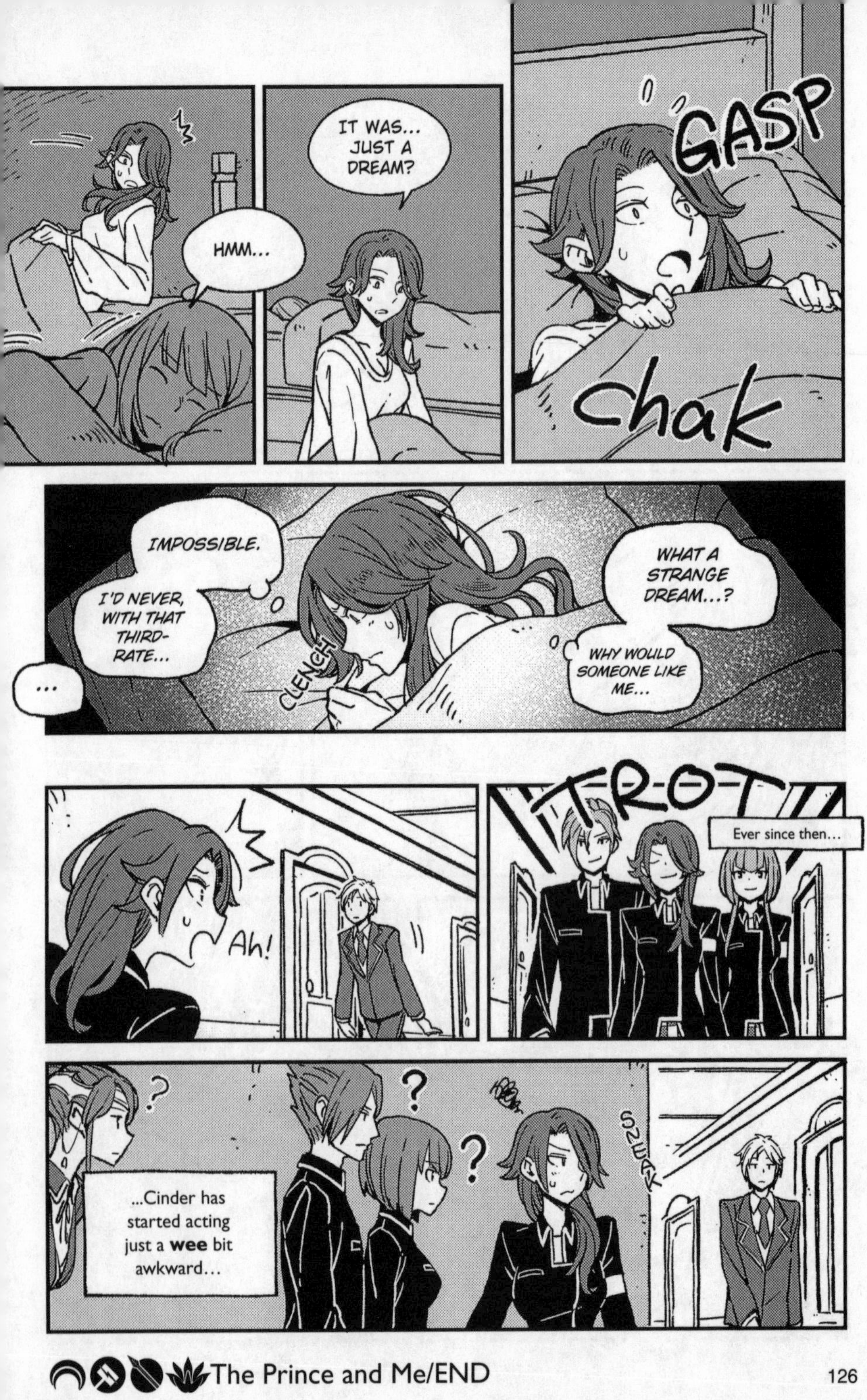
GASP
Chak
IT WAS... JUST A DREAM?
HMM...
WHAT A STRANGE DREAM...?
WHY WOULD SOMEONE LIKE ME...
IMPOSSIBLE.
I'D NEVER, WITH THAT THIRD-RATE...
CLENCH
...
TROT
Ever since then...
Ah!
SNEAK
...Cinder has started acting just a **wee** bit awkward...

The Prince and Me/END

A G Nonsuch

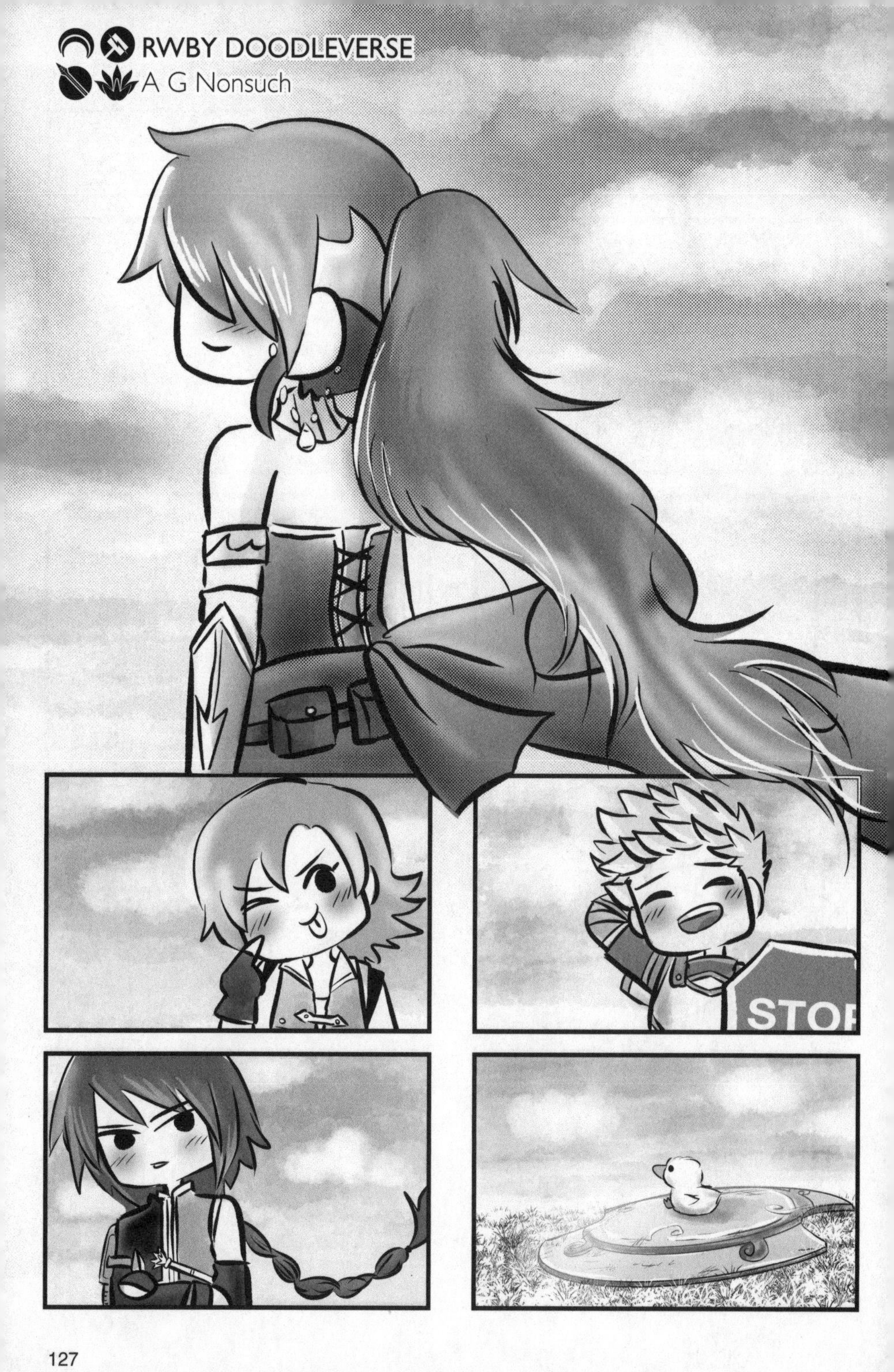
STOP

Movie Tickets 1

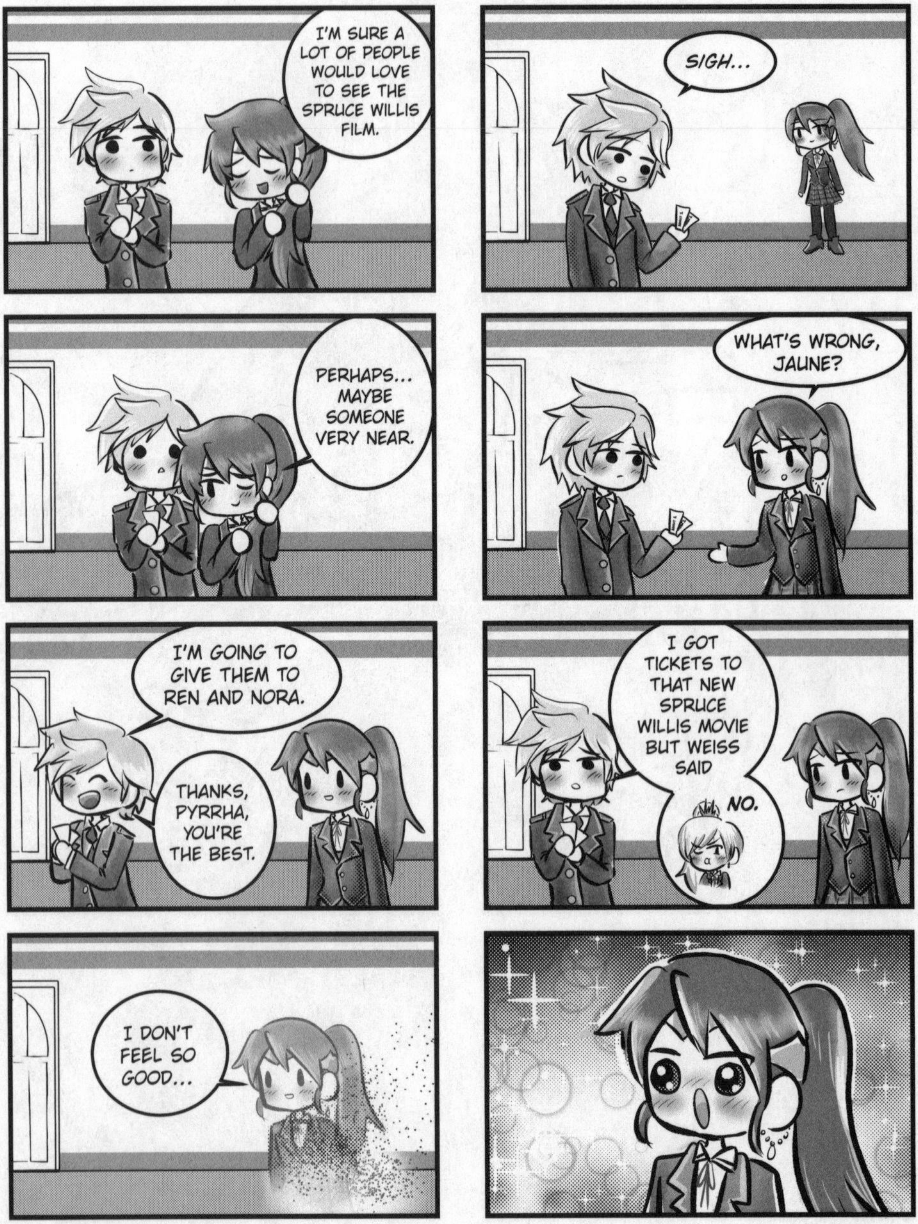
SIGH...
WHAT'S WRONG, JAUNE?
I GOT TICKETS TO THAT NEW SPRUCE WILLIS MOVIE BUT WEISS SAID
NO.
I'M SURE A LOT OF PEOPLE WOULD LOVE TO SEE THE SPRUCE WILLIS FILM.
PERHAPS... MAYBE SOMEONE VERY NEAR.
I'M GOING TO GIVE THEM TO REN AND NORA.
THANKS, PYRRHA, YOU'RE THE BEST.
I DON'T FEEL SO GOOD...

Movie Tickets 2

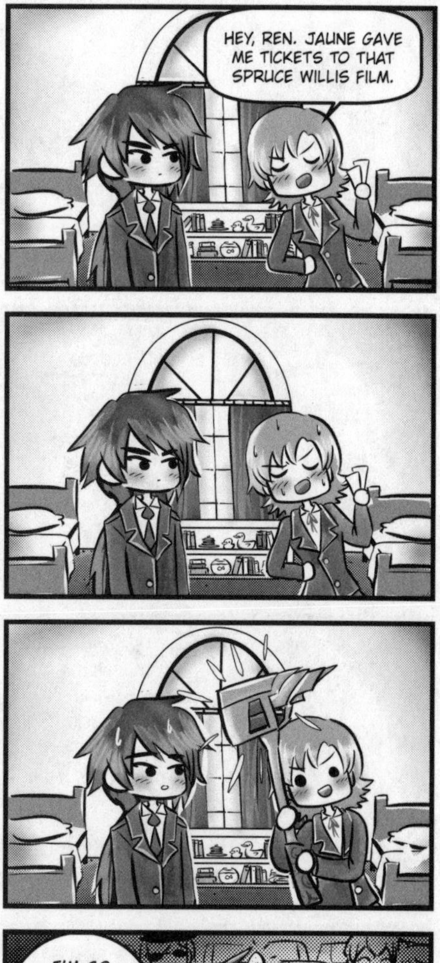
HEY, REN. JAUNE GAVE ME TICKETS TO THAT SPRUCE WILLIS FILM.
I'M SO GLAD WE DECIDED TO SEE THIS TOGETHER.

Movie Tickets 3

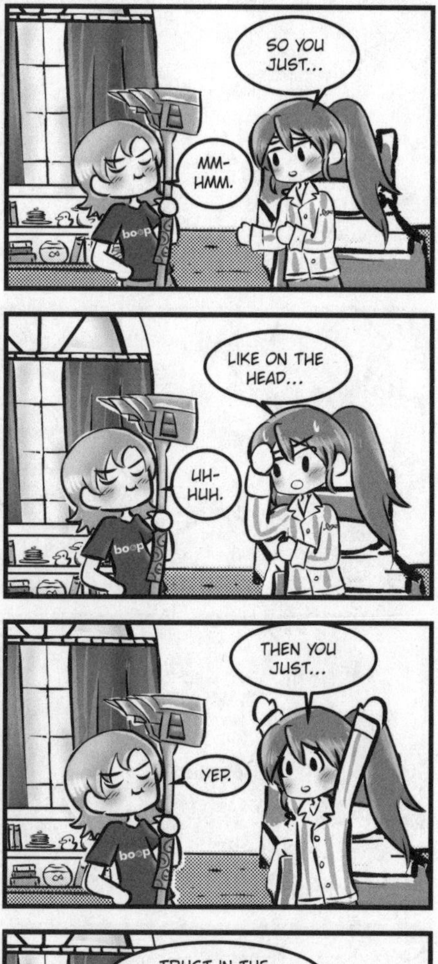
SO YOU JUST...
MM-HMM.
LIKE ON THE HEAD...
UH-HUH.
THEN YOU JUST...
YEP.
TRUST IN THE HAMMER, PYRRHA.

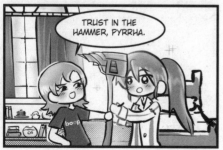

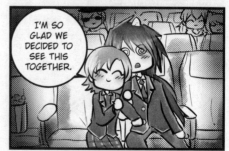

Movie Tickets 4

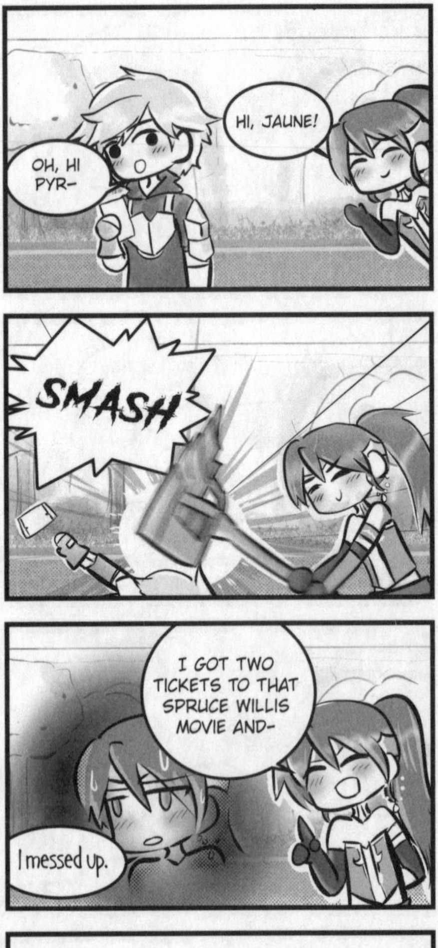
HI, JAUNE!
OH, HI PYR-
SMASH
I GOT TWO TICKETS TO THAT SPRUCE WILLIS MOVIE AND-
I messed up.
I'M SORRY!

Movie Tickets 5

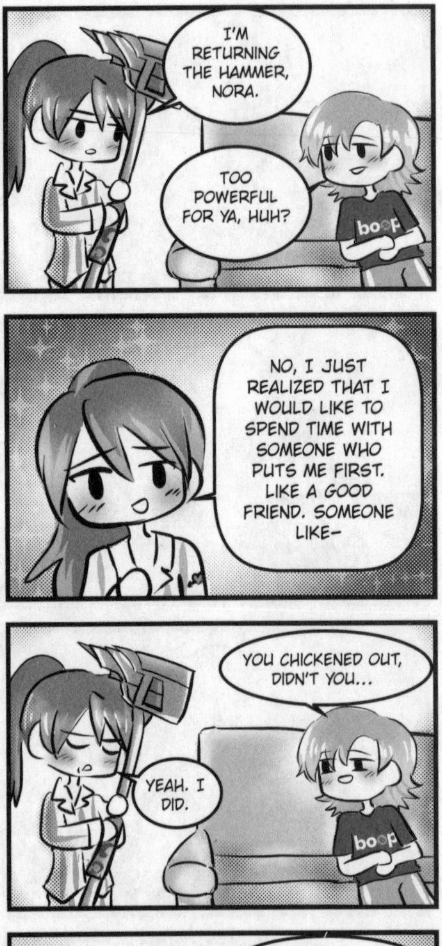
I'M RETURNING THE HAMMER, NORA.
TOO POWERFUL FOR YA, HUH?
boop
NO, I JUST REALIZED THAT I WOULD LIKE TO SPEND TIME WITH SOMEONE WHO PUTS ME FIRST. LIKE A GOOD FRIEND. SOMEONE LIKE-
YOU CHICKENED OUT, DIDN'T YOU...
YEAH. I DID.
boop
GIRLS' NIGHT?
GIRLS' NIGHT.
boop

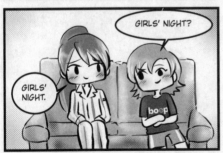

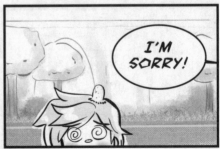

Dancing

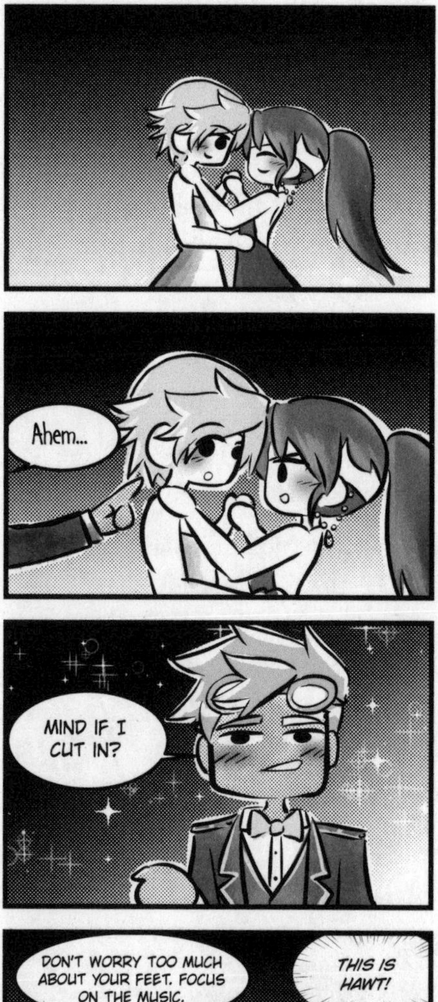
Ahem...
MIND IF I CUT IN?
THIS IS HAWT!
DON'T WORRY TOO MUCH ABOUT YOUR FEET. FOCUS ON THE MUSIC.

Pancakes

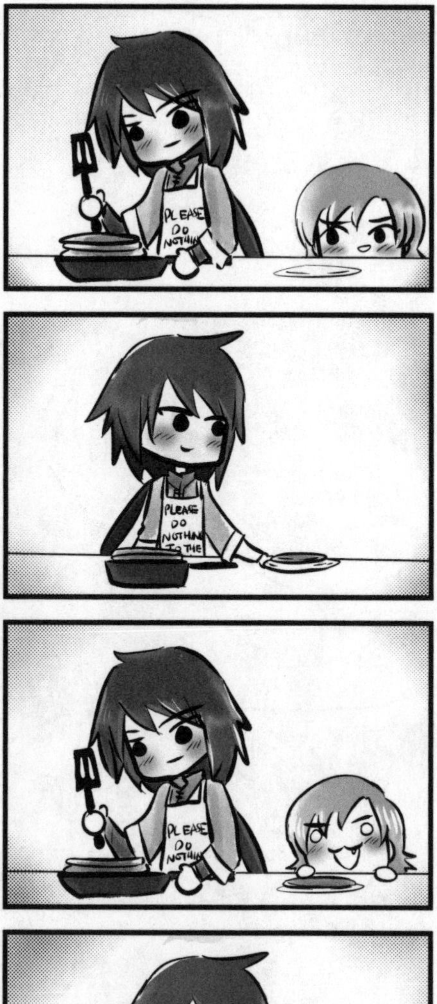
HUH?

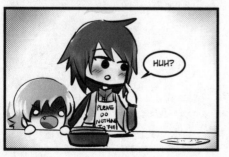

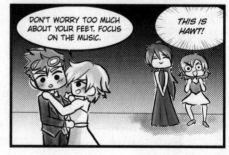

Dishes

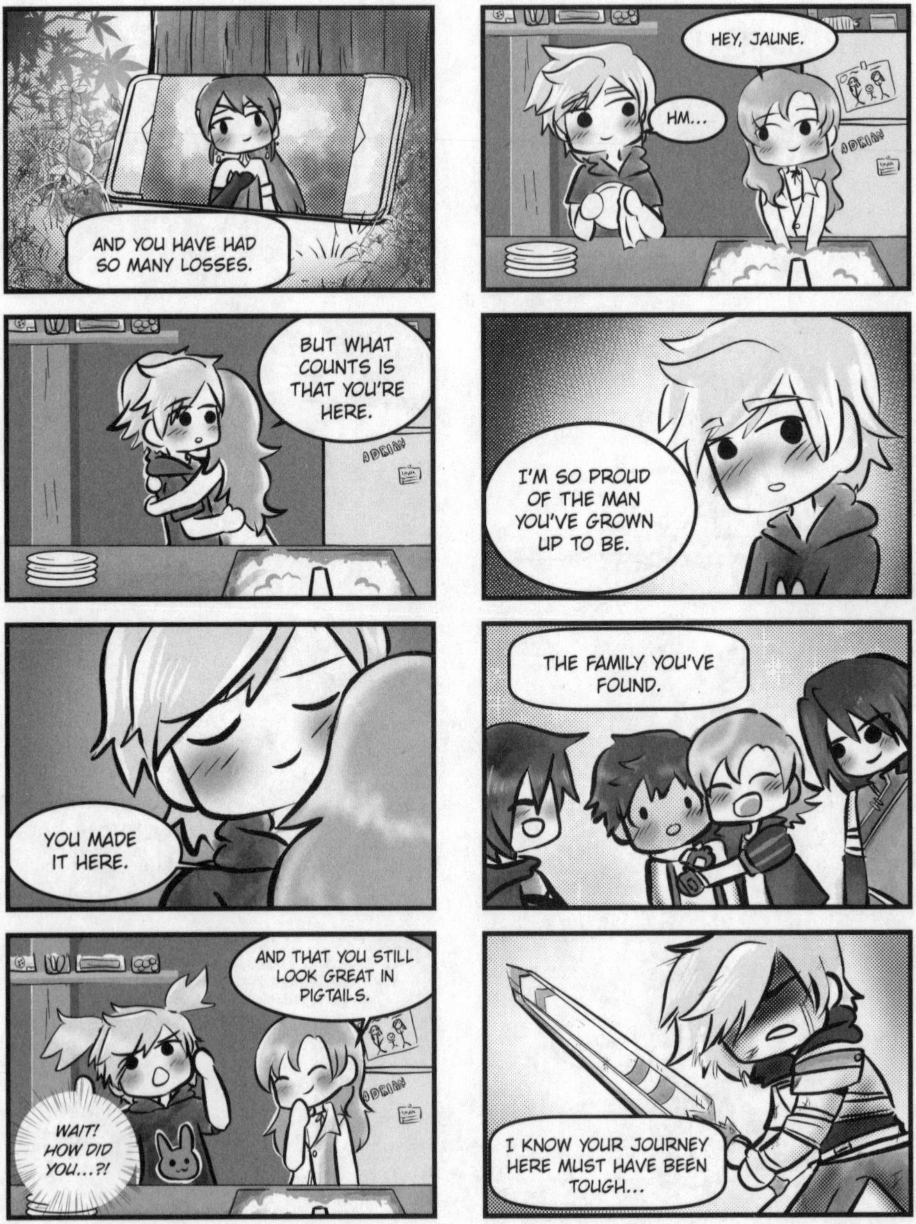
HEY, JAUNE.
HM...
I'M SO PROUD OF THE MAN YOU'VE GROWN UP TO BE.
THE FAMILY YOU'VE FOUND.
I KNOW YOUR JOURNEY HERE MUST HAVE BEEN TOUGH...
AND YOU HAVE HAD SO MANY LOSSES.
BUT WHAT COUNTS IS THAT YOU'RE HERE.
YOU MADE IT HERE.
AND THAT YOU STILL LOOK GREAT IN PIGTAILS.
WAIT! HOW DID YOU...?!

Pose

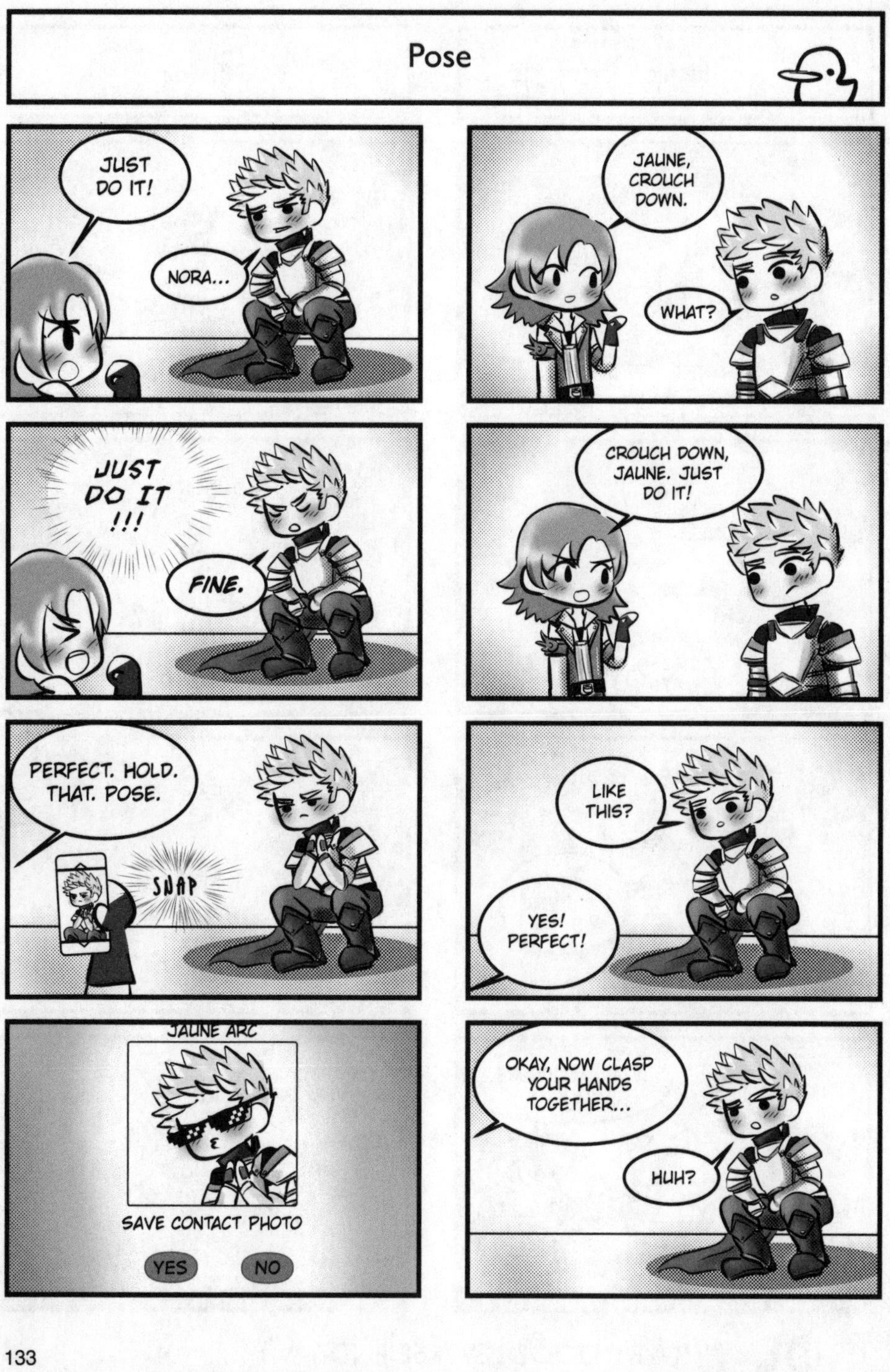
JAUNE, CROUCH DOWN.
WHAT?
CROUCH DOWN, JAUNE. JUST DO IT!
LIKE THIS?
YES! PERFECT!
OKAY, NOW CLASP YOUR HANDS TOGETHER...
HUH?
JUST DO IT!
NORA...
JUST DO IT !!!
FINE.
PERFECT. HOLD. THAT. POSE.
SNAP
JAUNE ARC
SAVE CONTACT PHOTO
YES
NO

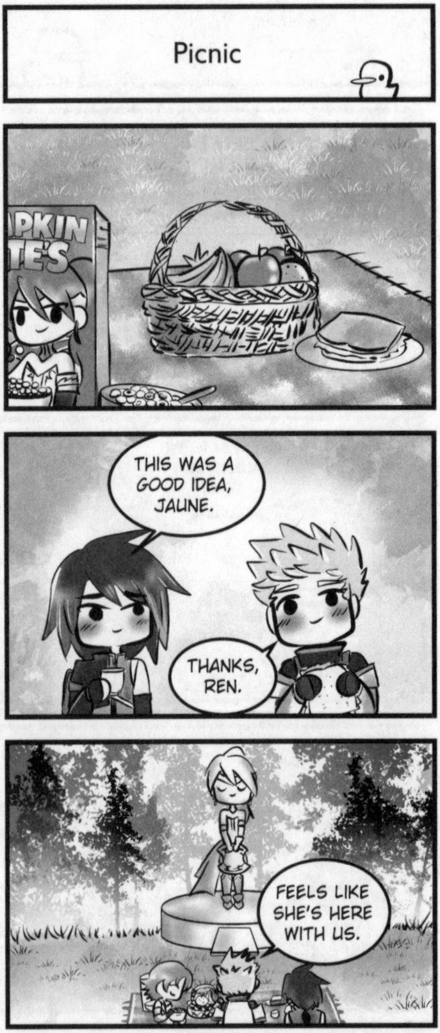
Picnic
THIS WAS A GOOD IDEA, JAUNE.
THANKS, REN.
FEELS LIKE SHE'S HERE WITH US.
NORA!
YEAH...AND SHE'S DELICIOUS.

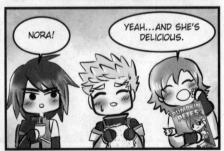

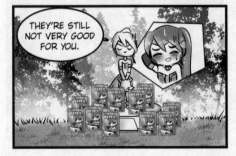

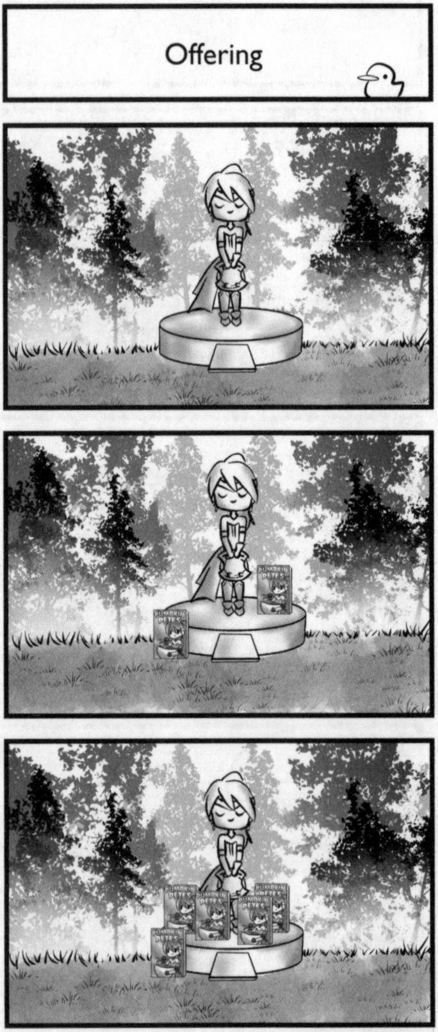
Offering
THEY'RE STILL NOT VERY GOOD FOR YOU.

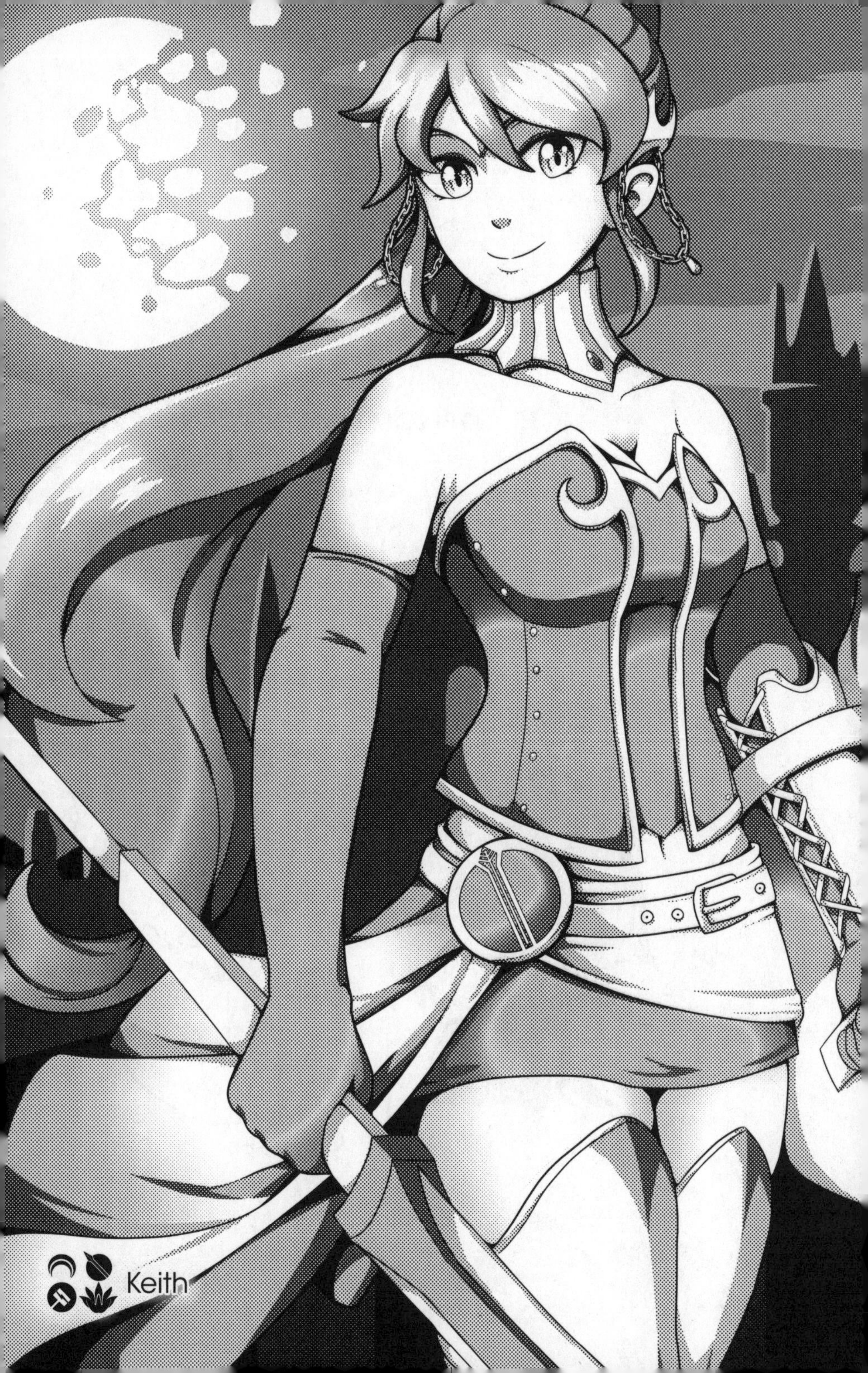
Keith

RWBY

OFFICIAL MANGA ANTHOLOGY

Volume 5

Shine

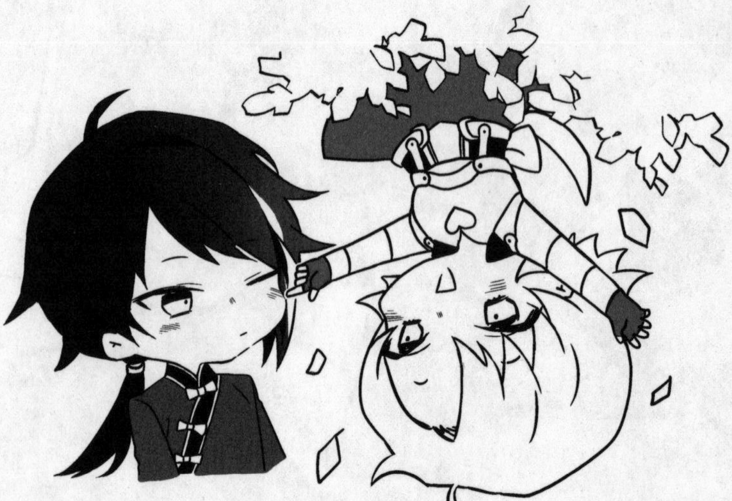

Ecru

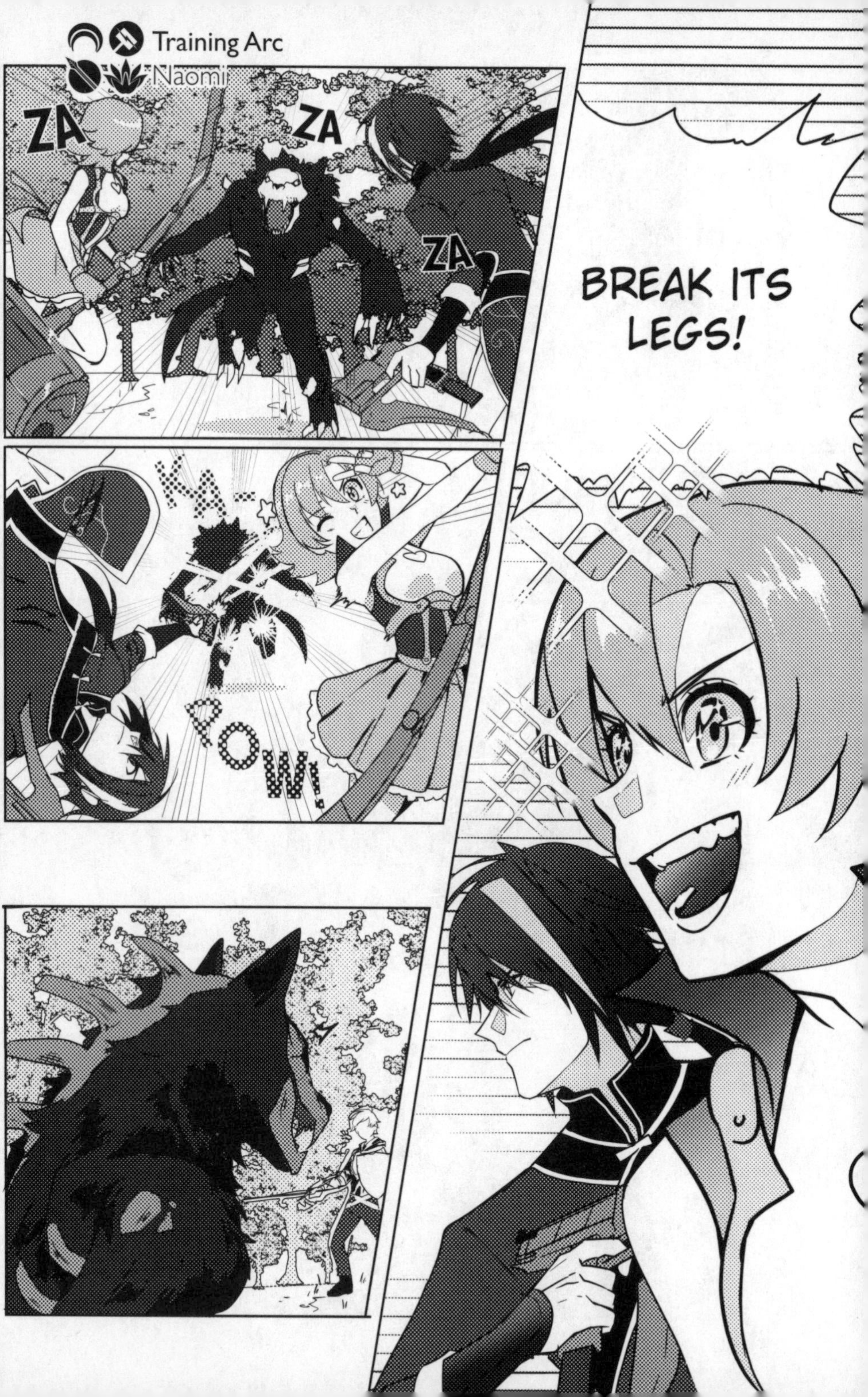
BREAK ITS LEGS!
ZA
ZA
ZA
KA-
POW!

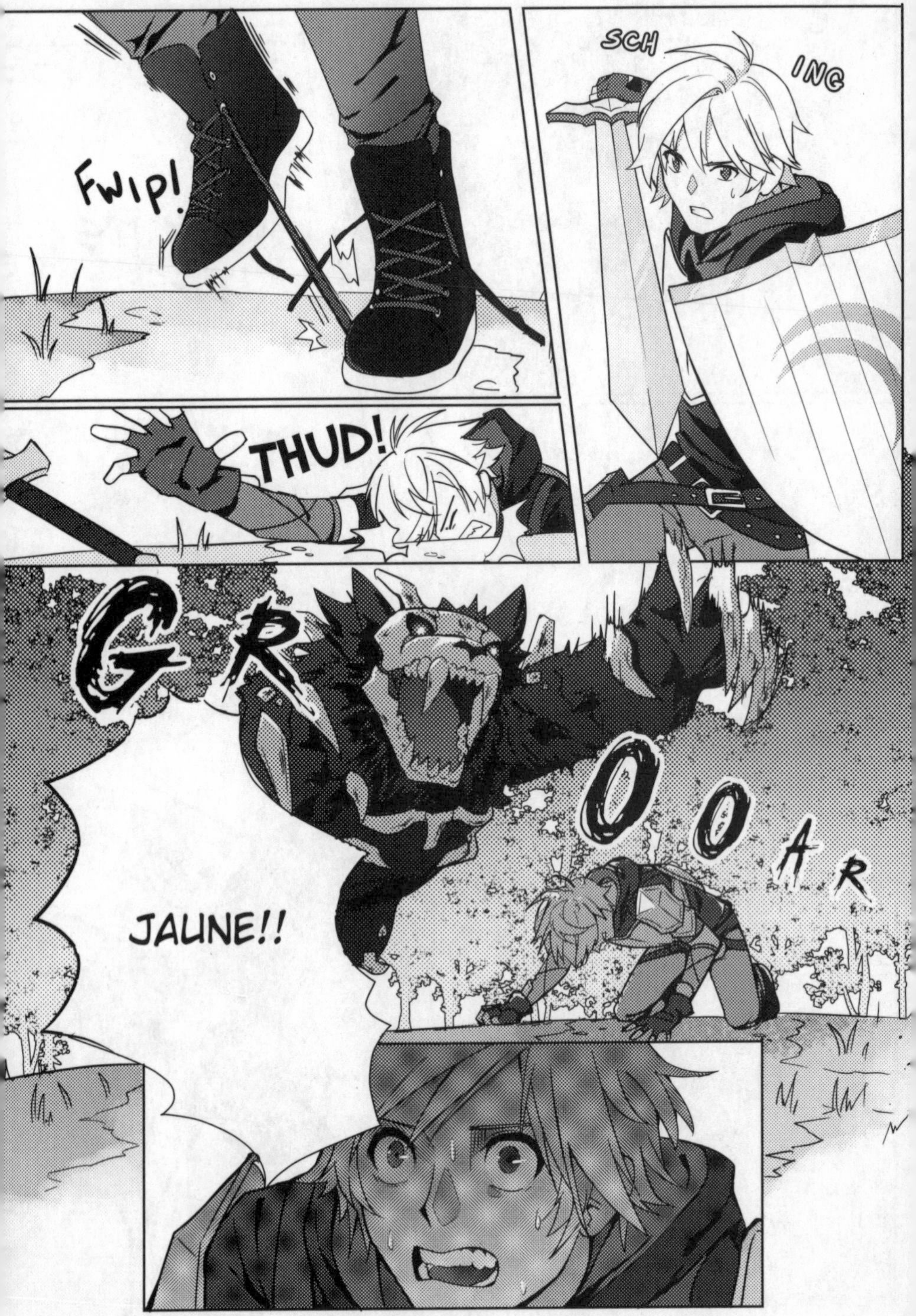
SCH
ING
FWIP!
THUD!
GROOOAR
JAUNE!!

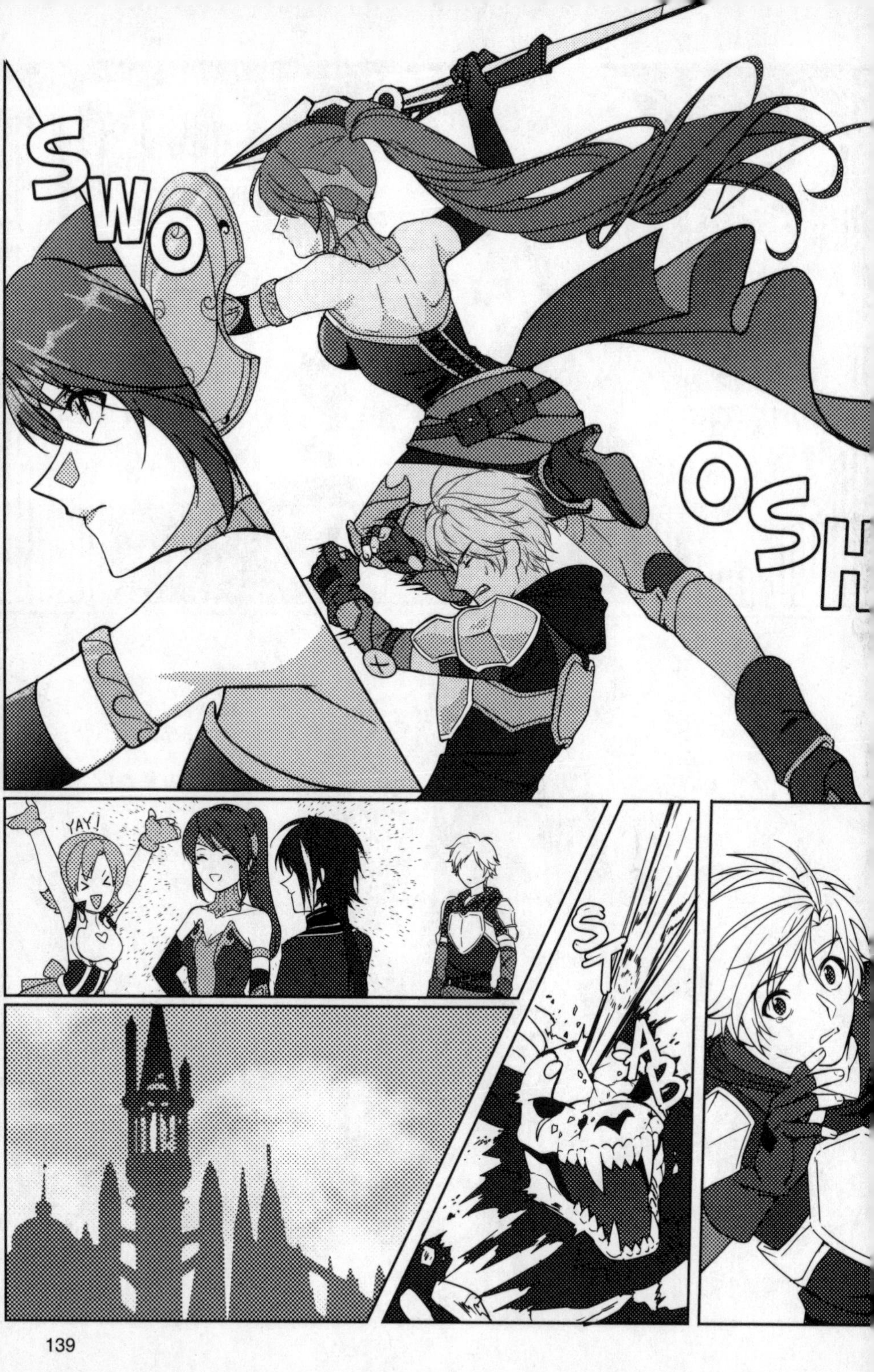
SWO
OSH
YAY!
ST
AB

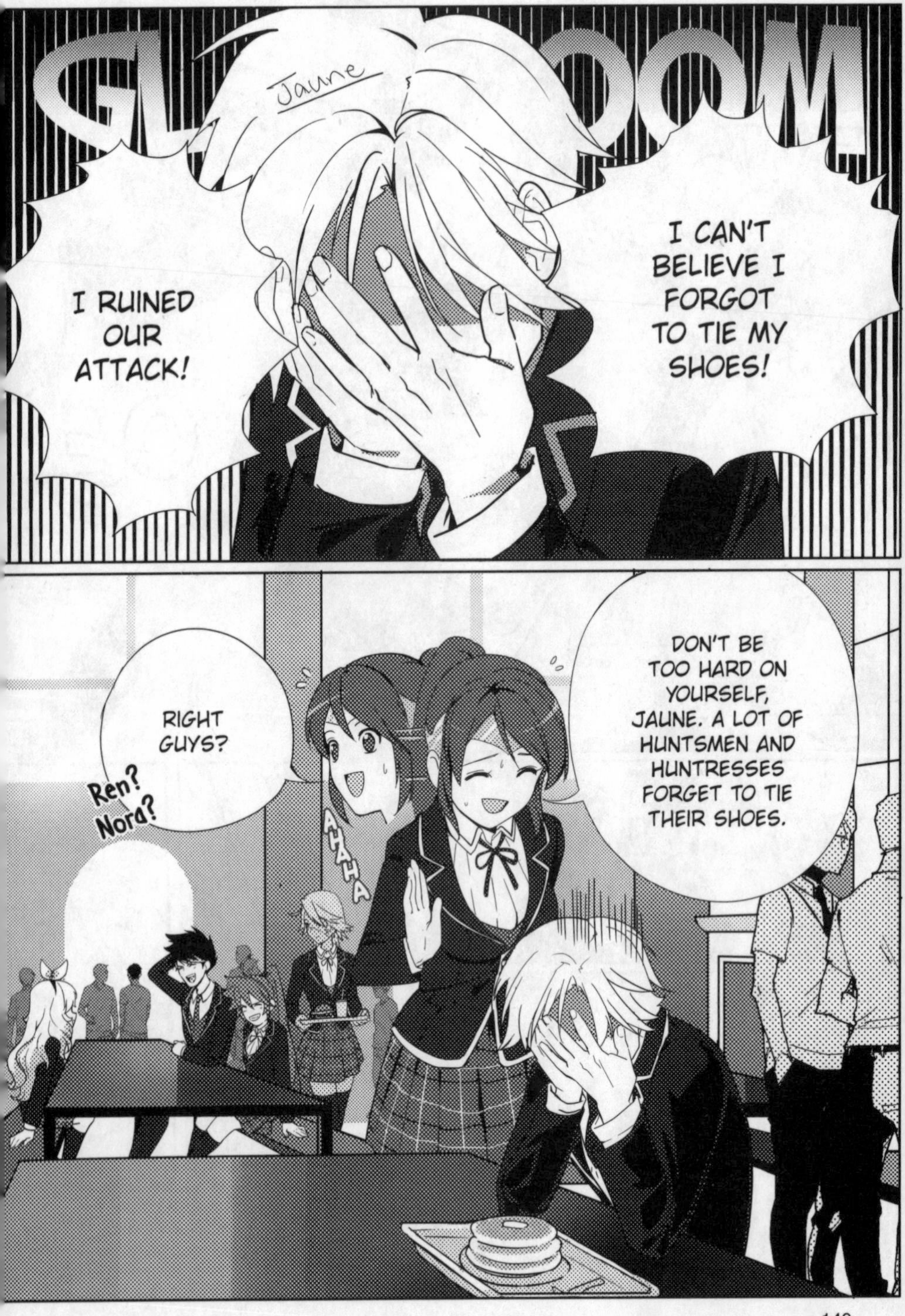
GL
OOM
Jaune
I RUINED OUR ATTACK!
I CAN'T BELIEVE I FORGOT TO TIE MY SHOES!
DON'T BE TOO HARD ON YOURSELF, JAUNE. A LOT OF HUNTSMEN AND HUNTRESSES FORGET TO TIE THEIR SHOES.
RIGHT GUYS?
Ren? Nora?
AHAHA

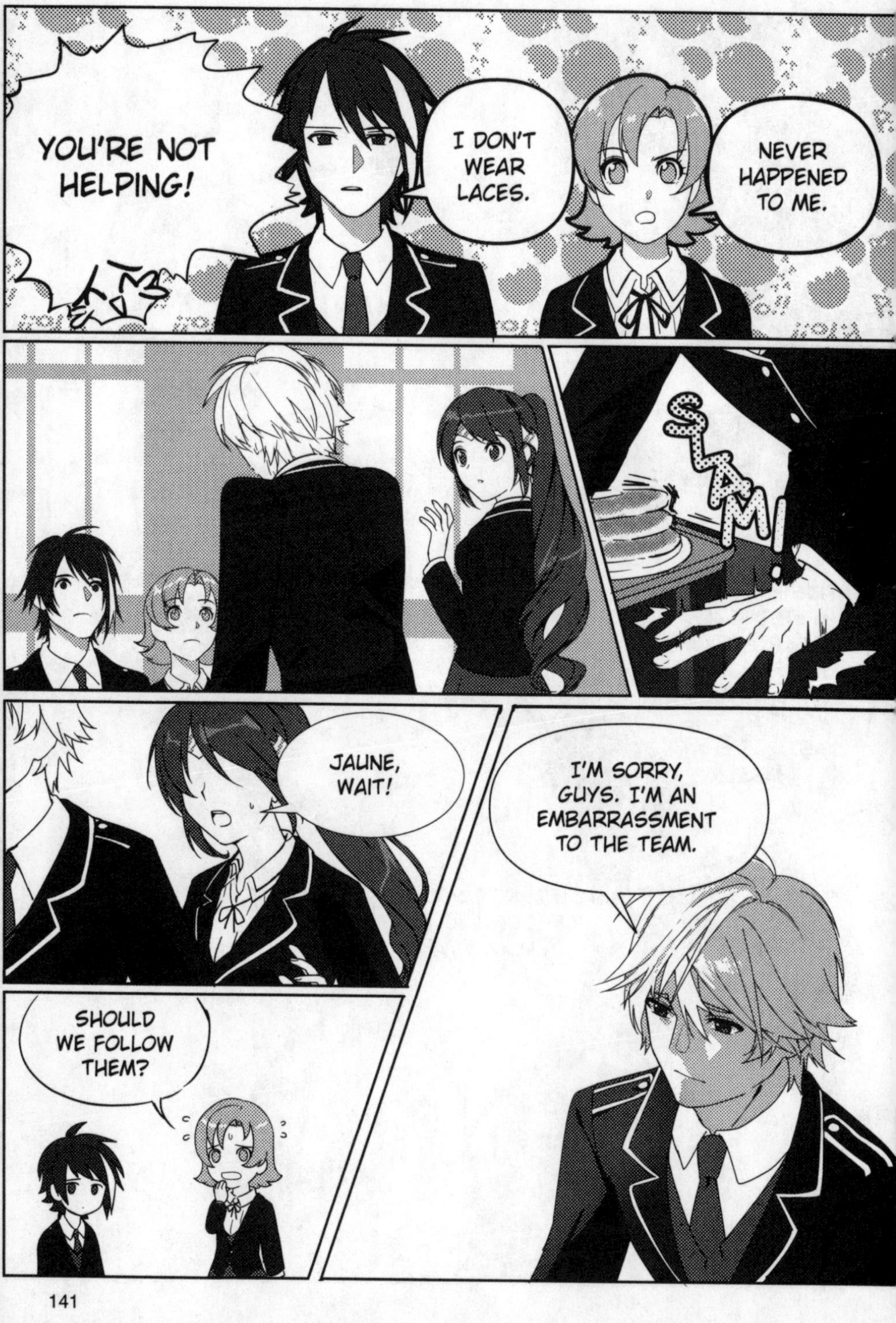
NEVER HAPPENED TO ME.
I DON'T WEAR LACES.
YOU'RE NOT HELPING!
SLAM!
I'M SORRY, GUYS. I'M AN EMBARRASSMENT TO THE TEAM.
JAUNE, WAIT!
SHOULD WE FOLLOW THEM?

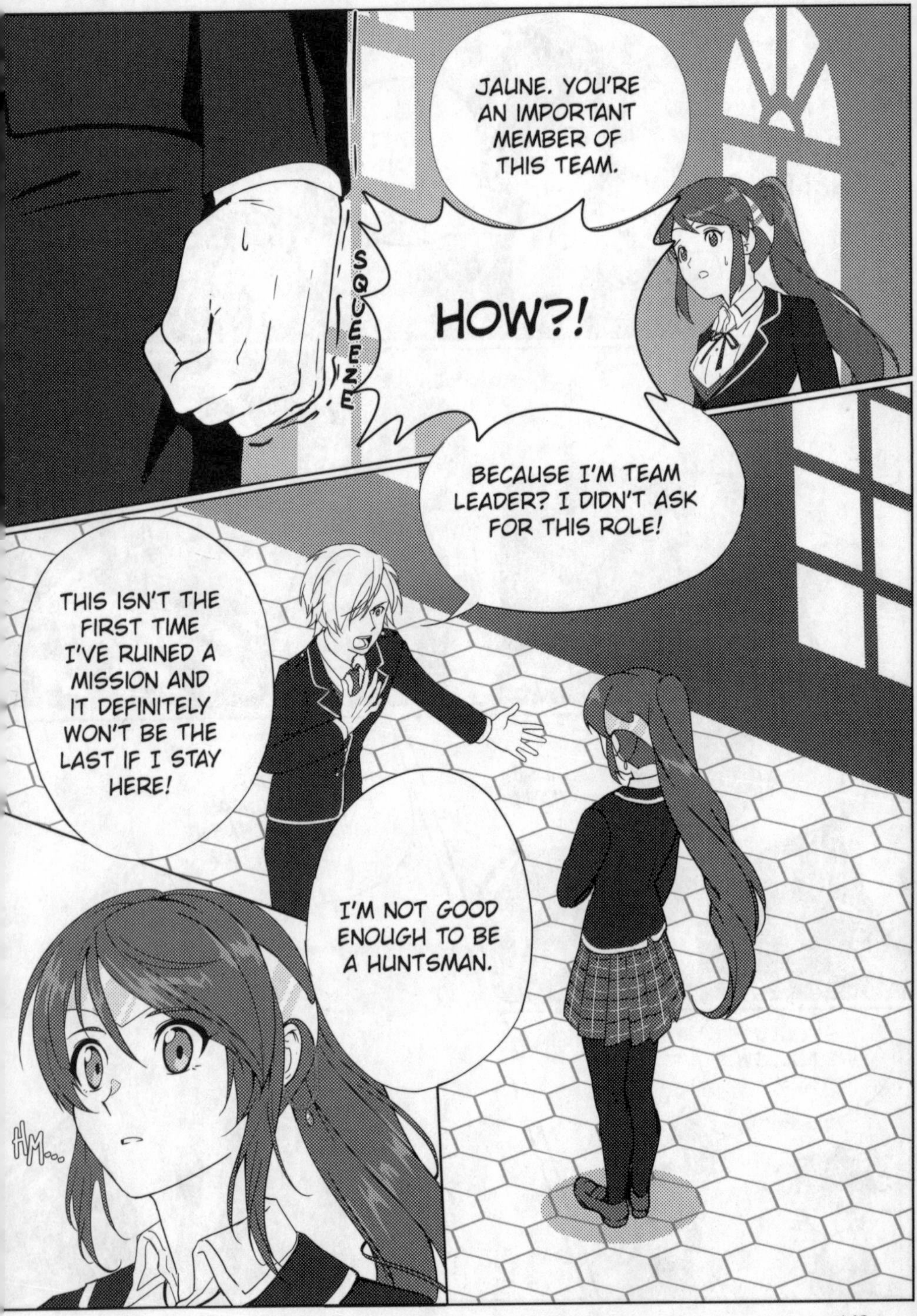
JAUNE. YOU'RE AN IMPORTANT MEMBER OF THIS TEAM.
SQUEEZE
HOW?!
BECAUSE I'M TEAM LEADER? I DIDN'T ASK FOR THIS ROLE!
THIS ISN'T THE FIRST TIME I'VE RUINED A MISSION AND IT DEFINITELY WON'T BE THE LAST IF I STAY HERE!
I'M NOT GOOD ENOUGH TO BE A HUNTSMAN.
HM...

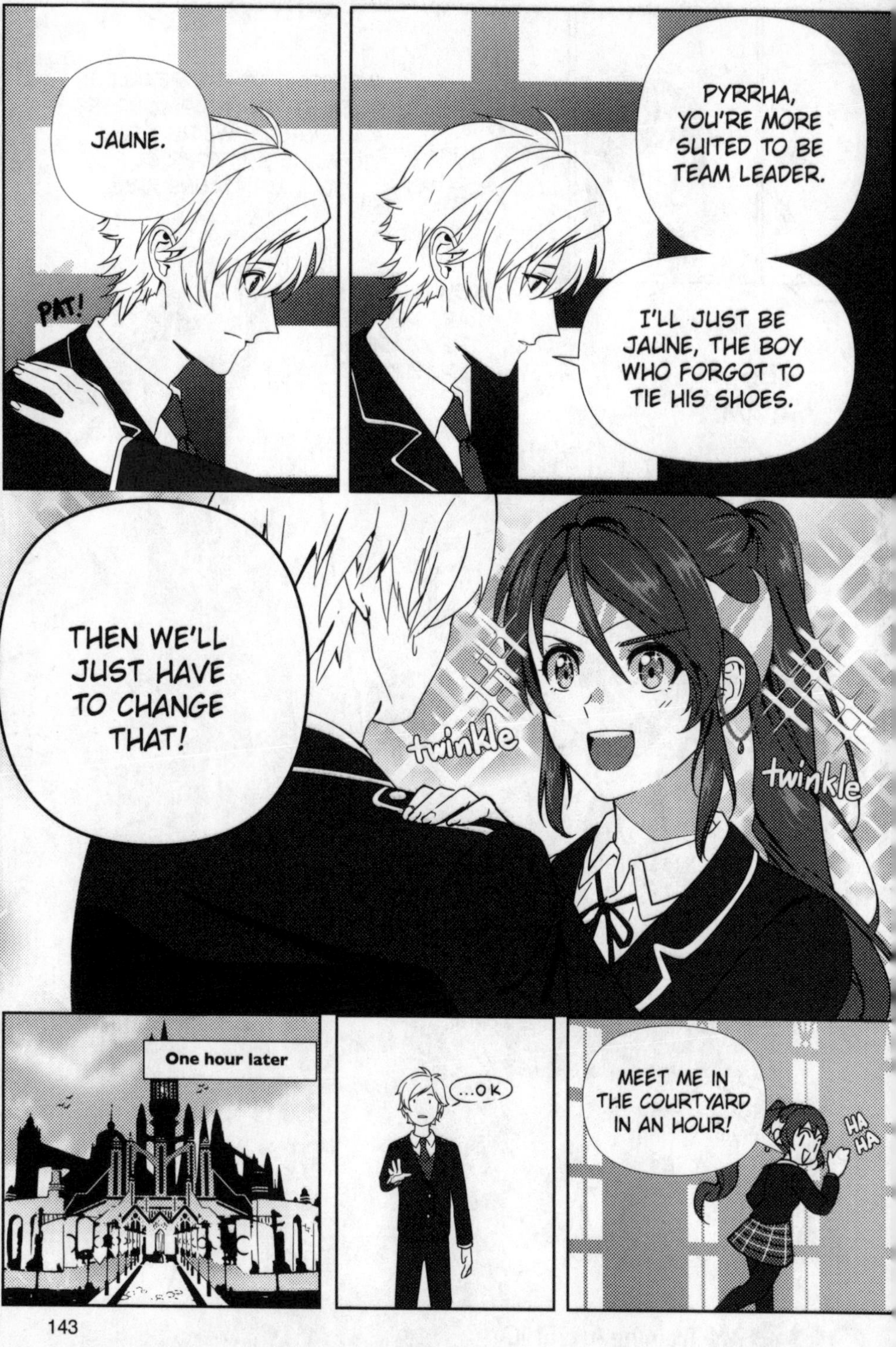
PYRRHA, YOU'RE MORE SUITED TO BE TEAM LEADER.
I'LL JUST BE JAUNE, THE BOY WHO FORGOT TO TIE HIS SHOES.
JAUNE.
PAT!
THEN WE'LL JUST HAVE TO CHANGE THAT!
twinkle
twinkle
MEET ME IN THE COURTYARD IN AN HOUR!
HA HA
...OK
One hour later

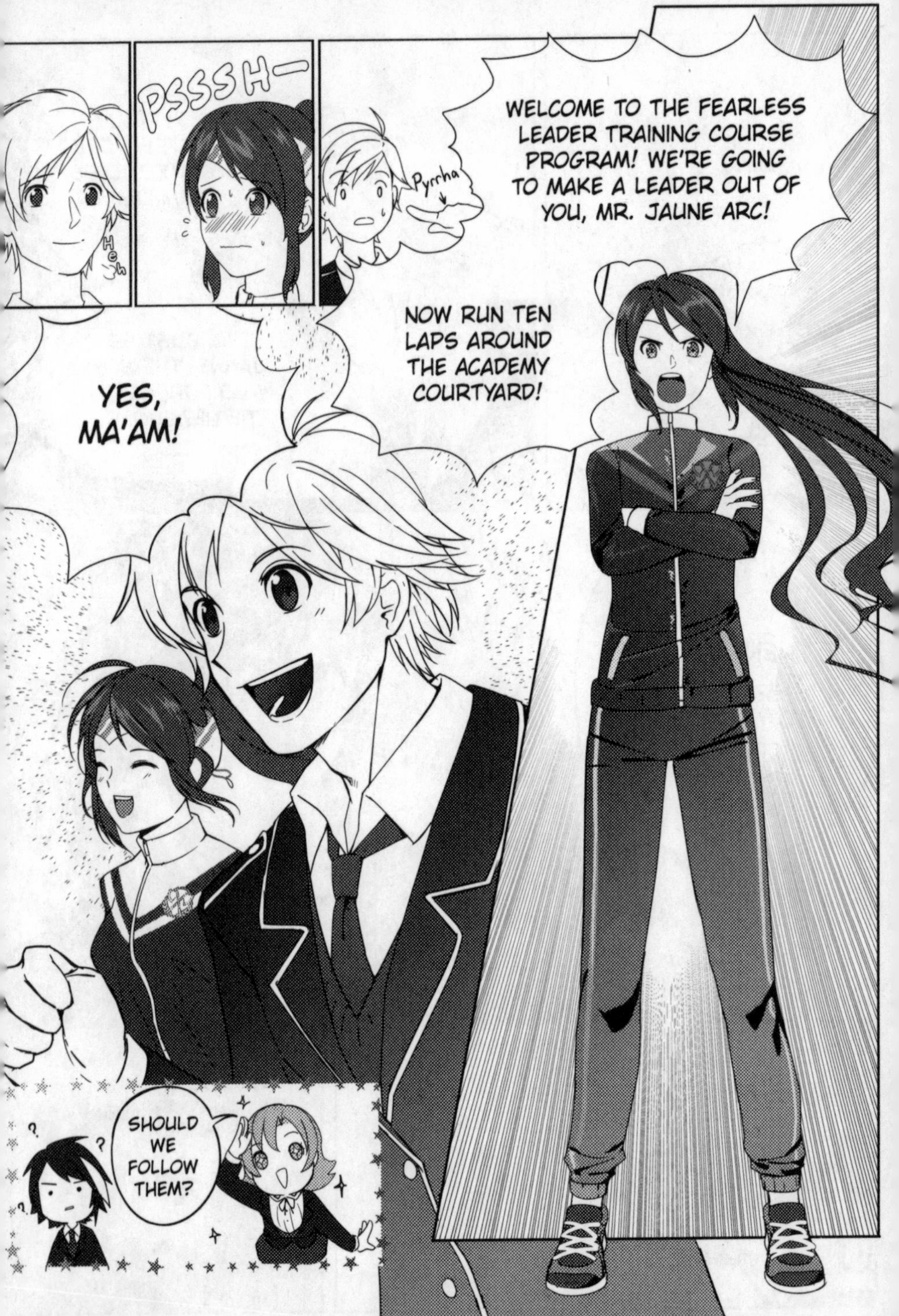
WELCOME TO THE FEARLESS LEADER TRAINING COURSE PROGRAM! WE'RE GOING TO MAKE A LEADER OUT OF YOU, MR. JAUNE ARC!
NOW RUN TEN LAPS AROUND THE ACADEMY COURTYARD!
Pyrrha
PSSSH—
Heh
YES, MA'AM!
SHOULD WE FOLLOW THEM?

Training Arc/END

Cereal Experiments Jaune

monorobu

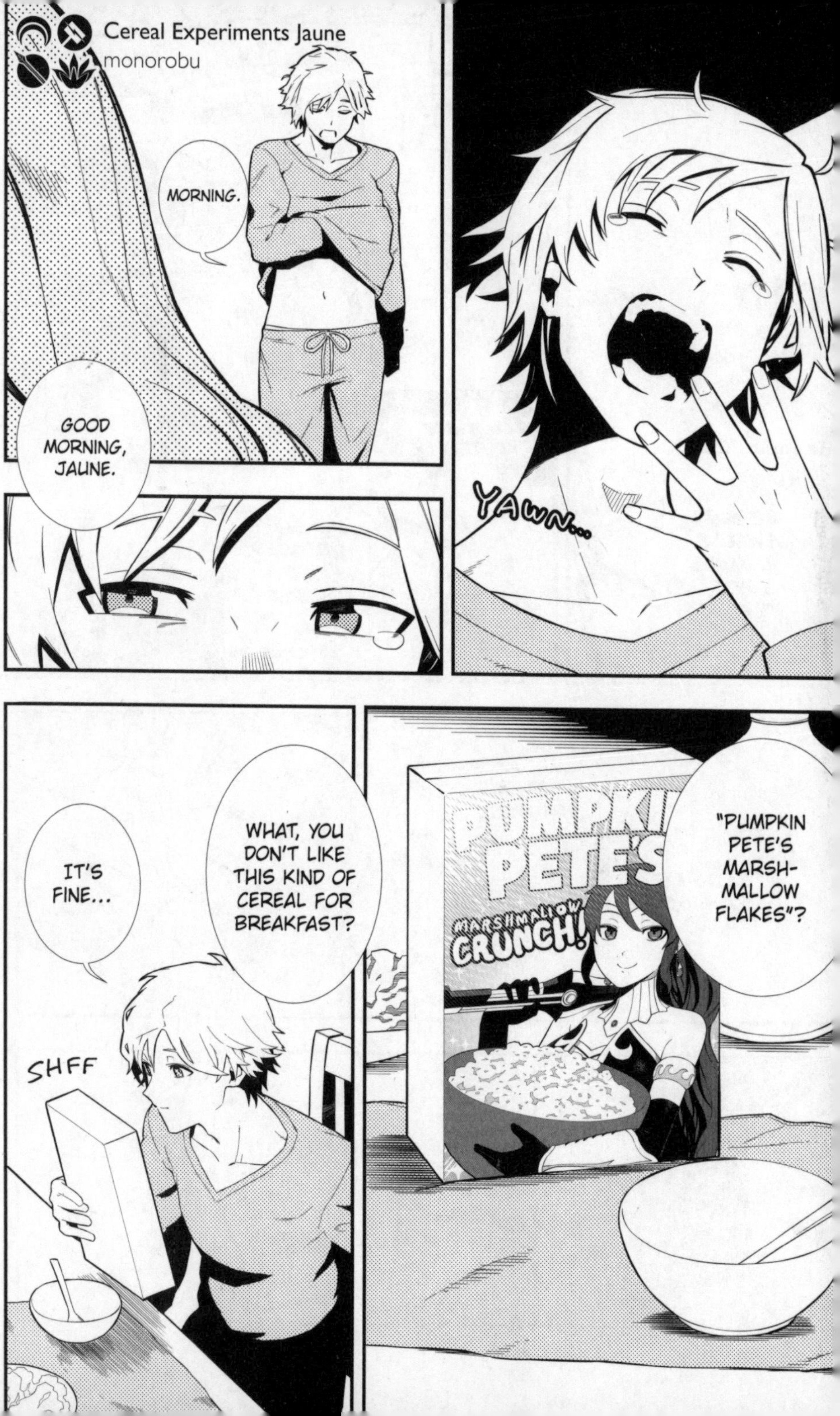
YAWN...
MORNING.
GOOD MORNING, JAUNE.
PUMPKIN PETE'S
MARSHMALLOW CRUNCH!
"PUMPKIN PETE'S MARSHMALLOW FLAKES"?
WHAT, YOU DON'T LIKE THIS KIND OF CEREAL FOR BREAKFAST?
IT'S FINE...
SHFF

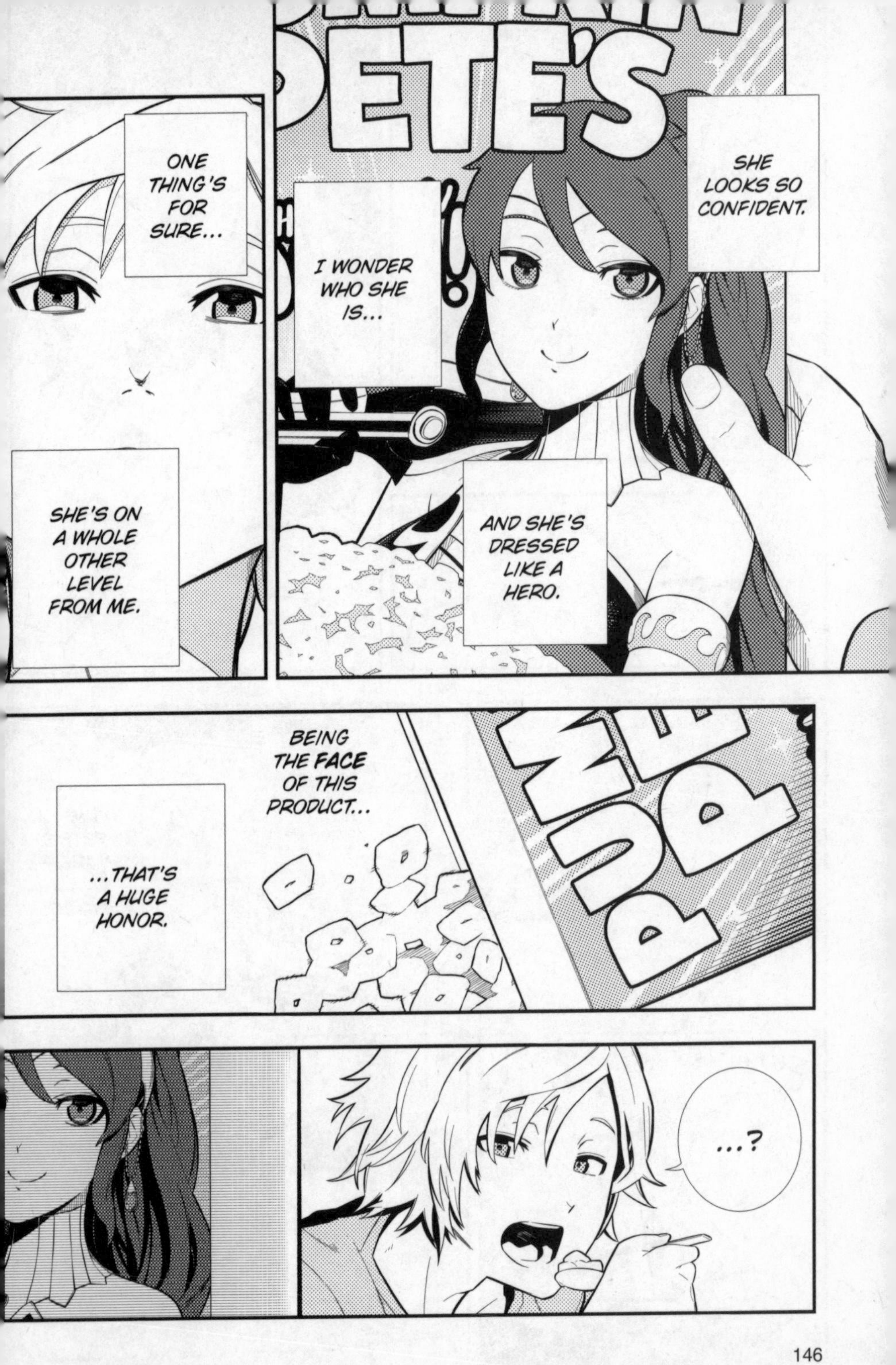
PETE'S
SHE LOOKS SO CONFIDENT.
I WONDER WHO SHE IS...
AND SHE'S DRESSED LIKE A HERO.
ONE THING'S FOR SURE...
SHE'S ON A WHOLE OTHER LEVEL FROM ME.
BEING THE FACE OF THIS PRODUCT...
...THAT'S A HUGE HONOR.
...?

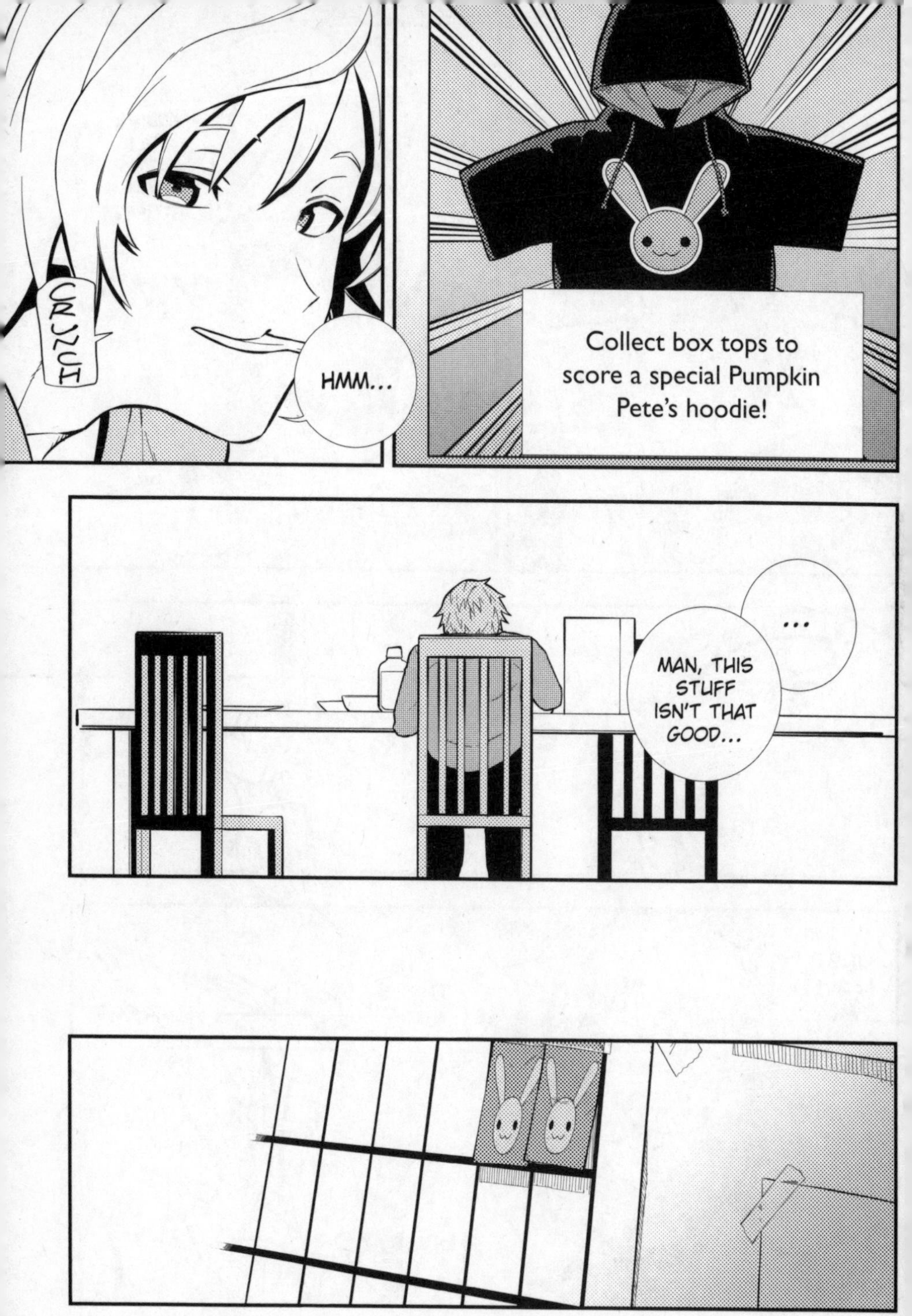
Collect box tops to score a special Pumpkin Pete's hoodie!
HMM...
CRUNCH
...
MAN, THIS STUFF ISN'T THAT GOOD...

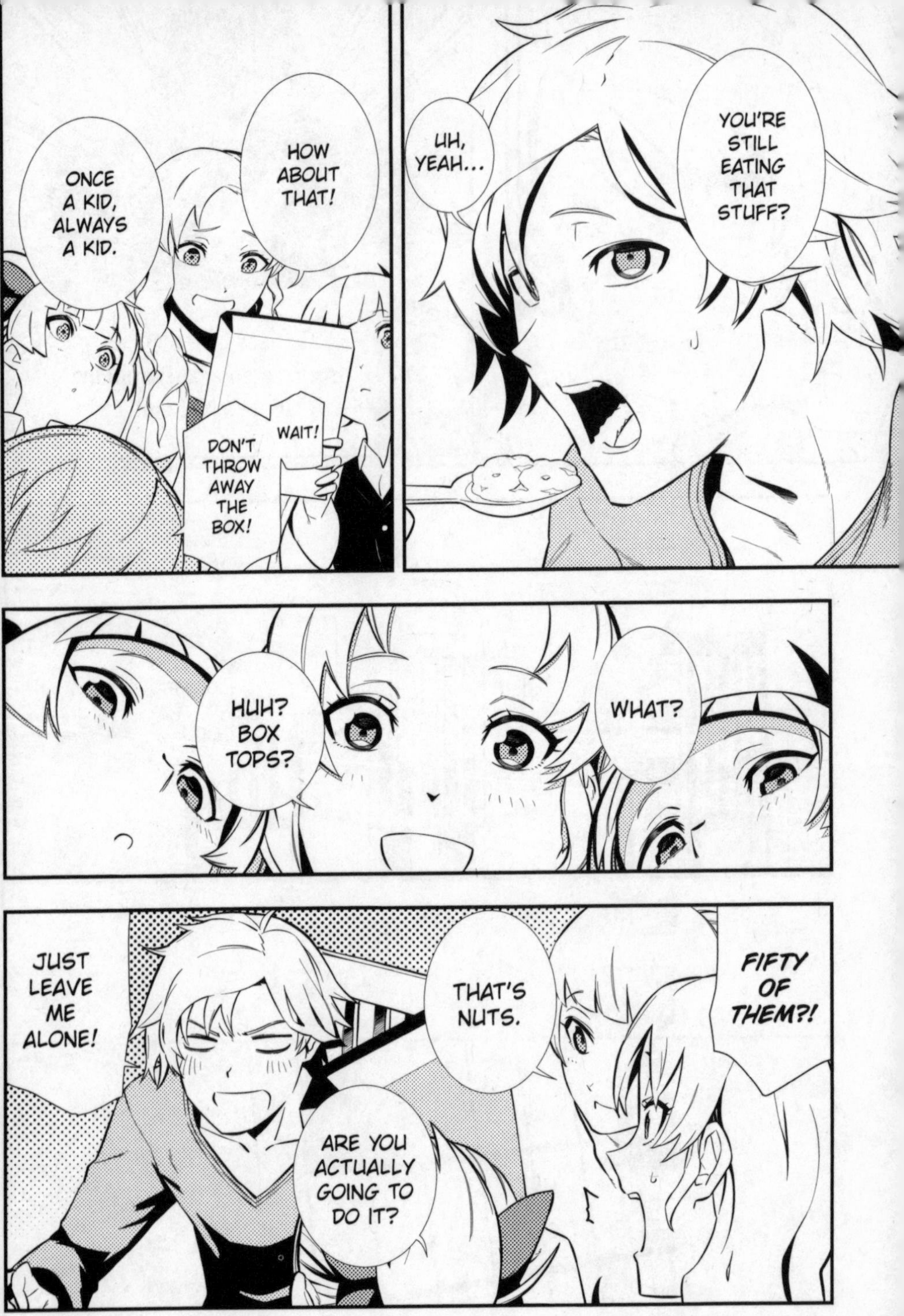
YOU'RE STILL EATING THAT STUFF?
UH, YEAH...
HOW ABOUT THAT!
ONCE A KID, ALWAYS A KID.
WAIT! DON'T THROW AWAY THE BOX!
WHAT?
HUH? BOX TOPS?
FIFTY OF THEM?!
THAT'S NUTS.
ARE YOU ACTUALLY GOING TO DO IT?
JUST LEAVE ME ALONE!

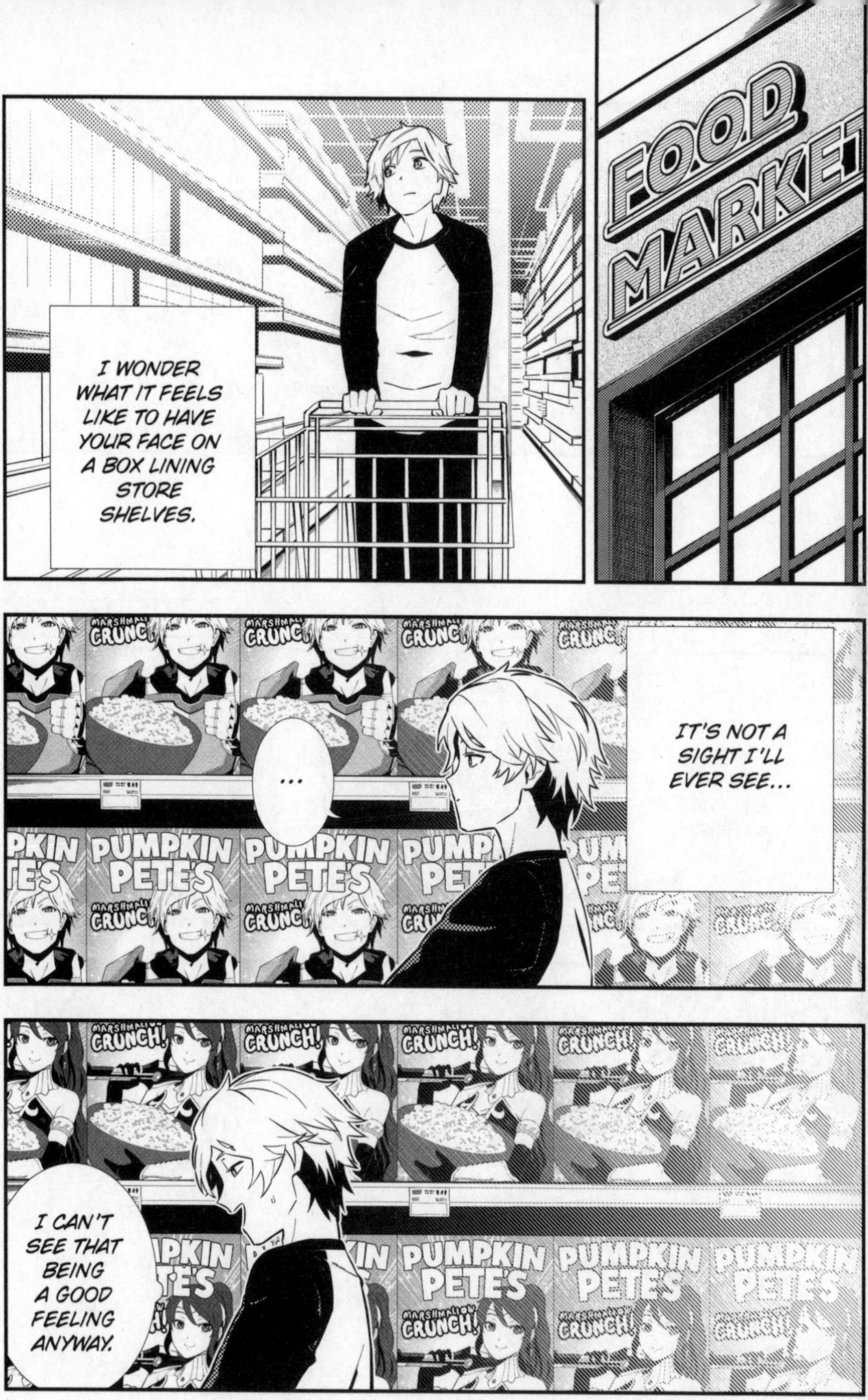
FOOD
MARKE
I WONDER WHAT IT FEELS LIKE TO HAVE YOUR FACE ON A BOX LINING STORE SHELVES.
IT'S NOT A SIGHT I'LL EVER SEE...
...
PUMPKIN PETE'S
MARSHMALLOW CRUNCH!
I CAN'T SEE THAT BEING A GOOD FEELING ANYWAY.

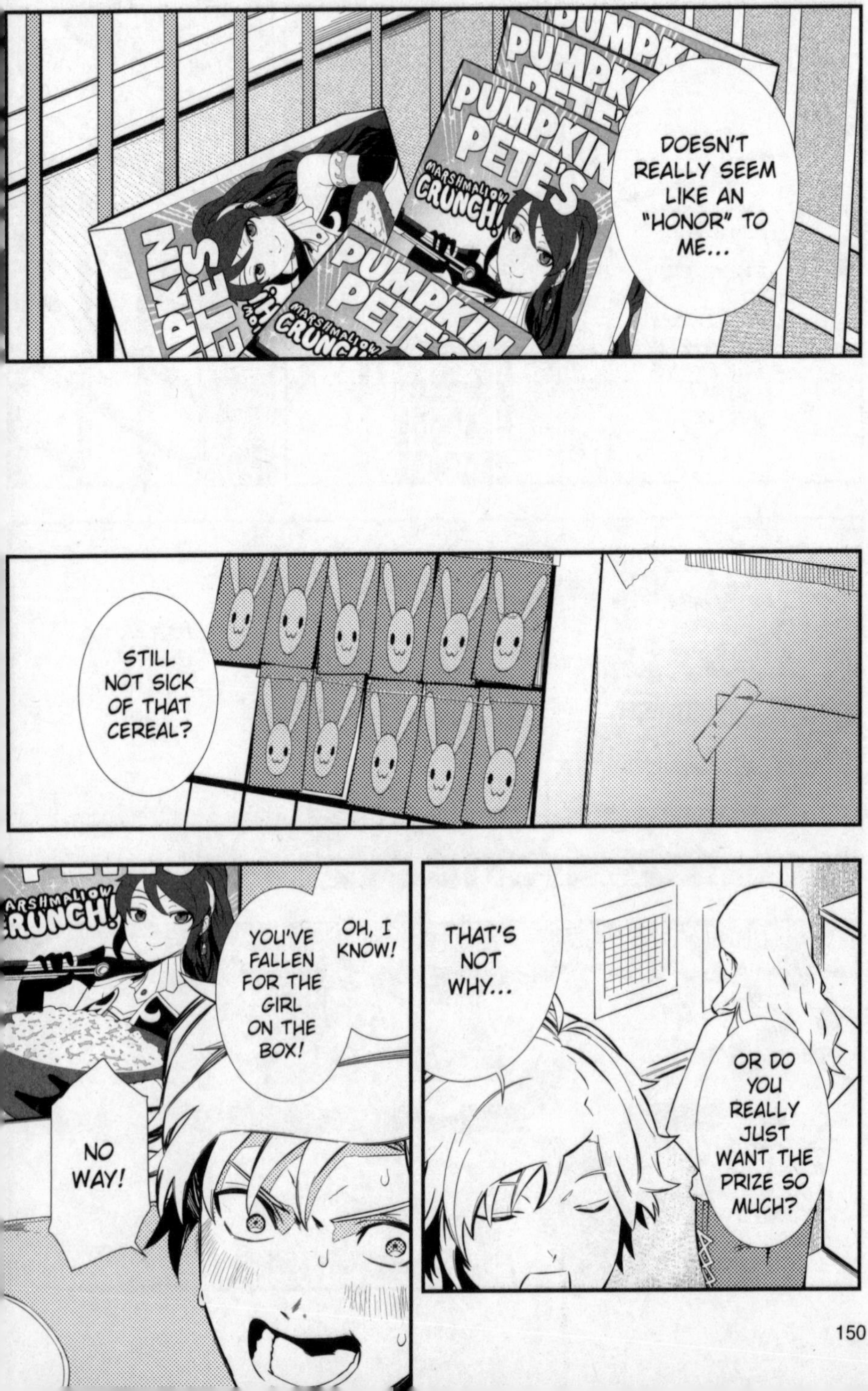
PUMPKIN PETE'S
MARSHMALLOW CRUNCH!
DOESN'T REALLY SEEM LIKE AN "HONOR" TO ME...
STILL NOT SICK OF THAT CEREAL?
THAT'S NOT WHY...
OR DO YOU REALLY JUST WANT THE PRIZE SO MUCH?
MARSHMALLOW CRUNCH!
OH, I KNOW!
YOU'VE FALLEN FOR THE GIRL ON THE BOX!
NO WAY!

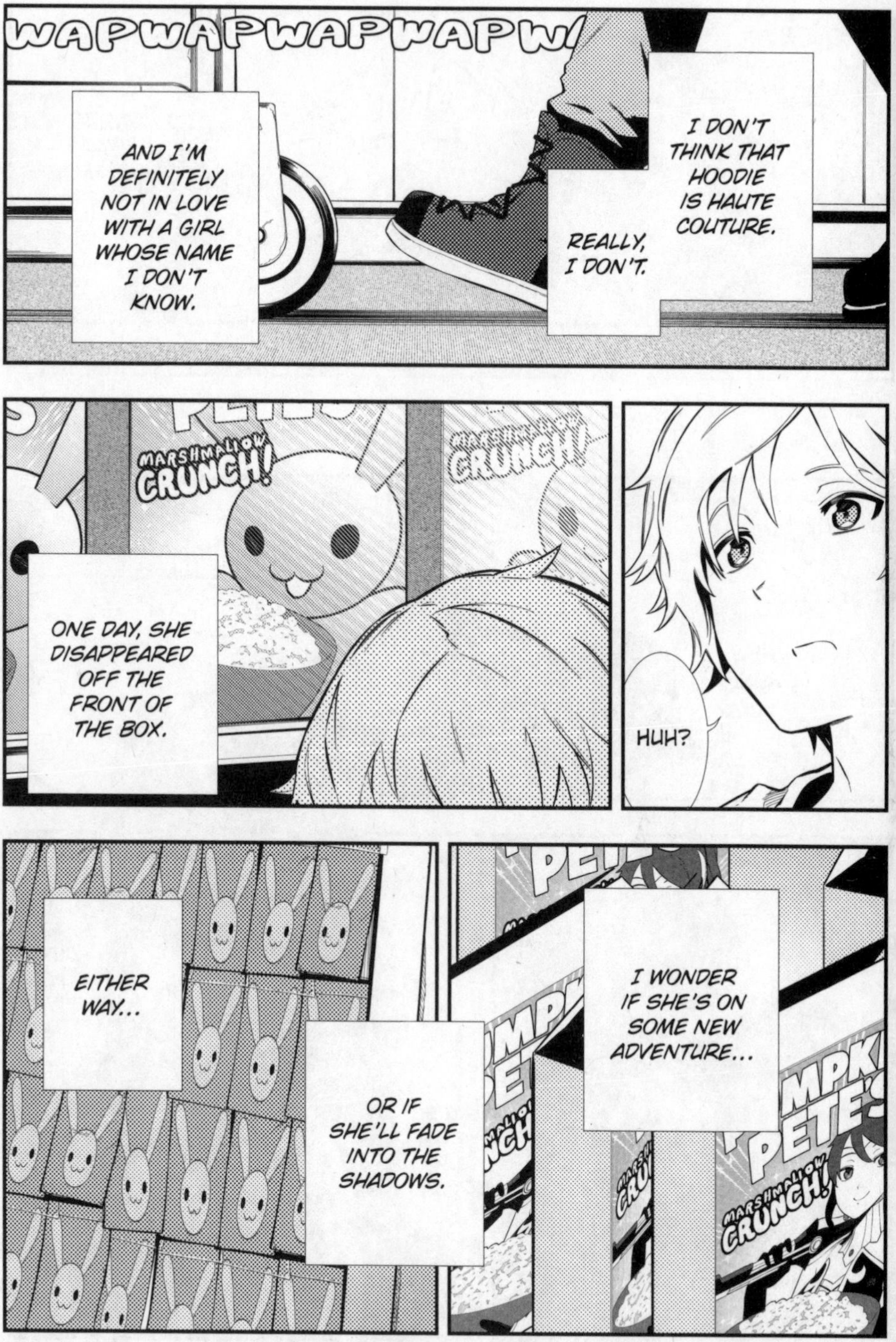
WAPWAPWAPWAPWA
I DON'T THINK THAT HOODIE IS HAUTE COUTURE.
REALLY, I DON'T.
AND I'M DEFINITELY NOT IN LOVE WITH A GIRL WHOSE NAME I DON'T KNOW.
HUH?
MARSHMALLOW CRUNCH!
ONE DAY, SHE DISAPPEARED OFF THE FRONT OF THE BOX.
I WONDER IF SHE'S ON SOME NEW ADVENTURE...
OR IF SHE'LL FADE INTO THE SHADOWS.
PETE'S
MARSHMALLOW CRUNCH!
EITHER WAY...

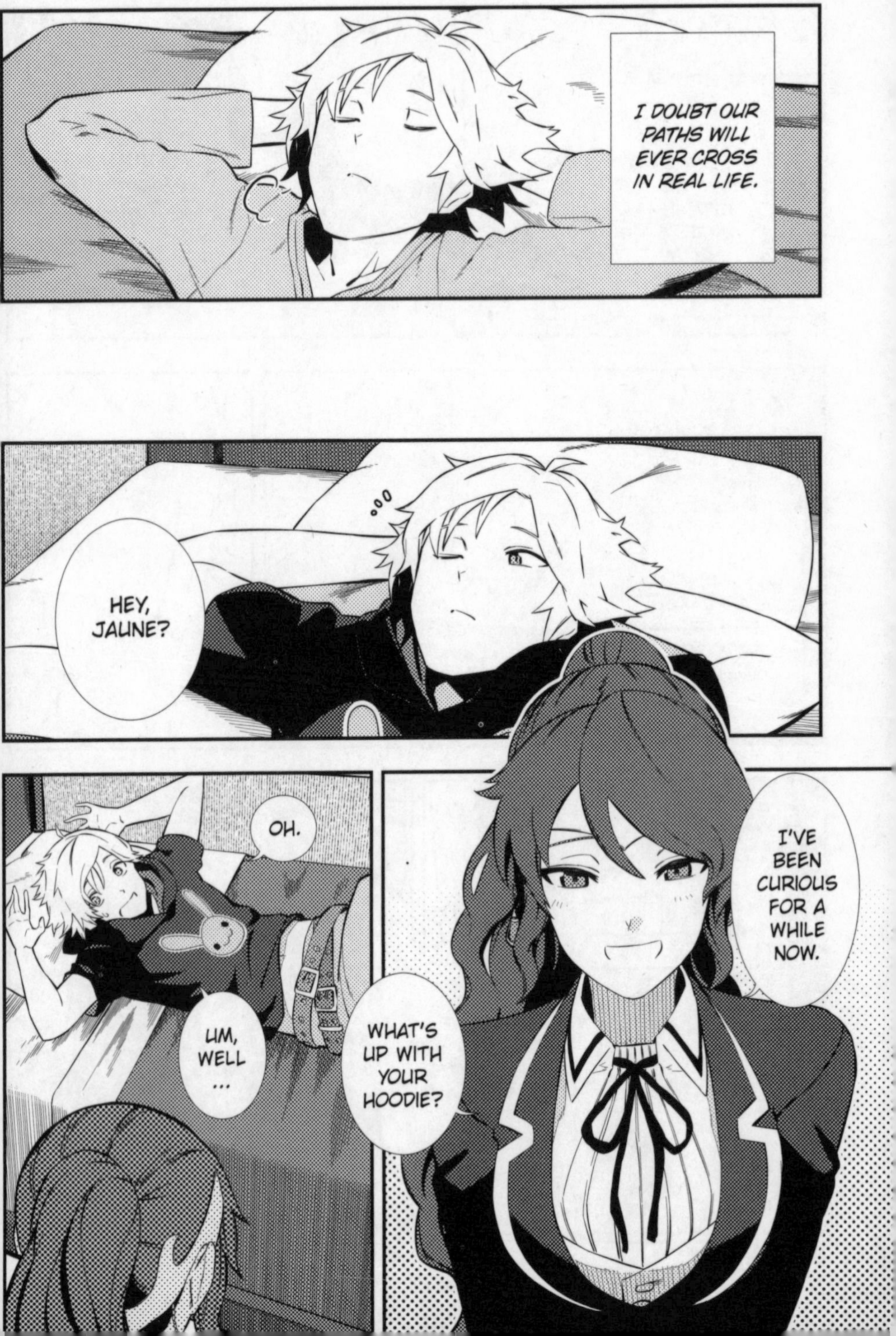
I DOUBT OUR PATHS WILL EVER CROSS IN REAL LIFE.
HEY, JAUNE?
I'VE BEEN CURIOUS FOR A WHILE NOW.
WHAT'S UP WITH YOUR HOODIE?
OH.
UM, WELL ...

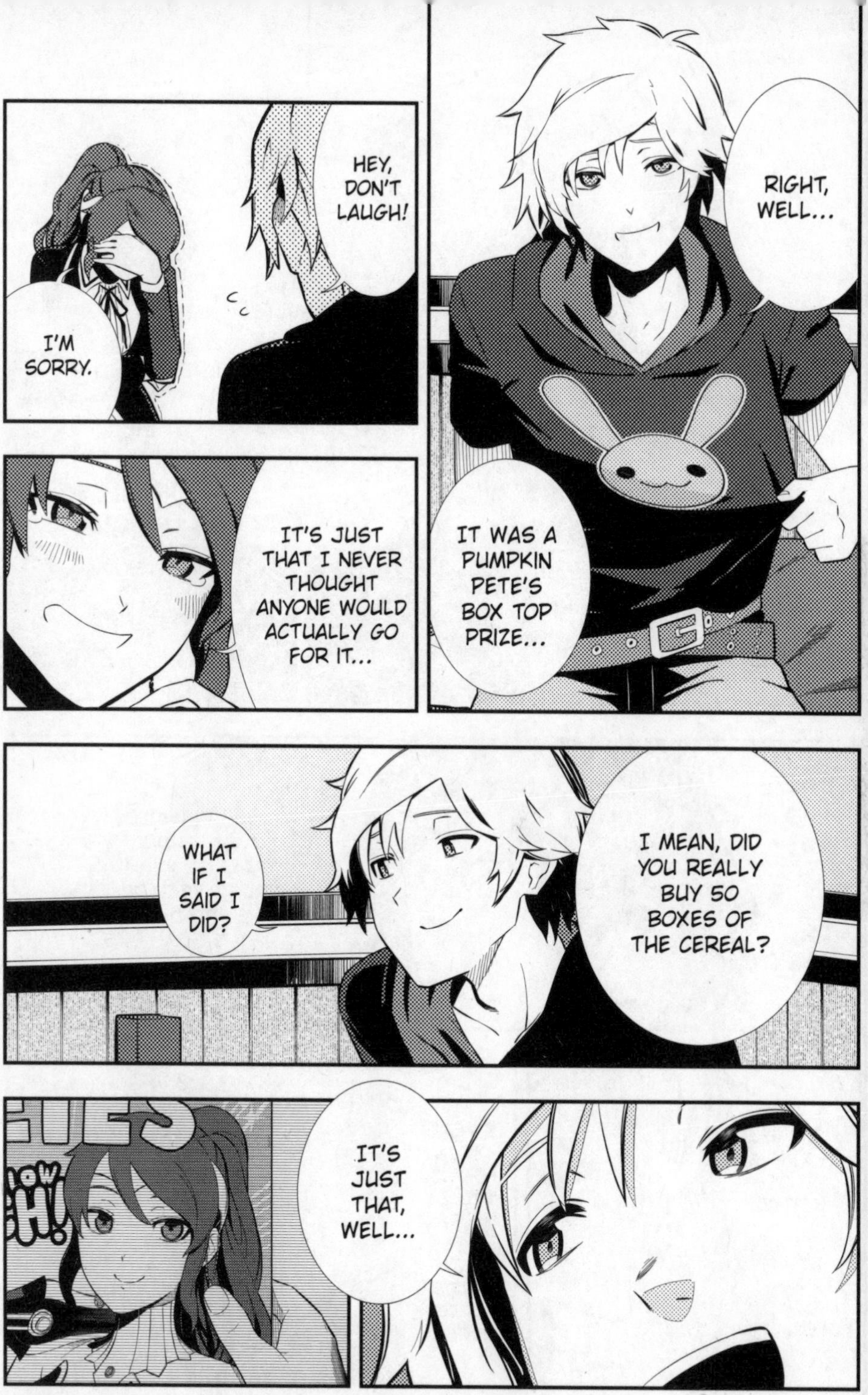
RIGHT, WELL...
IT WAS A PUMPKIN PETE'S BOX TOP PRIZE...
HEY, DON'T LAUGH!
I'M SORRY.
IT'S JUST THAT I NEVER THOUGHT ANYONE WOULD ACTUALLY GO FOR IT...
I MEAN, DID YOU REALLY BUY 50 BOXES OF THE CEREAL?
WHAT IF I SAID I DID?
IT'S JUST THAT, WELL...

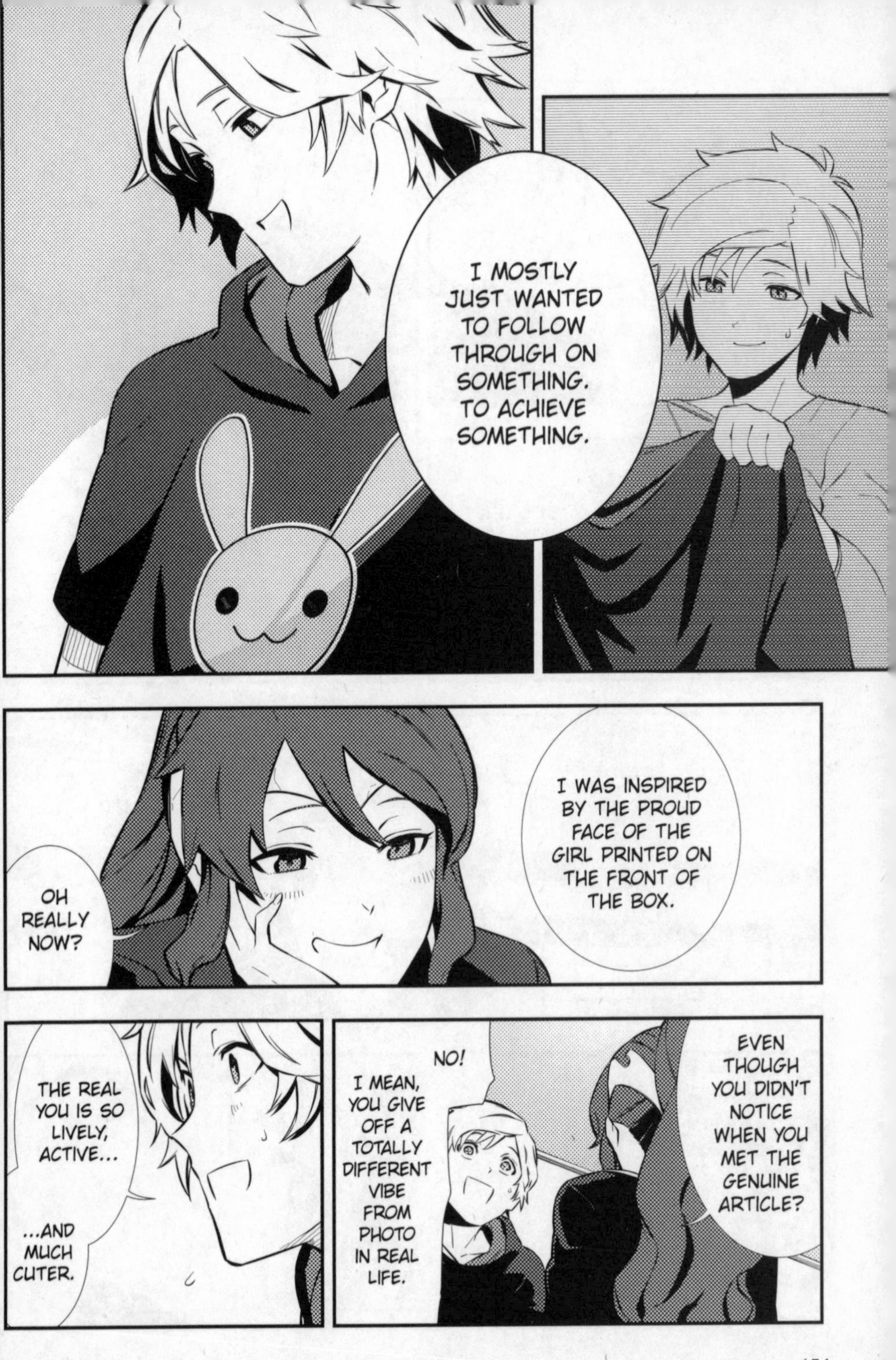
I MOSTLY JUST WANTED TO FOLLOW THROUGH ON SOMETHING. TO ACHIEVE SOMETHING.
I WAS INSPIRED BY THE PROUD FACE OF THE GIRL PRINTED ON THE FRONT OF THE BOX.
OH REALLY NOW?
EVEN THOUGH YOU DIDN'T NOTICE WHEN YOU MET THE GENUINE ARTICLE?
NO!
I MEAN, YOU GIVE OFF A TOTALLY DIFFERENT VIBE FROM PHOTO IN REAL LIFE.
THE REAL YOU IS SO LIVELY, ACTIVE...
...AND MUCH CUTER.

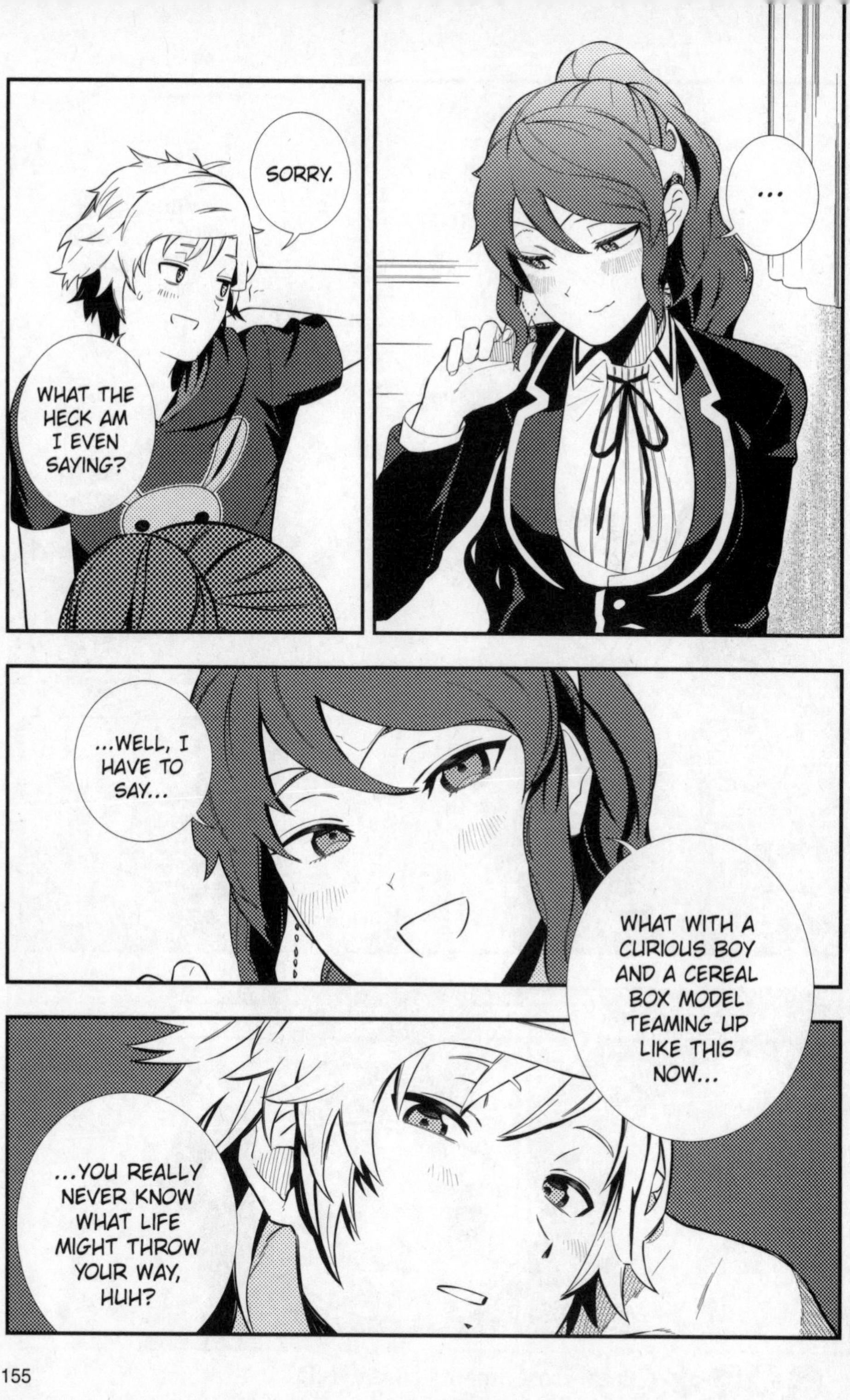
...
SORRY.
WHAT THE HECK AM I EVEN SAYING?
...WELL, I HAVE TO SAY...
WHAT WITH A CURIOUS BOY AND A CEREAL BOX MODEL TEAMING UP LIKE THIS NOW...
...YOU REALLY NEVER KNOW WHAT LIFE MIGHT THROW YOUR WAY, HUH?

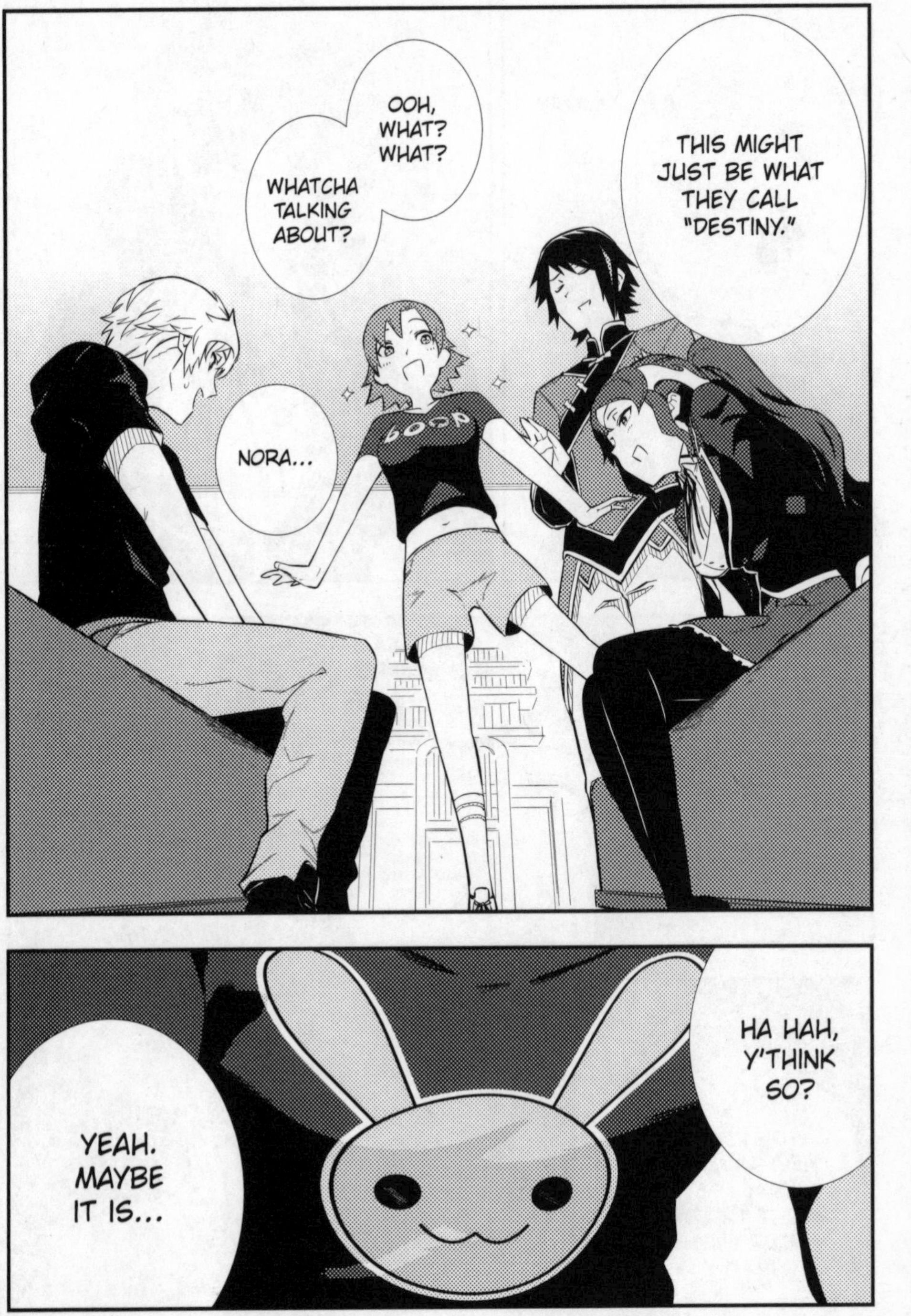
THIS MIGHT JUST BE WHAT THEY CALL "DESTINY."
OOH, WHAT? WHAT?
WHATCHA TALKING ABOUT?
NORA...
HA HAH, Y'THINK SO?
YEAH. MAYBE IT IS...

Cereal Experiments Jaune/END

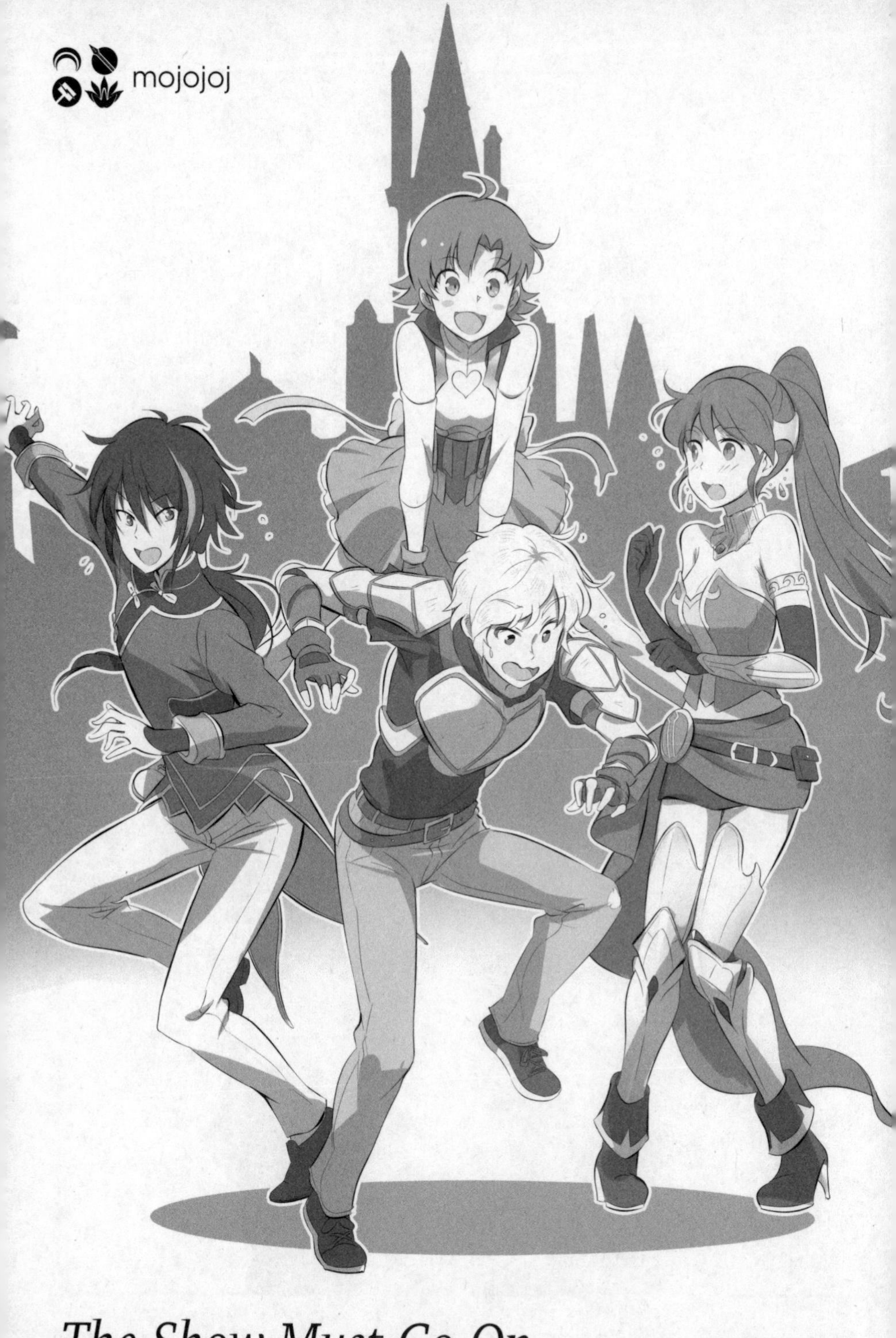
mojojoj

The Show Must Go On.

RWBY
OFFICIAL MANGA ANTHOLOGY
Volume 5

Shine

Ecru

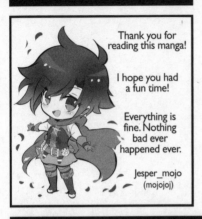

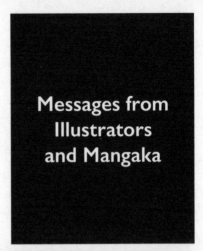

Messages from Illustrators and Mangaka

ILLUSTRATIONS + MANGA

Thank you for reading this manga!
I hope you had a fun time!
Everything is fine. Nothing bad ever happened ever.
Jesper_mojo
(mojojoj)

ILLUSTRATIONS

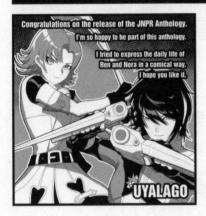

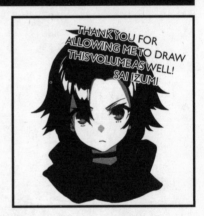

THANK YOU FOR ALLOWING ME TO DRAW THIS VOLUME AS WELL!
SAI IZUMI

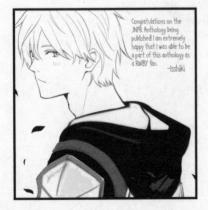

Congratulations on the release of the JNPR Anthology.
I'm so happy to be part of this anthology.
I tried to express the daily life of Ren and Nora in a comical way.
I hope you like it.
UYALAGO

Best Girl
Thank You!!
@Yujifantasia

Congratulations on the JNPR Anthology being published! I am extremely happy that I was able to be a part of this anthology as a RWBY fan.
-Isshiki

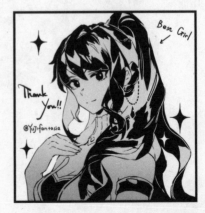

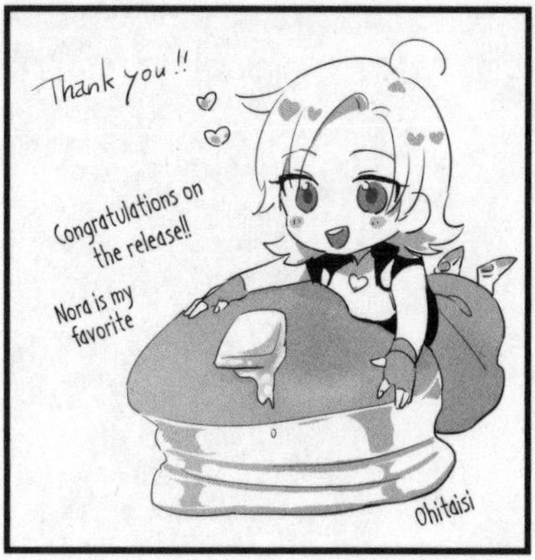
Thank you!!
Congratulations on the release!!
Nora is my favorite
Ohitaisi

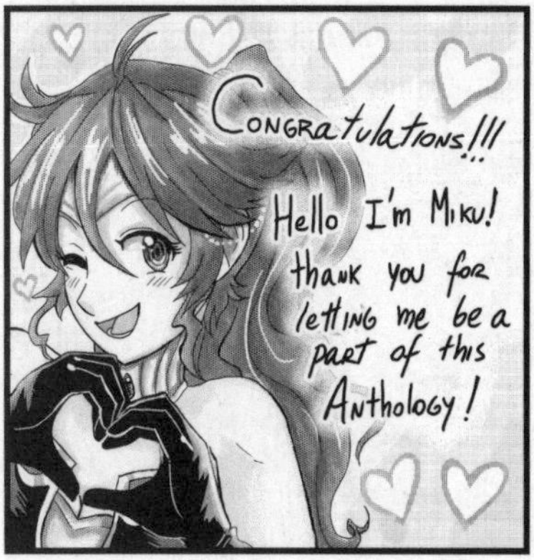
Congratulations!!!
Hello I'm Miku! thank you for letting me be a part of this Anthology!

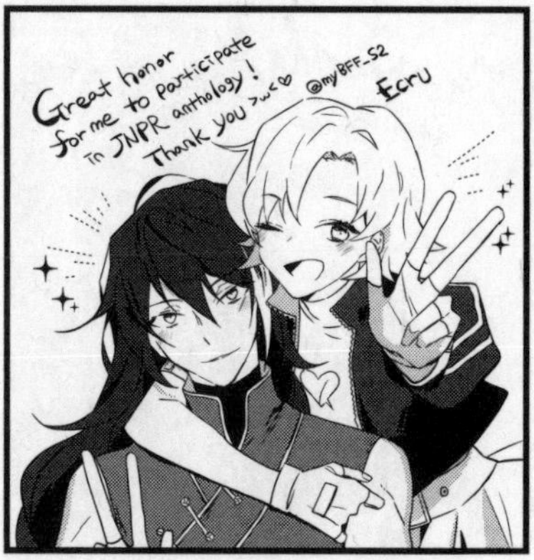
Great honor for me to participate in JNPR anthology!
Thank you
@myBFF_S2
Ecru

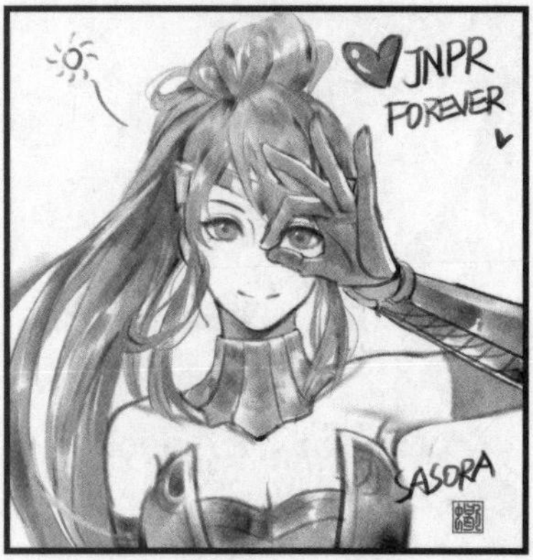
JNPR FOREVER
SASORA

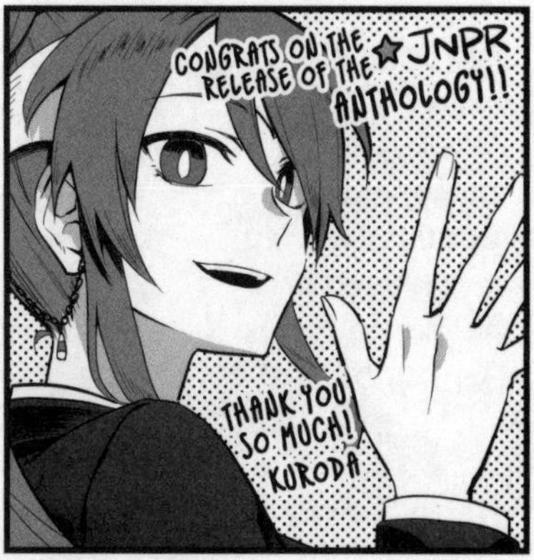
CONGRATS ON THE RELEASE OF THE JNPR ANTHOLOGY!!
THANK YOU SO MUCH! KURODA

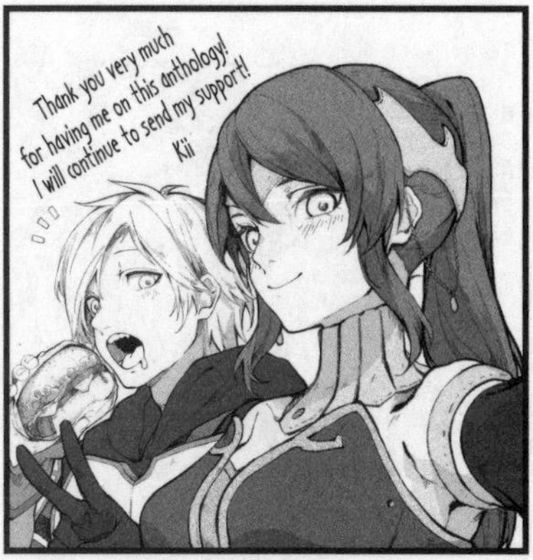
Thank you very much for having me on this anthology!
I will continue to send my support!
Kii

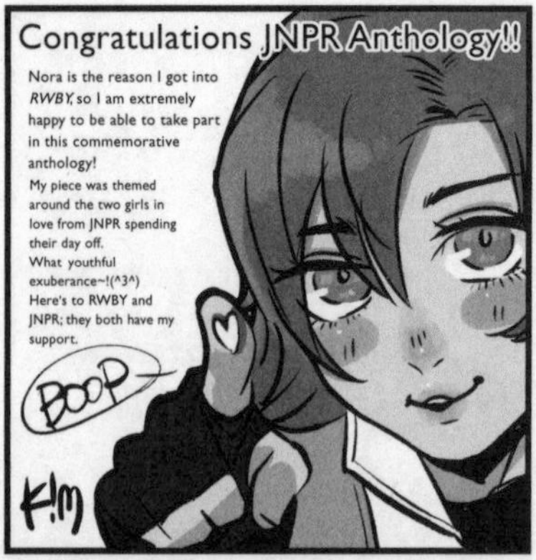
Congratulations JNPR Anthology!!
Nora is the reason I got into RWBY, so I am extremely happy to be able to take part in this commemorative anthology!
My piece was themed around the two girls in love from JNPR spending their day off.
What youthful exuberance~!(^3^)
Here's to RWBY and JNPR; they both have my support.
BOOP
K!m

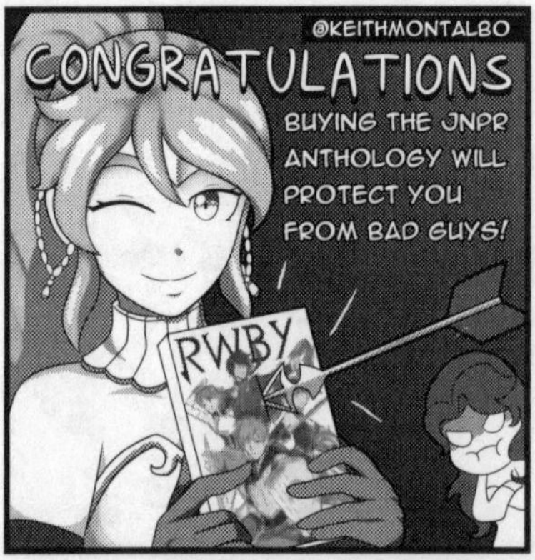
@KEITHMONTALBO
CONGRATULATIONS
BUYING THE JNPR ANTHOLOGY WILL PROTECT YOU FROM BAD GUYS!
RWBY

MANGA

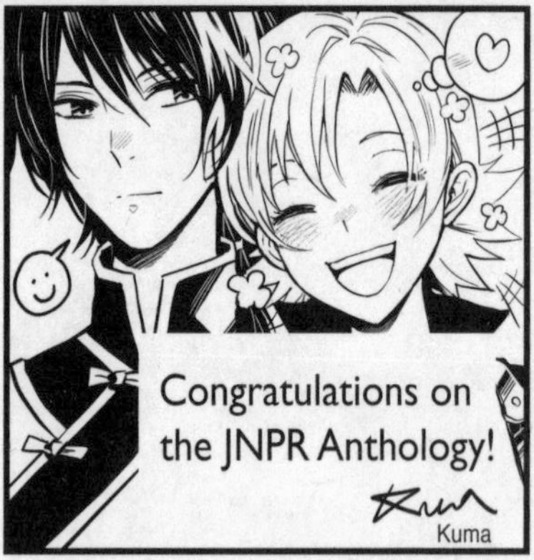
Congratulations on the JNPR Anthology!
Kuma

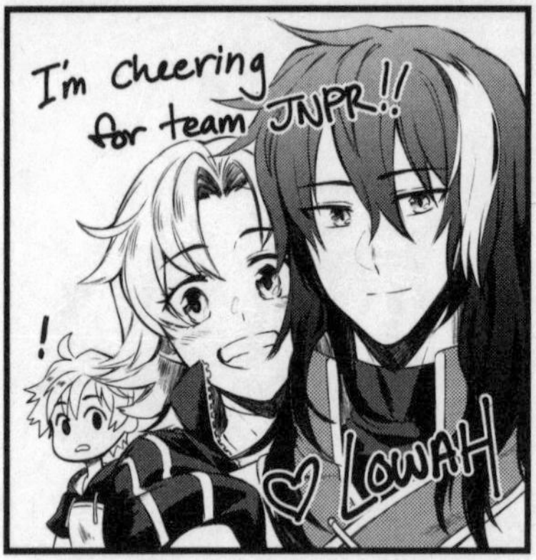
I'm cheering for team JNPR!!
!
LOWAH

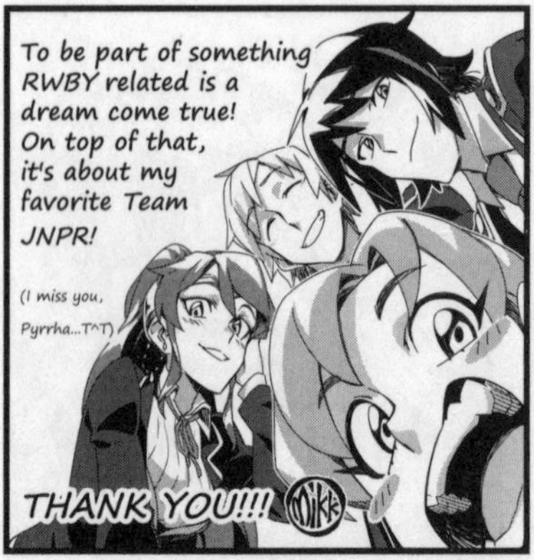
To be part of something RWBY related is a dream come true! On top of that, it's about my favorite Team JNPR!
(I miss you, Pyrrha...T^T)
THANK YOU!!!

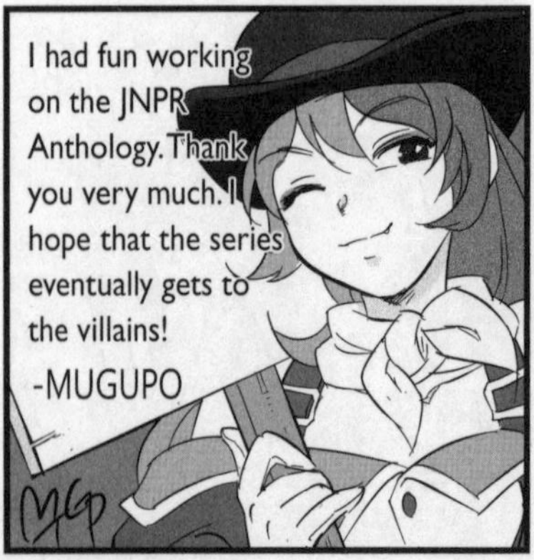
I had fun working on the JNPR Anthology. Thank you very much. I hope that the series eventually gets to the villains!
-MUGUPO

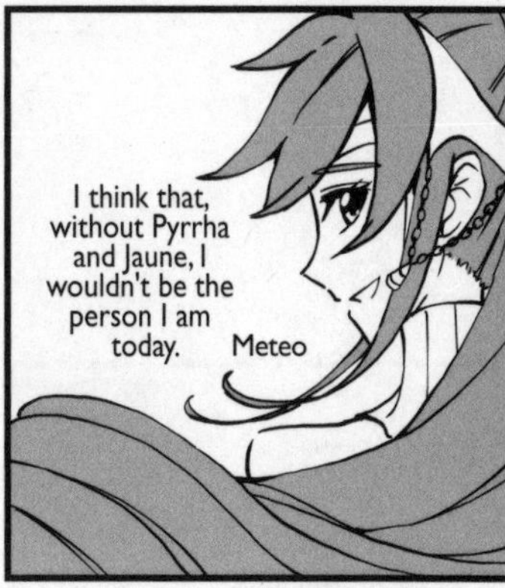
I think that, without Pyrrha and Jaune, I wouldn't be the person I am today.
Meteo

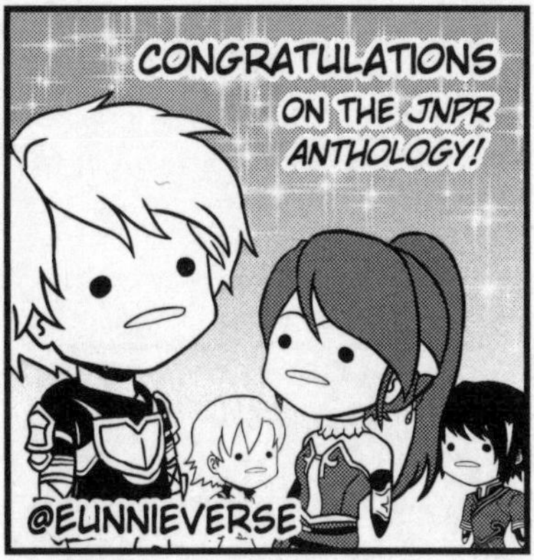
CONGRATULATIONS ON THE JNPR ANTHOLOGY!
@EUNNIEVERSE

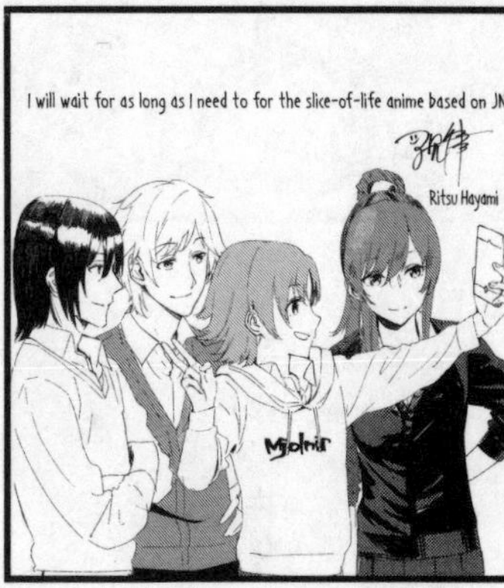
I will wait for as long as I need to for the slice-of-life anime based on JNPR.
Ritsu Hayami
Mjolnir

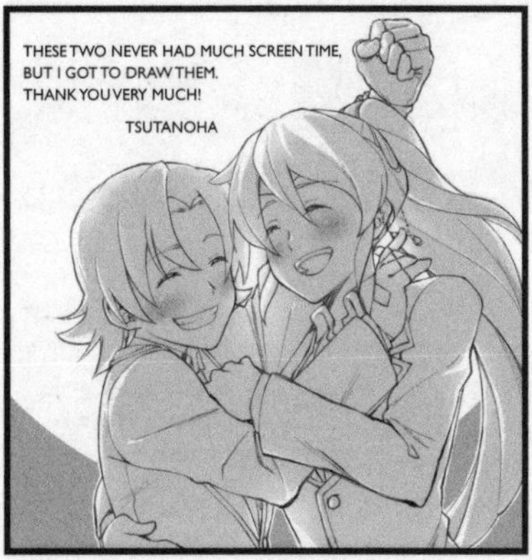
THESE TWO NEVER HAD MUCH SCREEN TIME, BUT I GOT TO DRAW THEM. THANK YOU VERY MUCH!
TSUTANOHA

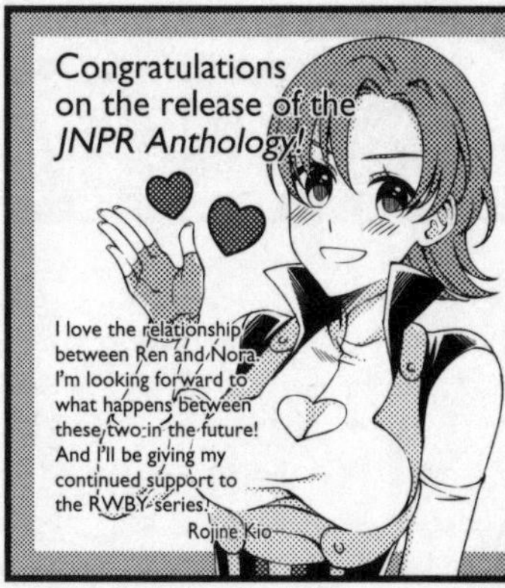
Congratulations on the release of the JNPR Anthology!
I love the relationship between Ren and Nora. I'm looking forward to what happens between these two in the future! And I'll be giving my continued support to the RWBY series!
Rojine Kio

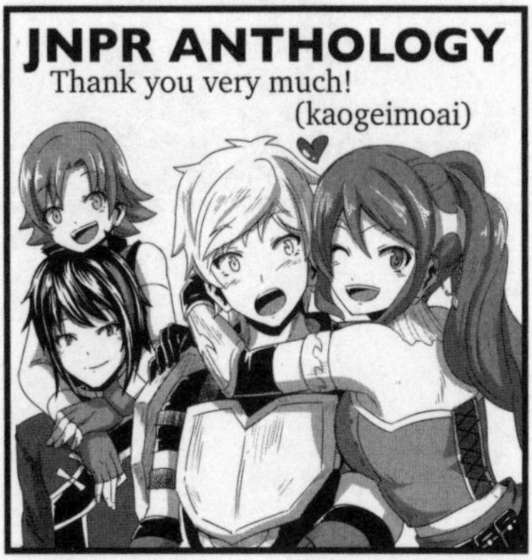
JNPR ANTHOLOGY
Thank you very much!
(kaogeimoai)

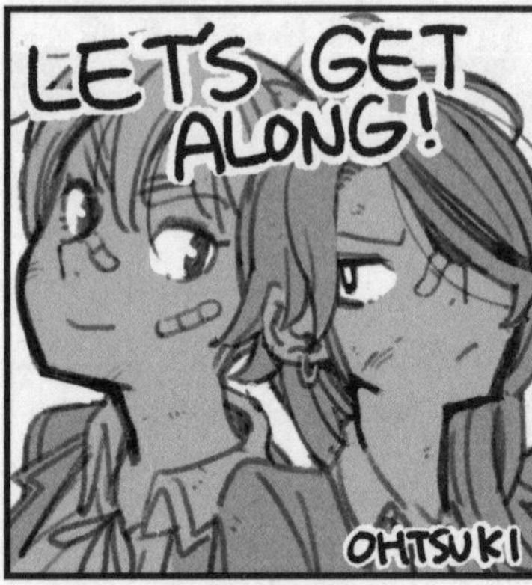
LET'S GET ALONG!
OHTSUKI

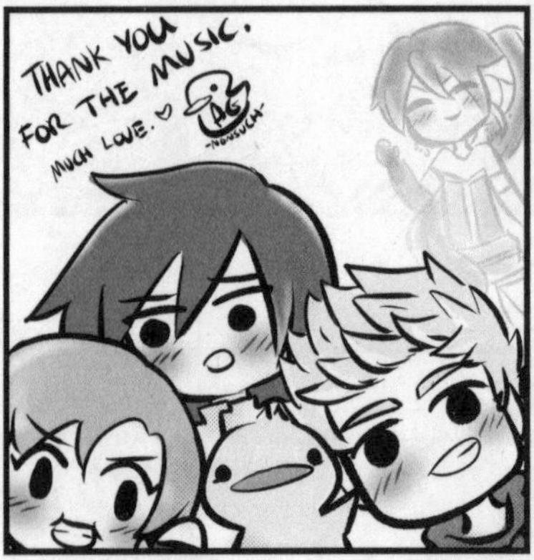
THANK YOU FOR THE MUSIC.
MUCH LOVE. ♡

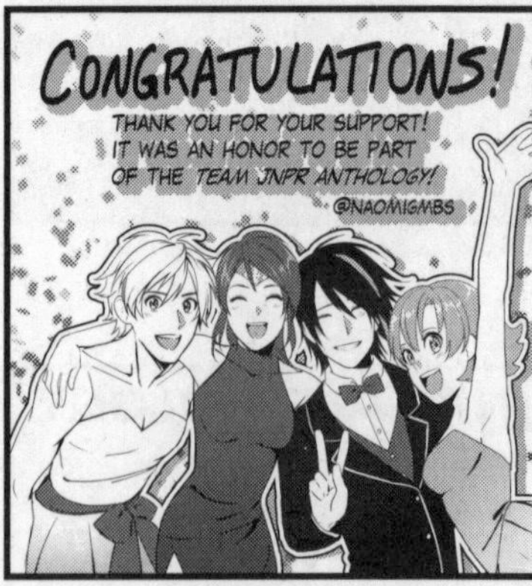
CONGRATULATIONS!
THANK YOU FOR YOUR SUPPORT! IT WAS AN HONOR TO BE PART OF THE TEAM JNPR ANTHOLOGY!
@NAOMIGMBS

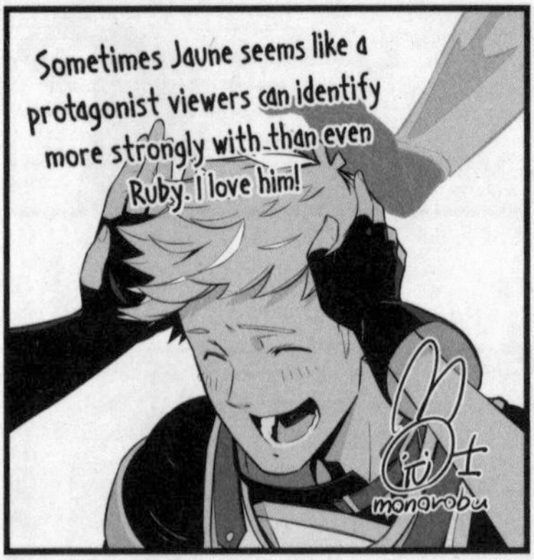
Sometimes Jaune seems like a protagonist viewers can identify more strongly with than even Ruby. I love him!
monorobu

I'll never forget the day I was asked to play Jaune Arc. Monty, Kerry, and I had taken our little idea for an anime and really started putting in the hours to make it more than just a "what-if." We'd been given the green light to actually develop the series outside of our free time. We were young, we were hungry, and we needed a supporting cast. The show would of course focus on four awesome female leads, but we wanted the series to have a wide cast of characters of all different shapes, sizes, and personalities.

We... definitely came up with too many characters, but some of the earliest ones included Sun Wukong, Dr. Oobleck, Penny Polendina, and Jaune, Nora, Pyrrha, and Ren of Team JNPR. Back then, we didn't have the luxury of hiring lots of well-established voice actors; we didn't even know if the series would be a complete flop or not. All we had was a dangerous amount of ambition and the small pool of talent and friends we already knew.

Monty liked how animated and energetic I was and asked me to read for a few of the male cast members. Even though it typically felt like goofing around back then, I was still nervous as I stepped into the booth for my audition. First up was my read for Sun. He was charming, playful, and most importantly...cool. I gave my read and stepped out of the booth. Monty stood in silence, thinking for a moment before finally telling me what he thought: "I think you might work better for a nerdier guy. Try Jaune." I was told I got the role as soon as I stepped out of the booth. Typecasting, am I right?

—Miles Luna

"She may be little but she is fierce" is the perfect quote that encapsulates Nora Valkyrie. She is an electric ball of strength and joy and I have loved her ever since I read her first line, "Wake up lazy butt!" Nora's trauma from childhood has made her perseverance on the face of adversity something to admire. Her love for her teammates and the good of humanity is a guiding light in this Grimm world. Her skills and the ability to steal a scene with her hilarious antics are unparalleled. I feel incredibly fortunate to have had the opportunity play this role and to know the positive impact she's made in the community that loves this story dearly and she will stay with me the rest of my life. I hope she's brought you as much joy as she has for me!

—Samantha Ireland

Samchild
boop!

"Are you really dead?!" is a question I never imagined hearing on an almost daily basis, but...here we are.

When the dearly missed Monty showed me the sketches of Pyrrha Nikos his first words were something to the effect of: "This is Pyrrha Nikos. This is who we want you to play. She's gonna die...," but it didn't register as being a huge deal. And, well, it wasn't. Because RWBY wasn't RWBY back then. It was clearly special, but eight years ago it was just a cool web series that I was thankful to be cast in. Characters die in shows all the time. The full weight of Pyrrha's death/impact didn't exist.

Fast-forward a couple of years and RWBY's popularity explodes. I was meeting the kindest fans at RTX and hearing them go on and on about how much they loved Pyrrha and how they wouldn't be able to handle it if anything ever happened to her...UH-OH. Every time someone would extoll her virtues, my heart would break for them because, well, I knew what we all know now. Looking these sweet souls right in the eye and NOT revealing the truth of her demise was probably the hardest and best acting I've ever done.

It touches my heart on every level that her popularity has continued to soar since the end of season three. I feel incredibly lucky to have gotten the chance to bring her strength, spirit, kindness, and occasional social awkwardness to life. Whenever I'm told that Pyrrha's an inspiration, I feel immensely proud. Plus, I'm a cereal, action figure, a custom race car, countless tattoos, and more. HOW AMAZING IS THAT?!

While her time with us was brief, her energy lives on and inspires us to love big, see the best in others, fight hard, and of course, to always believe in our own destiny.

Keep moving forward,
—Jen Brown a.k.a. Pyrrha Nikos

To all the those who made the *JNPR Manga Anthology*
possible, words cannot express just how grateful I am!
My joy at this anthology's release is overwhelming but I
am certain that my brother is smiling at these new stories
of his team's adventures and antics.

I am also certain that all those who love the world of
Remnant will find new laughter and tears as they read the
stories herein.

Thank you to everyone who made this possible and to all
those who continue to support the work that my brother
started!

—Neath Oum

About JNPR

Ein Lee

Are the early concepts for Team JNPR based on Monty's requests or your own original ideas?

Monty had an idea of what he wanted visually for Nora and Pyrrha. For Jaune and Ren he knew who they were as characters, but he wasn't as definite about their appearance, so he left them more to me.

Were there any characters that were completely your invention or were they all collaborative designs?

For team JNPR? Everything was based on Monty's ideas! A favorite *RWBY* character of mine, Neptune, was my idea (though, ironically, I didn't design him!). And Raven Branwen is based on my original samurai character, of the same name (originally, they were supposed to be the same character). I had some fun designs for Sun and Neptune's teammates Scarlet and Sage that went unused. And a bunch of other characters were originally descriptions from Monty that I turned into designs, like Penny, Cinder, Emerald, Neptune, Salem, Ozpin, etc.

What kind of design ideas did Monty give you?

Nora's original sketch actually had long hair (and high heels, I think. Monty put everything in high heels, ha ha), but her being high energy and based on the Norse god Thor, I figured short spiky hair would be more, err, electrifying.

For Pyrrha, Monty did a rough sketch of a girl with red hair in a miniskirt, and he told me he wanted her to be inspired by a Greco-Roman look, so I took the idea and ran with it, adding armor and trailing fabric for more movement when she moved in animation. It was certainly a challenge fitting the sexy pinup girl look that Monty loves so much (note the super-high platform heels!) with badass warrior, but I think the final result for her turned out really neat. Her design is simultaneously high drama with the opera gloves and shiny gold and red, but also suits her cool, paragon personality.

Jaune's description was basically goofy dork in homemade armor, and Ren was just quiet-Monty in universe-appropriate clothes.

And of course, each of them had to incorporate colors along the theme of their name— yellow for Jaune, bright colors (in this case, pink/orange) for Nora, green for Ren, red for Pyrrha.

What was your collaborative design process like with Monty?

It was so much fun, and really cemented my passion for character design. We'd chat on Skype to talk about *RWBY*, but often not, and it was a really organic collaboration that turned into a friendship that I'll never forget. When we discussed *RWBY*, it was often him telling me his new ideas for the show and seeing if I had any input. He was always so full of energy! Mostly for designing the characters though, he'd tell me about the character, some ideas he had for their appearance. I'd take notes and do a draft or two for him to see, and we'd refine the design from there until we had a final product.

From volume 4 of the show to volume 8, the character designs evolved quite a bit. Especially for Teams JNPR and RWBY. What kind of direction do you get from Rooster Teeth and the art directors on how to make those changes happen?

It was really just an exercise in giving established characters new outfits that were fresh but also identifiable as themselves. There are of course design elements tailored to story beats or in response to the story's changing environment, such as Jaune having red cloth around his waist after Pyrrha's death in memory of her, Blake cutting her hair short to signal a pivot/change, or the newest outfits for team RWBY/JNR all having long sleeves because the upcoming volume was going to take place in a cold environment.
For the outfit redesigns, I'd meet over video chat with Kerry, Patrick (the former art director who has since left) and the team to discuss upcoming story events and how that should be reflected in their designs. And of course, they'd tell me the things they wanted to see in the new outfits, and so on my end it's a lot of problem solving to try and incorporate as much of their ideas as I possibly can, and tell them what works visually and what doesn't.

The most important thing though, of course, as always, is that their outfits must look good!

RWBY OFFICIAL MANGA ANTHOLOGY 5

Shine

VIZ Signature Edition
Official Manga Anthology Vol. 5
SHINE
Based on the Rooster Teeth Series Created by MONTY OUM.

TRANSLATION David Evelyn
ENGLISH ADAPTATION Molly Tanzer
TOUCH-UP ART AND LETTERING Evan Waldinger
DESIGN Shawn Carrico
EDITORIAL ASSISTANCE Mayuko Hirao
EDITOR/PLANNER OF RWBY OFFICIAL MANGA ANTHOLOGY Yoshihiko Wakanabe
SENIOR EDITOR Joel Enos

COVER ILLUSTRATIONS Ein Lee & Meteo
BLACK & WHITE ILLUSTRATIONS Ohitashi, Miku, Sasora, Kuroda, Kii, K!M, Keith, mojojoj
SMALL ILLUSTRATIONS Ecru, Meteo

SPECIAL THANKS
Christine Brent and Geoff Yetter at Rooster Teeth

Printed in the U.S.A.

Published by VIZ Media, LLC
P.O. Box 77010
San Francisco, CA 94107

10 9 8 7 6 5 4 3 2 1
First printing, July 2021

VIZ SIGNATURE
vizsignature.com

VIZ MEDIA
viz.com

ratings.viz.com RATED T TEEN

PARENTAL ADVISORY
RWBY is rated T for Teen and is recommended for ages 13 and up. This volume contains violence and peril.

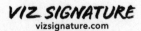

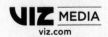

This book is my "thank you for *RWBY*"
to Monty, CRWBY, fandom and YOU!

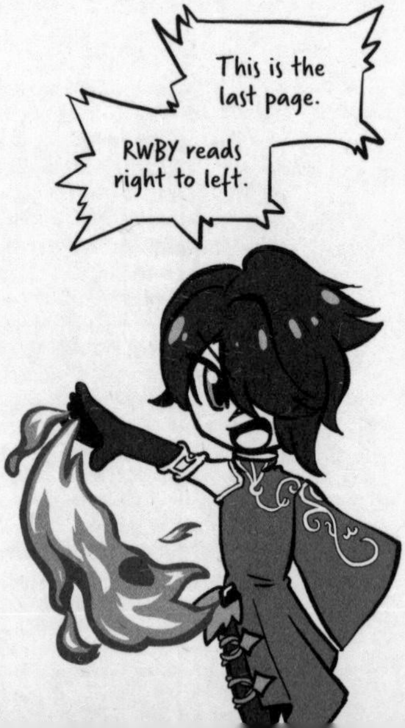
This is the last page.
RWBY reads right to left.

Meteo